D1187447

Murder in New Orleans

 HISTORICAL STUDIES OF URBAN AMERICA

Edited by Lilia Fernández, Timothy J. Gilfoyle, Becky M. Nicolaides, and Amanda I. Seligman
James R. Grossman, Editor Emeritus

A complete list of series titles is available on the University of Chicago Press website.

Murder in New Orleans

THE CREATION OF JIM CROW POLICING

Jeffrey S. Adler

The University of Chicago Press CHICAGO & LONDON

The University of Chicago Press, Chicago 60637
The University of Chicago Press, Ltd., London
© 2019 by The University of Chicago

All rights reserved. No part of this book may be used or reproduced in any
manner whatsoever without written permission, except in the case of brief
quotations in critical articles and reviews. For more information, contact the
University of Chicago Press, 1427 E. 60th St., Chicago, IL 60637.

Published 2019
Printed in the United States of America

28 27 26 25 24 23 22 21 20 19   1 2 3 4 5

ISBN-13: 978-0-226-64331-1 (cloth)
ISBN-13: 978-0-226-64345-8 (e-book)
DOI: https://doi.org/10.7208/chicago/9780226643458.001.0001

Library of Congress Cataloging-in-Publication Data

Names: Adler, Jeffrey S., author.
Title: Murder in New Orleans : the creation of Jim Crow policing /
Jeffrey S. Adler.
Other titles: Historical studies of urban America.
Description: Chicago : The University of Chicago Press, 2019. |
Series: Historical studies of urban America
Identifiers: LCCN 2018055528 | ISBN 9780226643311 (cloth : alk. paper) |
ISBN 9780226643458 (e-book)
Subjects: LCSH: Crime and race—Louisiana—New Orleans—History—
20th century. | Homicide—Louisiana—New Orleans—History—
20th century. | New Orleans (La.)—Race relations—History—20th century.
Classification: LCC HV6197.U62 L83 2019 | DDC 364.152/3097633509041—dc23
LC record available at https://lccn.loc.gov/2018055528

♾ This paper meets the requirements of ANSI/NISO Z39.48-1992
(Permanence of Paper).

CONTENTS

FIGURES

Introduction

Violence scorched daily life in New Orleans during the 1920s. Local surgeons treated so many gunshot wounds that they likened the city to a war zone. In fact, one physician calculated that the number of such victims treated at New Orleans's public hospital "rivals the casualties of many big battles."[1] At a time when homicide rates rose in the United States, and especially in American cities, lethal violence skyrocketed in New Orleans. By the middle of the decade, it ranked among the six most murderous cities in the nation. New Orleans was four times more violent than Pittsburgh, six times more than New York City, eleven times more than Milwaukee, and fifteen times more violent than Hartford. Early twentieth-century homicide experts dubbed Italy the "classic land of murder," yet New Orleans was nearly nine times more violent. In 1925, the city endured four times as many homicides as all of Canada, and its murder rate swelled to sixty-two times the English level.[2] By national and transnational standards, the streets of New Orleans were awash in blood.

During the next two decades, New Orleans experienced a raft of social, political, and economic changes, including the Great Migration of African Americans and the Great Depression, that should have fueled even higher levels of violence in the city, as race relations deteriorated, the local economy collapsed, and poverty worsened. Yet the local homicide rate tumbled by nearly two-thirds.[3] This book explores the dramatic rise and paradoxical fall in lethal violence in New Orleans between 1920 and 1945.

Shifts in both the level of deadly conflict and the nature of homicide reflected wider currents in local society. New Orleanians not only changed the frequency with which they butchered one another, but they also employed different weapons, slaughtered each other in different settings, and killed for different reasons during the Roaring Twenties, the Great Depression, and the World War II years. Although unique, intensely personal, and idiosyncratic circumstances triggered each homicide, violence ebbed and flowed in clear patterns, with particular kinds of conflicts rising or falling over time and in reaction to poverty, racial oppression, political instability, and a wide variety of other forces. Contrary to the plot lines of crime novels, films, or television programs, killers seldom snapped, ran amok, or suddenly became murderous monsters. Instead, violent acts typically erupted from within the rhythms of everyday life and occurred in ways consistent with broader social conditions and ideologies. Even when they committed brutal murders, New Orleans killers nearly always behaved according to—rather than apart from—their values, expectations, and needs. As a result, changes in the level and form of lethal violence represented ciphers, providing echoes of the pressures that buffeted ordinary early twentieth-century New Orleanians. Thus, charting these shifts offers insights into the racial, gender, class, and political ideologies of the era.

But murderous violence also generated powerful changes in New Orleans social and political life. Or, to be more precise, perceptions of local violence transformed family life, race relations, and the institutional landscape of the city. White reactions to African American homicide, for example, redefined policing and reshaped local legal institutions, though the perceptions that fueled these changes often bore scant connection to patterns of criminal behavior. New Orleans newspaper editors, voters, politicians, patrolmen, detectives, prosecutors, jurors, and judges responded to the crimes that they imagined more than those that actually occurred, producing a jarring disjuncture between crime and punishment in the city. Local law enforcers often cracked down on forms of violence that were rare and ignored the deadly crimes that were commonplace. In other instances, the locations of violent acts or the backgrounds of suspects, instead of the crimes themselves, dictated law enforcement and prosecutorial strategies. For some local politicians and parish prosecutors, this mismatch was purposeful and designed to mobilize voters or demonize specific groups. But more often the residents who cast votes, formulated public policy, policed the city, and imposed punishment unwittingly reacted according to their fears rather than to a dispassionate analysis of social problems or to the facts of a particular case. Therefore, although changing patterns of lethal violence sparked important shifts in the local criminal justice system, the link between crime and punishment was, at best, indirect.

This book explores the complex and often counterintuitive relationships between violence and reactions to violence and between crime and punishment.[4] Race played a crucial role in these alchemies, in part because New Orleans had the largest African American population of any southern city and in part because white residents, and the public officials they elected, defined order and social stability in explicitly racialized terms, though nine-tenths of local homicides occurred within racial lines. White city dwellers grappling with the challenges and changes of the era became transfixed by notions of interracial violence and by their worst nightmares about racial turmoil. Even in New Orleans, a city famous for its fluid racial boundaries, white residents increasingly saw urban life in black-and-white, defined crime in racial terms, and reconfigured local legal institutions to address their anxieties about race relations.[5]

Shifts in the composition of the city's population contributed to the development of this binary racial framework. By 1920, New Orleans, despite its multicultural reputation, had an unusually small proportion of immigrants; 7.1 percent of local residents were foreign born, compared with 36.1 percent of New Yorkers, 32.4 percent of Bostonians, and 29.9 percent of Chicagoans.[6] Ethnic affiliations remained rich and powerful in New Orleans, but more than most city dwellers in the nation, native-born white residents of the "Crescent City" shared a group identity. At the same time, and contributing to this racial bond, the ideology of Jim Crow encouraged white New Orleanians to perceive African American residents as a dangerous, distinct, undifferentiated mass. White city dwellers, and the criminal justice officials who represented them, understood violent crime as a starkly racial problem.

An analysis of homicide offers a unique perspective on the often-indirect relationship between crime and punishment. More than any other criminal offense, homicide is not socially constructed.[7] The legal definition of this crime has changed little over time. People often failed to report assaults, rapes, or property offenses, but not murders. Furthermore, for nonlethal crimes law enforcers frequently discouraged victims from lodging complaints and filing charges, and individuals disagreed on the boundary between lawful disputes and criminal altercations, insisting, for instance, that nonlethal wife beating or child abuse was a private matter. Likewise, most residents believed that men should be allowed to resolve their disagreements without interference—meaning that barroom brawls, sibling quarrels, or workplace fights that resulted in bruised cheekbones, broken noses, or chipped teeth did not constitute "crimes," in their minds. But dead bodies were another matter altogether, and corpses with gunshot injuries to the head or gaping stab wounds to the abdomen were nearly impossible to ignore. While nonlethal fights rarely or inconsistently attracted the attention of cops and prosecutors, citizens and local officials systematically reported the discovery of murder victims, and the deceased were recorded in police reports, coroner's files, and health department tallies—all of which, when it came to murder, tended to agree on the diagnosis.[8] Although not every death from criminal violence was investigated (or investigated thoroughly) and not every assailant was arrested, charged, or prosecuted, homicide victims were counted and identified.[9] As a consequence, criminologists, demographers, historians, and other scholars have concluded that homicide data are not skewed by a significant "dark figure" of unreported cases.[10] Hence, measures of homicide capture actual patterns of deadly violence. Though most violent encounters, regardless of intent, do not prove to be fatal, changing rates of homicide correlate to shifting levels of violent behavior, making homicide trends a particularly sound and revealing index of aggressive conduct.[11] Moreover, the variability of *punishment* becomes measurable when the definition of *crime* remains consistent.

Focusing on the years from 1920 to 1945 offers intriguing insights into the relationship between crime and punishment and the development of the criminal justice system. A remarkable assortment of seismic shifts struck American society during this period. The Great Migration transformed the racial and demographic composition of American cities; Prohibition challenged cultural boundaries and legal institutions; the Great Depression generated poverty, helped to transform the scope of government, triggered massive political changes, and connected disparate communities and regions to the larger nation; and World War II promoted the economic recovery of the era, led to the creation or expansion of massive military bases in and around cities such as New Orleans, injected new currents into politics, and contributed to the growth of the public sector. Furthermore, Jim Crow matured during this period, and the early rumblings of the civil rights movement became apparent.[12] A study of law and order during this era thus provides unusually clear perspectives, for example, on the relationship between crime and economic pressures or the influence of law enforcement professionalization on criminal justice.

At first glance, New Orleans would appear to be a curious focus for a study of the intersection of crime, race, and law. After all, the city seems sui generis—with Mardi Gras, Bourbon Street, bayous, and jazz. Upon closer examination, however, New Orleans becomes less alien and less unique. The broader political and economic forces of the era affected New Orleans as much as other American cities. Moreover, overall trends in local crime, race relations, and institutional development mirrored those of other major urban centers. New Orleans was exceptionally murderous during this era, though increases and decreases in local homicide followed the same patterns as in most big cities—but with more pronounced surges and contractions. Similarly, national currents in police and legal reform influenced New Orleans law enforcement and criminal justice institutions. Local and regional politics always affected the embrace of new wrinkles in crime fighting, but New Orleans officials typically imitated the glitzy trends of the day, such as the adoption of fingerprint identification and ballistics tests. Crime and punishment in early twentieth-century New Orleans echoed larger, wider patterns, though often in caricatured forms.

A crucial pragmatic factor also makes New Orleans a sound choice for studying the connection between violence and punishment in early twentieth-century America. A remarkable range of primary sources, from police files to trial records, has survived.[13] The depth and richness of this material make it possible to examine, with precision, the impacts of the Great Migration, the Great Depression, and World War II on lethal violence, as well as the influence of shifting patterns of homicide on local policing, prosecutorial discretion, convictions, and sentencing. Similarly, the extant sources provide the evidence to support analyses of the correlation between weapon use and criminal death, the link between rates of overall mortality and rates of homicide, and the connections among changes in violence, perceptions of crime, and trends in punishment.

In exploring these themes, and especially their interactions, this book charts the impact of violence on race relations and identifies the emergence of a disjuncture between crime and punishment and the rise of racial disparities in criminal justice. Such changes transformed policing, criminal prosecutions, and sentencing in the city. Racial biases were not new, though they assumed distinctive and enduring forms during this period, in response to the paradoxical mismatch between actual violence and white perceptions of violence in the city. Both the disjuncture between crime and punishment and the ferocity of racial disparities in criminal justice would grow more pronounced and become more engrained over the course of the twentieth century.[14] But the core shifts of the 1920–45 period eerily portended subsequent changes in the relationship between race and criminal justice, establishing the foundations for late-century patterns of police violence, trends in mass arrest, and the mass incarceration of African American citizens.

CHAPTER 1

"It's Only Another Negro Fight and Not Important"

A few minutes after 8:00 p.m., on January 18, 1923, twenty-five-year-old Richard Kenney fatally shot twenty-four-year-old Thomas Pepitone on a dimly lit New Orleans street. Both chauffeurs with criminal records and ties to a local gang, the former friends had tussled three times in the previous hour.[1] The initial skirmish occurred at the Olympia Pool Room, where Kenney had "playfully" jostled his friend as he entered. Pepitone, however, took umbrage and punched Kenney, and one of Pepitone's friends bludgeoned Kenney with a billiard cue, gashing his lip and loosening two of his teeth. Fearing that he was about to be "ganged," Kenney ran, pursued by Pepitone. When he finally outdistanced his rival, Kenney rushed to police headquarters and begged for protection. Captain Robert Stubbs advised Kenney to "avoid" Pepitone and suggested that he file a complaint.[2] A short time later, Kenney returned to the pool hall to retrieve his hat; Pepitone attacked him once again, this time with a billiard cue.[3] Unbeknownst to Kenney, Pepitone had suspected that he had "informed the police on him" about a previous criminal matter.[4] Robert Gonzalez, who knew both men, interceded and pulled the cue away from Pepitone, who quickly drew a knife. Gonzalez also wrestled the blade from the enraged Pepitone. Kenney then proposed that the men "go in the dark and fight fair."[5] Pepitone agreed, and they proceeded to a quiet spot on Iberville Street to resolve their differences with their fists.

Although both men had had run-ins with the law, the police considered Pepitone a particularly "hard customer."[6] Three years earlier, he had participated in a robbery-murder, but the district attorney had released him for lack of evidence.[7] He had also been repeatedly arrested on charges ranging from loitering to armed robbery.[8] Furthermore, twice Pepitone had failed to appear at court hearings, yet in all but one case the prosecutor or the judge had dropped the charges against him.[9]

When Kenney and Pepitone, accompanied by friends and assorted members of the city's Terminal Gang, found a secluded area suitable for settling their "difficulty with their fists," in a "fair fight," the latter suddenly brandished a sawed-off billiard cue and advanced toward his former friend. Surprised, Kenney reminded Pepitone of his "promise to fight fair with our fists only." Pepitone, however, bellowed, "I'm going to 'bust' your brains out." Anticipating that the fair fight might not be entirely fair, Kenney had hedged his bet. When Pepitone moved toward him, Kenney drew his .38 caliber revolver from his pocket and fired twice, hitting his cue-wielding adversary in the head.[10] The young gang member crumbled to the ground. Christian Burkhart, a local prizefighter and also a gang member with an extensive criminal record (and who, six months later, would himself be gunned down), stopped a passing motorist and had his friend transported to Charity Hospital, where Thomas Pepitone died three hours later.[11]

Richard Kenney fled from the scene of the shooting but returned to police headquarters and surrendered.[12] The next day, at a preliminary hearing, Kenney told the presiding judge that he shot in self-defense as the armed gangster advanced on him. Although a small crowd had followed the men from the pool hall to Iberville Street and observed the fatal encounter, once in the courtroom no one admitted to witnessing the shooting, and hence the defendant provided the only account of the killing.

The coroner's report, which was introduced at the hearing, directly challenged Kenney's version of the fight, stating that Thomas Pepitone had died from brain injuries caused by two bullets entering the back of his skull.[13] The police report also disputed Kenney's narrative and indicated that his shots "had taken effect in the back of [Pepitone's] head."[14] Similarly, a newspaper description of the fight noted that the victim had been shot in the head from behind, which left the police perplexed, the reporter added, "in view of the fact that Kenney claims he fired when Pepitone was advancing upon him." According to the *New Orleans States*'s account, "Kenney could not explain" the contradiction.[15] Nevertheless, Judge Alex O'Donnell accepted the shooter's story, found him not guilty because he had fired in self-defense, and released him.[16]

The Pepitone homicide occurred during a massive crime wave in New

Orleans, and the killing and the legal outcome revealed characteristic features of crime and punishment in New Orleans during the early 1920s. Violent encounters in the city seemed shorn of the rules and "etiquette" that southerners had long trumpeted.[17] As Richard Kenney discovered (and as his own behavior affirmed), notions of "honor" and "fair fights" may have been invoked rhetorically, yet they were roundly ignored; killers often ambushed their enemies, regularly shot unsuspecting, unarmed, even sleeping adversaries, and frequently stabbed or shot their victims in the back. Far from being shocked or outraged, journalists reported vicious murders with indifference. "A mere killing," the *New Orleans Times-Picayune* explained in 1923, "usually excites no more than passing interest."[18] Nor did cops, prosecutors, judges, or jurors respond with alarm to the epidemic of violence. To the contrary, they most often reacted with purposeful disinterest. Police officers conducted halfhearted investigations; prosecutors routinely dismissed charges against murderers; judges ignored forensic evidence, accepted wildly implausible explanations for violent crimes, and discharged killers; and the twelve white men who sat on Orleans Parish juries rarely convicted defendants in homicide cases, regardless of the class or the race of the killers.[19] In the rapid escalation to deadly force, the mismatch in weapons, the capacious assertion of self-defense, and the judge's blithe release of the killer, the Pepitone case was a typical New Orleans homicide.

Most important, the surge in violence, the casual responses of observers, the feeble reactions of law enforcers, and the feckless efforts of prosecutors, judges, and jurors fed one another, contributing to the city's skyrocketing homicide rate. A confluence of social and cultural changes, ranging from festering racial tensions to destabilizing demographic shifts, fueled the potential for conflict. As the criminal justice system actively ignored the wave of violence, New Orleanians looked to custom—rather than law—to resolve disputes and increasingly relied on aggressive self-help to settle arguments, redress grudges, even scores, and achieve justice, igniting an explosion in homicide in the city. This institutional breakdown encouraged working-class white New Orleanians, such as Richard Kenney, to bring guns to fistfights, to be prepared to use them, and to shoot their enemies in the back of the head. For African American residents, the combination of the social instability of the early 1920s and weak, indifferent legal institutions proved to be even more toxic, generating both a surge in homicide and a widening race-based gap in lethal violence. By 1925, African American New Orleanians made up slightly over one-fourth of the city's residents but nearly three-fourths of its killers.[20]

*

The 1920s spike in murderous violence was not confined to New Orleans. The United States experienced a jarring crime wave during the first quarter of the twentieth century, with the homicide rate jumping 45.3 percent. Between 1920 and 1925, lethal violence rose by 19.2 percent.[21] Violent crime increased particularly sharply in large cities. During the early 1920s, Detroit's homicide rate leaped by 40.9 percent, Philadelphia's by 45.3 percent, and St. Louis's by 57.1 percent. Chicago's homicide rate swelled by 58.7 percent.[22]

But, even by comparison, New Orleans was horrifically violent: its homicide rate soared by 139.5 percent between 1920 and 1925. By the middle of the decade, its rate of lethal violence was quadruple Philadelphia's, six times Buffalo's, and a dozen times Boston's. New Orleanians slaughtered one another twice as frequently as Chicagoans during the height of Al Capone's power, and the city had more homicides than the combined totals of Connecticut, Maine, Massachusetts, Rhode Island, and Vermont, though the population of New England was nearly twenty times greater.[23] To be sure, New Orleans was not America's "murder city," a distinction that belonged to Memphis, though it was one of the most homicidal urban centers in the nation during the exceptionally violent 1920s (see figure 1.1).[24] Noting that New Orleans had more homicides than London, England, with less than one-sixteenth the population, the *New Orleans Item* in 1922 looked forward to a time when the "unhappy, the jealous, and vicious will not turn their hands so readily to knife and pistol."[25]

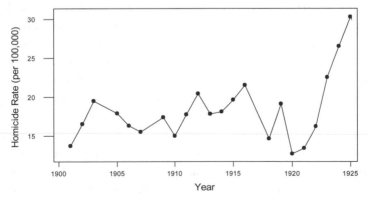

F I G . 1 . 1 . New Orleans Homicide Rates, 1901–1925. Source: Homicide Reports, Department of Police, New Orleans.

Nearly every form of lethal violence mushroomed in New Orleans during the early 1920s.[26] Gun homicide rates, for example, more than doubled, and knife homicide quadrupled. Street violence more than tripled, while killings in homes swelled fourfold between 1920 and 1925. Rates of homicide by men tripled and by women almost quadrupled.[27] The surge in local bloodshed also crossed racial lines. Between 1924 and 1926, the rate of homicide by men, by women, by white residents, by African American residents, by spouses, by acquaintances, and occurring in homes and on local streets peaked. The triggers for such violence were bound up in broader social and institutional forces, rather than more ephemeral changes, such as Prohibition or rum-running, whose influence on homicide was negligible.[28]

So violent was New Orleans during the early 1920s that observers insisted that the carnage became contagious. In many parts of the city, violence begot violence, and survival often required a quick resort to knives, guns, and deadly force.[29] Charity Hospital, the public medical-care facility, overflowed with the victims of violent crime.[30] In 1925, Rudolph Matas, the president of the American College of Surgeons, reported "the number of gunshot wounds of the abdomen treated at the Charity hospital yearly and collectively is larger than that of another other single institution of the same size and character in the United States and possibly the world."[31] As a result, the hospital emerged as a nationally renowned research center for the treatment of bullet injuries.

Myriad factors contributed to the rising tide of lethal violence, but demographic forces played a prominent role. The population of New Orleans surged during the 1920s, swelling by 18.5 percent and growing 30.3 percent faster than during the 1910s, as newcomers—including a massive flow of farmers from the lower Mississippi Valley—poured in from the surrounding region. Most were poor and young, with the proportion of New Orleans residents in their twenties hitting a peak during the early 1920s. And many were African American, for the city's African American population increased twice as fast as the white population during the 1920s. With this teeming population, and with sex ratios out of balance as a consequence of migration, New Orleans possessed the perfect demographic recipe for a spike in violence.[32] Not surprisingly, the city's homicide rate soared, and both victims and their killers were especially young during the early 1920s; nearly half were between twenty and thirty years old. On average, victims and killers in New Orleans were two years younger than their counterparts during the 1930s. Furthermore, two-thirds of those involved in homicides in this era either held unskilled positions or lived in households headed by unskilled workers;

across racial lines, lethal violence was concentrated among the poorest New Orleanians.

But population shifts, by themselves, did not trigger violence. Topographical conditions contributed as well, exacerbating demographic pressures and social tensions in the city. Swamps covered most of early twentieth-century New Orleans, precluding real estate development. As a result, during the 1920s the population remained confined to roughly one-quarter of the city's land, crowded on the high ground hugging the Mississippi River. The lion's share of the terrain to the north, between the river and Lake Pontchartrain, was either partially or entirely submerged. Although the city undertook efforts to drain the bayous of Orleans Parish, installing an electric pump in 1917, the reclamation process was slow.[33] As late as 1934, only 30 percent of the city's 366 square miles of land could support structures.[34] New Orleans's population density appeared modest in comparison with other large cities, with a level one-seventh that of Philadelphia, one-sixth that of Pittsburgh, and one-third that of Richmond.[35] But residents of the Louisiana city faced horrific overcrowding, since they were concentrated on limited high ground. This in turn created pronounced housing shortages.[36]

Under these demographic pressures, New Orleans's complex social geography began to collapse. Rich and poor, white and African American, native-born and foreign-born residents had long lived in close proximity there, contributing to the city's distinctive cultural tapestry.[37] African American New Orleanians, especially those working as servants, often resided near their employers, in an arrangement known as the "back-yard pattern."[38] Hence, as late as the 1920s, the city had low levels of racial segregation and no major African American neighborhoods. Instead, African American residents concentrated in small pockets near affluent white residents.[39] While New Orleans had a few ethnic neighborhoods, the city's foreign-born population was modest, and tiny clusters, rather than the large immigrant "colonies" of northern urban centers, predominated.[40] The bayous of the lower Mississippi Valley, moreover, prevented these pockets and clusters from expanding to accommodate newcomers during the early 1920s.[41] When migrants arrived in large numbers, living conditions deteriorated.

Death rates ballooned, and epidemiological and social crises overlapped. New Orleans's mortality rate climbed by 9.1 percent between 1920 and 1925. Deaths from heart disease soared, especially among poor and African American New Orleanians. The collision of demographic changes and ecological pressures contributed to social instability as well. The city's suicide rate, for instance, leaped by 48.6 percent between 1920 and 1925.[42]

Soon, the boundaries between these pockets crumbled. So too did boundaries between and within households. The housing shortage produced a spike in the number of families taking in lodgers, disrupting family life and sometimes sparking lethal violence. During the early 1920s, nearly half of the homicides occurring in homes involved people who were unrelated, such as conflicts between landlords and roomers. In 1924, for example, Charles Clay Howell fatally shot Lottie Oppenheimer while she ironed clothing in her kitchen. The twenty-five-year-old Howell had fallen in love with his landlady, a thirty-year-old widow. When he discovered that she felt differently toward him, Howell shot Oppenheimer three times and attempted to kill himself. In his suicide note, the killer lamented "that it was impossible to live in the same house with a woman he loved."[43]

Similarly, with a young population and a rising mortality rate, an increasing number of households included stepchildren, and friction often surfaced in newly blended families. Demographic change, therefore, sharply increased the potential for conflict and hence contributed to a surge in domestic homicide. Between 1920 and 1925, the proportion of homicides in which parents killed their children or stepchildren tripled.

The tensions of a blended household triggered Edward Woolfero's 1923 murder of Charles Robinson, his stepson. A fifty-two-year-old clerk, Woolfero attributed the violence to "family troubles."[44] In 1916, Woolfero, a widower, married Alice O'Rourke Robinson, a widow two years his junior.[45] Woolfero moved into his wife's Peniston Street home, which he shared with her teenaged children, Thelma and Charles. The dwelling belonged to his wife, though Woolfero declared himself the "head" of the household, because he was the husband and because he "paid for the running expenses" of the dwelling.[46] But he resented the children and bitterly complained that they "were running his home." In July 1922, Woolfero reached a breaking point and demanded that Charles Robinson leave the house and never return. "I stood him as long as I could," Woolfero explained at his murder trial, "and when I couldn't stand him any longer I sent him away."[47] Thelma Robinson, who had frequently butted heads with her stepfather as well, stopped speaking to him then, though she continued to live in her mother's home.[48] A World War I combat veteran and law student at New Orleans's Loyola University, Charles Robinson complied with the letter of his stepfather's edict and did not enter the house after his banishment. But on February 19, 1923, Charles Robinson visited his sister and mother to celebrate his twenty-third birthday. He carefully refrained from entering the house, remaining on the "gallery" (front porch).[49] When Woolfero, inside, saw Robinson on "his" property, he erupted in fury. Woolfero grabbed his .32 caliber Smith and Wesson revolver, charged out the front door of the house, and fatally shot Charles in the chest, as twenty-one-year-old Thelma recoiled in horror.[50]

Similar conditions fueled spousal homicide, the rate of which nearly quadrupled between 1920 and 1925. The full range of tensions challenging domestic harmony in New Orleans seemed to converge on Arthur and Leta Pichon's Royal Street apartment on the afternoon of February 14, 1922. A thirty-six-year-old sign painter, Arthur Pichon stabbed his thirty-year-old wife, plunging a hunting knife into her back once, into her left breast twice, and then into her face, cleaving her nose in an apparent attempt to disfigure her as she lay dying from the wounds that had pierced her heart.[51]

The murder ended a tumultuous three-year marriage, which had endured allegations of physical abuse—by both partners. Arthur's first wife, the mother of his two children, had died in 1919.[52] A short time later, the widower married Leta Ramires, at least in part "because he wanted to keep the children at home." But Leta bristled at this role, disliked Hilda and Arthur Jr., and often threatened to place her stepchildren—then eight and eleven—in an "asylum."[53] On one occasion, she left Hilda in a local orphanage for a week.[54] The children, at their father's murder trial, testified that their stepmother had frequently beaten them "till we were black and blue."[55] Arthur Pichon Sr. resented his wife's treatment of his children and began consuming large amounts of bootleg liquor. A year before he butchered Leta, Arthur was arrested for drunkenness and carrying a concealed weapon with which, he revealed, he planned to kill his wife and then himself.[56] Pichon was also suspicious of his wife's relationship with Tony Segura, the lodger in the room above the Pichons' apartment, and told police investigators that "most of their recent quarrels were the result of his wife paying a great deal of attention to one of the roomers."[57] The Pichon children as well had noticed that their stepmother doted on Segura and "would visit him when he called down to her to come up."[58] On the morning of February 14, 1922, Leta left twenty-five cents on the mantel and instructed her fourteen-year-old stepson to use the money to purchase bread and milk. When Arthur Jr. forgot, Leta scolded him.[59] Returning to the apartment inebriated and seeing his wife had "abused my little boy," Arthur Sr. exploded in rage. "I was so angered," he recalled, "by the repeated abuses to my children, of [sic] my wife's indifference toward me, of her attention to the other man, and of him [Segura]."[60] Pichon ordered his children to leave the house and then repeatedly stabbed his wife.

Eleven-year-old Hilda Pichon heard Leta begging for her life and found her stepmother "with a knife sticking in her head." She told police investigators, "Papa was very angry."[61]

More gruesome than most, the Pichon murder was hardly a typical homicide, though it was emblematic. It occurred in the home and between spouses. The violence erupted from tensions related to broken and blended families. And jealousy toward a lodger intensified the conflict.

Homicide increased for both white and African American New Orleanians during the early 1920s, though especially for the latter. The homicide rate for white residents more than doubled between 1920 and 1924—and then ebbed slightly in 1925. For African American residents, the rate nearly tripled. At the start of the decade, African American New Orleanians comprised 26.1 percent of the city's population, and they made up 27.3 percent five years later. But the proportion of local homicides committed by African American residents leaped from 45.5 percent to 73.4 percent.

The demographic and ecological pressures disrupting life in New Orleans during this era hit African American residents hardest, widening the racial disparity in lethal violence. The housing shortage and hence overcrowding, for example, proved more extreme. By the mid-1920s, the population density in African American pockets was more than twice that of white sections, and the proportion of African American households with lodgers was nearly double the white level.[62] Also reflecting the twin evils of overcrowding and poverty, the African American mortality rate, principally from disease, rose nine times faster than the white rate, which fragmented families, upset gender roles, and exacerbated inequality.[63] During the early 1920s, 87.9 percent of African American killers and 87.6 percent of African American homicide victims held unskilled jobs or lived in households headed by unskilled workers, compared with one-third of white assailants and victims.[64] Simply put, the social changes that contributed to the rising homicide rate among whites proved even more destructive for African American New Orleanians, dramatically increasing the potential for conflict and violence.

The operation of local legal institutions contributed to the increase in homicide. Law enforcers did little to discourage violent crime and largely left residents to settle their own disputes and to rely on street justice. During the early 1920s, as the city's homicide rate soared, fewer than one killer in seven was convicted.[65] In 1922, prosecutors secured convictions in one-eleventh of homicide cases. Nor was this meager conviction rate confined to homicides.[66] When victims survived violent attacks and their assailants were charged with "shooting, or stabbing, or striking with intent to kill," Orleans Parish district attorneys won convictions in one-ninth of cases.[67] St. Clair Adams, the president of the local bar association, concluded that "no city in America has worse protection from the criminal classes."[68]

New Orleans police officers typically had little difficulty identifying and apprehending most killers. Although they remained largely untrained and demonstrated greater interest in siphoning money from madams and gambling-hall operators and in defending the city's political machine than in fighting crime, policemen made arrests in more than three-fourths of homicide cases, in large part because killers usually did not bother to escape.[69] Many assailants remained at the crime scene until the police arrived, certain that they had acted appropriately and hence unconcerned about punishment. Others, such as Richard Kenney, were confident that they would be exonerated or acquitted and thus surrendered to the police. Moreover, killers, often covered in blood, were easy to identify. With a jocular tone, crime-beat reporters reveled in noting the number of times that assailants had been arrested but avoided punishment. For example, Robert Cass, who murdered John Muller in 1925 "because of pure meanness," had been arrested twenty-seven times before the "climax to [his] career of violence."[70]

Moreover, the toothless criminal justice system, largely reflecting (and exaggerating) notions of popular justice in New Orleans, eschewed punishing killers. Residents preferred private justice to the rule of law during the early 1920s, resented interference from patrolmen, and stridently defended their quick resort to violence. But neither in homes and the streets nor in police stations and courtrooms did New Orleanians rely on a code of honor, for exacting personal vengeance was unencumbered by rules. Killing trumped dueling, and street justice proved more desirable than state-imposed punishment or ritualized demonstrations of rectitude. Both Richard Kenney and Thomas Pepitone, in spurning the rules of a "fair fight," conformed to local custom.

Louis Daniels subscribed to this value system when he killed Eugene Fabre in 1926. While inebriated, the twenty-eight-year-old Daniels stumbled into the twenty-two-year-old Fabre in a crowded soft-drink establishment. After the usual exchange of insults, Daniels challenged Fabre to "go out and fight." The men left the barroom, walked twenty feet, and prepared to settle their differences. According to the police report, "When Fabre was in the act of pulling off his coat to fight, Louis Daniels retreated back, pulled his revolver out of his right hip pocket, and fired one shot, striking Fabre in the right eye, the bullet coming out the back of his head."[71] Likewise, Victor Ray London, furious about losing all of his money in a dice game, "called to [Fred] North to come out and 'fight like a man.'" As they descended a staircase leading to the street, where they would have a fair fight with their fists, London suddenly turned and fired five shots from his revolver, hitting North in the chest, abdomen, right leg, and left shoulder. As North bled to death, London rifled through his pockets and reclaimed the $3.50 he had lost in the dice game.[72] Again and again during the 1920s, New Orleans men challenged their adversaries to engage in fair fights and then ambushed them as they prepared to resolve their disagreements "like men."

Extended gaps in time frequently separated the initial dustup from the fatal encounter. While emotional wounds festered during these periods, assailants also frequently used the time in a more calculated manner and searched for firearms. Working-class New Orleanians often carried dirks (or knives), but they usually kept their guns at home—stashed under bedroom pillows or placed on living room mantels.[73] When trouble struck, a high proportion of the 75.1 percent of killers who used firearms dashed home to fetch their weapons, ran to the apartments of friends or relatives and borrowed revolvers, or even hurried to local pawnshops to procure shotguns. These men sought to even scores and kill their enemies, rather than publicly affirm their courage or defend their honor. On November 16, 1920, Gasper Baio, a merchant, and Victor Meador, a longshoreman, engaged in a heated dispute about a stove. The dockworker insisted that the shopkeeper had sold him a defective appliance. When Baio refused to "take it back," Meador "went home, got his pistol," returned to the store two hours later, and fatally shot Baio.[74] By the cultural standards of the 1920s, this was justice.

New Orleanians, both white and African American, embraced street justice, but white residents especially insisted that legal institutions should affirm their behavior. After shooting unarmed victims, sometimes in the back, they fiercely defended their righteousness. These killers implicitly and explicitly invoked white masculine privilege: the legal system, they argued, should protect, rather than contravene, the authority of white men to handle their own affairs and resolve their own disputes.

To witnesses, police investigators, crime-beat reporters, and later to prosecutors, judges, and jurors, white New Orleanians invoked capacious notions of self-defense, justifying murderous ambushes and acts of revenge, using weapons against unarmed adversaries, shooting enemies in the back, and virtually all manner of settling grievances.[75] For example, at 8:25 p.m. on August 27, 1922, fifty-one-year-old John L. Lenfant shot twenty-five-year-old Ralph Otillio in the back, chest, and abdomen, killing the day laborer.[76] The lethal encounter was the final chapter in a protracted feud. Eight years earlier, Lenfant had operated a saloon and had shot Otillio when the young man, then seventeen years old, his brother, and their friend attempted to "wreck" his barroom. Since that episode, the men, a reporter noted, had been "friendly enemies."[77] On the morning of August 27, they encountered one another on a street corner, and Otillio, according to his killer, attacked him. Lenfant "went to his home and armed himself" with a .41 caliber six-shooter and waited for his old nemesis. Mid-evening, the men crossed paths again, and Otillio struck Lenfant, knocking him to the ground. "I drew my gun," Lenfant told police investigators, "and fired. I was so excited I didn't know how many times I shot. I then got up and walked to the Fifth Precinct [police] station and surrendered." Lenfant explained to the desk sergeant, "I have no cause to be afraid. I did only what any other man would do under similar circumstances. I am sure I will be acquitted because I acted in self-defense. Otillio was a big man and I am only a little, old fellow."[78] Although Lenfant had secured his weapon in order to kill Otillio, had laid in wait to settle the score, had initiated the final skirmish, and had shot an unarmed man, an Orleans Parish grand jury exonerated him.[79]

Other white New Orleans killers invoked the "unwritten law" as a form of self-defense, claiming a husband was entitled to shoot his wife's lover in order to protect his home.[80] A forty-five-year-old clerk, John Wallace Daniels, explained that he shot Peter Holzarth because his thirty-seven-year-old neighbor had destroyed his home—by taking his wife for rides in his shiny new automobile, hence "stealing the affections" of the woman.[81] "If I had no children, I would not have shot Holzarth," the killer told the newspaper reporters huddled in his jail cell. "But I have four and I felt that it was my duty to protect them and—their mother."[82] There was nothing else for a man to do, he added, when another man tried to break up his home.[83] Similarly, Stanley Margiotta's attorney told an Orleans Parish jury that "a man's home is his castle," and therefore killing to protect it was an act of self-defense. A thirty-year-old saloon owner, Margiotta believed that thirty-six-year-old Samuel Lala, the father of nine children, had seduced his wife.[84] "For protecting his own home and fireside and the name of his wife from the advances of a man who was bent upon bringing shame and sorrow" on them, Margiotta shot his wife's unarmed traducer five times, including twice in the back. Margiotta then immediately surrendered at a nearby police station.[85] After deliberating the case for less than two hours, jurors acquitted the shooter, leading the *New Orleans States* to explain that the "unwritten law . . . had again won favor before a Louisiana jury, just as it had often scored in the past."[86] Prosecutors, judges, or jurors freed 84.6 percent of the white men who killed other white men out of jealousy during this period.

Some killers and their attorneys stretched the definition of self-defense in other directions. They invoked the "no duty to retreat" doctrine and insisted that if a (white) man believed that he was in danger, he was legally justified in resorting to deadly force, even if his assumption of the threat proved inaccurate or he had an avenue of escape available to him.[87] Judges sometimes balked at this argument, but jurors did not.[88] In homicides in which a white man killed another white man and claimed self-defense, prosecutors secured convictions in 2.6 percent of cases during the early 1920s; expansive self-defense assertions proved successful in the other 97.4 percent of cases.

When all else failed, white defendants could rely on jury nullification, which was explicitly enshrined in the state's constitution.[89] Judges routinely instructed jurors during this period that "you gentlemen are the sole Judges of the law and of the facts as to the Guilt or Innocence of the accused."[90] Thus, if the formal law, as stated in the criminal code of the state and explained by the trial judge, conflicted with jurors' sensibilities, members of juries possessed the authority to apply their own "principles of law."[91]

Prosecutors abetted popular justice for overlapping ideological, political, and pragmatic reasons. District attorneys possessed enormous, largely unchecked authority to dismiss charges in criminal cases. They acted unilaterally and were not required to explain or justify their decisions to "drop" cases, "eliminate" charges, or "dismiss" suspects.[92] Orleans Parish district attorneys during the early 1920s released more than half of all white homicide suspects before they faced grand juries, and only 21.3 percent of white defendants went to trial or agreed to plea bargains.[93] At the peak of the crime wave, in 1925, prosecutors released 61.3 percent of white homicide suspects before they could be indicted.[94] In some cases, district attorneys dropped charges because they saw little chance of securing convictions; occasionally they deemed the evidence "insufficient" to proceed to trial. More often prosecutors concluded that jurors, believing that the use of deadly force was justifiable, would acquit the defendants.[95] As elected officials, district attorneys sought public approval, and during the early 1920s white New Orleanians comprised 98.4 percent of registered voters.[96] Therefore, prosecutors, for both pragmatic and political reasons, pandered to white notions of popular justice.

But district attorneys in the age of Jim Crow also believed that white masculine privilege sustained social order. Thus, the New Orleans criminal justice system protected those who relied on private vengeance and valorized white masculine prerogative. The parish district attorneys in the early 1920s convicted 14.9 percent of white killers.[97] In cases in which white men killed other white men during this era, the conviction rate tumbled to 8.1 percent.

In preliminary hearings, grand jury proceedings, and criminal trials, judges, prosecutors, and jurors publicly endorsed white masculine privilege, and the message to white New Orleanians was unmistakable.[98]

The police also encouraged popular justice, sometimes even instructing white residents, including women, to take matters into their own hands. When these city dwellers complained that their homes or stores were burglarized, for instance, patrolmen and desk sergeants routinely instructed them to procure firearms and to keep them readily available—tucked under mattresses, hidden beneath the till in shops, or strategically placed under the bar in soft-drink parlors. On three occasions, burglars stole jewelry from Georgina Wilson's apartment. The fifty-five-year-old proprietor of a rooming house, whose husband was a ship captain and often away at sea, demanded protection from law enforcers. "The police," Wilson reported, "told me to get a gun and to use it." At 1:15 a.m. on January 8, 1925, she did exactly that. Feeling a hand on her leg, Wilson reached for the .38 caliber five-shooter that she kept in her bed and fired one bullet into the head of Simon Green, a fifteen-year-old "housebreaker." After the Seventh Precinct commander briefly confiscated the weapon, Wilson exclaimed, "I want my gun back." Charles Gill, an assistant district attorney, immediately instructed the police to release Wilson, since no charges would be proffered against her.[99]

But more often, white New Orleanians killed friends, neighbors, and relatives with the firearms procured for protection against home invaders. For example, Sidney Brewer, a thirty-one-year-old clerk with two children, fatally shot his neighbor Reginald Harris on March 15, 1922. At 10:15 p.m., Brewer heard rustling in the alley outside his bedroom and then saw the shadow of a man "through the glass and blinds" in his window. Fearing that Harris was a burglar, after a rash of recent home invasions in the neighborhood, Brewer "got his (12) gauge automatic Remington shot gun which was standing in the corner of the room and fired at the figure," only to discover that he had killed his neighbor, a thirty-six-year-old carpenter with four children.[100] An Orleans Parish prosecutor instructed the police to release Brewer without filing any charges.[101] During the early 1920s, 100 percent of the white men who killed other men in or around their homes were released, exonerated, or acquitted.[102]

Support from police, prosecutors, judges, and jurors for private vengeance and personal initiative, however, was not absolute, even for white men in New Orleans. Under specific circumstances, cops, district attorneys, and jurors embraced the rule of law—which also reflected popular white sensibilities. Wife killers, for example, confronted a very different criminal justice system than other white homicide defendants. During the early 1920s, 31.3 percent of white wife killers committed suicide. Of the remaining ones, 63.6 percent were convicted. Uxoricide violated notions of white respectability and masculinity, and hence the rules of street justice and private vengeance did not apply to white wife killers.[103]

But these murderers constituted the exception that proved the rule. Overall, during the early 1920s, only 11.2 percent of whites who killed someone other than a spouse were punished in court. As a consequence, New Orleans's criminal justice system remained purposefully toothless for white suspects, and the legal system helped to condition white men to take matters into their hands. Far from violating popular (white) cultural norms, Richard Kenney, who somehow shot his advancing attacker in the back of the head, and Sidney Brewer, who fired his shotgun at a shadow and killed his neighbor, acted in accord with white notions of justice, and New Orleans's legal institutions endorsed such conduct.

If the weak criminal justice system protected and reinforced the quick resort to popular justice and the violent resolution of private disputes for white New Orleanians, legal institutions encouraged aggressive self-help even more directly for African American residents. Law enforcers operated by fundamentally different rules when dealing with violence in the African American community. In homicide cases involving these New Orleanians, the criminal justice system proved to be even weaker, arresting, trying, convicting, and executing fewer killers during the early 1920s.

In the age of Jim Crow, the police became key guardians of the social and racial order of southern cities. They criminalized violations of racial etiquette and perceived challenges to the region's "caste" system.[104] In skyrocketing numbers, cops arrested African Americans for vagrancy, loitering, disorderly conduct, public drunkenness, and "being a dangerous and suspicious character."[105] Hence, African American communities endured endemic overpolicing for minor offenses.[106]

But New Orleans cops, prosecutors, judges, and jurors (all white until the 1940s) responded differently to African American felonies. The officials who generally overlooked white homicide demonstrated even greater apathy toward African American lethal violence. While they largely ignored white aggressive behavior to bolster white masculine prerogative, law enforcers dismissed African American lethal violence because they believed it was unimportant and unstoppable. They also felt confident that such bloodletting would remain safely confined within racial lines. At the same time that cops overpoliced African American communities for minor offenses, they underpoliced the same sections of New Orleans when the most serious crimes occurred.

Like their counterparts in other southern cities, white New Orleanians, particularly public officials, insisted that local violence was principally a "negro problem." According to Police Superintendent Guy Molony, "We have a rather high homicide record, but that is due largely to our great negro population. Most of the murders in New Orleans are committed by negroes."[107] Often responding to northern publications indicating that Memphis was "'murder-town' of the United States" and that New Orleans followed close behind, police superintendents, newspaper editors, and mayors insisted that such crime rankings maliciously misrepresented social life in the region.[108] Molony, for example, fumed that "were it not for the colored murders, New Orleans and the entire South would have an excellent record [for homicide]."[109] In 1925, the editor of the *New Orleans Item* reached the same conclusion, arguing that African American residents comprised the majority of local killers and their victims.[110] Similarly, a local surgeon estimated that two-thirds to three-fourths of those admitted to hospitals for gunshot wounds were African American.[111] These residents, according to city officials and many newspaper editors, were largely responsible for southern violence.

Most important, white officials argued that violent crime rarely crossed racial lines. "These murders," Molony explained in 1924, "are between negroes," something he said northern observers failed to understand.[112] And indeed, during the early 1920s, 94.2 percent of African American killers targeted other African Americans.[113] While African-American-on-white violence commanded enormous attention from white New Orleanians, such incidents were rare, comprising 3.4 percent of local homicides during the early 1920s.[114] The city's stratospheric homicide rate, white officials maintained, actually posed little danger to "peaceful" white residents.[115]

Thus, New Orleans law enforcers remained unconcerned about African American homicide, despite its explosive increase. At a time when prosecutors rarely convicted white killers, the conviction rate for African American killers was even lower; district attorneys convicted 13.5 percent of African Americans who committed intraracial homicides, compared with 18.6 percent of whites who did so.[116] Nor did the criminal justice system magically spring to life when African American men killed their wives. Prosecutors secured convictions in 25 percent of African American uxoricide cases, a rate less than half the comparable figure for white wife killers. Hence, although the overwhelming majority of early 1920s New Orleans killers escaped punishment, a higher proportion of white than African American residents were convicted. Even the execution rate was slightly higher for white killers—1.4 percent, compared with 0.9 percent.[117]

Both white and African American observers acknowledged that the normally languid legal institutions of New Orleans after the Great War barely responded to lethal violence in the African American community. The prevailing reaction to African American intraracial murder, according to the editor of the *New Orleans Item* in 1925, was that "it's only another negro fight and not important."[118] The ethnographers Allison Davis and John Dollard concluded that "a Negro's fighting only becomes really criminal and punishable if he fights a white man."[119] New Orleans's African American newspaper, the *Louisiana Weekly*, offered a blunter interpretation. "Just another nigger gone," the editor explained.[120]

Every level of the local criminal justice system was indifferent to African American intraracial violence. Cops complained that investigating African American homicides was an exercise in futility. In 1924, the police superintendent reported that "it is extremely difficult to convict a negro murderer."[121] City officials asserted that "the Negro will not give the police information leading to the arrest of dangerous crooks and criminals," conveniently justifying lackadaisical detective work.[122] The editor of the *Louisiana Weekly* reported that "it is common to hear one of our group say, 'If I kill a Negro, they [the police] won't do a thing.'"[123] In another editorial, the writer charged that "if a colored man kills a colored man, often little or no effort is made to capture the slayer."[124]

Patrolmen responded sluggishly to African American intraracial violence for other reasons as well. Again and again, in police investigations and in court testimony, street cops explained their approach to maintaining racial order: in walking their beats, investigating crimes, and testifying at murder trials, they divided the African American population into "Good Negroes" and "bad niggers."[125] "Good Negroes," in their eyes, accepted the racial hierarchy and, in their interactions with police officers, appeared docile, compliant, deferential, and submissive. These residents observed the rules of racial etiquette. In turn, cops defended "Good Negroes," viewing them as allies in the battle to safeguard the social order (and the racial hierarchy that sustained it). By contrast, "bad niggers" were "insolent and aggressive."[126] They refused to submit to the authority of police officers or to accept white supremacy. New Orleans policemen considered "bad niggers" volatile and potentially violent. In order to preserve social order, cops believed, such residents "must be 'taken care of'" and either arrested or punished "unofficially."[127]

But law enforcers, in determining whether to defend "Good Negroes" or apprehend "bad niggers," based their assessments entirely on African American residents' interaction with the police and white residents. Captain William Bell, for example, considered Milton Pierce a "Good Negro" and testified on his behalf at the thirty-eight-year-old teamster's murder trial. Prior to killing forty-two-year-old Alice Royal, Pierce had been arrested numerous times and had engaged in many fights, though he was never convicted.[128] When Mary Williams, Pierce's common-law wife, refused to obey his command to "come over to him," he hurled a brick at her. In the scuffle that followed, Pierce shot Williams once and shot Royal, her friend, three times, killing her. Nonetheless, the police released Pierce from custody. The district attorney charged the killer with murder anyway, and Captain Bell appeared as a character witness for him.[129] When Pierce's attorney asked the fourteen-year police veteran about the defendant's "reputation for peace and quiet," Bell replied, "I know that he has never given me any trouble." Reminded that Pierce had been arrested "several times," the police officer interjected, "But he has never given me any trouble; I have always known him to be a quiet negro."[130] For Bell, as for many of his colleagues, an African American whose homicide remained within racial lines and who appeared "quiet" and deferential toward white New Orleanians, particularly cops, was a "Good Negro" and posed no threat to the social order, regardless of his or her violent, even murderous, behavior toward African American New Orleanians. Vigorously investigating crimes committed by "Good Negroes" seemed entirely unnecessary. Between their indifference toward African American intraracial crime and police support for "Good Negroes," law enforcers did not aggressively investigate homicides involving African American residents. In 1925, when the city's homicide rate reached its apogee, New Orleans cops failed to make an arrest in 18 percent of homicide cases with an African American suspect, compared with 3.1 percent of cases with a white suspect. Ironically, the police made greater efforts to apprehend white than African American killers.

Orleans Parish district attorneys demonstrated similar indifference toward African American intraracial violence. Far from zealously prosecuting African American killers during the early 1920s, when local officials attributed the city's mushrooming homicide rate to the "Negro problem," district attorneys routinely released most African American suspects before they saw the inside of a courtroom, often indicating that the cases were "nolle prossed"—or criminal charges were abandoned.[131] In 1925, prosecutors "nolle prossed" 23.5 percent of African American homicide suspects, compared with 12.9 percent of white suspects. Relying on prosecutorial discretion, district attorneys also disproportionally "dropped" cases and "eliminated" charges involving African American suspects—before judges or jurors became involved in the proceedings.[132] While the public ritual of the hearing or trial allowed prosecutors to endorse white private vengeance, district attorneys more often dismissed charges against African American killers privately and silently, ignoring the violence rather than affirming it. Prosecutors usually refrained from explaining their decisions but sometimes insisted that they dropped such cases because they could not secure testimony from African American witnesses, an argument that African American residents dismissed as "bosh."[133]

Jurors also typically eschewed convicting African American defendants charged with killing other African American residents. Only the most gruesome, shocking homicide cases made it to trial; roughly two-thirds of suspects were released during earlier stages in the criminal justice process. Jurors, however, maintained unwavering apathy toward African American intraracial violence. "It is almost impossible to get a jury who will convict a negro for killing another negro," a law enforcement official complained.[134] Ethnographers reported that their informants throughout the region offered similar observations. "White juries do not tend to take Negro cases very seriously," John Dollard noted in his study of Indianola, Mississippi.[135] The rate of acquittal was higher in homicide cases with African American defendants than with white defendants.[136] Perhaps more significant, policemen and district attorneys assumed that white jurors would not convict African American killers, thereby justifying their perfunctory investigations and preemptive releases. Hence, expectations of juror indifference shaped the efforts of New Orleans law enforcers during the early 1920s, contributing to lower conviction rates for African American suspects in an era when the criminal justice system was already largely moribund.

New Orleans police officials, prosecutors, and courtroom observers saw scant logic in convicting African American suspects in intraracial homicide cases, except in the most horrific murders. Drawing from a blend of older assumptions about race and newer social-scientific perspectives, they often asserted that African Americans could not be held responsible for their behavior, since they lacked self-control and the innate capacity for "emotional restraint."[137] Impulsive and volatile, African Americans' behavior was fueled by raw emotion. "A great many among the negro race," explained Dr. Charles V. Unsworth, a local physician and alienist, possessed "a nervous condition in which an individual loses control."[138] By contrast to white criminals, whom white experts deemed purposeful and calculating, African American killers were "hot-blooded [and] temperamental," and their homicides "have usually found their impulse or their provocation in passion, jealousy, in depressed, neurotic or paranoic mentalities."[139] African American homicide, therefore, was "difficult," if not impossible, to prevent. "Doers of them [African American crimes] are not deterred as a rule, by fear of physical circumstances."[140] In his charge to the jury in an African American intraracial murder trial, Judge N. E. Humphrey made a similar argument, explaining that African Americans' actions "cannot be suppressed by any law of society."[141]

In short, New Orleans criminal justice officials believed that the rule of law and the threat of punishment would not discourage African American residents from engaging in violent behavior against one another.[142] "City fathers," according to a local African American newspaper editor, became accustomed to "winking at crime that only affects the Negroes."[143] Observers in other southern cities concurred. Memphis crime analysts, for example, wondered, "What is the effect [of court proceedings] upon the negro who, after all, has but the mind of a child?"[144] Similarly, Natchez ethnographers explained that white residents believed that "since the Negro knows no better and can act no differently, he should not be punished too severely, as long as he restrains himself in his relations with whites."[145] The African American *Louisiana Weekly* raged that "when Negroes kill Negroes, they are not punished."[146] At every level of the early 1920s New Orleans criminal justice system, law enforcers systematically ignored African American intraracial violence—while aggressively prosecuting these residents for loitering on street corners.[147]

Particularly for African American New Orleanians, violence was so endemic during the early 1920s, and legal institutions were so indifferent toward such crime, especially African American intraracial homicide, that self-help, even violent self-help, became a survival mechanism. Describing daily life for working-class African Americans in the city, a New Orleans ethnographer observed that "in a society where the law is administered by the upper caste, and does not offer protection to Negroes, it is a necessary survival-technique to learn this aggressive behavior."[148] As concentrated disadvantage—the layering of overcrowding, poverty, demographic instability, topographical pressures, and institutional failure—heightened the potential for conflict, African American residents recognized that they could not look to the legal system to mediate disputes.[149] "It is commonly known," an African American journalist noted, "that when one Negro violates the law by harming another of his group little or nothing will be done," and local ethnographers reported that their African American informants recognized that they "lived in a part of society which is largely outside of the protection of the white law."[150] Thus, African American New Orleanians, particularly working-class residents, learned to resolve disputes without involving white law enforcers.[151] "We did not want the cops to mix up in our quarrels," the young New Orleans trumpeter Louis Armstrong explained.[152] On the rare occasions when African American residents summoned the police to resolve domestic disputes, cops often did not respond, and when they did, patrolmen frequently arrested anyone they found, even the victim if the abuser had fled.[153] "Since he can hope for no justice and no defense from our legal institutions," a southern ethnographer recorded, "he must settle his own difficulties."[154]

Such self-reliance increased the likelihood that prosaic disagreements would escalate into violent, even deadly, conflicts. Writing about the same phenomenon in a Mississippi city, John Dollard described African American neighborhoods as "a kind of frontier where law is weak and each person is expected to attend to his own interests by means of personal aggression and defense." He concluded that "so long as the law does not take over the protection of the Negro person he will have to do it himself by violent means."[155] Routine interactions with cops and prosecutors, in short, conditioned African American New Orleanians to rely on self-help when trouble arose, and, in large numbers, men carried dirks in their pockets and women concealed ice picks and razors "in their bosoms," as the "best way to defend themselves."[156] When arguments flared, the residents sometimes reached for these weapons, much as white New Orleanians who purchased guns as protection against robbers more often used the weapons against family members during domestic disputes.

For African American New Orleanians, the sense of vulnerability and the resulting need to be prepared to act in self-defense grew more pronounced during the 1920s. While the inaction of local law enforcers encouraged, even necessitated, aggressive self-help and partially explained the race-based gap in local violence, social conditions rapidly deteriorated during the early 1920s, as demographic changes exacerbated African American poverty, overcrowding, household instability, and mortality. Daily life became more precarious, leaving these residents increasingly responsible for defending themselves.[157] One woman testified in a murder trial that she carried a knife to "protect myself." She added that "this is the way it was, if he [her abusive common-law husband] tried to hurt me I was going to hurt him."[158]

During the early 1920s, African American residents committed homicides with blades or ice picks at 8.8 times the rate of white New Orleanians. In 1925, the African American knife homicide rate was double the overall homicide rate for white residents. Perhaps more revealing, the process proved to be self-perpetuating; as violence soared, and as it was largely ignored by law enforcers, more African American residents carried knives for protection and brandished them during disputes. Between 1920 and 1925, the African American knife homicide rate soared by 951.5 percent.

These residents did not valorize ferocity or brutality.[159] But African American New Orleanians, ranging from newspaper editors to murder suspects, insisted that daily life compelled them to be ready to protect themselves, rather than relying on "an apathetic policeman for defense."[160] Social and institutional instability led working-class parents to prepare their children to fight. "Self-defense is one of the most necessary teachings," New Orleans ethnographers noted, for an African American child "lives in an atmosphere of violence. He lives, in fact, on a sort of frontier of American life where the man with the most courage and the most invulnerable arteries survives."[161] Some parents and grandparents even forced young children to resolve petty disputes with their fists in order to steel them for future, more serious conflicts.[162] According to one commentator, "Every boy or girl is taught to strike out in defense of his life, and to be certain to strike first."[163] "Everyday there were fights," Louis Armstrong recalled. "Seeing these sights going on all the time, we kids adopted the same method."[164]

African American New Orleanians, particularly working-class residents, often carried weapons to defend themselves and celebrated those who refused to submit. One fourteen-year-old African American girl defiantly told ethnographers, "I don't run from nobody—girl or boy. I either beat or get beat. I ain't scared of nobody."[165] Similarly, the young Armstrong revered "Black Benny" Williams. A renowned musician, Williams, according to the *New Orleans Times-Picayune*, "could make a trap drum do everything but talk."[166] Armstrong insisted that the drummer "would not bother anyone," but he yielded to no one, was fearless, and, when necessary, took on all comers.[167] At 2:30 a.m. on July 2, 1924, in a Gravier Street soft-drink establishment, Williams began dancing with twenty-four-year-old Helena Lewis, a prostitute. When the dance ended, Lewis stepped on the foot of Eva Paul, Williams's companion. The women argued, and Lewis challenged Paul to a fistfight. The twenty-three-year-old Williams interceded and "told her not to hit his woman." Perceiving this as a threat and a challenge, Lewis drew her knife and plunged it into Benny Williams's chest. He died four days later.[168] The police arrested Lewis on murder charges and then promptly released her on bail.[169] Two weeks later, half a block from the saloon where Lewis had stabbed Williams, Mary Sewell, a twenty-two-year-old prostitute, became embroiled in a dispute with Lewis, her neighbor, over the affections of a man, challenged her to a fight, and fatally shot her three times. The police failed to apprehend

Sewell. In less than three weeks, on a single street, and within a small social circle, two women, armed with both weapons and capacious assumptions about aggressive self-help, believed themselves to be in danger and committed homicide. Neither faced a judge or a jury for her crime. In a world with sky-rocketing levels of bloodshed, African American New Orleanians often antici-pated violence, carried weapons, expected their enemies to be armed, feared that hesitation could be fatal, and thus relied on preemptive self-defense.

The bodies of convicted killers testified to this "atmosphere of violence." When the Louisiana State Penal Farm at Angola admitted inmates, it recorded a "description and marks on person." Scars from bullet wounds and knife in-juries covered the arms, torsos, necks, and faces of the African American New Orleanians incarcerated at the facility. Twenty-three-year-old Willie Freeman, who was convicted of manslaughter for shooting his landlord in the head and had no previous prison record, had "2 cut scars over [his] left ear" as well as "cut scars" on his neck, over his right ear, and his left thigh.[170] Similarly, prison officials noted that twenty-eight-year-old Beatrice Washington, alias "Pig Iron," who fatally stabbed Hilda Mount in a dispute over money, had an "inch cut scar on chin, small cut scar insider corner left eye, cut scar left arm below elbow, shot scar left leg middle ways between hip and knee."[171] The readiness to fight and fierce self-defense insured survival but left residents' bodies blanketed with battle wounds.

If the systematic indifference of legal institutions encouraged African American New Orleanians to defend themselves, such self-reliance seemed to confirm what white policy makers, cops, prosecutors, judges, and jurors observed: that the resulting violence was unstoppable. Hence, better, fairer policing and legal protection for these residents would be needless and use-less. In short, the attitudes and assumptions of criminal justice officials made the stereotype of the knife-wielding African American appear self-fulfilling. One New Orleans police superintendent seemed cognizant of this paradox, arguing that the "negro [crime] problem" was at least partially "the fault of the [white] people themselves." Guy Molony explained that white residents "do not seem to expect the negroes to behave themselves as orderly as the law ex-pects them to." Hardly advocating social justice, he maintained that the "only cure" for African American violence was "hanging."[172]

Other commentators, however, recognized the wider effects of institutional discrimination. One white New Orleans newspaper editor, for example, ar-gued that race-based disparities in criminal justice, particularly inadequate police protection for African American residents, ultimately served to re-inforce the "sense of superiority" of "true believers in white-supremacy."[173]

Another observer of race relations concluded that "it is clear that this differential application of the law amounts to a condoning of Negro violence and gives immunity to Negroes to commit small and large crimes so long as they are on Negroes." John Dollard added that "one cannot help wondering if it does not serve the ends of the white caste to have a high level of violence in the Negro group."[174]

The low conviction and execution rates for African American killers did not cause lethal violence in the city. But the criminal justice system's anemic response to serious crime, particularly to lethal violence, deprived residents of a potential mechanism of dispute resolution, for African American city dwellers recognized that they could not rely on law enforcers or the courts. This realization bolstered the belief that aggressive self-help—carrying weapons and being prepared to use them—provided the most effective form of protection in African American New Orleans.

*

Lethal violence soared in New Orleans during the early 1920s, reflecting a collision of demographic, topographical, and institutional forces. As young, poor migrants from the region poured into the city, homicide rates skyrocketed, and both killers and victims became younger and poorer. Compared to their counterparts in 1910, for example, early 1920s New Orleans killers were, on average, three years younger and more concentrated at the bottom of the occupational ladder. In 1910, half came from low-working-class backgrounds, compared with three-quarters during the early 1920s. Moreover, living conditions rapidly deteriorated in New Orleans between 1920 and 1925, and the city's homicide rate more than doubled. Lethal violence, suicide, and mortality rates climbed for both white and African American residents.

But important race-based differences exaggerated the impact on African American New Orleanians. During the early 1920s, these residents experienced greater poverty, more pronounced overcrowding, and larger imbalances in sex ratios. Hence, many of the social "triggers" for violence and death proved to be more extreme for African American residents, whose homicide rates climbed 2.6 times faster, suicide rates rose 2.7 times faster, and overall mortality rates surged more than 9 times faster than those of white residents.

Legal institutions simultaneously contributed to the overall spike in homicide and widened the race-based gap in lethal violence. The city's criminal justice system accomplished little during this period, rarely punishing violent offenders. The informal rules followed by cops, prosecutors, judges, and jurors, however, depended on the race of the offender and the race of the victim. During this era, 87.3 percent of local homicides occurred within racial lines. Criminal justice officials, from street cops to jurors, were loath to convict white killers, believing that white men, who committed 94.9 percent of white homicides, should possess the authority to settle disputes themselves. Law enforcers endorsed popular justice and private vengeance, invoking any and every justification for releasing, exonerating, and acquitting white killers, such as Richard Kenney. The message from patrolmen and the district attorney and from judges and jurors was that white men could rely on their own initiative and aggressive self-help to settle disagreements. Such a legal philosophy helped to fuel the sharp increase in the white homicide rate. As social problems mounted during this period, more residents, especially working-class New Orleanians, redressed perceived grievances themselves.

For African American residents, the message from law enforcers was both similar and different. As with white killers, law enforcers demonstrated little interest in fighting crime or convicting African American killers. But the logic for discharging suspects or exonerating and acquitting defendants was race based, with policemen, the district attorney, judges, and jurors arguing that the criminal justice system could not deter African American intraracial violence and that, as a matter of public policy, such crime was unimportant if it did not affect white New Orleanians. During the early 1920s, as the city's violent crime rate rose, rates of arrest, indictment, conviction, and execution were lower for African American than for white killers. Recognizing that they had to protect themselves, more and more African American residents carried weapons, particularly knives, and depended on aggressive self-help to resolve conflicts and settle problems.

At the same time, the potential sparks for disputes—higher levels of poverty and overcrowding, greater imbalances in sex ratios, a larger proportion of family units destabilized by high mortality rates from disease and accidents, and a willfully indifferent criminal justice system—grew more pronounced for African American New Orleanians. Not surprisingly, while white homicide rates in the city rose, African American homicide rates skyrocketed.[175] Between 1920 and 1925, the race-based gap in violence expanded into a gulf, and the African American homicide rate ballooned to nearly eight times the white rate, providing convenient fodder for white supremacists who insisted that such evidence proved that African Americans were innately violent and that legal institutions need not and could not provide protection for African American New Orleanians.[176] If the criminal justice system told white men that they had the option to employ street justice, law enforcers conveyed to African American residents that they had to rely on self-help. The spiral of violence—and the race-based disparity in homicide—simultaneously reflected the operation of legal institutions and became self-perpetuating in the years after the Great War.

CHAPTER 2

"If You Hit Me Again I Will Stick You with This Knife"

Shortly after 8:00 a.m. on November 12, 1922, Silvia Hutton, a twenty-year-old African American housekeeper, walked into the Twelfth Precinct police station and informed Patrolman William Buse that she had just shot her husband, Willie. The couple had moved to New Orleans from Mississippi four years earlier and struggled to make ends meet. This morning, Silvia had started to build a fire, using pine kindling. Willie Hutton, however, insisted that she was doing it incorrectly and became increasingly belligerent, snarling that she used too much pine and not enough slower-burning wood. When Silvia failed to defer to her husband, Willie, a twenty-seven-year-old day laborer, exploded in rage and bludgeoned her with a piece of pine. According to police investigators, Willie then dashed to the bedroom "to get his winchester rifle and saying he was going to kill her." Silvia darted for the bedroom as well, grabbed the loaded .38 caliber revolver that she kept under her pillow, and discharged two shots before Willie could corral his cumbersome weapon and turn toward his wife. One of the rounds missed Willie, but the other penetrated his upper back, instantly killing him.[1]

The Hutton case was a typical domestic homicide in interwar New Orleans. Like the majority of the city's spouse killers, Silvia Hutton was African American, poor, and young. African Americans endured the lion's share of violence in New Orleans during this period, but intimate homicide was especially concentrated among these residents. Between 1920 and 1945, African American New Orleanians comprised 29 percent of the population and committed two-thirds of the city's homicides. They also made up 72.9 percent of the killers and the victims in spousal homicides.[2] During the 1920s, intimate violence was even more likely to erupt among African American New Orleanians, who comprised 27.2 percent of the city's population and three-fourths of the killers and the victims in spousal homicides.

Partly reflecting the demographic composition of New Orleans, African American spouse killers tended to be very poor and very young. The majority of African American husband killers were, like Silvia Hutton, domestic servants, and most wife killers worked as day laborers; 91.6 percent of African American spouse killers held unskilled positions or lived in households headed by unskilled workers, compared with 23.1 percent among white partner killers. Nearly half of the African American New Orleanians who murdered their domestic partners were also in their twenties, twice the proportion of white spouse killers. The mean age of African American spouse killers was 31.7 years, compared with 39 years for white partner killers. These trends, once again, were even more pronounced during the turbulent early 1920s, when the Great Migration reached its peak for the era. Between 1920 and 1925, almost two-thirds of African American spouse killers were under the age of thirty, and the mean age of these perpetrators was thirty.

More surprising, and in sharp contrast to overall historical trends in family violence, women committed the majority of spouse killings in African American New Orleans. Silvia Hutton was not an outlier. Wives were the assailants in 52.7 percent of domestic partner homicides. During the mid-1920s, when the city's overall homicide rate and its rate of family violence surged to their highest levels, the figure was 58.8 percent.

The Hutton shooting was typical of African American spousal violence in other ways as well. While disputes over kindling did not trigger large numbers of partner homicides, similarly prosaic quarrels routinely sparked domestic clashes during this period. The Huttons' lethal altercation reflected a deeper conflict over household power as Willie attempted to establish dominance and Silvia, at least in her husband's eyes, flouted his authority. A specific constellation of social pressures in New Orleans during this period roiled power relations and gender roles in African American households in ways that converted minor disagreements into deadly battles.

The collective impact of these escalating domestic quarrels redefined violence in interwar New Orleans, especially during the homicide explosion of the early 1920s. The African American spousal homicide rate more than quadrupled between 1920 and 1925, and during the 1920s this violence accounted for more deaths than drunken brawls, robberies, labor turmoil, and violence from organized crime and rum-running combined. In an era when machine-gun-toting robbers, both locally and nationally, generated hysteria, the African

American spousal homicide rate was eleven times the city's robbery-homicide rate.[3] Simply put, African American domestic violence fueled New Orleans's soaring rate of lethal violence.

Closely related, during the mid-1920s, African American homes and apartments were the most dangerous settings in New Orleans. Between 1920 and 1925, the rate of lethal violence there jumped nearly sixfold. Interpersonal conflict, especially homicide, is usually concentrated in public settings, such as streets, alleys, and barrooms, where besotted young men gather, strut, jostle, compete, and butcher one another to demonstrate their brawn and establish their status. But in the city of Bourbon Street and Mardi Gras in the 1920s, the African American home homicide rate was nine times the stranger-homicide rate, almost ten times the saloon homicide rate, eleven times the drunken-brawl death rate, and twenty-three times the local robbery-homicide rate.[4] More African American residents died from homicides in homes than on local streets during the mid-1920s. Even lethal fights between African Americans unrelated to one another disproportionately erupted in domestic settings, and homicides in homes occurred nearly as frequently between acquaintances as between spouses. During the mid-1920s, the death toll from male-on-male violence in African American homes was double that of male-on-female violence. Thus, a blend of social, cultural, demographic, institutional, and topographical forces transformed the normally safe havens of the family and the home into the most violent, homicidal social and physical spaces in the city.

In short, social conditions during the 1920s buffeted New Orleans's African American community, destabilizing household life. As a consequence, spousal violence soared, women committed the majority of African American spousal homicides, and nonrelatives fought and murdered one another in African American homes, in skyrocketing numbers. More than any other single factor, the changes and disruptions in African American family life and household relations ignited the overall explosion in lethal violence in early twentieth-century New Orleans.

*

The demographic composition of New Orleans changed during the 1920s, altering the population in ways that heightened the potential for lethal violence. Already possessing the largest African American population in the region, New Orleans gained thousands of newcomers, like Willie and Silvia Hutton, from the Great Migration. The city's African American population jumped by nearly thirty thousand between 1920 and 1930, increasing the size of the African American community by 28.4 percent during the decade, a rate of growth faster than that of African American Chicago and other major destinations of the Great Migration travelers.[5] Like most of the rest of those who fled the rural Deep South and moved to large cities, New Orleans's newcomers tended to be poor and young. But southern cities, such as New Orleans, attracted a particular segment of this migrant population.

Young, poor men, in search of factory jobs, typically left the region and resettled in northern industrial centers. They flowed out of Louisiana, Mississippi, Alabama, and Tennessee and poured into Chicago, Detroit, Cleveland, and Columbus. Labor agents, who sometimes deceptively recruited the migrants to break strikes in northern cities, also focused their efforts on young men.[6] As a consequence of these "pull" factors, Chicago's African American community in 1920 had 104.5 men for every 100 women. The imbalance was still greater in many other northern cities. Columbus's African American sex ratio was 113.4:100; Cleveland's was 119.2:100; and Detroit's African American population had 137 men for every 100 women.[7] Even a modest surplus of men usually contributed to mushrooming rates of homicide, and the surfeit of unattached young men helped to trigger spikes in African American violence in these cities, as the bachelors who resettled in industrial centers aggressively competed with one another for the attention of the much-smaller populations of young African American women. Chicago's African American homicide rate more than doubled during the early 1920s.[8] Similar demographic imbalances set off surges in drinking, gambling, carousing, and homicide in mining camps, immigrant neighborhoods, and other settings overflowing with boisterous young men.[9]

The migration process, however, unfolded very differently in southern cities. Lacking booming industrial sectors, these rapidly growing urban centers offered fewer factory jobs than their northern counterparts and hence attracted fewer young men. But African American women from the rural Deep South quickly found work in New Orleans, Memphis, and Atlanta, usually in domestic service.[10] Therefore, men more often moved to northern cities, while women more frequently settled in southern urban centers, creating communities there that had a dearth of young men and an oversupply of young women. In 1920, Atlanta had 85.8 men for every 100 women, while the sex ratio in Memphis was 89.7:100, and in Nashville was 83.1:100. New Orleans had 86.9 African American men for every 100 women in 1920 and 85.5 men for every 100 women a decade later.[11] For young residents, the imbalance proved to be more pronounced. In 1920, New Orleans had 77.1 African American men in their twenties for every 100 women in this age group, and the supply of men dipped to 73.6:100 in 1930.[12] For every four young African American women residing in New Orleans during the 1920s, the local community had fewer than three men.

Such a significant shortage of young men and surplus of young women should have pacified raucous bachelors, facilitated marriage, promoted family formation, fostered domestic stability, discouraged drunkenness, tamped down disorder, and reduced violence. But the toxic cocktail of race and region produced the opposite effect in New Orleans and other southern cities.[13] The imbalance in sex ratios strained gender roles and helped to spark spiraling rates of spousal homicide.

The uneven sex ratios redefined African American social life in southern cities. Many African American women there, particularly those in their twenties and thirties, lived on their own and supported themselves. Because of a combination of long-standing cultural traditions and the new demographic conditions, more than half of African American women in New Orleans held jobs, double the proportion of gainfully employed white women. Furthermore, African American women in the city worked outside the home at more than quadruple the rate of their white counterparts.[14] Married African American women often worked outside the home as well, at least partly because low wages mired their households in poverty. During the 1920s, married African American women were employed outside the home at six times the rate of white women in the city, and their jobs, as servants and cooks, were often more secure than the positions of their husbands.[15] For working-class African American women, in contrast to white—and especially foreign-born white—women, such employment patterns were routine.[16]

Similarly, African American women in New Orleans often headed their own households. In part, this was an effect of the shortage of African American men, though it also reflected the economic independence of the women.[17] In 1930, women headed 26.5 percent of African American households in New Orleans, compared with 17.9 percent of white households.[18] The disparity for young women, however, was much greater. African American women in their twenties and thirties frequently headed households, while white women who headed households were more often older and widowed. Thus, heading their own households was commonplace for young working-class African American women but was exceptional and tied to a life-cycle stage and a traumatic event for white women in New Orleans.

Not surprisingly, women who were employed, who enjoyed relatively greater job security than men in their cohort, and who ran their own households exercised economic autonomy. They routinely owned their homes or rented houses and apartments in their own names, also making them more independent. One African American woman told local ethnographers, "What's the use of havin' a fussin' man around when you're earning your own living anyway." "Mrs. Martin," the interviewer concluded, "is the undoubted head of the house; she pays the piper and calls the tune."[19] When the women did marry, their husbands frequently moved into their homes, which deprived these men of a traditional pillar of patriarchal authority.[20] Young African American men in New Orleans, who expected to "call the tune" in their homes, often found themselves supplicants—uncomfortably dependent on their wives for housing and sometimes for economic support.

In two other ways, the migration process steeled African American women, contributing to their self-reliance. First, with a significantly higher proportion of newcomers in the city, African American New Orleanians lacked the well-developed support networks that sustained white residents. Fewer relatives lived close by, and thus African American New Orleanians—poorer, younger, and more vulnerable to disease and death than white residents—were compelled to be self-sufficient during times of crisis.[21] At best indifferent, often hostile, social welfare institutions reinforced this need. Most private hospitals would not admit African American patients; the public hospital imposed draconian limits on beds for African American residents; and some physicians refused even to treat injured, bleeding African Americans during this period.[22] Over time, personal networks and community support mechanisms developed, but, particularly during the 1920s, African American New Orleanians, especially women, handled most problems on their own.[23]

Second, the legal system, with its willful indifference toward African American intraracial violence, also encouraged self-reliance. African American New Orleanians knew that they could not count on police officers to respond to their emergency calls or to mediate disputes. Though some patrolmen promptly answered such pleas for assistance, others ignored reports of murderous spousal violence in African American homes.[24] Such inconsistent responses taught African American New Orleanians to expect little from public institutions and to be prepared to defend and provide for themselves.[25]

If the daily realities of race relations and poverty in the Jim Crow urban South compelled African American women to be self-reliant, such autonomy weakened familiar forms of patriarchal authority. In households headed by women, and in marriages in which the wife was the primary breadwinner, men struggled to establish control and assert masculine privilege.[26] Even police indifference eroded African American men's perceived authority in their homes. Cops typically responded to white domestic conflict in ways that bolstered masculine privilege.[27] While patrolmen attempted to stop intimate violence among whites, they tried to do so while maintaining husbands' dominance. New Orleans police officers, all of whom were white men during this period, routinely refrained from arresting wife beaters, frequently blamed unfaithful wives for their partners' violence, and sometimes publicly expressed empathy for husbands who attributed their murderous acts to their wives' infidelity, insisting that the men, and not the women they shot, stabbed, and battered to death, were the real victims.[28] Thus, New Orleans policemen informally buttressed patriarchy, but only for white men. African American husbands enjoyed no such institutional support or solidarity from the cop on the beat.

At the same time, cultural traditions injected greater equality into African American domestic relations—and, in the process, eroded patriarchy. Early twentieth-century working-class African Americans in the region tended to form common-law unions rather than formal, state-certified marriages. For example, in her study of Indianola, Mississippi, during this period, the ethnographer Hortense Powdermaker found that "a licensed marriage in the lower or lower middle class is extremely rare."[29]

The terms of common-law unions were clear and straightforward. Couples consented to live together and present themselves as "man and wife."[30] In New Orleans, African Americans in common-law marriages specifically used this language.[31] Neighbors and friends employed precisely the same terms. For instance, Joseph Valmore reported to police officers investigating Charles Phillips's death that the victim and Mary Shields, his killer, "lived as man and wife."[32]

Moreover, the absence of mutual consent and the resulting end of cohabitation instantly dissolved these unions, making common-law marriages remarkably egalitarian.[33] Katherine Boyd informed police officers investigating a homicide that "Willard Rudolph told Lawrence Lomas that I was his wife, and I told him that it was not true[,] that I used to stay with him and I ain't lived with him for months."[34] Similarly, in describing the dissolution of her parents' common-law union, Edna Dunn stated her father was "out of our house now and what he does don't bother us none. It don't make any difference to me, but if he'd been home that would be different."[35] Without cohabitation, there was no marriage. One of the sociologist Charles S. Johnson's informants explained that "when you separate from your husband, you are already 'vorced."[36] Most important, because the union relied on mutual consent, its dissolution could occur unilaterally, giving husbands and wives equal control over the termination of the marriage.

The prevalence of common-law unions among African Americans reflected a combination of factors. In part, this domestic arrangement was a legacy of the pre–Civil War era, when state law did not recognize legal marriage for enslaved peoples.[37] Hence, domestic unions assumed informal structures.[38] Reconstruction politics, ironically, reinforced the appeal of common-law marriage among many African American southerners. While citizenship enabled freedpeople to establish formal, state-certified marital unions, this right came at a steep price, both literally and figuratively. Filing a marriage license at a local courthouse was expensive and beyond the means of many cash-strapped African Americans.[39] Furthermore, state certification of domestic unions ceded authority over family life to white government officials. African Americans were expected to conform their households to white middle-class standards of domesticity and sacrifice their capacity to define their own marital unions; without the permission of white officials, they could not enter into or dissolve domestic unions. Legal marriage, moreover, explicitly fortified patriarchal authority. When women consented to the terms of formal marriage, they lost control over their bodies, their contractual rights, their property (through coverture), and some parental rights.[40] The regulatory authority of the state in granting formal marriage licenses and in dissolving domestic unions, in short, was not benign. For many African Americans, accustomed to a more informal domestic arrangement and a more matrifocal household, access to state-certified marriage proved unappealing, and the benefits of common-law unions outweighed their new right to enter into expensive, patriarchal, formal marriages.[41]

Class-based notions of respectability also influenced the form of marital union that African American southerners chose. Despite the appeal of common-law unions, affluent African Americans typically opted for state-certified marriages. For these couples, the ritual and formality of the marriage ceremony affirmed status and represented a marker of middle-class respectability, complete with the gendered disparities built into such a domestic arrangement.[42] Early twentieth-century sociologists, such as E. Franklin Frazier, and white legislators in the South often associated legal marriages with bourgeois values, morality, family stability, sexual fidelity, and well-defined gender roles, whereas common-law unions, dismissively dubbed "putative marriages," implied instability, promiscuity, and "concubinage."[43] But working-class African Americans privileged the bond of affection and the spirit of mutual consent that undergirded common-law unions. Thus, African Americans of limited means most often opted for this domestic arrangement.[44] One of Powdermaker's Mississippi informants, for instance, explained that "a man is your husband if you live with him and love each other, but marriage is something for the outside world."[45] Some poor African Americans entered into formal marriages, and some working-class whites established common-law unions, though in modest numbers.

Louisiana law viewed common-law marriage in Janus-faced terms. On the one hand, the state did not recognize common-law marriage, considered common-law wives concubines, and treated common-law partners as fornicators and adulterers.[46] On the other hand, government officials typically perceived these unions in the same way as state-certified marriages. Census takers, for example, folded common-law partners, even those with different surnames, into the "married" category on their enumeration sheets. Similarly, police records, ranging from crime investigation reports to witness interview transcripts, used the categories interchangeably, sometimes describing partners as "common-law husband and wife" and simply as "husband and wife" within the same document. Coroners, when they listed the marital status of the decedent, ignored the distinction between informal and formal marriage. Judges were equally unfaithful to the legal difference. In homicide trials, where the formalities of the law were on full display, criminal court judges consistently rejected motions from attorneys to differentiate "paramours" from wives or to make "distinctions between legally married persons and persons living together." Nor was this a trivial matter in some trials, for judges explicitly ruled that a man was permitted to employ force for the protection of his "wife" from an informal marital union, even though common-law partners possessed "no legal relationship whatsoever."[47] In the everyday operation of the legal system, government officials ignored the distinction between state-certified marriages and common-law unions.

African American New Orleanians themselves simultaneously embraced and ignored the distinction between formal and informal domestic unions. Witnesses, killers, and dying victims of spousal homicide carefully identified the specific marital arrangement but then used familial terms more loosely. Bessie Walker, who fatally stabbed Rogers Matthews, told police investigators that the couple were common-law partners and that they lived "as man and wife."[48] More familial language, however, appeared in police records, newspaper accounts, witness interviews, and inquest documents relating to the homicide. Immediately after the deadly fight, for example, Walker's son frantically told a neighbor that "my Mamma cut my Daddy," though Matthews was not a legal or biological relative.[49] Walker's daughter described him as "her stepfather."[50] Newspapers mixed and matched terms when recounting the crime, sometimes describing the killer as the victim's "common-law wife" and other times omitting the modifier.[51]

Despite such fluidity, there were crucial distinctions between common-law and state-certified marriages, and these differences enhanced the common-law wives' authority in the household. First, because common-law unions were based on mutual consent, either spouse could terminate the marriage, bypassing filing fees, white judges and court clerks, legal formalities, and the middle-class, patriarchal framework that they supported.[52] Second, since husbands enjoyed no special property rights, wives lost no resources when these marriages ended. Women who owned houses or who held leases in their own names were not displaced. To the contrary, African American men often found themselves homeless when common-law unions dissolved.[53] After a three-week common-law marriage, for example, Ethel Joseph found that she and Ceopoles Johnson "were unable to get along, so I put him out of my house," leaving the forty-three-old man angry, humiliated, and with no place to live.[54] Likewise, Joe Neason's nine-month common-law marriage to thirty-three-year-old Ernestine Caldwell ended "when we had a fuss and she put me out."[55] For women such as Joseph and Caldwell, the custom-based terms of common-law marriage safeguarded their autonomy and protected their property, while for men such as Johnson and Neason, the dissolution process denied them patriarchal authority and left them searching for lodging. The enhanced symmetry in the power to terminate these marriages and in the financial impact of dissolution, by comparison to divorce proceedings, frequently worked to the advantage of African American women and to the disadvantage of African American men.

Thus, the definition and nature of common-law marriage shaped African American spousal homicide in interwar New Orleans. The mixture of imbalanced sex ratios, poverty, independent women, insecure men, hostility from legal institutions, and common-law marriage, however, proved to be volatile and bloody. Two-thirds of African American partner killings (and 70.2 percent of husband killings) occurred in common-law unions.[56] Moreover, in spousal homicides among common-law partners, the killers were disproportionately women. African American common-law wives committed 55.4 percent of spousal homicides, while women in formal marriages committed 47.5 percent of partner killings. The specific triggers that ignited deadly violence differed significantly in common-law unions as well.

Common-law partners often fought and killed one another in quarrels over household authority, the terms of which were negotiated in daily life, rather than embedded in law. While formal marriage granted husbands power over their dependents and their property, common-law marriage provided no such bulwarks for masculine privilege. At a prosaic level, partners defined and contested a wide range of household decisions, and minor disputes quickly became freighted with larger significance about control—literally, who made household decisions and who was the dominant partner was a zero-sum game.[57]

As a consequence, the threshold for conflict dropped. Seemingly trivial disputes laid bare larger battles over gender roles and household power. Again and again, African American men, anxious to establish their authority as men and husbands, demanded deference and obedience from women accustomed to autonomy and unwilling to submit.[58] Typically, a husband barked a command, his wife resisted, and then a deadly quarrel ensued. Oscar Pierce, a thirty-one-year-old peddler, for instance, attacked his thirty-one-year-old common-law wife, Agnes Davis, "for not coming to him when he called." She had informed him that she was "not in the habit of meeting him on [street] corners." Pierce then "told her that [he] would knock off her head off."[59] Similarly, thirty-two-year-old Edward Davis fatally shot his twenty-year-old wife, Lilly May Tucker, because she refused to come into the house when he insisted, while thirty-four-year-old Joseph Andrews killed Viola Lee, his thirty-year-old common-law wife, because "she refused to go downstairs" at his command.[60] To cops, crime-beat reporters, and proponents of white supremacy, the triggers for African American spousal violence seemed absurdly trivial, reaffirming their ideas about the emotional volatility and impulsiveness of these residents. But deadly quarrels about kindling and obedience were more complicated than these observers understood.

Arguments over dominance constituted the largest single trigger for deadly fights between common-law partners. More than a quarter of spousal homicides began with such a dispute. During the 1920s, 36 percent of common-law spousal homicides started when a husband issued an edict and his wife refused to comply. Lethal battles over control and dominance occurred nearly twice as often as the second-most-common spark, jealousy. In many instances, men's commands seemed unmistakably intended to force submission and demonstrate dominance. After returning home at 11:30 p.m., for example, thirty-eight-year-old, Mississippi-born James Taylor, according to police investigators, "undressed himself and in so doing dropped his trousers on the floor and told Ruby [Alexander] to pick them up, she refused to do so and they became engaged in an argument."[61]

The more egalitarian structure of common-law unions left lines of household authority undefined for working African American New Orleanians. As wage earners and often heads of households, African American common-law wives felt empowered and, at least in the quarrels that ended in death, typically refused to yield to their common-law husbands' expressions and threats of dominance. Men initiated the violence in the lion's share of these spousal homicides, usually in response to their wives' perceived insolence. When the women did not submit, prosaic quarrels turned violent.[62]

Again and again, common-law wives warned their husbands to desist or the women would respond in kind, though to the men such acquiescence would have connoted submission—and to a woman, no less. On January 14, 1923, for instance, Noah Matthews began beating Estelle Williams, and she cautioned him, "If you don't stop beating me I am going to cut you."[63] New Orleans ethnographers heard similar accounts from their informants. Edna Dunn explained that "her mother would not stand for her common-law-husband hitting her."[64] Another informant reported that "I told my daughter to take a gun to that nigger she's married to, if he bothers her again."[65]

Nor were these idle threats. African American common-law wives backed up their warnings with decisive, deadly actions. On May 17, 1930, seventeen-year-old Zelia Johnson explained that her drunken common-law husband began hitting her because he was dissatisfied with the meal that she had prepared for him. "I said god dam you[,] you hit me and if you hit me again I will stick you with this knife, then he hit me again and I stuck him."[66] Fannie Jackson offered a similar account of the death of her spouse. After her common-law husband, Richard Small, attacked her with a knife, "I told him 'if you cut me again I am going to kill you.' When he came after me the second time, I stabbed him under the heart."[67] In her statement to police investigators, thirty-nine-year-old Leona Walker described the vicious fight in which her common-law husband, Wandell Gettredge, attacked and taunted her and would not relent, despite her warnings. "My husband got in the bed and cursed me and slapped at me, and I told him if he would hit me again he won't like it, and he hit me again. . . . I got out of bed and got the iron in the kitchen and came back with the iron, and he said to me, I 'wouldn't be no woman if I wouldn't hit him,' and [I] slammed him in the head with the iron and I kept on hitting him with the iron."[68] The autopsy revealed that Walker's blows with the flatiron fractured Gettredge's temporal bone and upper right maxilla, lacerated the right side of his face, and caused multiple contusions and a cerebral concussion.[69]

While these lethal fights were usually spontaneous, rapidly spiraling from arguments and threats to abuse and finally to fatal retaliation, they typically did not occur in isolation and nearly always represented the last in a long series of violent clashes over household power. On October 7, 1939, Percy Payton, a thirty-seven-year-old day laborer, and his common-law wife, Lucille

Betz, visited Sam Moon's Place, a barroom. At 9:15 p.m., Payton turned to the thirty-four-year-old Betz and commanded her to "give me some of what you are drinking."[70] She responded by roaring, "I'll give you something," pulling a four-inch pocketknife "out of her bosom [*sic*]," and driving it into Payton's chest. The blade pierced the right ventricle of his heart.[71] When bar patrons gasped at her deadly response, Betz snarled, "I'll [*sic*] killed that M.F. and I'm glad he is dead." She later confided to a local journalist that the couple had lived together "as man and wife" for a decade and had often fought, usually over the allocation of household resources. Two weeks before the fatal stabbing, Payton had beaten her so badly that she "had gone to the 12th Precinct police to ask help to stop the abuse. No policeman came to her house." A few days later, the couple fought again, and Payton broke Betz's jaw and loosened three of her teeth. Five days prior to the homicide, they bickered over money, with Payton demanding that Betz "had better buy him liquor or he would break her jaw again." Determined to "protect herself," she began carrying the pocketknife that she stabbed Payton with when he ordered her to share her beverage.[72] The neighbor of another common-law couple whose marriage ended when the wife fatally stabbed her husband told police investigators that "they have been having these fights three or four times a Month for the longest."[73] Like dozens of spousal homicides, the final, lethal encounter was unplanned but was the result of sustained, violent conflict.

Many African American common-law wives, like Lucille Betz, carried weapons and were willing to use them. And, like Percy Payton, many common-law husbands discovered that their demands and violence elicited forceful, deadly resistance. According to police investigators, forty-five-year-old Gordon McKay attacked his seventeen-year-old common-law wife and died in the process. "He made a grab for her," the officer recorded. "He slapped her in the face and he kicked her and [she] pulled from her bosom a pocket knife and stab [*sic*] Gordon McKay."[74] Edward Francis met a similar fate on June 13, 1931, shortly after the laborer began beating his common-law wife, thirty-year-old Helen Clark, because she made too much noise and woke him from a drunken stupor. Dressed only in his "underclothing and socks," according to the police report, "he continued to beat her, she shoved him away and he, being under the influence of liquor, fell to the floor and Helen drew a knife from her bosom and pounced on him," fatally stabbing him.[75] In her statement to the police, Anna Nelson explained that she killed her common-law husband, Nelson Corner, in self-defense. "He struck me in the chest and he said 'You god dam son-of-a-bitch I'm going to kill you' and he come at me to hit me again and had something in his hand that he had taken out of his pocket, and I had my ice pick in my belt on the left side, and I took it out with my right hand and stuck him"—in the clavicle, chest, forehead, face, and wrist, according to the autopsy report.[76]

More often, abused common-law wives were unarmed when the abuse began, reached for the closest weapon to defend themselves, and employed it with deadly force. Two-thirds of homicides between common-law partners occurred in the home, and 68.8 percent of African American husband killers used sharp instruments, particularly kitchen implements, such as knives and ice picks. Descriptions of the final, lethal fights were remarkably similar to one another. At 11:00 a.m. on March 2, 1924, the inebriated Henry Long chased Susie Harris, his common-law wife of four years, through the house, beating her as she tried to flee. When the fight progressed to the kitchen, Harris "picked [up] from a table in the room a bread knife and stabbed him" in the neck, shoulder, and chest.[77] After Louis Bruneau struck Rosie Baptiste, she "secure[d] an ice pick which was on the table in the same room, and with same stabbed her paramour," while Dora Taylor "secured an Ice Pick from the sideboard" and impaled Edward Sanders with it.[78] When Archie McGee, a thirty-nine-year-old longshoreman, struck Sarah Gates with a chair, the thirty-nine-year-old domestic servant "picked up a pair of scissors which she was using to make a quilt" and "stuck him on the left side of the neck."[79] Estelle Brown "managed to get the pocket knife off of the trunk"; Ethel Joseph "grabbed a knife from the table"; Dorothy Pruitt "picked up a paring knife off of the kitchen table."[80] Although the violence was unplanned, deadly weapons abounded, within easy reach, in every household.

By contrast, common-law husbands, who, more often than not, were the ultimate victims in the domestic violence that they initiated, typically relied on guns. While men usually began the physical confrontations by punching or bludgeoning their partners, blows from fists accounted for only 4.8 percent of African American common-law wife killings. Blunt instruments, ranging from chair legs to bottles, produced another 3.2 percent of common-law uxoricides. Over half of the African American men who killed common-law wives used firearms. But these husbands seldom carried the weapons. Rather, they kept their guns on mantels, stored in closets, or stashed under bedroom pillows.[81] When disputes spiraled out of control, and particularly when husbands' slaps and punches failed to cow their defiant wives, the men often rushed to fetch their firearms. Fred Miller, for example, told police officers investigating the death of Victoria Doneght, his common-law wife, that he "went to a bedroom, obtained his revolver, returned to the kitchen and shot the woman three times."[82] In most cases of African American common-law spousal homicide, however, women grabbed the closest knives or ice picks and employed lethal self-defense after they were struck. Thus, common-law wives generally dispatched their abusive partners with paring knives, meat cleavers, or scissors before their husbands had secured their revolvers. Even though guns inflicted lethal injuries more often than carving knives or ice picks, African American women killed preemptively, which likely accounted for the higher proportion of husband killings.

In one other way, common-law marriage contributed to the carnage from spousal homicide. Early twentieth-century white observers, such as the ethnographer John Dollard, believed that jealousy seared common-law unions. In these informal arrangements, he argued, husbands exercised less proprietary control over their wives' bodies and hence more often resorted to violence. "Since the Negro cannot hold his woman by force, say, of a strong family institution, he must do it by personal force instead," Dollard explained.[83] But common-law unions in early twentieth-century New Orleans were often stable and long lasting, and jealousy and the violence of proprietary sexual control triggered only one-fifth of African American common-law spousal homicides, a far lower proportion than Dollard predicted.[84] Because separation ended the union, common-law wives most often immediately dissolved the marriage and tossed their partners into the street as soon as they suspected infidelity. Put differently, extramarital affairs signaled the end of "consent" and therefore the end of the union. As a result, there were relatively fewer lingering marriages that were slowly torn asunder by jealousy and allegations of infidelity.

But the suddenness of dissolution occasionally led partners, nearly always men, to contest the finality of the couple's separation. In the 20.7 percent of the common-law spousal homicides triggered by jealousy, a recently jilted man encountered his ex-wife, sometimes with her new partner, sparking a violent confrontation. On August 24, 1928, after their two-year common-law marriage dissolved and thirty-one-year-old Viola Lee returned to "her rightful [i.e., legal] husband," thirty-four-old Joseph Andrews declared that "he could not live without her" and shot her five times, four of them after she crumpled to the ground.[85] Lee and Ernestine Caldwell's twelve-year union ended in 1938, and both then formed new common-law marriages. When Lee saw Ernestine with her new partner, he bellowed, "I should kill you both," and fatally shot her in the abdomen. The city's African American newspaper, which had middle-class sensibilities, termed these deadly, jealousy-infused quarrels between former partners "common-lawism."[86] But in fact such triggers for spousal homicide were unusual in African American common-law marriages.

For the one-third of African American spousal homicides that occurred in formal marriages, the etiology of lethal violence was very different. While formally married killers and victims tended to be young and poor, they were slightly older and slightly wealthier, probably reflecting the class-based aspirations of those who opted for state-certified marriages. Among legally married African American spouse killers, 86.8 percent came from households headed by an unskilled worker, compared with 95.1 percent for the common-law assailants. Nearly all of these modest differences were gender based. Demographically, wife killers in formal and informal domestic unions were virtually identical. Husband killers, however, varied. Women in legal marriages who killed their domestic partners were nearly two years older than those in common-law unions. Furthermore, 81.5 percent of the formally married African American women who killed their partners lived in households headed by unskilled workers, whereas the comparable figure for common-law wives was 97.1 percent. In short, husband killers were young and poor, but those in legal marriages tended to be slightly older and slightly wealthier. The youngest and poorest women proved to be particularly unwilling to submit to their partners' patriarchal demands, while relatively older wives and those not quite as mired in poverty more often lived—and killed—in state-certified marriages.

For African American New Orleanians in formal domestic unions, sexual jealousy and tensions surrounding dissolution—rather than issues revolving around household authority—constituted the leading sparks for spousal homicide, accounting for 29.7 percent and 25.6 percent of partner killings. Moreover, men committed 52.5 percent of African American spousal homicides between legally married partners, compared with 44.6 of homicides between common-law partners. For those who invested in the rituals of legal marriage—complete with the gender ideology it represented and buttressed—the collapse of the marital unit and sexual control loomed especially large. At least judging by the triggers in domestic homicides, separation was particularly devastating for legally married African American husbands, who most often killed wives for infidelity or for refusing to reconcile after leaving them.

Frequently, such men tracked down their wives, begged for or demanded reconciliation, and then shot those who rejected them. Half of women killed by their legal husbands had left their partners, compared with one-quarter in common-law uxoricides. Sometimes, fury from infidelity combined with anger over separation. On August 6, 1925, thirty-one-year-old Charles Butler accused his wife, nineteen-year-old Lilly Butler, "of keeping company with another man," and she left him. Six days later, Charles followed his estranged wife to her mother's house and asked for a reconciliation. When Lilly refused, he shot her in the right temple.[87] Similarly, Eddie Palmer, a forty-eight-year-old deckhand, tracked down his forty-two-year-old estranged wife, Juanita, at her sister's house, tried "to get her to return home with him," and when she refused shot her in the head, chest, abdomen, and right hand. He also shot and killed his sister-in-law, Ella Despinasses.[88]

Unlike the overwhelming majority of common-law wife killings, these were premeditated acts. Nearly two-thirds of the murderers used guns, which they brought anticipating that the women might reject their pleas for reconciliation. For example, on August 8, 1929, Sam Miles, a twenty-seven-year-old day laborer, borrowed a .38 caliber revolver, and the next day he went in search of his twenty-three-year-old wife, who had left him and moved in with a friend. When he found her, Miles began "pleading with his wife to come back to him." Morise Miles refused, "telling him that he treated her to [*sic*] mean to go back with him; and she would rather die." Sam Miles immediately "drew his revolver" and shot and killed both his estranged wife and her friend Rachel Jefferson.[89] For men in formal marriages, much more than for husbands in common-law unions, uxoricide was a purposeful act, carried out in response to humiliation.[90]

When legally married African American women killed their husbands, they also frequently planned the violence. Whereas more than two-thirds of common-law wives used knives or other sharp objects, usually relying on the first weapon they could reach during a violent quarrel, 58.6 percent of formally married women who killed their husbands used guns. They most often shot their partners either in acts of jealous revenge or in self-defense, having armed themselves in anticipation of being attacked by their spiteful, violent partners. Spontaneous lethal battles over household authority, such as Willie Hutton's homicide, occurred among married couples, but jealousy was the leading trigger when legally married women killed their partners. On September 11, 1926, for example, thirty-two-year-old Florence Mackie, accompanied by her sister, followed her husband of eight years to the home of his lover and asked the owner of the house to summon Leonze Mackie to the street. When he appeared, she shot him in the chest with a .38 caliber revolver.[91]

Finally, the interaction among the social geography of New Orleans, imbalanced sex ratios, and the racial climate of the city, particularly during the 1920s, also contributed to the death toll from homicide in African American homes.

Compounding the pressures generated by family formation in overcrowded areas without adequate housing stock, African American households disproportionately included "nonfamily persons."[92] Poverty and the concentration of African Americans in small, bounded pockets of the city compelled many families to take in boarders, usually young single men.[93] In 1930, nearly one African American household in six had a lodger, double the proportion of white households in the city.[94] Moreover, because young single newcomers comprised a large share of their community, African American families were smaller, with fewer children, than white families.[95] As a consequence, African American homes and apartments contained a higher proportion of adults, often unrelated to one another. Furthermore, lodgers tended to reside in homes with few children and in homes headed by women, precisely the households where the lines of household authority were most ambiguous and where domestic violence was most likely to erupt. Contemporary observers worried that lodgers might "constitute a disruptive factor in family life."[96]

The presence of so many non-family-members created two problems, both of which fueled violence. First, the mix of unrelated adults in cramped, overcrowded homes blurred the boundaries between private space and public space. Particularly during the 1920s, New Orleans offered relatively few leisure spaces that African American residents were permitted to use. In 1928, for example, the city had one playground "for Negroes," compared with seventeen for white residents. Downtown and French Quarter saloons and restaurants tended to provide sections for African Americans, awkwardly walled off from the main drinking areas and dining rooms. As a result, a wide range of leisure activities that normally concentrated in public settings were displaced, and African American New Orleanians often held card games, for example, in their houses and apartments, bringing more and more unrelated young men into crowded private, domestic space. Some of the quarrels that ordinarily erupted in barrooms exploded in homes. On November 19, 1922, for instance, an African American steamboat roustabout, known only as Uncle George, lost money in a dice game held on the second-floor "gallery" (balcony) of a rooming house on South Rampart Street. Angry about his losses, Uncle George chased forty-four-year-old Joe Gilbert, a roustabout who resided in the building, from the gallery through the rooming house to a stairway, where he bludgeoned his coworker to death with a wooden plank.[97] Violent disputes over dice or craps games constituted the third-leading trigger for homicides in African American homes during the early 1920s, accounting for nearly one-tenth of these deaths. Furthermore, lethal violence in African American homes occurred as often between acquaintances or neighbors as between domestic partners.

Second, the presence of lodgers and the porous boundaries of African American private space added to the fragility of 1920s African American family life. Jealousy was the second-leading spark for African American home homicides during the early 1920s.[98] In many instances, husbands, already insecure about their authority, worried that the bachelors boarding in their homes and apartments would take advantage of domestic tensions and become sexually involved with their wives. In some cases, these fears were well founded. Late in October 1924, Thomas Smith, a forty-nine-year-old carpenter, bickered with his wife, Ella, and the couple separated. Two weeks later, on November 4, he "returned and stated that he wanted to make up with her." As they talked, thirty-seven-year-old Andrew Williams, a day laborer, knocked on the door and asked to come in. Ella Smith "told him he could not as Tom was there." Williams replied, "How come. I cant [sic] come in[?] I was here tonight." A moment later, Williams shot and killed Thomas Smith.[99]

Such encounters proved to be especially deadly because they occurred in homes, which often had guns in them. During the mid-1920s, 64.1 percent of African American New Orleanians who committed homicide used firearms. But in African American homicides taking place in private residences and between acquaintances, 87.5 percent of killers shot their victims. Moreover, while friends, witnesses, cops, and especially saloonkeepers often interceded in disagreements erupting in public settings before they became violent, the disputes unfolding in homes escalated beyond the gaze of observers. A quarter of all African American homicides between acquaintances during the bloody 1920s occurred in homes, and more male-on-male homicide than male-on-female or female-on-male homicides took place in domestic settings.

Disputes in homes, therefore, more often involved guns and resulted in bloodshed and death. Thus, the mix of ecological conditions, demographic pressures, and economic forces that weakened the boundary between public and private space in African American New Orleans pushed social life into homes and, in the process, increased the lethality of quarrels.[100] In 1925, the African American home homicide rate soared to 8.3 times the white rate.

*

By the mid-1920s, homicide in New Orleans reached its highest level for the era, as did spousal homicide, lethal violence by women, and deadly violence in homes. Moreover, the gap between African American and white homicide ballooned. In 1920, the African American homicide rate was 4.9 times the white rate. Five years later, it expanded to 7.8 times the white rate. Furthermore, in 1925, the African American spousal homicide rate was 7.1 times the white rate, and the African American husband-killing rate exceeded the white one by 22.8-fold.

A confluence of forces contributed to the surge in African American violence and especially ignited the explosions in spousal homicide, lethal violence by women, and deadly fights in homes. Demographic factors, however, played a central role. The Great Migration brought thousands of young, poor African Americans to New Orleans during the 1920s, increasing a segment of the population with high rates of victimization from violent crime. Sex ratios in the city fell increasingly out of balance as a result of the flow of newcomers, with young working-class women far outnumbering young men in the African American community. A high proportion of these women secured employment, supported themselves, headed their own households, owned or leased their houses, and became self-reliant.

Cultural and historical forces reinforced the autonomy of working-class African American women in New Orleans during this period. These women preferred common-law unions over formal, state-certified marriages, since such arrangements enhanced their authority in household life. Accustomed to autonomy and participating in a marital form that afforded them relative equality, African American wives often resisted their husbands' demands for control over household resources and household authority—or, as the city's African American newspaper said of one spousal homicide, it occurred as a common-law husband struggled to establish himself as the "ruling mogul of that shanty."[101] The men, however, clashed with self-reliant partners who often refused to yield to masculine privilege. As a result, the lion's share of African American spousal homicides occurred in common-law unions, and, more often than not, husbands began the quarrels and wives ended them—with ice picks and paring knives.

Institutional factors also contributed to the violence in African American homes. The courts largely ignored these bloody battles and left African American residents to handle their own problems, abetting reliance on aggressive self-help. Police indifference reinforced the ambiguous lines of household authority that sparked domestic quarrels. When law enforcers responded to domestic violence complaints in white homes, they typically aimed to stop the conflict without undermining masculine privilege. Hence, patrolmen strengthened patriarchal authority in white marriages and reduced uncertainly about domestic power. By ignoring conflicts in African American households, cops reinforced the symmetry or ambiguity in domestic authority that helped to elevate trivial disagreements about routine matters into more serious fights about dominance.

Ecological conditions, particularly during the 1920s, fanned the flames of domestic discord as well. Because African American New Orleanians in the age of Jim Crow lived in overcrowded pockets, surrounded by white neighborhoods, and were trapped in poverty, many residents took in lodgers. The high proportion of unattached people living in cramped quarters added to spousal tensions and weakened the boundaries between private and public space for African American residents. As boarders became a source of friction and a focal point for jealousy, and as dice games and craps games brought more outsiders into African American households, the potential for conflict and violence rose. Moreover, these clashes unfolded close to the weapons that residents stored in their homes, increasing the likelihood that guns, rather than fists or bottles, would be employed. With these layers of tensions and public activities occurring in private space, African American homes became the most homicidal settings in the city by the mid-1920s.

In sum, ambiguous lines of household authority and fluid boundaries separating public and private space combined to strain gender roles during the early 1920s and fueled an explosion in African American violence. In the years immediately after the Great War, an enormous, race-based gap, especially in spousal violence, homicide by women, and deadly fights occurring in New Orleans homes, emerged. These disparities fluctuated over time but persisted through the 1920s, 1930s, and early 1940s.

CHAPTER 3

"She Made Me Her Dog"

At 2:10 p.m. on October 27, 1927, three New Orleans police officers discovered one of the most grisly crime scenes in the city's history. Fifteen minutes earlier, Nedda Douglas, an African American resident of an Ursuline Street rooming house, had alerted the police that something seemed amiss in her white neighbor's apartment. At seven the previous evening, one of the inhabitants, twenty-nine-year-old Henry Moity, had warned Douglas and her common-law husband not to "get scared if they heard the children crying early in the morning." Douglas did indeed hear wails coming from the Moitys' apartment shortly after midnight. But the next morning she heard nothing and saw no one from the household. Concerned because three adults and three children lived in the cramped upstairs rooms, and because Henry, a sign painter, and Theresa, his twenty-six-year-old wife, had recently quarreled, Douglas entered the apartment, "saw blood on the bed," and summoned the police.[1]

The cops encountered a scene of unimaginable carnage. Blood covered the walls, saturated two mattresses, and pooled on the floor. The policemen noticed a large trunk, with a machete sitting suspiciously atop it. Opening it, they found the body of twenty-seven-year-old Leonide Moity, Henry's brother Joseph's wife. Her head had been severed from her shoulders; her upper and lower jaws had been crushed; her "disarticulated" arms, legs, and left hand had been tucked under her torso. Moments later, the policemen spotted a second trunk, this one containing the mutilated body of Theresa Moity, Henry's wife. Theresa's head had also been severed; her arms were cut off at the shoulder and her legs at the knee; one hand was badly mangled and the other chopped off at the wrist.[2]

The police immediately identified Henry Moity as the principal suspect. Their investigation took them to the home of Alcee Lecamu, Henry Moity's sister. She revealed that three weeks earlier her brother Joseph, a thirty-two-year-old day laborer, had separated from his wife, Leonide, left the Ursuline Street apartment they had been sharing with Henry's family, and moved in with her. Moreover, at 2:00 a.m. on October 27, according to Lecamu, her younger brother, Henry, had mysteriously dropped off his three children, five-year-old Theda Anna, three-year-old Gloria Swanson, and two-year-old Henry Calvin, and disappeared without explanation. Three days later, a deputy sheriff in Lockport, Louisiana, thirty-five miles southwest of New Orleans, captured the fleeing suspect and returned him to city authorities. Henry Moity initially offered a confusing "yarn" about a sailor butchering the women.[3] But the loquacious suspect quickly recanted, confessed to beheading and dismembering his wife and sister-in-law as they slept, and then provided police detectives, traffic cops, the district attorney, newspaper reporters, and anyone else who would listen with detailed accounts of the crime and rambling explanations for his actions.[4]

According to his six confessions, Henry Moity's world began to crumble when his family migrated to New Orleans.[5] Henry, Joe, and their wives hailed from New Iberia, Louisiana, an impoverished town 130 miles west of New Orleans. Henry and Theresa Alfano were "childhood sweethearts."[6] But Theresa married another man. At the age of sixteen, however, she separated from her husband and moved in with nineteen-year-old Henry, who had completed two years of schooling and worked as a day laborer. They lived together "as man and wife" until Theresa secured a divorce, at which time the teenagers married.[7] Henry served in the navy during World War I, grew bored with military life while stationed in Charleston, deserted after a furlough, and received a dishonorable discharge in 1921.[8] When he returned to New Iberia, his wife and her friend "Leonie" Lee, who had married Joe Moity, clamored to resettle in New Orleans. The young women had become fascinated by reports of the city's "bright lights and its big stores."[9] Soon, the Moity brothers, their young wives, and their children moved to the city.

But "city life was too much" for Theresa and Leonie, and their indecent behavior, according to Henry Moity and his siblings, led to the women's murders.[10] The Moity brothers also fared poorly in New Orleans, neither securing a stable or well-paying job, despite the prosperity of the mid-1920s. Henry found work as a sign painter and Joe as a laborer, but the two couples and their five children lived huddled together in a tiny apartment, on which they often could not pay the rent.[11] Even as Henry and Joe struggled to support their families, Theresa and Leonie, according to testimony at Henry's murder trial, became "dizzied by city life as though by a heady wine."[12] They began "running around with other men" and neglecting their children.[13] Theresa and Leonie also "taunted" their husbands, flaunting their infidelity and causing neighbors to laugh at the beleaguered brothers.[14] Henry stated that the women "said they were going out and make some money, because me and Joe couldn't make any."[15] More than once, Henry caught his wife with other men.[16] Court testimony described how Henry had swallowed his pride and begged Theresa to "again become the kind of wife and mother she had been before they came to New Orleans." But she "laughed at him, and said she would slap his face with money she had gained by prostitution."[17] "I'd come home," Henry admitted, "and find the kids alone with nothing to eat—it was awful."[18] When Theresa Moity announced her intention to leave Henry, the despondent, cuckolded young husband first considered killing himself and the children but then hatched a plan to slaughter his wife and sister-in-law, who he believed had lured his spouse into a spiral of debauchery.[19]

Hamstrung by Moity's repeated, salacious confessions, his lawyer, Chandler Luzenberg Jr., a former parish prosecutor who represented a number of high-profile murderers during this period, posited an insanity defense, arguing that "Henry was driven mad by her infidelity." Defense co-counsel James A. Lindsay, also a prominent attorney and politician, explained that the defendant "loved his wife. He learned of her infidelity and pled with her to mend her ways," yet "she laughed at him." Lindsay asked the jurors "is it any wonder that the fractured mind of Henry Moity gave way, and that he committed a crime of which he would before have been incapable?"[20] The Orleans Parish jury, however, convicted Henry of murdering Theresa Moity, and he subsequently pleaded guilty to murdering Leonide Moity. Judge J. Arthur Charbonnet sentenced him to consecutive life terms in prison.[21]

New Orleanians condemned the killings but embraced the killer. Moity remained unrepentant, convinced that his actions were justified. During one of his confessions, he explained, "I am not sorry that this happened. That woman drove me crazy."[22] After his conviction, Moity insisted that deputies need not handcuff him, declaring, "I'm a law-abiding citizen. I'm not a criminal."[23] His relatives concurred. Leon Moity, his father, called Henry "a good boy. The women drove him to it. He was forced to do it."[24] Joe Moity, who told journalists that "he was sorry his brother killed his [Joe's] wife but that he was personally glad to get rid of her," added that Henry "was always a jolly boy until his wife went wrong."[25] The police officers who interrogated Henry Moity, detectives who had "heard confessions time and again," also "seemed unanimous in expressing sympathy for the man, in spite of the horrible crime."[26] Similarly, Dr. George Roeling, the parish coroner and a fierce proponent of law and order, held Theresa and Leonide Moity largely responsible for their own beheadings. "When they came to New Orleans," he concluded, their "sudden reaction led them into indiscreet actions which caused their murder."[27]

The public agreed. The *New Orleans States* estimated that half of the local population held "sentiment in favor of Moity."[28] Even the jurors who convicted Henry Moity considered him a victim of circumstances. When the killer applied for clemency, after serving seven years at the Louisiana State Penal Farm, ten of the twelve jurors submitted petitions in his support. More than one thousand New Orleanians also signed petitions endorsing clemency for the military deserter who had decapitated and dismembered his sleeping wife and sister-in-law, crammed their bodies into steamer trunks, abandoned his children, and fled into the night.[29]

The murders of Theresa and Leonide Moity were hardly typical New Orleans homicides. Between 1920 and 1945, only 1.3 percent of local killers slaughtered their victims with axes or machetes, and no other New Orleans killer hacked off his victims' heads and limbs. Moreover, only 1.5 percent of local homicides had more than a single victim. Just one other white spouse killer also murdered other family members. Nor did many other New Orleans killers gain such notoriety, confess so frequently, attract as much popular sympathy, or revel in the voyeuristic publicity surrounding their crimes.

In other ways, however, Henry Moity's "diabolical" actions on October 27, 1927, reflected common elements of white spousal homicide.[30] If the brutality of his crimes was unique, the sparks that ignited Moity's explosion of violence were not. Similar tensions, pressures, and quarrels, blending romantic love and murderous rage, fueled dozens of white spousal homicides, particularly during the turbulent 1920s. Again and again, white New Orleanians killed their domestic partners after the women announced their intention to separate. Moreover, men committed the majority of white spousal homicides, and their crimes were typically premeditated.

As with African American spousal murder, a collision of demographic changes, economic pressures, institutional practices, and cultural forces shaped white intimate violence in New Orleans from 1920 to 1945. Furthermore, the chaotic transformations of the 1920s, the inconsistent responses of legal institutions, and the resulting pressures on gender roles roiled domestic relations across racial lines. For both white and African American New Orleanians, spousal violence exploded during the early 1920s and constituted the leading single source of homicide.

But the constellation of pressures that rocked family life unfolded in race-specific ways. Economic forces and police practices, for instance, affected white and African American households differently. Thus, the frequency and morphology of spousal homicides among white and African American residents were distinct. Even the specific triggers that generated the final, lethal skirmishes between husbands and wives assumed race-specific patterns. Although New Orleans's racial hierarchy played no direct role in Henry Moity's decision to behead his wife (and sister-in-law) with a machete, his spousal homicide stood apart from those committed by African American residents and shared much with other white partner killings, echoing the omnipresent imprint of race on daily life in the Jim Crow urban South.

*

White and African American spousal homicides were similar in some ways. Both soared during the early 1920s, with rates quintupling for the former and more than quadrupling for the latter residents. Moreover, for the 1920–45 period, the white partner-killing rate peaked in 1926, while the African American spousal homicide rate hit its highest level in 1925. Furthermore, in a city renowned for its alcohol consumption and raucous saloon culture (even during Prohibition), white residents killed their spouses at three times the rate of white saloon homicides, while African American New Orleanians slaughtered their domestic partners at four times the rate of African American barroom killings. Quarrels about patriarchy and masculine privilege also triggered deadly spousal conflict in white and African American and households alike.

But these similarities paled in comparison with race-based differences in such violence. Despite roughly comparable surges, African American partner killing erupted with far greater frequency. Between 1920 and 1925, spousal violence accounted for 20.9 percent of African American homicides and 13 percent of white homicides. In addition, during the mid-1920s, the African American spousal homicide rate swelled to nearly six times the comparable figure for white New Orleanians.[31]

The profiles of white and African American spouse killers and victims differed in more than race. White residents who committed partner homicide, for example, were more than seven years older than their African American counterparts, averaging 39.1.[32] White victims were older as well, with a mean age of 36.6 years, while the average for African American spousal homicide victims was 32.1 years. Similarly, white spouse killers were wealthier. Whereas 41.2 percent of white spouse killers lived in households headed by unskilled workers, the comparable figure for African Americans was 91.6 percent. These differences partly reflected the overall composition of the city's white and African American populations, though white spouse killers were more concentrated among middle-aged and relatively more affluent residents than the larger white population (or than white killers in general), just as African American killers were younger and poorer than the larger African American community. Other differences also set white spouse killers apart. For instance, husbands committed 61.6 percent of white intimate-partner homicides, but wives committed 52.7 percent of African American spouse killings.

Furthermore, the triggers that ignited spouse killings, the weapons employed to dispatch partners, and the postviolence responses varied by race. In white households, jealousy and separation constituted the leading sparks. By contrast, prosaic battles over household authority, such as Silvia and Willie Hutton's deadly quarrel about kindling, produced more African American spousal homicides than any other specific trigger. When domestic disagreements mushroomed and anger turned to rage, white New Orleanians overwhelmingly reached for guns, shooting their victims in 77.9 percent of spousal homicides. African Americans more often relied on ice picks and knives and stabbed their spouses in 47.3 percent of such crimes.[33] Economic factors contributed to the gap—ice picks were less expensive and more accessible than firearms. But other forces assumed more significant roles in weapon choice. White spouse killers also reacted differently after they murdered their partners. Nearly half immediately attempted suicide, compared with one-twentieth of African American spouse killers.[34]

These contrasts reflected larger, wider racial differences in domestic life and spousal conflict. Just as the gender ideals linked to common-law marriage influenced the morphology of African American spousal homicide, the social and cultural norms associated with formal, state-sanctioned domestic unions shaped white family violence. Two-thirds of African American partner killings occurred among common-law partners, compared with one-fifth among white New Orleanians.[35]

White spousal homicide assumed two distinct forms in New Orleans between 1920 and 1945. In 59 percent of these killings, the partners lived together at the time. The morphology of these homicides was unique. The age and class backgrounds of those involved, the specific triggers for the violence, and the killers' explanations for slaughtering their cohabiting spouses stood in sharp contrast to the factors connected with deadly violence between estranged partners.

White New Orleanians who killed cohabiting spouses were typically in their thirties and came from working-class backgrounds. The mean age of these assailants was 37.5 years. Their victims had a similar demographic profile, with an average age of 38.9 years. Furthermore, 39.5 percent of killers and victims came from households headed by unskilled workers and an additional 50 percent from households headed by semiskilled or skilled workers. White New Orleanians who murdered their cohabiting partners, in short, were not young newlyweds struggling with the transition to married life, and they were not the poorest residents of the city.

The lion's share of white spousal homicides occurring in intact marriages were bound up with men's systematic use of violence in the service of patriarchal control—what sociologists have called "patriarchal terrorism."[36] These husbands routinely employed coercion and force to maintain dominance. The leading single spark for spousal homicide was jealousy. In one-third of the killings, husbands accused their wives of infidelity, triggering the lethal altercations. Forty-nine-year-old Jack White, for example, became furious when his wife "got into a conversation" with another man at a dance.[37] He renewed the quarrel later at their home, asking thirty-eight-year-old Pearl White if she intended "to be true to him," and then fatally stabbed her.[38] Similarly, according to Annabel Hanselman, her thirty-five-year-old husband, Frederick, attacked her "because I was dancing with one of his friends."[39] These men rarely had specific evidence that their wives were unfaithful.

Instead, allegations of infidelity and, in fact, most explanations for the men's use of violence were pretexts, intended to justify assertions of dominance. Battles over money, for example, provided husbands with convenient opportunities to affirm patriarchal authority and to underscore their wives' dependence. Robert Mariner told police investigators that he became angry when his wife "returned without sugar for which he had given her 50 cents."[40] The forty-five-year-old sailor explained that he "grabbed hold of her and gave her a good shaking," killing the woman. Patrolmen at the crime scene found "a large smear of blood on the wall" and a bag containing a pound of sugar on the floor.[41] Similarly, one woman told detectives that "I asked my husband to give me the automobile keys and some money, as I wanted to go get some groceries, and he said that he was not going to give me any money because it was his money . . . my Husband got up from the tabel [*sic*] and he struck me with his fist and he grabbed my hair with both hands, and began pulling me around the kitchen."[42] In these homicides, husbands instigated disputes over money to highlight their wives' dependence and coerce their submission.

More often, however, no specific challenge to husbands' authority—real or imagined—triggered men's murderous assaults on their wives. The husbands beat their wives without any provocation or explanation. Forty-six-year-old Amelia Reike disclosed to police investigators that her drunken husband, Frankie, repeatedly assaulted her. First he was dissatisfied with dinner, and at bedtime he attacked her after screaming, "Got [*sic*] damn it[,] you got to get out of the bed." He then pulled the covers off of her and tossed her onto the floor. When she closed the bedroom window, because she was cold without a blanket and sitting on the floor, Frankie Reike "got up and told me to open the window. I opened the window," she explained, "and he came to me and started beating me up."[43] Women in such marriages lived in constant fear that their husbands would inexplicably erupt in homicidal rage.

In these fatal quarrels, wives did not question their partners' behavior or contest patriarchal authority—in contrast to wife killings in African American New Orleans. White battered women usually complied with their husbands' demands and endured vicious attacks nonetheless. Many dying victims lamented that there was nothing they could do to placate their partners.[44] He "had the worst temper of any man in the world," one woman explained. "He would get mad at trifles."[45] When a police captain asked thirty-six-year-old Eugenie Cressy, as she lay dying, why her husband, Max, a patrolman at the docks, had attacked her, the woman replied, "For nothing."[46]

In nearly every case of spousal homicide involving cohabiting white New Orleanians, a long history of domestic abuse preceded the final skirmish. Forty-four-year-old Virginia DeMaggio described her marriage as "20 years of torture," telling police investigators that she and her husband, a grocer, "hadn't been married long before he began to abuse me. Sometimes he would slap me, then he would strike me with his closed hand. Later he began to kick me. I couldn't do anything."[47] In her statement to police investigators, on March 12, 1922, Maude Kippers revealed that her husband, a thirty-one-year-old night watchman, "has abused me from the day we have been married until now. He kicked me and grabbed me by the hair and dragged me all over the floor and kicked me and punched me."[48] Some wife killers defiantly acknowledged the endemic abuse. Fifty-two-year-old Frank Cutala, a scissors grinder, unapologetically recounted "daily quarrels and occasional fistic encounters" with his fifty-five-year-old wife, Mary, telling a detective, "I don't care if they hang me now that I've gotten her out of the way."[49]

Neighbors often described endless fights and told police investigators that they became inured to the screams coming from the next apartment. On April 14, 1921, the residents of Bartholomew Street heard twenty-six-year-old Philipine Hughes cry, "My God, Sam, don't do it; don't do it," followed by the sound of three gunshots. They told police detectives that the couple frequently quarreled, and "for that reason they did not pay much attention to Friday morning's verbal outbreak which preceded the shooting."[50] Similarly, Mrs. G. Weiss testified that Mildred Welch screeched, "'Don't hit me Bill,' then it was quiet for a few minutes, then the loud talking began again and I heard Mrs. Welch scream 'don't choke me you are killing me.'" Accustomed to hearing such cries, Weiss asked her husband to turn up the volume on their radio.[51]

The level of violence typically escalated over time. Victims, often in their dying declarations, explained that early in their marriages their husbands had slapped them, and over time punching and kicking replaced slapping. But only 4.1 percent of these assailants used their fists, and 8.7 percent relied on blunt instruments to kill their spouses. Abusive husbands, in short, seldom committed uxoricide during the first violent quarrel with their spouses. Nor did they graduate from spouse beater to wife killer by landing one additional, deadly blow during a routine violent argument. Rather, the level of brutality rose over time, and the men eventually turned to firearms, ending their marriages with the pull of the trigger.[52] In murders occurring among white cohabiting spouses, 69.4 percent of killers used guns.[53]

Most often, these homicides were premeditated, even though years of abuse preceded the last quarrel. Wife killers did not carry guns in their homes. In early twentieth-century New Orleans, men stored their weapons in closets or on mantels. Although white city dwellers in intact marriages who committed uxoricide did not carefully plan their crimes, neither did they merely grab the closest weapon in the heat of the moment, which would have been a kitchen knife, ice pick, bottle, or chair. Instead, when the brutality of the domestic violence surged, the men purposefully fetched guns and shot their wives. One-third used shotguns.

Ironically, most fatal encounters between cohabiting white spouses did not result in wife killings, even though men nearly always initiated the violence. Rather, patriarchal terrorism proved to be more deadly for men than for women.[54] Wives killed husbands in 53.1 percent of homicides occurring among cohabiting partners.[55] For all of the public discourse about demure, submissive southern white women, New Orleans wives fought back.

White husband killings were reactive. The women employed lethal violence to save their own lives.[56] In nearly every such homicide, white women in intact marriages who killed their husbands had suffered many years of abuse. Ida Dietz, for example, told the Orleans Parish district attorney that her husband, Fred, a fifty-eight-year-old carpenter, "had beaten and abused me nearly every day for four years," while Josephine Corso testified to a jury that her husband, Anthony, "beat me . . . all the time I lived with him, nine years."[57]

To persuade cops and prosecutors of the abuse that they had endured before fighting back, many husband killers revealed physical evidence, peeling back their clothing to expose the welts and scars that covered their bodies. Eleanor Fontana showed detectives bruises and cuts all over her body and explained that Dominick Fontana "has abused me like that for four years."[58] Similarly, Sara Kellaway reported that "my back looked like a map of Europe in black and blue."[59] "I loved him and didn't want to do it," Lillian Rodwell explained, "but he kept beating me, and he's so powerful I was scared. Why just look at these bruises."[60]

Many of these women had turned to the police for help before resorting to lethal self-defense. Lillian Rodwell reminded detectives investigating Thomas Rodwell's death that "she had been forced on several occasions to call the Ninth Precinct police station for protection from her husband," himself a patrolman assigned to that station.[61] But beat cops usually either failed to respond or intervened halfheartedly. This mainly reflected the working-class backgrounds of policemen, who identified with the men and the gender hierarchy that undergirded patriarchal terrorism.[62] In some cases, patrolmen had a special bond with the wife beaters and found themselves uncomfortably investigating the deaths of their colleagues, such as Thomas Rodwell.

Many New Orleans policemen ignored domestic violence complaints. Mrs. John Porter repeatedly sought police protection from her husband. Initially, she turned to the neighborhood patrolman, Arthur Leninger, who "told me he could do nothing for me." When Porter telephoned the Third Precinct Station and pleaded for help, the clerk also insisted that "he could do nothing for me."[63] Porter persisted until an irate Patrolman Leninger arrested her on a charge of "conduct unbecoming," leading the abused wife to conclude that "in the future I will not rely on police protection. If my husband annoys me I will protect myself."[64]

More often, patrolmen responded to complaints from white women but sought to mollify the violent husbands and refrained from encroaching on their relationships with their spouses. One week before Henry Moity beheaded his wife, Theresa Moity had summoned the police to their apartment, reporting that her husband had threatened her with a gun. The beat cop, "Whitey" Dakin, spoke with the couple until they "smoothed things over."

Dakin then urged Henry to behave himself, assured the sign painter that "I am not going to arrest you," and departed.[65] When abused women finally killed their attackers, policemen frequently quipped that they were not surprised. Captain James C. Scripps, for example, responded to the report that Carrie Lenard had fatally stabbed her spouse by remarking, "This isn't any shock to me—I could see it coming. They were almost getting to be regular customers of ours."[66]

Believing that they had exhausted other options for addressing the abuse, the women killed out of desperation.[67] Parish prosecutors, police detectives, and criminal court jurors heard familiar accounts from these New Orleanians. "I had to kill him. I had to kill him," thirty-three-year-old Odile Bouligny told an Orleans Parish district attorney.[68] "I remember thinking that I've got to kill him, because if I don't kill him, he'll kill me."[69] On November 28, 1927, Josephine Corso recounted a comparable tale of desperation. The twenty-seven-year-old woman "told a jury she shot and killed her husband to save her own life." Corso "described how her husband's fingers reached for her throat as he cried out, 'You —— I'll choke you!' His fingers were almost at her throat, she said, before she shot him."[70] Maude Kippers divulged to the New Orleans police superintendent, "I was desperate for I knew he was a beast when in a rage."[71] Admitting to a police investigator that she hoped her abusive husband would die, Eleanor Fontana "touched a dark purple bruise on her left shoulder" and said, "It will be the last scar he gives me—or any other woman."[72]

Longtime victims of domestic violence, the women reached their breaking points and resolved to defend themselves. The homicides were not planned as much as they were premeditated. These women determined that their husbands might kill them during the next "rage" and hid guns in anticipation of shooting in preemptive self-defense.[73] As her husband kicked her, for example, twenty-two-year-old Annabel Hanselman lunged for the Colt .38 caliber revolver that she had stashed under her pillow "to protect herself."[74] Elizabeth Haag concealed her .38 caliber pistol under a mattress.[75] Likewise, Eleanor Fontana kept a revolver under her bed. "I just knew he would come home drunk and when he's drunk, he picks on me." She explained to police detectives, "I told him never to hit me again. I knew I would kill him if he ever did. That's why I had the gun. I have thought of it for a long time. Any woman would."[76] Odile Bouligny kept her emergency weapon "hidden under the sideboard."[77] At a time when women rarely carried firearms, 80.8 percent of the white women who killed live-in husbands used guns. As with white wife killers, the nearest weapon was usually a meat cleaver or an ice pick. These women, however, anticipated that they would need to defend themselves and were prepared to do so should the need arise—and it did.

In nearly every such husband killing, the abused wife brandished the revolver, pleaded with her spouse to desist, and then shot the man as he ignored her warnings and continued to advance. According to the *New Orleans Times-Picayune*, when Frank Clark, a forty-four-year-old blacksmith, lunged at his wife, the forty-two-year-old woman grabbed her .25 caliber revolver and "told her husband if he attempted to strike her she would fire; he failed to heed her words, and she fired."[78] Another husband killer told police detectives that "he approached me with his fists closed. I begged him not to hit me again and that if he did I would shoot. He came and I fired."[79] Thirty-eight-year-old Carrie Lenard offered a similar description of the death of her husband. After George Lenard, a thirty-eight-year-old painter, began beating her, she "warned him not to hit me again, telling him if he struck me again I would stab him. Despite my warning he advanced on me and raised his hand again as if to strike me. It was then that I lunged at him with the knife and drove the blade into his chest." The distraught killer told police investigators, "I told him I'd give it to him. I told him he was going to get it."[80]

But why did some battered women kill their cohabiting abusers, while others endured the beatings and often died at their abusers' hands? In most ways, white husband killings resembled white wife killings. Similar people in similar circumstances using similar weapons committed these homicides against live-in spouses. The average age of the men who killed their cohabiting wives, for example, was 41, while the mean age of men killed by their wives was 39.7. The timing of husband killing also echoed the timing of wife killing. In white spousal homicides occurring between live-in partners, 30.8 percent of the former took place on weekends, compared with 33.3 percent of the latter; both were concentrated on Sundays and late in the evening, when spouses were most likely to interact—and quarrel.

Despite the parallel morphologies, a few differences in spousal homicides among cohabiting couples distinguished white husband killers from white wife killers, providing hints about why some wives fought back. Although these spouse killers came from the working class, the men who killed their live-in wives were poorer than the women who killed their cohabiting husbands. For example, 54.6 percent of white wife killers held unskilled positions, while 26.9 percent of husband killers came from households headed by unskilled workers. Concentrated in the upper tier of the city's working class, women who killed their cohabiting partners were three times more likely to come from households headed by skilled workers.[81] Put differently, white men who murdered their live-in wives were poorer than those who were killed by their wives, and white women who employed deadly force to stop their abusive husbands tended to be relatively wealthier than wives killed by their domestic partners. Women who killed their cohabiting spouses were also younger, by nearly four years.

Patriarchal terrorism appeared to have been more normative among older and poorer white New Orleanians, reflecting long-standing working-class notions of a masculine prerogative to employ violence as a mechanism of control. Younger and wealthier women, less invested in plebeian custom, more often resisted abusive partners and relied on deadly self-help—and their hidden .38 caliber revolvers—to protect themselves. But even the wives who killed their battering husbands had nearly always endured years of violence at their hands. Thus, the differences in age and class between cohabiting killers and victims represented slightly alternate cultural sensibilities among white working-class New Orleanians.

Spousal homicides involving separated white partners were different enough to constitute their own category. Many women in unhappy marriages left their husbands, though doing so often failed to protect them.[82] To the contrary, estranged white wives were at heightened risk in the hours, days, and weeks after they left their husbands, and 41 percent of white partner killings occurred after the woman had moved out of the family home.[83]

Killers and victims who were separated were distinctive. The murderers tended to be older and relatively wealthier than those who killed cohabiting partners, while their victims were younger. Husbands committed 86.7 percent of the white spousal homicides involving estranged partners, compared with 46.9 percent of killings between cohabiting partners.[84] The men who killed their estranged wives were also two years older than those who murdered cohabiting partners, with the mean age for the former group 43, and were twice as concentrated in their forties.[85] The women they murdered were, on average, nearly six years younger than those killed by cohabiting men. Moreover, husbands who murdered their estranged wives tended to be wealthier than their counterparts in intact marriages. Most were clustered in the upper tier of the working class, and nearly one in four held a white-collar job, compared with 9.1 percent of cohabiting wife killers. Even the instruments of death varied. In uxoricides involving separated partners, 92.3 percent of killers used guns, nearly always small revolvers (and never shotguns), compared with 56.5 percent among cohabiting partners. The aftermaths of the murders differed as well, with 73.1 percent of estranged wife killers but 47.8 percent of cohabiting wife killers attempting suicide after slaughtering their partners.[86]

In numerous, overlapping ways, the separation itself triggered these spousal homicides. Many white New Orleanians lived together unhappily for years, and then husbands murdered their wives immediately after they separated; 55.8 percent of all white wife killings occurred shortly after the spouses separated. The women nearly always left their husbands in such spousal homicides, instantly usurping power over their marriage and shattering the men's sense of masculine authority. The partners had often quarreled without violence, until the wife separated from her husband. Soon thereafter, he murdered her. Other marriages had endured domestic violence, but the men progressed from slapping and punching to shooting only after their wives departed. Even unions poisoned by allegations of infidelity avoided murderous violence until the women announced their plans to leave. Henry and Theresa Moity were typical in this regard. According to testimony at her killer's trial, Theresa had long tormented Henry, boasting of her assignations with other men.[87] Although Henry once had threatened Theresa, he had never struck her. But half a day after Theresa revealed her intention to leave him, Henry purchased a machete and beheaded her. "Thinking of what my wife was about to do," he explained, "I planned out" the killing.[88] In arguing for a murder conviction, Eugene Stanley, the Orleans Parish district attorney, also emphasized the timing of the violence, reminding the jury that "Henry killed his wife not because she was unfaithful but because she was about to leave him."[89]

In three-fourths of these homicides, the violence occurred immediately after the estranged wife rebuffed her husband's plea for reconciliation. Witness testimony at murder trials, suicide notes, killers' confessions, and other sources described how men begged, beseeched, and pleaded with their estranged spouses to return home. When the women refused, the men instantly began shooting. James Guerra, for example, followed his estranged wife to her mother's house and "pleaded for his wife to return to him. She refused."[90] According to the *New Orleans Times-Picayune*, "when he saw that his attempts were of no avail he whipped out a pistol, fired point blank in her face."[91] Similarly, on February 12, 1922, Seymoure Godwin tracked down his estranged wife and asked her "about returning home to him." The moment Louise Godwin rejected his plea, Seymoure drew a small-caliber revolver from his pocket and shot her in the right eye.[92]

Children often watched or heard their father beg for reconciliation and then murder their mother when she rejected his plea. From his jail cell at the Fifth Precinct station, thirty-eight-year-old Ivan Ferguson, a banana checker, told reporters that he asked his estranged wife, twenty-six-year-old Margueret

Ferguson, "if she would make up with me." When the woman "replied that she would not be seen dead with me," he produced a Colt .38 caliber revolver and shot her in the right temple.[93] Police officers at the scene interviewed the only witness to the crime, four-year-old Emily Jane Ferguson, who wept, "Papa shot Mama."[94] From her bedroom, twelve-year-old Catherine Cairis heard her father, a forty-three-year-old machine worker, ask her mother "to take him back, and he said that if she didn't she'd be sorry." The young girl told Captain Edward J. Smith that her thirty-two-year-old mother, Josephine, "said 'what are you going to do, kill me?' and he said 'No.' Then they went into the kitchen, and I heard a lot of noise. It sounded like dishes falling. I heard her holler 'Catherine.' I saw my mother on the floor with blood all over her."[95]

The killers' pleas, as they begged their estranged wives to consider reconciliation, laid bare the husbands' desperation, for they used language, made promises, and evinced emotions entirely unbecoming an early twentieth-century working-class man.[96] Masculine authority and dominance fueled patriarchal terrorism, but separation and divorce transformed husbands into supplicants, beseeching their wives to give them another chance and vowing to mend their ways. Marital stability, rather than spousal domination, represented a core component of masculinity for these men, and the collapse of their households left them feeling emasculated, helpless, and fully at the mercy of their stridently independent wives. Condido Badua and James Guerra described how they "pleaded" with their wives to come home, and Seymoure Godwin, in a suicide note, stated that he had "begged Louise to come back to me."[97] Forty-two-year-old Edward Harmeyer pledged to "reform, get a job, and quit drinking," while Charles Holloway promised his wife that if she returned "he would buy her new clothes and refurnish the home," offering to repair their union through consumption.[98]

Other desperate husbands attempted to use their new emotional dependence as a tool for manipulation and threatened to kill themselves unless their estranged wives gave them another chance. Young Catherine Cairis described how her father "told my mother if she didn't come back to him he would drink poison."[99] For these wife killers, separation abruptly inverted the gender hierarchy, turning patriarchy on its head and making the men weak and dependent. Henry Moity admitted that Theresa had "made me her dog."[100] In begging and pleading for their spouses to come home, the men explicitly ceded power and authority to their wives.

The women's explanations for leaving their husbands deepened the men's humiliation and despondence. Physical abuse alone rarely prompted the women to separate. Some police investigations and trials revealed that the men had battered their spouses, but such cases were unusual, and few women left their husbands because of domestic violence.[101] Instead, the wives insisted that they separated because their husbands had failed as men. These women, in dying declarations but especially in the tense discussions in which they refused to reconcile with their estranged husbands, stated that the men were poor providers, grounding the collapse of their marriages in the men's inability to meet class- and gender-based ideals.[102]

Their husbands had fallen short as breadwinners. When estranged spouses bickered because the wife refused to reconcile, the men often became volatile, and the women sometimes mocked them with cutting references to entertaining other men.[103] But, until that point, the wives mainly explained that the marriage was irrevocably broken because the men had not adequately supported the family.[104] Ivan Ferguson attributed his wife's decision to leave to the couple's recent financial difficulties. "I made good money up to last September, but since then I have not done so well."[105] A neighbor confirmed this explanation to police investigators, indicating that Margueret had, in fact, "separated from her husband because he has failed to support her."[106] Ernest Goodwin, a cop, told jurors that "I lost my head when she said she was able to earn her own living and did not need me or anything I had."[107]

In the emotionally charged conversations that preceded the murders, in suicide notes, and in court testimony, the men who murdered their estranged wives revealed their investment in middle-class domestic ideals, such as companionate marriage, and their sense of deep, raw humiliation. Whereas working-class men who killed cohabiting wives often celebrated their brutality—as testimony to their manliness—and conveyed little concern about providing for their families, the men who murdered estranged spouses feared that they had failed as providers, as husbands, and as men. Their wives' decisions to leave them publicly exposed these shortcomings. Friends, neighbors, and their estranged wives "laughed" at them, they told police detectives and jurors. Such reactions, for example, haunted Henry Moity, who insisted that because his family lived in a "dingy" apartment, because Theresa had announced that she was abandoning him, because his wife was "running around with other men," and because he had been consigned to cooking for his children, "people on the corner [were] looking at him and laughing at his shame." In one of his confessions, the killer explained that, hours before beheading his wife, he had discussed his plight with Nedda Douglas. The humiliation of feeling his African American neighbor's pity and hearing her "sympathizing with him" proved to be unbearable and convinced him to follow through with his plan to butcher his wife and sister-in-law.[108]

Nor did these killers act impulsively. To the contrary, nearly all of the homicides of estranged white wives were premeditated. Many killers discussed their plans with friends and acquaintances. Henry Moity told two neighbors, including Douglas, that he was considering killing his wife.[109] Others wife murderers revealed to police investigators that they had planned the violence. Joseph Pennino admitted to local detectives that "I'd been considering killing her for a long time," while Edward Harmeyer, in his formal statement to the police, confessed that "he had planned the killing."[110]

The men often made meticulous preparations. Since the spouses no longer lived together, the husbands had to arrange to meet their estranged partners. Some simply went to the homes where their wives now resided, typically the women's parents' or siblings' houses, while others concocted ruses to lure their estranged spouses to their deaths. Seymoure Godwin called his sister-in-law's home and "told his wife that her little child Eugenia Godwin had met with a serious accident and for her to go at once to 626 Julia Street and see the child." When Louise Godwin arrived at the address, he implored her to reconcile and immediately shot her when she refused.[111] Whereas cohabiting wife killers usually shot their partners late at night, more than a third of men who murdered their estranged partners killed their victims early in the afternoon, when they tracked down the women.

Many murdering husbands drafted suicide notes or put their financial affairs in order before asking their wives to "return home," unmistakable indicators that the men expected to kill their wives and themselves. Seymoure Godwin's suicide note, addressed to his brother, included detailed information about insurance policies, burial preferences, and instructions for the care of "my darling baby," two-year-old Eugenia.[112] Condido Badua's preparations shocked even veteran cops. After fatally shooting his wife, the baker waited for police investigators to arrive at his father-in-law's house, explained that "I had planned to kill her and then myself," and handed Corporal John Kirchem a printed card containing his "farewell message." "Good-bye forever; may you live long and see many more. Forgive me and forget me not," the card began.[113]

Anticipating that their estranged wives would reject their pleas, these wife killers came prepared to kill the women. Shortly before he slashed his wife's throat, Edward Harmeyer asked his son to run to the neighborhood barbershop and "have a keen edge put on the razor." The devastated ten-year-old boy later told policemen, "Daddy said he wanted to shave, but he didn't."[114]

Hours before committing his crimes, Henry Moity went to a hardware store to purchase a meat cleaver to butcher his wife. The store clerk told him that she had no such cutlery but said "I've got this," selling Moity the sugarcane machete he used to dismember his wife and sister-in-law.[115] Ivan Ferguson stole his landlord's .38 caliber revolver; Ralph Uribe pawned an overcoat to procure the .45 caliber automatic revolver he used to kill his estranged wife; Joseph Pennino borrowed a friend's .38 caliber revolver; Joseph LaFaso and George Warthan both purchased small handguns just before they met with and murdered their spouses.[116] These men expected to execute their wives immediately after they spurned the reconciliation request. Moreover, they needed small, concealable weapons, since they planned to give their spouses an opportunity to restore domestic order before resorting to murderous violence.

At odds with their working-class backgrounds, and in stark contrast with the men who murdered cohabiting partners, husbands who killed estranged wives consistently and publicly affirmed their "love" for their spouses. Usually in the moments immediately before or immediately after they fatally shot the women, and nearly always in suicide notes, these men spoke and wrote of romantic love. Thirty-year-old William D. Wiggins, who slashed his twenty-year-old wife's throat three times, explained his actions in a suicide note. "Love is the cause of it all," he wrote. "For I love Viola. I love her better than I can tell."[117] Ivan Ferguson, who killed his wife in the presence of their young daughter, explained that "I did it because I loved her," while Condido Badua told a police corporal that "I just shot my wife because I loved her."[118] Other men proclaimed their love for their wives as the women bled to death. After Ralph Uribe shot his wife in the head, a witness watched as the killer "knelt down by June and started to cry and said 'Oh June I shot you and I love you'[;] he then went to the kitchen and got a glass of water[,] came back and moistened her lips."[119]

Most of these wife killers insisted that they could not go on living without their beloved partners (and victims). Nearly three-fourths of the white men who killed their estranged partners attempted suicide, 80 percent of them successfully. Without the women they murdered, their lives were empty and meaningless. Suicide notes and confessions overflowed with the language of emotional dependence and with references to the men's unwavering "love" for their victims. Emile Rouyer, for example, wailed, "I love her still. If she's dead, I still love her. I wish I were dead."[120] Similarly, Alfred K. Lincoln stated that "I couldn't bear being without her . . . I couldn't bear the thought of living without her," just as George Warthan confessed to police investigators that

"I could not live without her."[121] Patrolman Ernest Goodwin sobbed to his fellow cops, "She refused to live with me and I couldn't live without her."[122] Such expressions of love, though they came from men who murdered their estranged wives, stood in contrast to the sentiments of husbands who killed their cohabiting spouses, such as Charles Ney. On his way home to slaughter his wife, Ney remarked to a cab driver, "My wife is an old battle ax and I am going to get rid of her."[123]

For the men who killed their estranged wives, the murders—and accompanying suicides—were simultaneously expressions of romantic love and reassertions of patriarchal authority, indicating that their break with working-class notions of masculine prerogative was incomplete. The killers often explicitly framed the murder-suicides in proprietary terms. Through homicidal violence, the humiliated, hitherto helpless men reestablished permanent, undisputed control over their wives and their marriages.[124] The women no longer dictated the fate of the union, and if the men could not have their estranged partners, then no one else would. Seymoure Godwin's suicide note explained that "it would be better for us to be dead than to live like this."[125] Similarly, immediately after his estranged forty-year-old wife, Hurl, rejected his plea for reconciliation, sixty-seven-year-old Alfred Lincoln seized authority over their union, announcing, "Well, I may as well end it all for both of us." Lincoln then asked if he could "kiss her good-bye." As they embraced, he shot her in the chest and then shot himself.[126] Oliver Stevens unequivocally conveyed his proprietary intentions, telling his sister-in-law that "if he could not have her [his wife] nobody else would, and that they would both die together."[127]

Demographic factors contributed to such motivations, exaggerating the emotional weight of marital dissolution for these killers. Concentrated in their forties and stalled at the upper tier of the city's working class, men who murdered their estranged wives failed to achieve middle-class financial stability or material expectations. Their setbacks in the workplace proved to be particularly crushing and emasculating when their wives left them for this reason.

The killers were overwhelmingly longtime New Orleanians. With close ties to the neighborhood and the community, their disappointments in the workplace and failures in the home became well known (or, more important, the men believed that their misfortunes became well known), deepening the men's despondence. Hence, their perceptions of neighbors "laughing" at them proved to be emotionally devastating and often appeared in wife killers' suicide notes and confessions.[128]

The women they murdered were also established residents of the city. More than four-fifths had lived in New Orleans for over a decade, compared with 45.5 percent of white wives killed by cohabiting husbands. Such deep ties to the community made separation a viable option, since the women were likely to have relatives living nearby with whom they could stay. But this option proved to be double edged, for these wives also faced increased short-term threats of spousal homicide, as their assertions of independence often produced violent backlashes from the men they left.[129]

The age of the women played a crucial role in the spiral of emotions contributing to wife killing. Three-fourths of the estranged victims of New Orleans wife killers were under 40, compared with 56.5 percent of women murdered by cohabiting husbands. The mean age for the former group was 32.2, whereas the average age of cohabiting victims was 38. Young wives likely had heightened expectations for emotional fulfillment and financial stability, particularly during the Roaring Twenties, when the economy boomed and when popular culture celebrated consumption. Reflecting the shifting mores of the era, younger women were probably more independent as well, making them willing to leave their marriages and adding to their husbands' insecurities and possessiveness.[130]

The collision of these factors helped to transform marital dissolution into spousal homicide and especially homicide-suicide. The cocktail of older husbands with languishing careers, younger wives, and exaggerated expectations often proved to be deadly. A significant age gap heightened the potential for women to leave unhappy marriages and for men then to kill their estranged partners. On average, cohabiting white wife killers were three years older than their victims, whereas separated wife killers were nearly eleven years older. Furthermore, among separated couples, the greater the age difference, the higher the proportion of homicide-suicides. When the killer and victim were within five years of age, 57.1 percent of murderous husbands committed suicide. When the gap exceeded a decade, 78.6 percent of killers took their own lives, and when the age disparity topped fifteen years, 88.9 percent of husbands shot themselves after murdering their estranged wives.

Crime-beat reporters sometimes snidely noted the age gulf. For example, the *New Orleans Item* described how forty-year-old Seymoure Godwin fatally shot his "young and pretty wife Louise Godwin, 23," on February 12, 1922.[131] The newspaper offered a more scandalous depiction of forty-five-year-old Charles Holloway's murder of his eighteen-year-old wife. Three weeks after Robbie Holloway left her husband and refused to reconcile, stating that "my love for you is dead," Charles shot her and then himself. The reporter noted that, according to a friend of the victim, Robbie had admitted that "I married such an old man because I wanted to get away from home."[132]

Middle-aged men disproportionately responded to their young wives' decisions to abandon them and their marriages with threats, guns, and suicide.

*

The social, demographic, and institutional forces of the early twentieth century, particularly during the 1920s, fueled spousal homicide in New Orleans but affected African American and white couples in different ways. The social instability of the era roiled family relations for many New Orleanians, across racial lines. Thus, rates of spousal violence skyrocketed, and by the mid-1920s, when the city's homicide rate reached its high-water mark, spousal killings were the leading source of lethal violence, for both African American and white New Orleanians. Although the rate of increase was similar for the groups, African American spousal homicide occurred at dramatically higher levels. Four overlapping factors contributed to this gap.

First, demographic differences between African American and white New Orleanians influenced rates of spouse killing. While the city was a lodestone for rural southerners during this era and New Orleans's population swelled by 18.4 percent during the 1920s, the flow of African American migrants far outpaced the arrival of white newcomers. New Orleans's white community thus had better-balanced sex ratios and a smaller population of single young residents—and uneven sex ratios and a high proportion of young people fueled conflict and buoyed rates of violence. In 1930, the city had ninety native-born white men in their twenties for every one hundred white women but only seventy-four African American men in their twenties for every hundred African American women.[133] Such a pronounced demographic imbalance contributed to discord in African American households.

With a more demographically balanced population, white New Orleanianss also had larger families. The median white family in 1930 was 26 percent larger than its African American counterpart.[134] As Emily Jane Ferguson and Catherine Cairis discovered, some men murdered their wives in the presence of their children, but more often parents refrained from such violence when young sons and daughter were in the household. Furthermore, older children often intervened in domestic quarrels and sometimes even employed lethal violence to protect their mothers. Such efforts did not eliminate domestic violence and on occasion merely substituted patricide for uxoricide, but the frantic efforts of children frequently interrupted the cycle of escalation. Therefore, having larger families and more older children, white families experienced lower rates of spousal homicide.

In multiple ways, white women benefited from having deeper ties in the community, though this disparity fell over time as the city's African American community matured and developed its own support networks.[135] But, particularly during the 1920s, white women more often had local relatives to shelter them. To be sure, separation did not always protect women, though it often saved lives.[136] Most white husbands did not stalk and hunt their estranged wives. Furthermore, men who followed their partners to the homes of relatives often encountered the women's brothers, brothers-in-law, and fathers, who insured the safety of estranged wives, making separation a sound strategy in most—but not all—cases. More often newcomers to New Orleans, African American wives had fewer family members living close by; hence separation, and the protection it afforded, was less feasible for them.

Second, white husbands experienced relatively fewer threats to their authority. Common-law marriage, with its more fluid and egalitarian structure, remained uncommon among white residents. Overwhelmingly living in formal marriages, white husbands enjoyed the legal bulwarks of patriarchy, such as coverture. With a clear, institutionally supported web safeguarding their authority, white men less often confronted challenges for household control.[137] Similarly, in 1930, married white women worked outside the home one-fifth as often as African American women and headed households one-third less frequently.[138] As a consequence, white women remained more financially dependent on their spouses. Thus, the combination of legal institutions and economic factors enhanced white men's authority in the house, reduced white women's autonomy, and strengthened the gender hierarchy for white New Orleanians.[139]

Third, New Orleans cops buttressed patriarchal authority for white residents but not for African American residents. Across racial lines, policemen sometimes ignored domestic violence complaints, leaving abused women to defend themselves. But patrolmen more often responded to calls from white women. When the police intervened in domestic disputes, as Whitey Dakin did after Theresa Moity reported that Henry had threatened her, these law enforcers usually tried to "smooth things over," which entailed calming frightened wives but rarely arresting abusive husbands. Such intervention in domestic quarrels interrupted the spiral of violence in some instances. As with the Moitys' fight, the cop's arrival ended the quarrel, though it failed to prevent the violence. This reluctance to arrest and charge menacing white husbands, however, strengthened the gender hierarchy and discouraged white women from challenging their spouses' authority. Such a police strategy for mediating domestic disputes also invited white women to defer to patriarchal authority—and was probably intended to do so. By contrast, ignoring domestic violence calls, which was the usual response to complaints lodged by African American women, led abused women to rely on self-help, often with the aid of ice picks and paring knives. Hence, New Orleans cops encouraged white women to submit to their husbands but unwittingly encouraged African American women to defend themselves, widening the racial disparity in spousal homicide.

Patrolmen bolstered the authority of white husbands in other ways as well. Despite the popular perception that white men eschewed police interference in their households and relied on personal initiative, many sought help from law enforcers. Again and again, these men summoned the beat cop when their wives were unfaithful and asked the patrolmen to arrest their wives' lovers. And policemen frequently obliged. In 1924, for example, Condido Badua saw his wife "walking with another man" and had the home wrecker arrested.[140] Henry Moity employed the same strategy to discourage his sister-in-law, Leonie, from meeting with her lover, having him arrested, charged with loitering, and sentenced to thirty days in the parish jail.[141] Cops who resisted arresting abusive husbands routinely arrested men suspected of seducing married women. Such police actions provided unmistakable institutional support for white husbands.[142] By shoring up the gender hierarchy among white New Orleanians, law enforcers discouraged white women from contesting household authority. They offered no comparable support for African American men, leaving these residents to rely on more informal and ultimately more violent methods for negotiating authority within the domestic sphere.

Fourth, economic pressures, particularly the deeper, more intractable poverty experienced by African American residents, played a central role in the race-based gap in family violence. African American men's struggles to provide for their families, often in combination with women's employment and economic independence, unsettled gender roles, transforming minor quarrels into pitched battles over authority. Many white residents struggled as well, and white wives often separated from husbands who failed as breadwinners. But white working-class families were relatively wealthier than African American New Orleanians. Confronting less endemic (if still formidable) poverty, white husbands and wives engaged in deadly fights at lower rates.

In short, the cumulative effects of racial discrimination shaped spousal homicide in early twentieth-century New Orleans. The social, economic, and cultural changes of the era, particularly during the 1920s, whipsawed white New Orleanians, such as Henry and Theresa Moity, heightening expectations but not necessarily transforming daily realities. These pressures, especially for slightly older husbands who married younger women, produced deadly conflict as white men's embrace of romantic love and their efforts to fulfill proprietary masculine expectations collided with women's assertions of independence. As a consequence, white spousal homicide soared during the early and mid-1920s. But the grinding poverty and entrenched institutional discrimination of Jim Crow New Orleans fueled far greater domestic tensions among African American residents. Thus, spouse killing surged throughout the city, though it tore through African American homes at almost six times the rate of white households.

CHAPTER 4

"Give Me the Gat"

At 8:00 p.m. on April 15, 1930, Harry Jones, a twenty-four-year-old African American dockworker known as "Butter Beans," fatally stabbed twenty-one-year-old Joseph Isom, an African American day laborer.[1] This was their fourth violent encounter of the day. Twelve hours earlier, Isom, whom neighbors called "Kuse," had approached Jones at the corner of Third Street and South Rocheblave Street and asked him for a nickel. Although the men knew one another, Jones rebuffed the request. "I told him I did not have any money," the killer later explained, "and that he should go to work and get some money." Angered by the surly response, Isom snatched a stick from a small child and swatted Jones across the face. The two men then traded punches until Jones picked up a brick and hammered Isom.[2] Thirty-two-year-old Joe Glenn, an African American day laborer who knew both combatants from the neighborhood, quickly intervened. "I took the brick away from Butter Beans," he testified to police investigators, and separated them.[3] Jones began walking away, but Isom and his friends chased him. When they caught up with Jones, the men pummeled him with their fists. After breaking free, Jones "ran into a ladies [sic] house, and they threw bricks in[to] the house."[4]

A dozen hours later, as Harry Jones left his uncle's house, the men crossed paths again, one block west of their initial fight. Isom, a short, burly man who outweighed Jones by forty pounds, intentionally "bumped into Butter Beans and asked him why he hit him [with a brick] this morning." They exchanged punches, grabbed bricks and hurled them at one another, and both brandished knives and slashed at their opponents. Thirty-eight-year-old Horace Williams, an African American sewage worker who lived nearby and knew both men, told a police clerk that "I then got in between them and tried to separate them, when Butter Beans reached over my shoulder and stabbed Kuse."[5] The blade of his pearl-handled knife penetrated the left side of Isom's neck, and Jones sliced in a downward direction, severing his victim's subclavian artery and piercing his left lung.[6] Joseph Isom staggered across Fourth Street, collapsed on the sidewalk, and died from blood loss and shock before the ambulance arrived. Jones, who surrendered to the police a day later, suffered from a stab wound to the abdomen, a second wound to his chest, a third to his right arm, and a fourth to his left hand.[7]

The deadly street fight between Harry Jones and Joseph Isom bore the characteristic features of early 1930s New Orleans homicides. Lethal violence had changed dramatically over the course of the previous decade. During the early and mid-1920s, when the city's murder rate skyrocketed, homicides generally involved domestic partners, occurred in homes, and were committed with handguns. Moreover, because the violence tended to erupt in private dwellings, witnesses were rarely present, and hence observers seldom interceded. By the early 1930s, homicides, particularly among African American New Orleanians, more often occurred between acquaintances and in the streets, and killers increasingly relied on knives rather than revolvers. Furthermore, because the lion's share of lethal encounters shifted to public settings, other residents observed the fights and frequently attempted to intervene. Over the course of Butter Beans's clashes with Kuse, for instance, Joe Glenn had broken up one fight, and twelve hours later Horace Williams had attempted to separate the men a second time.

New Orleans homicide changed in counterintuitive ways during the late 1920s and early 1930s. The relationship between killers and victims shifted markedly, as did the settings for lethal violence and the choice of weapon. But the rate at which New Orleanians slaughtered one another also abruptly changed. Many of the ingredients that combined to trigger the explosion in deadly violence during the early 1920s persisted, and new sources of social tension generated searing problems in the city. Race relations deteriorated in New Orleans during this period; disparities in law enforcement and daily life increased, and racial inequality grew more pronounced. The social instability of the Roaring Twenties and Prohibition should have sparked additional violence as well. Moreover, the local (and national) economy crumbled during the late 1920s, beginning with a modest recession in 1926 and culminating in the Great Depression. Poverty and unemployment ballooned, hitting the city's African American community with particularly devastating force.[8] This catalog of social, legal, political, and economic forces created the perfect formula for an epidemic of murder in a city already enduring soaring rates of bloodletting. And yet New Orleans violence plummeted.

Between 1925 and 1933, the city's homicide rate plunged by 52.8 percent. Nearly all forms of lethal violence became less common, even as the economy spiraled downward and institutional racism, political oppression, and social instability metastasized. New Orleans's reputation for violence persisted, though its national ranking for homicide tumbled. In 1925, the city had the sixth-highest homicide rate in the United States, vying for the top position with other southern urban centers, such as Memphis and Birmingham.[9] Eight years later, New Orleans ranked twenty-ninth in homicide.[10] In short, a set of social and economic conditions that should have fueled violence in New Orleans simultaneously transformed the character of homicide in the city and reduced the frequency with which local residents butchered one another. No single factor produced this sea change. Instead, demographic shifts, ecological forces, and economic pressures combined and interacted to redefine lethal conflict as the Roaring Twenties gave way to the Great Depression.

*

Social conditions in New Orleans in early 1920s seemed to augur a continued surge in violence and an ever-increasing death toll. In the years after the Great War, the city's homicide rate mushroomed, jumping two-and-one-half-fold between 1920 and 1925, and New Orleans possessed many of the tensions, fault lines, and pressures for this trend to persist. In fact, social conditions in New Orleans seemed ideal for the death toll from violence to rise.

Race relations, for example, worsened as Jim Crow matured. Whereas a blend of entrenched "racial etiquette" and vigilante justice had maintained the city's racial hierarchy earlier in the century, public policy and the state increasingly assumed this function.[11] Lawmakers, for example, worked to stunt African American electoral influence. In 1921, after the US Supreme Court struck down the "grandfather clause," which had attempted to restrict the franchise to men whose grandfathers had been eligible to vote, Louisiana legislators provided local registrars of voters with a new tool for preserving white political domination: the "understanding clause."[12] Parish officials could require those seeking to vote to interpret an arcane paragraph from the state constitution, enabling the registrars to deny the franchise to applicants who failed this virtually unpassable test. As a result, the number of American Americans voters in New Orleans sank. Between 1920 and 1934, the city's African American population grew by 36.1 percent, and the roll of registered voters swelled by 56.3 percent. The number of African American residents registered to vote, however, fell by 57.8 percent. In 1920, African American New Orleanians comprised 26.1 percent of the local population and 3.2 percent of registered voters. Fourteen years later, 29.6 percent of residents but only 0.8 percent of registered voters were African American.[13] This mirrored statewide trends, where the proportion of African American registered voters slipped from 1.2 percent to 0.3 percent.[14] The Louisiana Democratic Party's all-white primary system cemented white control over electoral politics. In New Orleans, 97 percent of registered voters belonged to the Democratic Party, ensuring that the winners of Democratic primaries triumphed in general elections. African American residents could not participate in these primaries until the mid-1940s.[15]

Such systematic disfranchisement had pernicious effects on daily life for African American residents. White residents maintained nearly complete control over the criminal justice system, and African American New Orleanians remained excluded from the municipal police, criminal court juries, and the bench. Lawmakers, policemen, prosecutors, and judges recognized that they served and were beholden to an all-white constituency.[16] If unresponsive, hostile legal institutions encouraged aggressive self-help and thus violence, then the increasing disfranchisement of African American New Orleanians should have contributed to the city's homicide rate.[17] Denying the franchise to African American residents also had palpable economic consequences. In 1932, as local unemployment rates reached high-water levels, municipal officials attempted to restrict jobs at the wharf to registered voters, an unambiguous ploy to prevent African American laborers and longshoremen from securing work in the city's largest industry.[18]

Similarly, elected officials used the expanding authority of local government to impose racial segregation in housing and public accommodations. Even though race-based zoning ordinances had been recently struck down by the US Supreme Court, New Orleans enacted such a measure in 1924.[19] Other municipal ordinances established racial segregation in saloons and restaurants, on city streetcars, and in myriad other realms of daily life.[20] During the late 1920s, New Orleans had forty-six kindergartens for white children and none for African American children.[21]

Race-based disparities increased as white New Orleanians harnessed the burgeoning power of the state to codify and bolster white privilege. These inequities extended to the sick and injured, and New Orleans's public hospital maintained rigid racial quotas, confined African American patients to overcrowded "colored" wards, and "doubled up" beds in the African Ameri-

can portions of Charity Hospital.[22] Physicians at the public hospital and ambulance drivers casually denied treatment to bleeding African Americans.[23]
Not surprisingly, the mortality rate for African American patients at public
facilities soared to twice that for white patients.[24] In combination, such measures exacerbated African American poverty, alienated these residents from
municipal government, and insured that they were more likely to die from
treatable injuries than white New Orleanians, all of which should have contributed to violent death in the city.[25] If racial discrimination and inequality, exclusion from public accommodations, and overt biases in policing
and criminal justice contributed to violence, then the upward trajectory of
New Orleans's early 1920s homicide trends should have continued and even
accelerated.

Prohibition, bootlegging, and rum-running should have buoyed lethal violence in the city as well. New Orleans emerged as one of the nation's leading importing centers for illegal liquor during the 1920s. Each year, smugglers transported thousands of cases of alcohol from Cuba, the Bahamas,
and British Honduras to the small deep-water islands near the mouth of the
Mississippi River.[26] From there, shipment to New Orleans was quick, easy,
and difficult to intercept. One writer counted eighty-five different routes
from these tiny islands to New Orleans warehouses, concluding that it was
virtually impossible for federal agents to stem the flow of demon rum. From
New Orleans, local criminal networks distributed the smuggled liquor across
the country. "Gathered in New Orleans," the reporter Harry T. Brundidge
explained in 1925, "are the owners or representatives of the syndicates, the
rum-runners, the shore men, the bootleggers, the sea captains, the boat crews,
the power boat and truck drivers, the hooch makers and mixers, the bottlers,
the label counterfeiters, and all the rest of the motley mob which have made
bootlegging one of America's greatest industries."[27] Clashes between criminal gangs contributed to violence in Chicago and Detroit, the nation's other
major importing centers for illegal hooch, but not in New Orleans—or at least
not during the late 1920s and early 1930s.[28]

Nor did the economic collapse of the late 1920s and the 1930s increase
local violence. Manufacturing fell by 50 percent in the city between 1929 and
1933, and nearly every sector of the local economy faltered.[29] Unemployment
surged, and joblessness frayed the fabric of family life. If poverty and blistering class and racial divisions spawn interpersonal conflict, then the economic
crisis should have produced rising levels of violence. Yet, even as New Orleanians suffered through the longest and deepest economic downturn in US
history, the city's homicide rate spiraled downward (see figure 4.1).

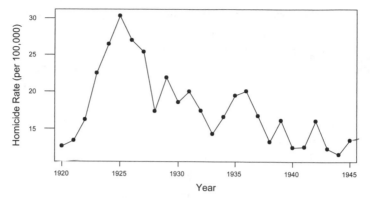

F I G . 4 . 1 . New Orleans Homicide Rates, 1920–1945. Source: Homicide Reports, Department of Police, New Orleans.

Between 1925 and 1933, New Orleans's homicide rate fell by more than half, from 30.3 per 100,000 residents to 14.3. The decrease crossed every social, spatial, and demographic boundary. The rate for men tumbled by 57.6 percent and for women by 56.7 percent. The African American homicide rate dropped by 65.2 percent, while the white rate sank by 37.5 percent. Lethal violence between acquaintances dipped by 48.8 percent, between strangers contracted by 63.1 percent, and between spouses slumped by 58.3 percent. Homicides committed in homes decreased by 54.2 percent and on streets by 57.2 percent.

Why did lethal violence in New Orleans plunge during the late 1920s, despite the social turmoil that roiled daily life? Moreover, why did the sharp drop in homicide continue through the depths of the Great Depression? And what was the relationship between the decrease in the rate of lethal violence and the shifts in the form or nature of deadly disputes?

Some of the pressures that fueled the early 1920s crime wave abated or even reversed during the late 1920s and early 1930s. Prohibition and organized crime, for example, contributed modestly to the city's death toll during the early 1920s and negligibly thereafter. In the age of Al Capone, New Orleans experienced scant violence from the production, distribution, or sale of illegal alcohol. During the early 1920s, deaths from rum-running and organized crime accounted for 4.4 percent of New Orleans homicides. By the mid-1920s, the figure had fallen to 2.3 percent, and Prohibition-related crime sparked 0.4 percent of local homicides during the closing years of the decade. The most violent year for such gangland violence was 1921, when clashes between rival criminal networks triggered four murders.

New Orleanians rejected the crusade to outlaw alcohol and flouted Prohibition. National observers dubbed New Orleans "the wettest spot in the country."[30] By comparison, one prominent journalist quipped, New York, Chicago, and San Francisco were merely "damp."[31] The undercover Prohibition agent Izzy Einstein concurred. He conducted an informal survey in which he recorded how long it took him to obtain an alcoholic beverage in each city he visited. New Orleans captured the top spot, as Einstein secured illegal booze within thirty-five seconds of arriving in the city.[32] A more formal tally, conducted by the *Literary Digest* in 1930, revealed that New Orleanians opposed restrictions on alcohol by a margin of fourteen to one.[33]

Through the Prohibition years, New Orleanians imbibed freely. In 1925, a newspaper analyzed police data and concluded that "New Orleans is getting drunker and drunker."[34] During the first five years of America's "Noble Experiment," arrests for drunkenness more than quintupled.[35] Police officials conceded "that there is so much liquor and so much desire to drink it that all they can do is put the drunks away as quietly as possible."[36] More concerned with controlling gambling than with enforcing an unpopular law, cops typically overlooked smuggling, bootlegging, and the distribution and sale of illegal alcohol.[37] Nor did federal agents, who never numbered more than forty in the city, significantly interfere with New Orleanians' love of hooch.[38] Even during Mardi Gras, when demand spiked and suppliers had to supplement smuggled whiskey with the "made-overnight stuff," alcohol remained readily available. Far from expressing outrage, newspapers rejoiced at the "quality of the liquor."[39]

New Orleanians, however, made a few cosmetic concessions to the Volstead Act; saloonkeepers renamed their businesses "soft-drink stands," and restaurant owners sometimes dispensed whiskey in coffee cups.[40] Moreover, in official correspondence, policemen occasionally maintained the charade. Investigating a murder in which an inebriated, boisterous patron killed the bartender who attempted to eject him from a saloon, Sergeant Herman Stupey termed the setting a "soft drink establishment" and described the altercation as "an argument started about a bottle of Coca Cola."[41] By the late 1920s, even such rhetorical nods to the Eighteenth Amendment fell into abeyance. Saloons sold illegal liquor openly, and bootleggers operated out of a storefront across the street from police headquarters.[42]

With a huge supply of illegal alcohol on hand and local law enforcers showing little inclination to interfere with their business, smugglers and rum-runners were scarcely different from other New Orleans entrepreneurs. No vast criminal gangs competed to control the decentralized, well-stocked local marketplace; few bootleggers needed to employ force to protect their stashes, since both consumers and law enforcers ignored the Volstead Act; and thus the death toll was small at the start of Prohibition and fell thereafter.[43] Homicides occurring in "soft-drink stands" and resulting from drunken brawls echoed larger trends in New Orleans violence, rising during the early 1920s and plunging during the late 1920s. The saloon homicide rate dropped by two-thirds between 1925 and 1933. At its peak, 1920s gangland violence accounted for roughly one-sixth of homicides in Chicago and Detroit.[44] But in New Orleans, such crime sparked one-twenty-fifth of homicides during the early 1920s and one-two-hundred-fiftieth of killings by the end of the decade.

Demographic forces, which had helped to fuel violence in the early 1920s, played a different role during the late 1920s and the 1930s. Regional migration patterns had increased the potential for violence in the years after the Great War, when waves of disproportionately young, single, and poor newcomers had flooded New Orleans. With the economy reeling during the late 1920s and early 1930s, few young newcomers moved to New Orleans. The rate of white population growth decreased by nearly two-thirds, and the rate of African American population growth slumped by half. By the late 1920s, natural increase, rather than migration, accounted for most of the city's growth.

This demographic change transformed the population in ways that depressed the conditions sparking deadly conflict. Sex ratios began to balance, and the proportion of young adults in the city contracted.[45] Between 1930 and 1940, the segment of the population comprised of residents in their twenties fell by 10.8 percent. The contraction was twice as great among African American New Orleanians.[46] With a larger share of the city's population consisting of older, more settled residents, New Orleans's homicide rate tumbled. If the demographic composition of the city in the years following World War I heightened the potential for aggressive, violent behavior, the population shifts of the late 1920s and the 1930s produced a more restrained environment.

The reconfiguration of the population also changed family life in ways that reduced domestic conflict. With the arrival of fewer young men, the number of lodgers plunged. The proportion of white households with boarders decreased by 44 percent, and the proportion in African American households dipped by 47.4 percent.[47] Lethal violence fueled by jealousy dropped accordingly, from one-sixth of African American homicides in the early 1920s to one-ninth by the early 1930s. Similarly, better-balanced sex ratios and fewer young migrants contributed to family formation, particularly for African American New Orleanians. The proportion of young African American residents who married increased.[48] African American fertility rates rose, and median household size for African American New Orleanians increased by 26.6 percent.[49] With a higher proportion of both children and relatively older adults and with a rising proportion of married residents, household life became more settled, reducing the likelihood of deadly conflict between jealous husbands and lodgers as well as between domestic partners.

Shifting employment trends for African American women contributed to the decrease in spouse killing. The high rate of employment of African American women during the early 1920s had enhanced their autonomy, lowered their tolerance for assertions of patriarchal authority, and simultaneously ignited men's coercive expressions of masculine privilege. By the late 1920s, however, some of these sources of domestic friction had begun to wane. The proportion of African American women in the labor force fell from 51.4 percent in 1930 to 43.4 percent in 1940, as the collapse of the economy compelled white residents to lay off their servants and cooks.[50] By comparison with the demographic turbulence of the post–World War I years, the domestic sphere in New Orleans, especially for African American residents, became more stable, dousing some of the sparks that had ignited spousal homicide.[51]

These demographic shifts did not produce domestic harmony or eliminate violence, though they contributed to decreases in rates of homicide between partners and occurring in homes, both of which slumped by more than half between the mid-1920s and the early 1930s. Similarly, the rise and fall of Prohibition notwithstanding, shifts in rates of saloon homicide and drunken-brawl homicide, both of which surged during the early 1920s and plunged between the mid-1920s and early 1930s, varied directly with the proportion of young men in the New Orleans population. As migration to the city slowed and as the proportion of bachelors dipped, daily life became less disorderly and less murderous.[52]

Ecological changes dovetailed with demographic shifts during the late 1920s and early 1930s and also helped to depress local homicide rates. Until this period, swamps covered most of the city, resulting in overcrowding on the higher, drier ground near the Mississippi River and producing the "back-yard pattern" in which African American New Orleanians lived in close proximity to white residents, tucked into shacks and dilapidated houses. But the drainage efforts begun during the late 1910s increasingly made the northern sections of New Orleans habitable, and by the late 1920s the developed portions of the city extended nearly to Lake Pontchartrain.[53] New subdivisions offered larger homes and catered to more affluent residents, and the combination of market forces and restrictive covenants insured that only white New Orleanians could take advantage of the physical expansion of the built-up parts of the city.[54]

The construction of a sea wall to shield these new residential areas from Lake Pontchartrain and the publicly funded development of the lakefront, beginning in 1926, unleashed white flight in the city.[55] Affluent white residents fled from the older, densely packed, heterogeneous sections of New Orleans. The internal migration had a sorting effect on the city, accelerating the formation of class- and race-based neighborhoods.[56] Even without the benefit of the local racial zoning ordinance, which the US Supreme Court struck down in 1927, New Orleans became increasingly segregated during by the early 1930s. The construction of a massive public housing project in the 1930s further separated African American residents from white New Orleanians.[57]

At the same time, Jim Crow continued to undermine the city's fluid, multiracial culture and gradually forged a binary racial hierarchy. White New Orleanians began to see their city in black-and-white and attempted to squeeze the local Creole population into an undifferentiated "Negro caste." Describing the "socially traumatic experience of [Creole residents] being forced, like American Negroes, to assume the role of a lower-caste population," the ethnographers Allison Davis and John Dollard explained that "the colored Creole group is merging socially and biologically with the American Negro group." Davis and Dollard concluded that elite Creole New Orleanians "are now treated in all respects like Negroes by the local whites."[58] Over time, this compelled middle-class African American and Creole residents to "attend Negro schools, churches, and associations; and they intermarry with Negroes."[59] Policemen, prosecutors, judges, and other government officials adopted a binary racial worldview, and legal documents, ranging from arrest reports and interviews with crime witnesses to coroners' designations, divided New Orleanians into "whites" and "Negroes" or "Coloreds," a shift that coincided with rising residential segregation and Louisiana courts' embrace of a "one-drop" definition of racial identity.[60]

Such an ecological and cultural transformation had complex effects on local violence. The combination of falling levels of population growth and an increasing housing stock reduced overcrowding for white New Orleanians. More space, fewer lodgers, and greater domestic privacy eased some of the tensions that had fueled domestic violence, contributing to a 54.3 percent drop in white spousal homicide between 1925 and 1933 and a 19.5 percent fall in the rate at which white residents killed one another in their homes.

While African American New Orleanians remained in the older sections of the city and continued to live in crowded, dilapidated housing stock, the emergence of neighborhoods provided a springboard for community development. Haltingly, class divisions within the city's African American community faded. Civic organizations, such as the NAACP, struggled with this transformation. From its inception in 1915 through the 1920s, a Creole elite had led the group. Its highborn, well-bred leaders preferred to work within the existing power nexus and to rely on their personal connections to powerful white New Orleanians to ameliorate the worst facets of racial oppression. Reluctant to jeopardize their bonds with white officials, these "racial progressionists" reacted cautiously to grotesque police brutality and to prosecutors' indifference toward African American crime victims, frustrating non-Creole African American professionals and alienating working-class African American residents, who rarely joined or supported the civil rights organization.[61] The local branch of the NAACP even failed to register its opposition to the ordinance restricting dock employment to registered voters, explaining that it hoped that the courts would "nullify" the statute and hence the organization's leaders would not need to butt heads with municipal officials.[62]

During the 1930s, two overlapping changes occurred. First, a younger, more strident generation of African American community leaders, such as the local attorney A. P. Tureaud, came of age and demanded more forceful challenges to Jim Crow.[63] And second, at least episodically, diverse, multiclass coalitions galvanized around specific issues, in part reflecting the ways in which racial segregation concentrated these residents in neighborhoods and contributed to a shared experience for African American New Orleanians.[64] In 1930, for example, after Charles Guerand, a drunken off-duty patrolman, brutally murdered Hattie McCray, a fourteen-year-old African American dishwasher who spurned his sexual advances, a cross-section of African American residents contributed to a fund to hire a private attorney to assist with the prosecution of the killer.[65] Similarly, civil rights groups began organizing rallies against police brutality and seeking legal remedies to endemic abuse.[66]

Concrete changes from these collective efforts came incrementally and grudgingly, though this larger process of community building had a significant impact on African American violence.[67] The consolidation of civil rights organizations, the development of cohesive neighborhoods, and the growth of nuclear and extended families provided crucial support networks for African American New Orleanians.[68] Institutions attempted to provide legal protection for criminal suspects and support for crime victims, and impoverished residents found sources of food and lodging.[69] Furthermore, as the city's African American community matured and as families grew and relatives more often lived nearby, abused women had new options. Rather than resorting to self-help, they could seek refuge with relatives and escape domestic violence. This strategy sometimes failed, and angry husbands continued to stalk their estranged partners and butcher them. But separation often protected the victims of domestic violence and hence reduced rates of spousal murder.

Changing patterns of homicide during the late 1920s and early 1930s hint that community organization and family formation reduced domestic homicide. First, the African American wife-killing rate fell by 51.1 percent between 1925 and 1933. Second, the proportion of separated partners who were killed doubled during this period. Since most women who left their abusive marriages likely avoided lethal violence, this increase probably reflected an overall surge in separations. With the gradual development of the African American community, battered women increasingly gained the option of leaving their violent husbands.

Third, the proportion of African American residents killed by relatives rose during this period. Ironically, this signaled a decrease in spousal homicide. In many of these deadly encounters, fathers, brothers, and sisters shot or stabbed the men abusing their daughters and siblings. Nineteen-year-old Leona Peters, for example, killed her brother-in-law, Henry Sambrone, as he attacked her sister, on November 12, 1931. During the previous evening, Sambrone, a thirty-nine-year-old African American tinsmith, had brutally beaten his wife. According to the police report, Edna Sambrone fled "to her sister's house to keep away from her husband and further beatings by him." The next night Henry Sambrone broke through the door of Peters's house, "wrestled with Edna Sambrone, his wife, and struck her in the mouth." When Peters demanded that her brother-in-law "get out of the house," he bellowed "he was getting out of nothing" and resumed his attack on his estranged wife. Leona Peters grabbed her double-barreled 12-gauge shotgun from the chifforobe and fired once from a distance of five feet, striking her brother-in-law in the chest, fracturing three of his ribs and lacerating his right lung.[70]

In a similar homicide, fifty-two-year-old Jessie Lewis, an African American construction worker, shot and killed his brother-in-law, Joseph Gomez, a thirty-seven-year-old laborer. Gomez and Lewis's sister, Ada Williams, had lived "as man and wife" for three years. On October 4, 1929, the couple fought and separated, and Williams moved in with her brother. Six days later, Gomez went to Lewis's second-floor apartment and attacked Williams. Lewis interceded, roaring, "'Don't hit my sister,' whereupon . . . Joseph Gomez said 'it wouldn't be a pity [if] I would kill both you S.B.s, and struck Jessie Lewis.'" The construction worker reached under his pillow, seized his revolver, and fired three times. Gomez died thirty minutes later.[71]

The combination of a sharp drop in the African American spousal homicide rate, an increase in the proportion of African American women killed by estranged husbands, and a surge in the percentage of raging husbands killed by their wives' relatives suggested that an expanding support system offered greater protection for domestic violence victims. In some instances, such as the Sambrone and Gomez killings, a deadly fight still occurred, and a third party committed the homicide. But more often this growing web of protection likely gave pause to abusive husbands and reduced the death toll from domestic abuse.[72]

By comparison with the atomized residential patterns of the early 1920s, African American New Orleanians increasingly lived in nuclear units, in neighborhoods, and close to relatives. Jim Crow policies, explicit discrimination, and the resulting racial segregation contributed to this emerging social geography. Yet this social geography also facilitated the development of familial and community support systems that displaced some domestic violence, as relatives employed force to stop murderous husbands, and reduced spousal homicide.

Demographic and ecological shifts interacted to reduce domestic violence in other ways as well, particularly for African American New Orleanians. The reconfiguration of home and neighborhood life helped to produce a 62.8 percent drop in the African American spousal homicide rate from the mid-1920s until the early 1930s. But the household violence rate decreased even more sharply, plunging by two-thirds between 1925 and 1933 (see figure 4.2). Furthermore, the proportion of all African American homicides occurring in homes contracted, falling from a peak of 44.1 percent in 1924 to 30.3 percent nine years later. When the flow of newcomers decreased and family formation accelerated, African American domestic life became increasingly privatized. Outsiders and nonrelatives gradually disappeared from African American homes. As a consequence, nonspousal homicide in African American homes plummeted. Deadly quarrels between men in African American homes fell by one-third, and homicides between acquaintances in private residences dropped by half—from 32.2 percent of home homicides to 16.7 percent. When acquaintances and lodgers left domestic space, jealousy-fueled conflicts decreased.

Other sources of violence in the home also fell. During the early 1920s, before African American neighborhoods fully emerged, a broad range of leisure activities remained concentrated in private space. Boarders, for example, drank, played cards, and threw dice in African American homes. As the number of lodgers decreased and public, neighborhood recreational space expanded, such activities, and the disorder that they spawned, left African American households. During the mid-1920s, drunken brawls sparked

6.9 percent of the lethal violence occurring in African American homes. By the early 1930s, the figure had dropped to 3.8 percent. Similarly, the proportion of home homicides triggered by card and dice games fell from 9.3 percent to 3.4 percent. Some of this violence merely migrated from private settings to public locations, such as the streets and neighborhood saloons. But as family life became more private, quarrels involving nonrelatives increasingly left African American homes. By the early 1930s spousal violence accounted for the lion's share of deadly quarrels in the home, and the African American spousal and home homicide rates converged, with the sharp reduction in the latter mainly reflecting the drop in home homicides between non-family-members (see figure 4.2).

When demographic and residential trends shifted, African American men spent more time in public settings, and women established greater control over household life. African American spousal homicide dropped, but wife killing fell more sharply than husband killing. Between the mid-1920s and the mid-1930s, the rate of spousal homicide by men fell by 46.7 percent, compared to a 30.1 percent dip by women, and the proportion of spousal homicides committed by women rose from half to two-thirds.

The changing locus of African American violence also lowered the body count. When young single men left their homes and more often socialized, imbibed, bickered, and fought in public, homicide rates in domestic space plummeted. But the concentration of men on street corners and in barrooms did not generate a surge in public murders, even though such settings emboldened working-class bachelors and encouraged the kind of strutting and competition that typically buoyed homicide rates. To the contrary, street and

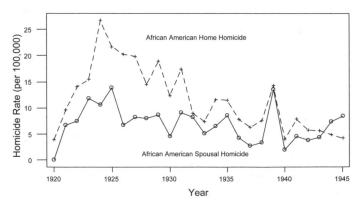

FIG. 4.2. African American Spousal and Home Homicide Rates, 1920–1945. Source: Homicide Reports, Department of Police, New Orleans.

saloon homicide also fell. While this violence dropped in part because the city had a decreasing proportion of raucous young men, some quarrels were simply displaced. Fights over card games that had erupted in crowded homes during the early 1920s flared on street corners and in alleys by the early 1930s. But men also fought differently on the streets and in the barrooms.

When these New Orleanians moved their disputes into public settings, they frequently left their guns behind at home. During the late 1920s, African American men used firearms in 65.3 percent of home homicides but 52.7 percent of street homicides. Again and again, aggressive men insulted one another, exchanged threats, squared off, and then dashed home to find their revolvers. For example, when a dispute erupted at a fish fry held in a dance hall, one of the combatants vowed to "return later and start plenty [of] hell." He ran home, "returned to the dance with a nickel plated revolver in his hand," and opened fire. Twenty-seven-year-old Cecil McNair died from a bullet wound to the abdomen in the ensuing hail of gunshots.[73] White New Orleanians faced the same challenges as fights moved to public settings. When Fred Kelly became embroiled in a dispute with Jules Saik on Dumaine Street on August 15, 1929, he threatened, "I'll fill you full of lead." Then both men scurried for their guns. Saik instructed his fourteen-year-old son "to go upstairs to get the gun." Dimitry Saik ran into the house but quickly returned to the sidewalk, frantically reporting, "I couldn't find it."[74] In the meantime, Fred Kelly, a twenty-eight-year-old ruffian with an extensive police record, turned to his friend and shrieked, "Give me the gat. Give me the gat."[75] Finally, Jules Saik hurried into his house, located his revolver, and returned to the street; the shooting began, leaving Saik dead.[76] In many instances, however, the frenzied search for guns interrupted the cycle of escalation, and the men failed to reconvene and act on their murderous bluster.[77]

In addition, most New Orleanians involved in violent altercations were less patient than Fred Kelly and Jules Saik. Instead, like Henry Jones and Joseph Isom, they opted to fight immediately and relied on the first weapons they could reach—bricks, bottles, bats, and knives. By the early 1930s, knives surpassed guns as the weapon of choice in African American street homicides, and by the mid-1930s, blades produced more saloon homicides than bullets. Mortality rates for cuttings, brick assaults, and fistfights, however, were far lower than those for bullet wounds.[78]

Therefore, because the changing locus of fights reduced access to guns in the heat of the moment, homicide rates dipped, even if the number of fights remained constant. But the number of violent disputes did not remain fixed. Rather, the volume of such altercations dropped as the proportion of young bachelors in the city fell and the raucous nightlife of the early 1920s faded. The combination of the contraction in the size of the most violent population, the decrease in immediate access to firearms, and the lower mortality rate from punches and stabbings than from bullet wounds produced a drop in homicides. As one local prosecutor noted, quarrels mainly turned deadly when one of the combatants "happened to have a revolver at a psychological moment when he engaged in a fight."[79] By the late 1920s, fewer bellicose young men "happened to have a revolver" when they clashed.

The shift to street fights and "cutting scrapes" reduced death rates in another way as well.[80] Friends, acquaintances, bartenders, and even cops were more likely to observe public fights and more often interceded before deadly injuries were inflicted, just as Joe Glenn broke up the initial skirmish between Joseph Isom and Henry Jones. More than two-thirds of home homicides involved only the killer and the victim, whereas roughly half of deadly street fights involved at least three parties, one of whom typically attempted to act as a peacemaker. Similarly, third parties more often attempted to separate brawlers armed with bricks and knives than those brandishing firearms. These trends overlapped and reinforced one another. When violent disputes migrated to public settings, gun use fell, mortality rates from injuries dropped, and noncombatants more frequently restrained the participants before an assault became a homicide. For all of the performative bombast of back-alley brawlers, street fights were less deadly than home fights.

The drop in firearm homicide accounted for most of the volatility in New Orleans's homicide rate during this era. Between 1920 and 1925, when the homicide rate jumped by 139.5 percent, the gun homicide rate spiked by 128.8 percent. But from 1925 to 1933, the homicide rate plunged by 52.8 percent, and the city's gun homicide rate fell by 63.3 percent (see figure 4.3). Lethal death also varied directly with the percentage of killers employing firearms. When the proportion of homicides committed with guns rose, the homicide rate soared, and when the proportion dipped, the rate spiraled downward. New Orleanians committed more than three-fourths of homicides with firearms during the early 1920s; by 1933, the figure had dropped to 55.4 percent—and in 1940, only 39.3 percent of local killers shot their victims. During the years for which New Orleans's homicide rate exceeded twenty (per 100,000 residents), two-thirds of killers shot their victims. By comparison, in the years when the rate fell below fifteen, fewer than half of assailants used guns.

Nor was this correlation unique to New Orleans. H. C. Brearley and Frederick L. Hoffman, the nation's leading experts on homicide during the 1930s, documented the relationship between guns and violent death. "Even

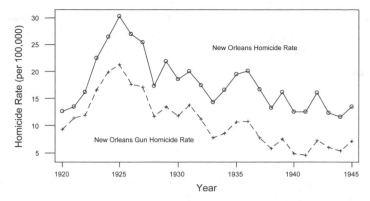

F I G . 4 . 3 . New Orleans Homicide and Gun Homicide Rates, 1920–1945. Source: Homicide Reports, Department of Police, New Orleans.

a casual examination" of American data on violence, the sociologist Brearley explained in 1932, "will reveal a tendency for the lower homicide rates to be associated with a smaller percentage of firearms slayings."[81] Hoffman demonstrated that cities with low proportions of gun homicides had modest homicide rates, while urban centers with high proportions of gun use led the nation in lethal violence.[82] In New Orleans and across the nation, when the proportion of killers using guns dropped, homicide rates decreased.

In part, gun deaths in New Orleans plummeted because of shifts in the social geography of recreation and violence, but firearm homicide also fell because the supply of revolvers contracted during the late 1920s and the 1930s. Policemen, however, had scant effect on the reduction in gun violence or the supply of firearms. Early twentieth-century Louisiana had lax gun laws.[83] The *New Orleans States* noted that "under the existing regulations the only requirements for the purchase of deadly weapons are that the purchaser shall be more than eighteen years old and have the purchase price."[84] The state's criminal code prohibited Louisianans from carrying concealed weapons, though New Orleans cops enforced this law rarely and selectively.[85] When the city's racial hierarchy appeared unstable, or particularly when an African American resident was accused of committing a high-profile crime against a white New Orleanian, police authorities often launched highly publicized raids on African American saloons and arrested patrons on concealed-weapon, vagrancy, or loitering charges.[86] Thus, municipal officials and cops used the state's concealed-weapon law to bolster white supremacy more than to reduce gun violence, embarking on law-and-order crusades to preserve their definition of "order" rather than to enforce the concealed-weapon law.[87]

Nonetheless, criminal justice officials, editors, and community leaders routinely attributed violence to "gun toting." In 1923, for example, Police Superintendent Guy Molony told a Bible class that "gun-toting [was] one of the chief menaces" his department confronted "in its efforts to enforce law and order."[88] During the mid-1920s, as the homicide rate climbed, grand jury reports typically featured bromides for reducing violence. A 1925 report concluded by "deploring the gun-toting habit and recommending speedy trials with capital punishment for those convicted of major crimes."[89] A year later, Dr. Rudolph Matas, the city's most prominent surgeon, became so alarmed by the mounting death toll from "pistol toting" that he proposed organizing "an Association Against the Pistol."[90]

But mayors, police superintendents, journalists, and civic leaders rejected efforts to enact stronger laws to control guns and combat violence. Insisting that the "only way to put a stop to murder is hanging," Superintendent Molony declared that "state regulations for the sale of firearms would be of no aid in the homicide solution." The police chief argued that "from the mail order houses the persons could obtain the weapons, even though they were forbidden in the state."[91] National experts agreed that mail-order houses enabled consumers to skirt state and local restrictions.[92] In 1925, Hoffman, for example, bemoaned that "mail order houses furnish weapons to any one, old or young, sane or insane, good or bad, without the least difficulty," and in 1927 the former New York City police commissioner William McAdoo reached the same conclusion.[93] Three years later, Julius Rosenwald conceded that Sears, Roebuck and Company sold more than $3 million worth of firearms annually, prompting him to "discontinue the sales for the good of the country."[94] With so many inexpensive pistols already in circulation, Molony warned, tighter restrictions on firearms "would simply deprive the law-abiding citizens of the rights of carrying a gun; while the other element would do just as he pleased in the face of any laws."[95] Thus, Molony denounced the evils of pistol toting, but, like other police and city officials, he made scant effort to tighten restrictions or to enforce Louisiana's concealed-weapon law.

Yet two very different sets of market forces reduced the supply of cheap guns in the city and thus contributed significantly to the drop in homicide. New Orleans was awash with cheap handguns during the early 1920s, though such weapons became less plentiful later in the decade. For as little as five dollars, mail-order catalogs offered a wide variety of pistols.[96] Newspaper advertisements during the early 1920s identified private sellers willing to sell "guaranteed revolvers" for the same price.[97] Local pawnshops offered "cheap 'Saturday night' weapons" for as little as two dollars, while individuals, though private sales, could purchase revolvers on street corners and in saloons for even less.[98] Guns had street value, and anyone in need of quick cash could easily find a buyer for a pistol along Canal Street or at the docks. After Henry Moity decapitated his wife and sister-in-law in 1927, he fled into the bayous. Desperately needing money as he went on the lam, he sold his gun on the street for $1.50.[99]

Many of the revolvers offered in catalogs, newspapers, shops, and back alleys during the early 1920s were military surplus equipment. Police clerks frequently noted that confiscated or recovered murder weapons were "army" or "military" weapons. On July 27, 1921, for example, Sergeant Joseph Perret described the gun that Michael Droucourt used to kill Joseph Harris as a "U.S. Army made, 1917" revolver, "marked 'United States Property.'"[100] Similarly, Captain James Dimitry noted that Henry Wilson shot Hugh Macelus with a "Colt 32 calibre, six shooter, army special revolver," while police investigators recovered a Colt Army .38 special from the grocery store where Stanley Margiatta fatally shot Sam Lala for seducing his wife.[101] Mail-order houses during the early 1920s also touted their products' connections to the Great War. F. H. Brooks Inc., of Evansville, Indiana, for instance, placed advertisements in New Orleans newspapers for military weapons. For "less than half the pre-war prices," Louisianans could purchase a "military model." This was "a man's gun, built for hard service."[102]

Although these weapons remained in circulation for many years, "army specials" and "military automatics" disappeared from police reports by the late 1920s. Moreover, fewer advertisements for any revolvers appeared in New Orleans newspapers, and mail-order houses largely stopped selling pistols.[103] With cheap military weapons no longer flooding the market and fewer local firms or national catalog companies offering handguns, the price of revolvers rose in New Orleans, typically doubling by the early 1930s.[104] The police department's stolen property files also documented the rising price of pistols, as gun owners usually valued their filched property at ten dollars or more by the late 1920s.[105] Rampart and Canal Street pawnshops and private residents continued to sell inexpensive handguns, often for as little as three or four dollars, but even this modest figure represented a 100 percent increase since the early 1920s.[106] Thus, the drop in the proportion of homicides committed with guns, which correlated with the plunge in New Orleans's homicide rate, coincided with a decrease in the supply of firearms and an increase in the price of such weapons.

Gun use in New Orleans homicides varied with the class of the killer. The poorer the assailant, the less often he or she used a firearm; instead, the poorest New Orleans murderers disproportionately stabbed or bludgeoned their victims. For example, 56.6 percent of killers holding unskilled jobs relied on guns, compared with 69.5 percent of skilled assailants, 76.5 percent of those with low-white-collar positions, 84.6 of killers in high-white-collar occupations, and 100 percent of the killers holding professional positions. To be sure, cultural forces assumed some role in this pattern, for young toughs in plebeian New Orleans, particularly African American ruffians, took pride in "juggin" (i.e., stabbing) their enemies, as an expression of masculine ferocity.[107] But economic factors proved to be the principal factor in weapon choice.

Gun use by the poorest New Orleanians slumped when the price of revolvers rose. For killers in skilled or white-collar jobs, across racial lines, firearm use changed little over time, suggesting that the higher price tag had scant effect on more affluent assailants. By contrast, for killers from low-working-class households, the proportion of homicides committed with guns plummeted as the price of a weapon increased. During the early 1920s, when revolvers were cheap, 68.4 percent of killers holding unskilled jobs shot their victims. By the late 1920s, the proportion dipped to 61.8 percent, and the figure fell to 42.9 percent during the late 1930s.

But the price of the weapon was not the only factor in the affordability of guns. As the economy crumbled during the late 1920s and as unemployment rates skyrocketed, fewer working-class residents had the disposable income to purchase even a cheap revolver. Thus, fewer such New Orleanians carried revolvers, and therefore not as many residents possessed firearms when fights erupted, contributing to the drop in the gun homicide rate, which in turn spearheaded the sharp decrease in the overall rate of lethal violence.

Because this tangle of market forces principally influenced the poorest New Orleanians, shooting homicides by African American residents tumbled fastest. During the interwar era, 85.8 percent of African American killers held unskilled jobs, compared with 33.5 of white killers. The politics of Jim Crow exacerbated this gap, as New Deal programs funneled relief assistance to white New Orleanians. During the Great Depression, for example, the jobless rate among African Americans soared to twice that of white New Orleanians, and poor-relief benefits were more modest.[108] Whereas gun use by white killers holding unskilled positions dipped during the late 1920s and the 1930s, revolver use by African American New Orleanians rocketed downward. From the early 1920s until the late 1930s, the proportion of white killers holding unskilled jobs who relied on firearms dropped from 69.2 percent to 51.7 percent, while the proportion of African American killers in unskilled positions who used guns plunged from 67.2 percent to 39 percent (see figure 4.4).[109]

Gun violence, as a consequence, plunged, decreasing by 77.2 percent between 1925 and 1940. The city's African American firearm homicide rate fell by 87.4 percent, and the comparable rate for white New Orleans dwindled by 58.9 percent (see figure 4.5). The drops were incremental and cumulative because older guns remained in circulation, even as the price rose and the supply contracted. Similar shifts in market conditions occurred throughout the United States during this period, and the gun homicide rate dropped nationally. Mortality rates from accidental shootings and gun suicides also fell during the 1930s, indicating a wider reduction in access to firearms.[110] Hence, changes in the price and supply of firearms, exaggerated by local demographic

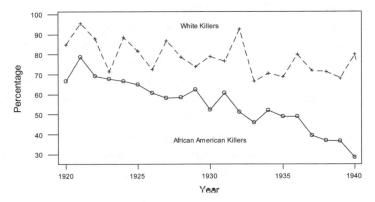

FIG. 4.4. Proportion of Homicides Committed with Guns, 1920–1940. Source: Homicide Reports, Department of Police, New Orleans.

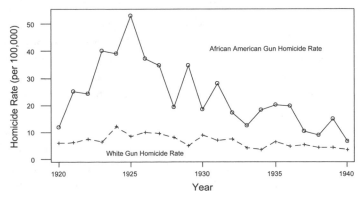

FIG. 4.5. African American and White Gun Homicide Rates, 1920–1940. Source: Homicide Reports, Department of Police, New Orleans.

changes and by the effects of the Great Depression, produced a sharp drop in gun violence, particularly for African American New Orleanians.

Over time, New Orleans killers increasingly struggled to secure firearms. Anna Elmar, Cleo Wiley, and Louise Philips committed premeditated homicides during the 1930s. A fifty-four-year-old white housekeeper, Elmar killed her common-law husband of nine years, George Bensfield, a day laborer. Frightened of her abusive partner, Elmar had given a neighbor, Anselmo Garcia, a five-dollar bill and asked him to buy her a gun and bullets. He purchased a .32 caliber revolver and ten cartridges for her.[111] Nine days later, on August 15, 1938, Elmar fatally shot her husband in the chest.[112] On December 7, 1935, eighteen-year-old Cleo Wiley, an African American servant, became embroiled in a dispute with Mabel Slack, a seventeen-year-old African American waitress. The women quarreled over the attentions of a man in a Melpomene Street restaurant. Slack grabbed a bottle and smashed it on Wiley's forehead. Before Wiley could respond, thirty-two-year-old Louis Smith intervened, whisking her out of the restaurant and walking her home.[113] But as soon as Smith left, Wiley "went into a store and bought a pocket knife [with] one blade for 25 cents." She then returned to the restaurant, and, "with out saying a word," stabbed Slack in the chest, puncturing her right lung.[114] After her common-law marriage to Sam Hollins disintegrated, twenty-nine-year-old Louise Philips, an African American servant, spent thirty-five cents on a "long bladed knife, commonly known as a Texas Jack Knife," and stabbed her husband in the chest, right arm, and right shoulder.[115]

These murders reflected broader trends in New Orleans homicides during the 1930s. Relatively wealthier and, on average, seven years older, white killers, such as Anna Elmar, could still scrape together five dollars for a handgun. By comparison, poorer, younger African American killers, such as Cleo Wiley and Louise Philips, more often settled grudges with inexpensive knives. Even in premeditated killings, class and race shaped weapon choices. During the depths of the Great Depression, many African American residents could not afford firearms, but abused wives, jealous lovers, embittered acquaintances, and besotted enemies could purchase a bladed weapon in any hardware store or pawn shop for a tiny sum.

Most New Orleans homicides, however, were not premeditated, and killers relied on the closest available weapons.[116] As a consequence, homicides occurring in homes more often involved guns, where pistols and rifles were usually stored. Yet, even in killings taking places in domestic settings, assailants increasingly turned to bladed weapons, for ice picks, meat cleavers, carving knives, razors, and scissors were present in every household, whereas

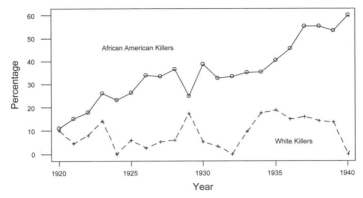

F I G . 4 . 6 . Proportion of Homicides Committed with Knives, 1920–1940. Source: Homicide Reports, Department of Police, New Orleans.

guns gradually became scarce. When African American violence moved to the streets, the shift from shootings to cuttings accelerated. In 1925, the African American gun homicide rate was three times the knife homicide rate. By the mid-1930s, more African American killers used bladed weapons than firearms. Similarly, between 1925 and 1940, the proportion of African American homicides committed with knives rose from one-fourth to nearly two-thirds (see figure 4.6). But, because knife wounds were less often fatal, the homicide rate dropped, especially for African American New Orleanians.

In short, changes in the composition of the African American community, in family and neighborhood life, and in access to guns combined, producing a sharp drop in lethal violence, despite worsening racial inequality and discrimination and the collapse of the economy. The economic crisis of the era accelerated these changes. By the early 1930s, African American violence was increasingly concentrated in public settings where guns were less common and where the likelihood of outsiders, ranging from friends to cops, intervening in fights was greatest. Violent quarrels among African American New Orleanians persisted but became less deadly. Furthermore, these shifts were self-perpetuating. When revolvers became relatively less common on the streets of the city, fewer young men felt a need to carry guns and more witnesses were willing to attempt to separate the combatants. As the Great Depression wore on, and as market forces limited access to firearms, the African American gun homicide rate plunged, pulling the city's overall homicide rate down with it (see figure 4.7).

These shifts crossed racial lines, though the drop in white violence was more modest. Slower population growth, better-balanced sex ratios, the

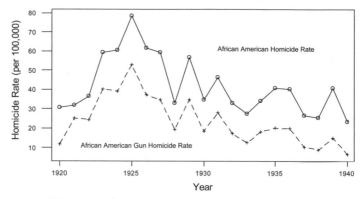

FIG. 4.7. African American Homicide and Gun Homicide Rates, 1920–1940. Source: Homicide Reports, Department of Police, New Orleans.

decline of lodging, and the development of new residential areas helped to produce a one-third decrease in New Orleans's white homicide rate between the mid-1920s and the early 1930s, compared with a two-thirds drop in the African American rate. White households had included fewer boarders than African American homes, and crowding had been less extreme. Thus, the impact of the shifts in white household structure and family life on interpersonal violence proved to be smaller than those experienced by African American residents.

Changes in gun homicide unfolded in the same way. Market pressures had a smaller effect on white residents, and especially white killers, who were relatively wealthier than their African American counterparts. Socioeconomic status, therefore, exerted less influence on the weapon choices of jealous, angry, drunken, and feuding white assailants, as handguns were less often priced out of their reach. Between the mid-1920s and the late 1930s, the proportion of low-blue-collar white killers using guns fell by 15 percent. By comparison, the proportion of African Americans in unskilled jobs who committed homicide by shooting dropped by 40.2 percent. In addition, two-thirds of white killers held semiskilled, skilled, or white-collar jobs (compared with 14.2 percent of African American killers), and gun use did not drop over time for these more affluent New Orleanians. Therefore, white gun murder decreased, while African American firearm violence plummeted. Between the mid-1920s and the early 1930s, the white gun homicide rate dropped by 50.3 percent, while the African American firearm homicide rate plunged by 76.3 percent (see figures 4.4 and 4.5).

In sum, a peculiar layering of seemingly unrelated demographic, ecological, and economic pressures produced a dramatic drop in New Orleans violence at a time when social pressures appeared to be perfectly aligned to fuel an explosion in homicide. New Orleanians did not suddenly live more harmoniously during the late 1920s and the 1930s. Nor did the economic crisis of the era generate unity, provide a salve to invidious social and racial divisions, or inculcate greater faith in the ability of legal institutions to mediate conflict. Rather, residents of the city increasingly interacted, quarreled, and fought in settings and with weapons that yielded lower death tolls from such clashes. The drop in violence did not occur among all groups uniformly, but homicide rates fell across every social and spatial boundary in New Orleans.

*

During the late 1920s and the early 1930s, New Orleans homicide changed dramatically and paradoxically. The high-profile, purported triggers for interpersonal violence, such as Prohibition, organized crime, inequality, and the Great Depression, did not generate increased homicide. To the contrary, in a period of blistering racial discrimination, searing political oppression, and soaring levels of poverty, violence plummeted. The deep economic crisis of the era profoundly affected violence, but in surprising and indirect ways. By slowing population movements and especially by making it more difficult for the poorest residents to afford firearms, the Great Depression redefined the locus for violent conflicts and limited access to inexpensive handguns. In combination with changes in the social ecology of New Orleans, these forces sharply reduced homicide. Between 1925 and 1933, the number of violent deaths dropped from 127 to 66.

Although Harry Jones's knife thrust into the neck of Joseph Isom on April 15, 1930, proved fatal, Butter Beans and Kuse's fight did not yield a sudden death. The men clashed four times over the course of the day, using fists, bricks, and finally knives, and twice outsiders attempted to separate the bachelors. By comparison with early 1920s altercations, which more often erupted in homes and with guns, such violence was far less likely to add to the parish coroner's caseload. In short, homicide, especially by African American residents, plunged during the late 1920s and early 1930s.

White New Orleanians, however, particularly city officials, cops, and parish judges and prosecutors, saw these changes in criminal violence very differently. Just as white residents acknowledged the core role of guns in murders and yet eschewed any effort to fortify or even enforce existing firearm restrictions, they recognized that New Orleans's homicide rate was falling but perceived a crisis in law and order. Similarly, policy makers and law enforcers possessed data documenting the decreasing rate of African American violent crime, though they imagined only growing threats from African American criminals. If the changes in lethal violence in New Orleans were counterintuitive, white city and parish officials responded to the changing face of criminal violence in equally paradoxical ways.

CHAPTER 5

"The Iron Hand of Justice"

Julius Roberts personified white New Orleanians' fears of African Americans during the late 1920s and the 1930s. On April 13, 1929, at approximately 7:30 a.m., the twenty-one-year-old African American laborer robbed a grocery store and murdered the white proprietor, forty-nine-year-old Annie Flink, and her fourteen-year-old son, Henry, bashing in their skulls with an ax.[1] Twice each month, on the fifteenth and the thirtieth, section hands at a nearby railroad yard cashed their paychecks at the grocery, and the day before the robbery Annie Flink had withdrawn $5,700 from the Whitney Central Bank for this purpose.[2] This was the age of celebrity bandits and high-profile bank robbers, the era of Sacco and Vanzetti, Bonnie and Clyde, John Dillinger, and Pretty Boy Floyd.[3] Cops assumed that the killings were collateral damage from a well-coordinated heist. Inexplicably, Mrs. Benjamin Purcell, the white neighbor who found the Flinks' bodies, had reported that they had been shot, leading policemen to suspect that heartless bandits had executed them.[4] But when other neighbors reported that they had noticed Julius Roberts leaving the store around 7:30 a.m. with an ax, the police refocused their investigation. Detectives searched the suspect's house and found bloodstained overalls. Roberts soon admitted that he had killed Annie and Henry Flink.[5]

Roberts's confession, which was printed in local newspapers, made the murders even more horrifying for white New Orleanians, because the killer knew his victims and committed the crimes impulsively. He had grown up a few blocks from Flink's market and as a child "used to play around the store."[6] He had even worked for Annie Flink, and Henry Flink had known Julius Roberts his entire life.[7] In his statement, Roberts blamed "mookers" or "muggles" (colloquial terms for marijuana cigarettes), explaining that "I was smoking mookers Saturday and went out of my head."[8]

On the spur of the moment, Roberts decided that "Flink's [store] ought to be a good place [to rob]."[9] He located an old ax under his sister's house, walked to the small grocery, and asked Henry for a pack of cigarettes. As the boy handed him the cigarettes, the tall, wiry Roberts swung the weapon with all his strength and struck Henry above the right eye with the flat side of the ax, caving in his frontal bone. After the fourteen-year-old crumbled to the floor, Roberts hammered him again, above his left ear, fracturing Henry's parietal bone. Annie Flink, a New Orleans native whose husband had died a year earlier, heard the commotion and hurried to the front of the store. When she reached the counter, Roberts bludgeoned her on the top of the skull twice with the bladed side of the ax, cleaving her occipital and parietal bones. Annie Flink fell face-first and died instantly, and Henry, his cranium crushed, succumbed six hours later.[10] Seemingly unaware of the payroll money, Roberts snatched the small Hershey's Kisses box that Flink used for loose change and dashed off with $5.23. Just outside the grocery, he accidentally dropped the plasterboard box and fled with a few quarters, dimes, and pennies.

Described by journalists as a "blood-thirsty scoundrel" and the "fuddle-brained negro who swung the ax to secure a few paltry coins," Julius Roberts, better known in the neighborhood as "Doo-Doom," violated the racial etiquette of Jim Crow New Orleans in the most vicious ways.[11] More than mobs, cops, laws, courts, or the Louisiana State Penal Farm at Angola, the unwritten rules of racial comportment were supposed to preserve social stability. White and African American residents knew and generally performed their racially inscribed roles, the former group asserting paternalistic authority and the latter, at least outwardly, appearing deferential and submissive.[12] New Orleans had experienced no lynchings in recent memory, in large part, according to whites, because residents honored core boundaries and upheld the etiquette undergirding the racial hierarchy. But Julius Roberts flouted all of this. Not only did he kill respectable white residents, but he slaughtered two people he knew—a widow and a child, no less. White New Orleanians worried about bandits and holdups during this period, but Doo-Doom Roberts, and killers like him, proved much more frightening. Roberts confessed that he had gone "plumb crazy," leading many white residents to wonder if their African American neighbors might suddenly kill them as well.[13] During the late 1920s, murder—to white residents—no longer seemed harmlessly confined to African American households. To the contrary, it bled across racial lines.

In the white imagination, an irrational, drug-crazed African American resident had turned on decent white residents for no reason. This explanation also tapped the mushrooming national panic about predatory crime, such as the Leopold and Loeb thrill killing of fourteen-year-old Bobby Franks in Chicago in 1924, Edward Hickman's kidnapping, sexual mutilation, and murder of twelve-year-old Marion Parker in Los Angeles in 1927, and Andrew Kehoe's school bombing in Bath, Michigan, which claimed forty-five lives, also in 1927. Not surprisingly, in late 1920s Louisiana, the face of senseless violence was African American. Thus, Julius Roberts's minute-and-a-half killing spree ignited a crime panic among white New Orleanians—or, rather, it yoked a local crime panic to the national crime wave.

The timing of the panic was curious, for lethal violence was plummeting at this very moment. Between 1925 and 1929, New Orleans's homicide rate fell by 27.6 percent. Three factors nonetheless led white New Orleanians to become alarmed about robbery-homicide and interracial violence. First, violent crime became more visible in the city, even as it became less common. Because deadly violence in local homes dropped particularly sharply during this period, homicide in public settings comprised an increasing proportion of murders and hence captured disproportionate attention from reporters and law enforcers. Since African American New Orleanians committed two-thirds of the city's homicides and their violence had been concentrated in private settings, these crimes had been largely invisible to white residents. Most local newspapers devoted perfunctory attention to African American domestic violence, typically describing such bloodshed, if at all, in one-paragraph stories buried in interior pages. White readers barely noticed African American homicide. But robbery-homicide, particularly by African American New Orleanians, was public and visible. Second, because such crimes were rare, they seemed especially shocking and therefore commanded front-page attention and banner headlines in white newspapers, exaggerating the impact of the most atypical violence. Local newspapers termed the threat from holdups "intolerable" and described an "epidemic of bank robberies."[14] And third, fears of African American predators became self-perpetuating. As white New Orleanians worried about flagging racial boundaries, black-on-white violence appeared more menacing, regardless of its actual frequency.

Although homicide decreased precipitously, white New Orleanians demanded protection from bandits and particularly from African American robbers. City officials and white newspaper editors, who had long dismissed the stratospheric local crime rate as merely a "negro problem," suddenly considered violence a formidable threat to social order, public safety, racial stability, and white supremacy.[15] In turn, law enforcers responded to the crime panic in ways that transformed New Orleans's criminal system during the early 1930s, establishing practices that redefined race relations in the city for decades.

*

Robbery became the signature crime of the era. Although the number of these crimes increased in New Orleans during the late 1920s, robberies, and particularly robbery-homicides, remained uncommon. New Orleans had half as many reported robberies as Cincinnati and Kansas City, one-third as many as Philadelphia, one-fifth as many as St. Louis, and one-forty-third as many as Chicago. The local robbery rate was less than half that of the nation's major urban centers.[16] Even after New Orleans's robbery-homicide rate doubled during the late 1920s, murderous holdups accounted for only one-twentieth of homicides. But white residents perceived a different reality. At least in part, J. Edgar Hoover conditioned New Orleanians to see gun-toting bandits lurking in every alley. He exploited the threat from murderous robbers to generate support for the Federal Bureau of Investigation and, in the process, transformed small-time hoodlums into celebrity criminals and connected isolated holdups to a national crime wave.[17]

Robberies, especially bank robberies, were glaring public crimes. Bandits followed the money and often struck stores and banks in the heart of the central business district. Adding to the sizzle of such crimes, holdup men routinely hit their targets during business hours, brandished guns to cow their victims, and then climbed into fast cars and disappeared. Only in the loosest sense did Julius Roberts's brutal-but-bumbling crime resemble the predations of big-time bandits. The core similarity, in the minds of white New Orleanians, was that robbers, like him, preyed on respectable white folk.

Bandits capitalized on the regimen of the marketplace, learning the rhythms of commerce and using them to their own advantage. While Julius Roberts insisted that only muscle memory and the haze from his muggles cigarettes directed him to Annie Flink's small grocery market, less than a year later two more deliberate, hooded white bandits entered Frank and Joseph Pipitone's grocery store and "commanded every one in the place to throw up their hands."[18] To demonstrate his resolve, one of the bandits fired a bullet into the floor. The robbers knew that the Pipitones had between $4,000 and $7,000 in small bills on hand in order to cash paychecks for workers at the nearby American Can Company.[19] When forty-four-year old Frank Pipitone, an Italian immigrant, resisted, Claude Cefalu shot him in the abdomen and the chest.[20] After seizing the cash, the robbers dashed to the street, where an accomplice was waiting in a stolen Buick to whisk them away.[21]

Bandits targeted banks on their busiest days, often immediately before pay-days or holidays. These were audacious, flamboyant crimes. At 1:07 p.m. on December 24, 1930, for instance, two white men robbed the Canal Bank and Trust Company in the heart of the city's business district, the third time this branch had been hit since 1926.[22] Their faces hidden behind blue handker-chiefs, Jules Van Hoven and Otto Deeters charged into the lobby, pointed their revolvers at employees and customers, and "commanded all of them to stick them up." As nineteen-year-old Deeters climbed over the wire cage sepa-rating patrons from tellers and began stuffing cash into a pillow slip, Patrol-man Ernest A. Grillot happened to walk by the front of the bank. Twenty-year-old Van Hoven shot the policeman in the chest. The bullet pierced Grillot's badge and passed through the thirty-three-year-old veteran cop's left lung and heart, killing him—and symbolizing the helplessness of law enforc-ers, whose shields, literally and figuratively, failed to protect them or the law-abiding public.[23]

When detectives apprehended and interrogated bandits, the robbers re-vealed that local financial institutions offered "easy money."[24] The suspects explained that the city's booming economy, inept cops, and vulnerable targets made New Orleans a magnet for professional criminals from across the na-tion. Bank robbers from Chicago, the urban center most associated with vio-lent crime, flocked to the Louisiana city, according to the leader of one such robbery gang, "because they could make big money in the South holding up banks, as they carried large amounts of cash and were poorly guarded."[25] The bandits who struck the Canal Bank and Trust Company in 1930 and killed Raymond Rizzo and Herman Taylor told investigators that they stole an auto-mobile and traveled from Chicago after hearing that "New Orleans banks can be easily robbed."[26] Even if police records did not support reports of a mass migration of seasoned bandits, a New Orleans newspaper in 1930 announced that "with state and federal governments taking a definite stand and making a definite effort to put a stop to Chicago crime, a lot of racketeers and other persons of low classes will leave there and come here."[27] Similarly, Louisiana attorney general Percy Saint announced that draconian anticrime measures in New York were "driving northern bandits to New Orleans."[28]

These bandits were killers. "The criminals who specialize in this business," the *New Orleans Times-Picayune* reported in 1931, "have made it evident that murder is a part of their plan and purpose. The mere flourish of guns for purposes of intimidation no longer contents them."[29] Assistant District Attorney J. Bernard Cocke concurred, insisting that "every bandit is a potential murderer, willing and armed to kill."[30] A "new generation" of holdup men, a national expert concluded, "will shoot and kill a merchant because they don't like the looks of his face."[31] Though committing only 2.4 percent of New Orleans homicides during the late 1920s and early 1930s, white bandits haunted the local business elite and their customers.

But a second and still more menacing class of murderous robbers also preyed on respectable white New Orleanians. Julius Roberts belonged to this group: African American robbers. White bandits were seen as hardened killers, and their crimes were purposeful. By comparison, African American robbers were said to murder for no reason.[32] These criminals committed one-third of local robberies and 48.3 percent of robbery-homicides during the late 1920s and early 1930s.[33] Although their murders accounted for only 2.3 percent of the city's lethal violence, with victims such as Annie and Henry Flink, they cast long shadows.

For white residents, robberies by African American New Orleanians were particularly terrifying for three reasons. First, the holdups targeted whites. During the late 1920s and early 1930s, three-fourths of robberies and four-fifths of robbery-homicides by African Americans had white victims. By comparison, in homicides not involving robbery, whites comprised 3.9 percent of the victims of African American killers. Holdup men seldom targeted African American New Orleanians, who had relatively little wealth, owned few stores, and rarely worked as bank tellers, clerks, or paymasters.

Second, African American bandits typically robbed neighborhood shopkeepers and street peddlers for tiny hauls of cash. On March 21, 1932, for example, twenty-one-year-old Leaval Hubbard and twenty-two-year-old Sanders Watkins, both African American, decided "to make some money."[34] Just after 9:00 p.m. the two men stood outside Edward Melancon's grocery on Magnolia Street and bickered about robbing it, Hubbard arguing that "that man ain't got no money" and Watkins insisting that they proceed.[35] After Hubbard entered the store, drew his .38 caliber revolver, and instructed Melancon to "get them up," Watkins plucked $1.87 from the cash register. When the forty-nine-year-old shopkeeper resisted, Hubbard, who had committed five other recent robberies, shot him in the abdomen. With Melancon collapsed on the floor, dying, Watkins rifled his pockets and found another $12; the killers netted $13.87.[36] Similarly, three seventeen-year-old African American residents robbed and shot fifty-one-year-old Jacob Vildhinsen, a tamale vender. The trio had planned to stick up a drugstore, but there were "too many people in the place." Seconds later, "they saw the hot tamale vender and decided to rob him." The teenagers shot the Dutch immigrant in the chest and escaped with $1.65—or 55 cents apiece.[37]

Third, by targeting neighborhood grocers and street venders, African American robbers ignited a furious backlash from a cross-section of white New Orleanians. Their crimes seemed especially vicious and gratuitous. Contemporary observers attributed the apparent willingness of African American criminals to kill ordinary citizens for pennies to racial difference. Exaggerating the acumen of white bandits, police officials and newspaper editors insisted that these criminals were clever, disciplined, and professional; they generally killed for large hauls and meticulously planned their heists. By contrast, white New Orleanians argued, African American robbers lacked the discipline and intellectual acuity to pull off complex capers. Instead, they acted on impulse and struck the nearest white victim when the urge for lucre surfaced.[38]

The families of the victims of African American robbers were also particularly sympathetic, and crime-beat reporters seized on this narrative angle, inflaming white passions and selling newspapers in the process.[39] Just as Julius Roberts's crime left twelve-year-old Charles Flink an orphan, Leaval Hubbard's brutality sent Edward Melancon's family into a heart-wrenching tailspin, which newspapers voyeuristically chronicled. Before the robbery, the *New Orleans States* noted, income from their small grocery did not provide "much in the way of luxuries," though the "necessities were there—and the Melancon family was happy." But after Hubbard's vicious, senseless crime, the murdered shopkeeper's widow became "gravely ill"; "creditors took over the little store"; they were forced to move to a small, cramped house; O'Neil, the oldest of the five Melancon children, "became the sole support of the family"; and fourteen-year-old Lloyd issued a public plea for help in securing a job.[40]

A volatile mixture of anxiety about crime, outrage at the predations of white bandits, and terror expressed by panicked white New Orleanians transformed policing and criminal justice in the city during the late 1920s and early 1930s. In the years after the Great War, many big-city police departments had professionalized, establishing training academies, imposing bureaucratic command structures, and embracing "scientific" crime fighting.[41] But not New Orleans, where institutional change moved in reverse, and city officials abolished formal training for new officers.[42] During the early 1920s, local cops devoted scant attention to crime fighting, in part because white residents believed that violence principally remained confined among African American residents.[43] Other tasks, ranging from providing muscle for the political machine to managing the French Quarter's vice industry, commanded police attention. According to one New Orleans official, the police department was more "a political organization, devoted to blackjacking recalcitrant voters into line[,] than a police department. It was an effective political club," Commissioner of Public Safety Stanley Ray explained, "but an ineffective police force."[44] As violent crime rates swelled during the early 1920s, police budgets contracted, and the number of cops on the street dropped.[45]

The robbery panic, however, triggered a sea change. New Orleans officials discovered violence and vowed to get tough on criminals.[46] Police Superintendent Thomas Healy pledged in 1925 to "stamp out lawlessness" and promised "a drive against bandits."[47] Again and again, municipal leaders announced that they would take "drastic action to stop hold-ups."[48] Police chiefs and mayors seized on military metaphors.[49] In 1929, Superintendent of Police Theodore A. Ray declared "war on bandit gangs."[50] The next year, he launched a "war on holdups," and Ray's successor, Hu Myers, proposed a "new war on bandits."[51]

The city's crusades never professionalized law enforcement in New Orleans, but they militarized the police. Municipal officials, for example, purchased "machine guns to combat the depredations of bandit gangs."[52] In 1929, Police Superintendent Ray went a step further and introduced a high-speed motorcycle with a sidecar specially designed to hold a policeman wielding a Thompson submachine gun. This crime-fighting tool, Ray crowed, could fire fifty large-caliber bullets in half a minute and would be deployed to every robbery scene.[53] The *New Orleans Item* dubbed the contraption the "death-dealing machine," while the *New Orleans Times-Picayune* predicted that "bandits who prey on pay rolls and commercial houses in New Orleans will be greeted in the future with slugs from a new submachine gun."[54] "Advanced warfare is now claiming the attention of the police department," one journalist concluded.[55]

More important, Ray ordered policemen to "shoot to kill" when they encountered bandits.[56] While the superintendent did not establish overall training, he demanded that patrolmen "learn how to shoot bandits."[57] "Shoot to kill," Ray preached in 1929, "but watch out for innocent people."[58] Moreover, when cops killed holdup men, Ray and his successors promoted the shooters and issued citations specifically for "killing bandits."[59] According to one newspaper editor, cops who shoot and kill "deserve, and usually receive, not only the support of their superior officers but the approval and support of the people."[60] Municipal law enforcers had killed suspects before the robbery panic of the late 1920s, but "shooting to kill" quickly became a marker of police professionalism and effective crime fighting.

The surge in banditry proved to be short-lived. Robbery and robbery-homicide crested during the early 1930s and then plummeted. Between 1931 and 1934, New Orleans's robbery rate dropped by half and then inched downward until the 1940s.[61] The robbery-homicide rate followed a similar trajectory, peaking in 1930 and then plunging by 70.2 percent during the next four years. In 1930, robbers killed eleven New Orleanians and wounded another dozen citizens, and holdups produced 12.9 percent of local homicides.[62] During the remainder of the decade, robbers committed twenty-two murders, accounting for only 3 percent of homicides.

The sudden decrease in robberies, robbery-homicides, and particularly bank heists led many New Orleanians to credit the new crime-fighting methods.[63] "We congratulate the police," one newspaper editor announced.[64] "Shoot to kill" had saved the city from desperadoes. "Since the police department launched an intensive drive against bank holdups," another editor observed in 1932, "no bank has been molested."[65] Two years later, the district attorney, noting the "splendid work on the part of the New Orleans police department," announced that "bank, pay roll and other forms of robbery have practically been stamped out."[66] A 1938 visitor concurred, writing that "hold-ups, frequent only a few years ago, are now rare."[67] More than aggressive policing, the Great Depression likely accounted for the drop, since many downtown banks closed, payroll receipts sagged, and commerce slowed in the city. New Orleans's sharp fall in robbery rates also mirrored national trends, suggesting that local crime-fighting measures did not, by themselves, reduce banditry.[68] Nonetheless, commentators attributed the plunge in robberies to the willingness of the police "to meet bandits and hold-up men on an equal or better footing."[69]

The lion's share of the decrease in robbery, and particularly in robbery-homicide, was in crimes by white bandits. From 1920 until 1926, white robbers committed five murders. Between 1927 and 1930, they killed thirteen residents, and from 1931 until 1940, white robbers fatally shot five New Orleanians. Thus, more than half of murders by white bandits between 1920 and 1940 occurred during a four-year period. Between 1930 and 1940, the white robbery-homicide rate tumbled by 84.2 percent.

Robbery-homicide by African American New Orleanians decreased slightly, dipping at one-third the rate it fell among whites. Despite Ray's shoot-to-kill orders and his death-dealing motorcycle, African American banditry continued. These robbers killed nine victims between 1927 and 1930 and twelve between 1931 and 1940. After 1930, when the number of white robbery-homicides plunged, the proportion of such murders committed by African American residents skyrocketed—but largely because white robberies fell. Between 1927 and 1930, white criminals committed 59.1 percent of the city's robbery-homicides, whereas from 1931 to 1940, African Americans were responsible for 72.2 percent of these crimes.

During the 1930s, white New Orleanians conflated robbery with African Americans. In part, the decrease in high-profile bank robberies, which were usually committed by white bandit gangs, reflected police priorities. City officials had focused their "war on bandits" on the central business district, promising that the "shotgun squad," for example, would keep career criminals "in the outskirts" of the city. Police chiefs even established "deadlines" at the boundaries of the downtown commercial zone, and cops arrested "bandits and crooks" who ventured into this area.[70] Concentrating police efforts near the largest banks and commercial houses, however, did little to protect shops on the "outskirts," such an Annie Flink's grocery. Moreover, the economic collapse of the 1930s shuttered banks and large commercial firms but did not close corner markets, which remained targets for robbers. Therefore, shifts in policing and changes in the local economy combined to safeguard banks and reduce white banditry yet had a more modest impact on African American and small-scale robberies.

Criminal justice officials, however, linked the persistence of African American robbery-homicide to deeper, more foreboding shifts in city life. White New Orleanians perceived an increasing threat from African American residents, even as African American homicide rates plunged. Nor did the proportion of homicides in which African American residents killed whites increase. Between 1920 and 1940, 94.5 percent of African American homicides remained within racial lines. Furthermore, Doo-Doom Roberts and Leaval Hubbard notwithstanding, robbery-homicide by African American New Orleanians remained rare, accounting for 1.6 percent of the city's homicides from 1931 to 1940, and only seven white residents died at the hands of African American bandits during this ten-year span. But the surging proportion of robbery-homicides committed by African American New Orleanians, in combination with the high visibility of these crimes, made a stronger impression on white residents than did the number or the rate of such murders. Cops, as well as crime-beat reporters and municipal officials, insisted that African American residents preyed on their white neighbors, often tracing this violent behavior to the demise of older mechanisms of racial control.

The institutional bulwarks of racial hierarchy seemed to be crumbling, which allegedly enabled African Americans to become bold, aggressive, and predatory. In 1927, for example, the US Supreme Court overturned New Orleans's racial segregation ordinance, opening the floodgates to dreaded "race mixing."[71] Furthermore, a 1931 legal challenge to Orleans Parish's use of the state's "understanding clause" to preserve the racial purity of the voting rolls jeopardized white control over electoral politics, a threat compounded by Huey P. Long's meddling.[72] Long, who battled New Orleans officials over patronage and hoped to weaken the local political machine, announced that he would help African American New Orleanians to register to vote, prompting a local official to charge that "Senator Long is deliberately planning to destroy white supremacy in Louisiana."[73] Civil rights leaders' attacks on the exclusion of African American residents from criminal court juries magnified white anxieties about the collapse of the institutional structures of racial control during the late 1920s and the early 1930s.[74]

Even the physical expansion of the city seemed to undermine the racial order. When New Orleanians resettled in newly drained areas, more residents, white and African American, commuted to the stores, factories, and warehouses along the Mississippi River, increasingly traveling in automobiles. This form of transportation, however, roiled customs of racial deference. On crowded streets, particularly at night, drivers could not always identify one another's racial backgrounds. Yet white drivers expected African American "automobilers" to grant them the "racial right of way."[75] If African American drivers passed them or, worse still, cut them off in traffic, white vehicle operators considered such actions to be expressions of overt racial aggression.[76]

The anonymity of the streets, where the conventions of "racial prerogative" faltered, fueled numerous altercations, sparking race-inflected disputes in which African Americans appeared—to whites—to transgress core behavioral boundaries.[77] On August 23, 1927, for instance, Andrew Wiebelt, a twenty-seven-year-old white security guard, fatally shot Lilly Johnson, a forty-three-year-old African American resident, after a minor traffic dispute. Albert Johnson, the African American driver of a vehicle, testified in court that Wiebelt bellowed at him, "Nigger, put your lights on." Wiebelt claimed that Johnson responded by screaming, "Suck my arse, you white mother fuckers."[78] Enraged, Wiebelt followed Johnson as he drove home. As Johnson exited his automobile, Wiebelt drew a gun and fired multiple shots at him, one of which struck and killed Johnson's mother, Lilly, as she sat on the front porch of her house.[79]

Similar skirmishes over racial etiquette erupted on streetcars, where white riders attempted to enforce racial custom, demanded deference from African American riders, and fought—and sometimes killed—over access to seats, collisions in cramped aisles, and the placement of the screens that separated white from African American passengers.[80] In such a charged climate, jostles in crowded public settings seemed neither accidental nor incidental.[81] Rather, they represented expressions of racial defiance and revealed the new boldness of African American New Orleanians. Disputes over space and racial convention particularly marred Mardi Gras celebrations during the early 1930s, leading to fights, homicides, and, among white New Orleanians, trepidation.[82] According to local whites, as racial boundaries crumbled, African American New Orleanians seized the opportunity, flouted convention, and attacked white residents. One attorney took to the radio in 1935 to warn that respectable white residents "don't want these baboons mixing with white people and being turned loose on the streets of New Orleans to kill."[83]

Fearing the collapse of white supremacy, frightened by African American defiance and predatory crime, and encouraged by the apparent effectiveness of aggressive policing, white New Orleanians embraced cops as guardians of a beleaguered racial order. City officials also looked to police, hoping that the rule of law, rather than popular justice or mob violence, would shore up the social order.[84] Municipal and criminal justice leaders increasingly encouraged aggressive policing, even beyond shooting bandits. Long considered political operatives more than law enforcers, New Orleans cops became crime fighters in a city in which predatory crime and social disorder had become even more racialized.

During the late 1920s, the New Orleans police began to shoot to kill. Between 1928 and 1930, the police homicide rate rose by two-thirds, and the proportion of New Orleanians who died at the hands of cops more than doubled. The spike in deadly police shootings, however, had no correlation with the city's homicide rate (see figure 4.1). Between 1925 and 1930, the lethal violence rate tumbled by 36.7 percent, yet the police homicide rate leaped by 64.3 percent. Rather than pivoting to aggressive policing in response to violent crime, New Orleans patrolmen and detectives employed deadly force in reaction to the robbery and robbery-homicide surge and the panic that it triggered, even though holdups accounted for only 5.3 percent of homicides during the hysteria. Trends in police homicide in interwar New Orleans roughly tracked patterns of robbery-homicide (see figure 5.1).[85] Both the police homicide rate and the robbery-homicide rate peaked in 1930.

The link between white banditry and law enforcers' use of deadly force was particularly strong. When white robbers prowled New Orleans and killed

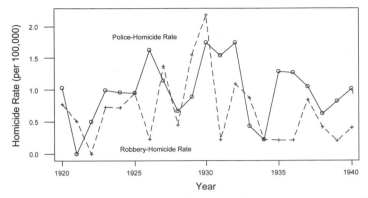

F I G . 5.1. Police Homicide and Robbery-Homicide Rates, 1920–1940. Source: Homicide Reports, Department of Police, New Orleans.

their victims, cops employed lethal violence against them; when white banditry waned, so did police homicide against whites.[86] In 1928, white robbers committed no murders. Two years later, they killed six of their victims. During this period, the rate at which law enforcers killed white New Orleanians tripled. By comparison, during the 1931–40 period, when white robbers committed only a handful of murders, the rate of police killings of whites fell by half.

New Orleans cops generally used lethal force against white residents who were suspected criminals and carried weapons. Robbery or burglary suspects comprised nearly half of the white victims of police homicide. During the early 1930s, the proportion rose to almost two-thirds. Similarly, 46.9 percent of these victims had guns and another 6.3 percent carried knives between 1920 and 1940, and during the early 1930s, 66.7 percent possessed firearms and 16.7 percent had dirks. In 1930, every white resident killed by cops was a suspected robber with a gun.

Vernon Floyd was a typical white victim of New Orleans police homicide. On April 27, 1930, the twenty-year-old racetrack laborer participated in a crime spree. With two accomplices, Floyd stole a Star Checker Cab and held up a store. The robbers escaped with $100 and immediately headed to a second target. As two of the criminals entered George Reynolds's grocery store, brandished revolvers, and seized $300, thirty-three-year-old Raymond Credo, an off-duty patrolman sitting on his front step across the street, recognized Floyd as a "police character" (i.e., a known criminal). Credo grabbed his gun and waited for the holdup men to emerge from the store. When Floyd and Robert Davidson left the grocery but ignored Credo's command to "halt," the cop opened fire, hitting Floyd in the chest and killing him. Davidson suffered a bullet wound to the jaw but survived.[87] The third bandit, who had remained in the stolen taxi during the robbery, fled when the shooting began. Four days later, Police Superintendent Theodore Ray promoted Credo to corporal for killing Vernon Floyd.[88] To be sure, local cops were often reckless, sometimes misidentified criminals, and occasionally fired indiscriminately into crowds, though they typically shot in the general direction of white felony suspects.

Police shootings of African American New Orleanians also mirrored robbery-homicide trends, but with a twist. When African American bandits killed their victims, such as between 1930 and 1932 and between 1935 and 1937, the number of African American suspects killed by cops exploded (see figure 5.2).[89] The African American robbery-homicide rate rose by 69.2 percent between 1928–29 and 1930–32, and the rate at which policemen killed African American residents ballooned by 406.3 percent. Between 1930–32 and 1933–34, however, the rates dropped by 81.8 percent and 82 percent respectively. The African American robbery-homicide rate rebounded by 219 percent between 1933–34 and 1935–37, while the rate at which cops killed African American residents swelled by 256.2 percent. When African American robbery-homicide rose during the 1930–32 period, one-tenth of African American homicide victims were killed by local law enforcers. By comparison, when African American robbery-homicide dipped during 1933–34, police killings accounted for one-fiftieth of African American homicide deaths. The peaks and troughs of violence by African American robbers, in short, corresponded to surges and contractions in police violence against African American suspects.

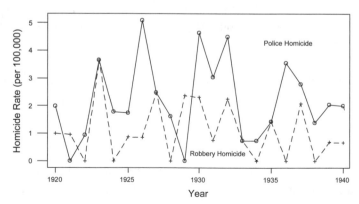

FIG. 5.2. Rates of Police Homicide against African Americans and Robbery-Homicides by African Americans, 1920–1940. Source: Homicide Reports, Department of Police, New Orleans.

Yet the African American New Orleanians who died at the hands of cops were not typically robbery or burglary suspects. Whereas 47.2 percent of whites killed by law enforcers were suspected robbers or burglars, only one-third of African Americans killed by policemen were suspects in such crimes.[90] Instead, cops killed nearly two-thirds of African Americans for more ambiguous reasons; policemen considered them "disorderly" or insisted that they were engaged in "suspicious conduct" and shot them while making the arrest. Furthermore, 25.4 percent of African American victims carried guns, compared with 46.9 percent of whites killed by municipal law enforcers. During the early 1930s robbery-homicide spike, which fueled a police homicide spike, 13.3 percent of African Americans shot by New Orleans policemen carried firearms, compared with two-thirds of white victims of police homicide. The connection between African American robbery-homicide and police homicide was indirect; the trends fluctuated together, though the individual homicides were largely unrelated. The robbery panic conditioned—and encouraged—New Orleans cops to shoot to kill and provided a justification for a liberal use of deadly force against African American New Orleanians.

If the "police character" Vernon Floyd was a typical white victim of aggressive law enforcement, Milton Battise was a typical African American victim. Battise was not suspected of committing a serious crime, had no criminal record, and was unarmed. Just after midnight on June 29, 1930, an "old Ford touring car" with "about five or six negroes" passed a vehicle on the outskirts of New Orleans driven by an older white couple. The white driver and his wife complained to a cop that the African Americans "had cursed them and abused them" as they sped past. Motorcycle officers Irvin Karl and George Mamola located the automobile and attempted to arrest the driver and the other occupants for "disturbing the peace," "using obscene language," and "annoying a motorist and his wife." One of the passengers, however, failed to comply and "started to run."[91] Twenty-one-year-old Milton Battise, according to the policemen, "ignored their command to halt and made a threatening move toward his back pocket."[92] Fearing that Battise was reaching for a gun and hence that their lives were in danger, Karl and Mamola discharged their revolvers. One of the bullets struck Battise in the back of skull, instantly killing him—and challenging the cops' assertion that their lives were endangered, for the suspect was running away from them. When investigating officers examined Battise's body, they found no weapon but discovered a half-pint flask of whiskey in his back pocket.[93] If Battise did indeed reach for his pocket, it was likely to ditch the illegal hooch.

Again and again, New Orleans cops apprehended African Americans for "loitering" or "disturbing the peace" and killed them for making threatening motions. Policemen shot Edward Liles for "reaching his hand into a pocket as if to draw a weapon," Paul Henry for "reaching to his pocket," Oscar Brooks because he "shoved a hand into his bosom," Dave Hughes for "putting his left hand in his left hip pocket," and Winston Thomas when he "reached for his trouser pocket."[94] Like Milton Battise, none of these men carried a gun. Cops asserted that the furtive "hip-pocket move" placed their lives in jeopardy and hence justified the shootings.[95]

A confluence of overlapping factors contributed to patrolmen's use of deadly force with African Americans suspects. Reflecting prevailing notions of racial difference, law enforcers believed that African Americans were, by nature, violent and unpredictable and thus feared their ambiguous movements.[96] Patrolman John Dowsky, for example, noticed Louis Parenton's "right hand at his hip." He felt that "the negro was about to draw a weapon . . . and fired two shots."[97] The sensational, widely publicized murderous behavior of men such as Julius Roberts and Leaval Hubbard reminded local cops of the risks they faced in African American neighborhoods, and therefore African American robbery-homicide and African American shootings at the hands of New Orleans policemen followed the same rhythms.

Encounters between local cops and African American suspects also typically occurred at night, on the streets, and in African American neighborhoods, adding to police perceptions of vulnerability. Moreover, as police administrators saturated downtown areas with patrolmen, outlying parts of the city, particularly those with large numbers of African American inhabitants, remained underpoliced, leaving residents and cops there feeling isolated.[98] In 41.7 percent of the fatal police shootings of African American New Orleanians, the confrontation involved only the killer and his victim, whereas 20.8 percent of cases with white victims were one-on-one interactions. Surrounded and outnumbered in African American neighborhoods at a time when racial controls appeared to be disintegrating and when the residents seemed to be emboldened, local policemen felt besieged and reacted accordingly, a response permitted by Louisiana criminal law, endorsed by police and criminal justice officials, and roundly supported by white New Orleanians.[99] Police violence, the *Louisiana Weekly* explained, "has its roots in fear."[100]

Class ideologies abetted this deadly reaction. Poorly paid and uneducated, New Orleans cops had little status.[101] Describing the "typical Southern policeman," the sociologist Gunnar Myrdal suggested that "it is not difficult to understand that this economically and socially insecure man, given his tremendous and dangerous authority [as a cop], continually feels himself on the defensive."[102] Especially during the Great Depression, when poverty eroded the material foundations of white supremacy, working-class whites, including policemen, demonstrated greater zeal, even desperation, to preserve their superiority and affirm their authority, and, as the *Louisiana Weekly* noted, the police "have been taught, by custom and tradition, that the club and the gun are symbols of their authority."[103] Thus, law enforcers used their service revolvers in response to perceived insolence or defiance from African American suspects. But, because cops saw violations of racial etiquette as symptoms of the larger collapse of white supremacy, even minor transgressions by African American residents represented threats to law and order. In short, when "shoot to kill" became a defensible law enforcement method, New Orleans policemen relied on deadly force to preserve their position in the fragile racial order.[104] Particularly on the streets of the city and at night, one observer of the New Orleans cops explained, "when a policeman attempts to make an arrest, he must win. If he loses the struggle he is through; he has lost everything."[105]

African American residents became the principal victims in police shootings. During the robbery panic, from 1927 to 1930, half of the New Orleanians killed by cops were white.[106] By the early 1930s, a decisive shift had taken place. From 1931 to 1934, two-thirds of victims were African American, and by the late 1930s, the proportion had climbed to 76.9 percent.[107] From 1931 to 1940, the city's African American police homicide rate swelled to five times the white rate.

Police violence emerged as a mechanism of racial control, purposefully deployed to inculcate fear and establish dominance. Patrolman Lawrence Terrebonne used this tool with unusual bluntness. On August 5, 1933, Terrebonne, while investigating a disturbance, inexplicably attempted to arrest every African American patron in a restaurant. To encourage submission, the thirty-eight-year-old cop commanded the customers to line up and "slugged" a few "over the head with the butt of a pistol" to accelerate the process. According to the *Louisiana Weekly*, forty-one-year-old Gerald Singleton then attempted to "dispose" of a gun he was carrying. Terrebonne immediately shot Singleton in the shoulder. When the other suspects became agitated, the cop stood over Singleton and bellowed, "It's not my custom to shoot a 'Nigger' once and stop. I always follow the first shot with a second shot, and the second shot means another dead 'Nigger'; I've killed three 'Niggers' already, and you're lucky you're not the fourth one."[108]

New Orleans police officers, knowing that they had the support of parish district attorneys, rarely hid their deadly use of force. To the contrary, they rejoiced in such fine police work.[109] Yet neither police files nor coroner's records contained records of Terrebonne's three victims. While his assertion of killing "three 'Niggers'" was fabricated, Terrebonne's hyperbole was instrumental, serving to intimidate African American suspects and affirm racial dominance. Similarly, African American residents called Detective William Grosch and his partner, who killed eight suspects between them, the "killer twins," and Grosch reveled in reminding African American suspects of this reputation. When he encountered or anticipated defiance, Grosch apprised the suspect of his name or responded decisively and then publicly celebrated it.[110]

During the early 1930s, robbery and robbery-homicide rates plunged, but the aggressive policing methods launched to control banditry persisted and shifted. Just as city officials increasingly associated predatory crime with African American residents, local law enforcers transformed the "war on bandits" into a war on African American suspects. Police use of nonlethal force followed the same trajectory and the same logic, emerging first as a tool against white robbers, becoming a badge of law enforcement prowess during the late 1920s, increasingly victimizing African American New Orleanians by the early 1930s, and gradually developing into an instrument of racial dominance. The boundary between crime control and racial control faded over time. During the 1930s, when familiar methods of racial deference appeared to falter, the city's criminal justice system filled the void.

Police brutality was hardly new in interwar New Orleans. Cops had long relied on rough justice and billy clubs to impose "order" on the streets, though ideas, practices, and legal sensibilities shifted during the early twentieth century.[111] Reformers across the country increasingly denounced police brutality and particularly demanded that cops abandon coercive interrogation methods—the "third degree." During the 1920s, legal scholars and activists called for the elimination of such "grilling" and "sweating," and judges overturned criminal convictions based on coerced confessions.[112] Louisiana lawmakers, in the state's 1921 constitution, specifically prohibited "any treatment designed by effect on body or mind to compel confession of crime."[113] This movement culminated in 1931, when the Wickersham Commission exposed and denounced police violence, triggering a national scandal with its descriptions of the "third degree." The commission's volume on the topic, entitled *Lawlessness in Law Enforcement*, revealed the systematic use of cruel, sadistic interrogation methods.[114] Police departments throughout the country publicly rejected the use of coercion to elicit confessions.

But New Orleans cops, just as they embraced police shootings as professional law enforcement, celebrated aggressive, violent interrogation methods. Like their counterparts elsewhere, many policemen bristled at the reform impulse and insisted that tough interrogation techniques were indispensable when dealing with hardened criminals.[115] New Orleans police officials simultaneously denounced and endorsed torture as a form of interrogation. When asked about the third degree in the abstract, police administrators vehemently denied that local cops employed such methods. Police Superintendent Guy Molony, for example, insisted that there was "positively no 'third degreeing' of criminals in New Orleans."[116] Yet when violent, even sadistic practices secured confessions from robbers and murderers and "solved" major cases, officials bragged about their uncompromising interrogation methods. Seven months after affirming his opposition to the third degree, Molony announced that he elicited the confession from one murderous robber using "a modern, up-to-date 'third-degree.'"[117] Likewise, Police Chief George Reyer contended that "the third degree is not permitted in the New Orleans police department, has not been and will not be tolerated," but he oversaw a surge in coerced confessions.[118]

During the late 1920s, the use of the third degree expanded as the robbery panic gripped the city. Even as city officials acknowledged that grilling and sweating violated state law and insisted that such methods did not occur in New Orleans, the "war on bandits" encouraged cops to secure confessions at any cost, and newspapers endorsed the use of third-degree interrogation techniques on vicious hoodlums. In an editorial entitled "Against Third Degree," the *New Orleans States* termed the practice "intolerable" but added that "where habitual and murderous criminals are picked up as suspects in violent crimes against society, the public is usually disposed to turn its head in the other direction if the police have to use some coercion in extracting confessions."[119] In another Janus-faced denunciation, the editor conceded that "there should be some license granted to the authorities in their effort to protect themselves and the community from the bandits, gunmen, murderers and their [*sic*] like."[120]

In short, violent interrogation methods, like shooting to kill, became an accepted, even admired, police technique as the robbery panic unfolded. When a defense attorney asked Detective John Grosch—the brother of the "killer twin" William Grosch—about his stature as the "best third degree artist in the country," the thirty-five-year-old cop, known on the streets as "Third Degree Grosch" and as "Bulldog Johnny Grosch," sheepishly denied that he possessed any such reputation and then gloated that he "had secured more than 300 confessions" from suspects.[121] He later boasted to the local Rotary Club that "if it were not for the 'third degree' methods by which I have forced legal admissions in cases where I had every reason to be sure of the guilt,

New Orleans would today be delivered over to organized and brutal crime."[122] Whereas earlier forms of police brutality occurred in dark alleys, now cops beat suspects in precinct houses and as a form of professional crime fighting. "Whatever methods they [the police] use," a newspaper editor argued, "the long series of bank and pay roll robberies holdups has been ended." When there were "complaints of third degree," legal authorities should "give due reflection to the right of the public to set up its defense against the wanton taking of human life."[123]

John Grosch's bravado notwithstanding, detectives recognized the legal ambiguity of the third degree and devised a justification for ignoring state law. Constitutional safeguards, they argued, pertained to suspects who were charged with a crime. When "no formal charge" was filed, protections against coerced confessions did not exist, and aggressive interrogation techniques were lawful and indeed crucial for crime fighting.[124] Thus, policemen simply delayed filing charges against some criminals. In other cases, New Orleans cops hid their brutality and masked evidence of vicious abuse, moving suspects from precinct to precinct so that relatives and defense attorneys could not locate them and stashing brutalized suspects in unlikely places—dubbed keeping them "on ice"—until their contusions began to heal and their welts started to fade.[125] Moreover, the coroner prohibited all other doctors from examining prisoners held in the parish prison to make it difficult for suspects to document their injuries.[126]

New Orleans cops employed a range of methods to secure confessions—or in response to perceived defiance. Detectives flogged suspects with rubber hoses, kicked and punched them, particularly in the genitals, lashed them with wire cables, and threatened to shoot them. For African American suspects, and even African American witnesses who were not considered cooperative, they staged mock lynchings. To encourage eleven-year-old Eddie Johnson to provide testimony implicating seventeen-year-old Willie Williams in a robbery, cops "placed a belt around his neck and threatened to hang him."[127] Likewise, detectives at the Tenth Precinct placed a rope around Charles Johnson's neck "and lifted him up for about ten minutes, beating him while suspended in the air," to persuade the African American suspect to confess to assaulting a white woman.[128]

Many New Orleans cops, particularly Detective William Grosch, favored the "one-way ride."[129] Detectives would drive a suspect to a secluded stretch of highway, place a gun against his temple, and suggest that he admit his guilt and sign a confession. In January 1934, after Vernon Guichard refused to confess to killing Harry Paul Chaison, detectives beat him over the head with their billies. When he maintained his innocence, Guichard said, they "took me to some isolated place which I think is on the old basin and there one of them placed a pistol to my head and said that if I didn't tell them I killed the white man, find or make the gun that was used, that they were going to blow my G—— brains out and throw me in the water."[130] On at least two occasions, Grosch killed the suspects taken "on a ride." Afterward he insisted that they had made furtive movements during these trips.[131] Such executions burnished Grosch's reputation as a maniacal interrogator and led subsequent suspects to confess before the detective could load them into his vehicle.[132]

The most notorious police station was the Twelfth Precinct, better known as the "damnable 12th."[133] Captain James Burns commanded the precinct from 1928 to 1931. The 300-pound cop became a local celebrity for donning a white dress, wearing a wig with long curls, and "gamboling" at the annual police minstrel show, earning him the nickname "Buttercup."[134] Law enforcers and judges revered Buttercup Burns for his "amiable disposition and kindliness."[135] But a very different Captain Burns surfaced when he conducted interrogations. Burns frequently instructed his officers to heat an iron stove poker and sodomize prisoners until they became cooperative. During one such session, he ordered a patrolman to "burn the nigger and make him tell us where he got that watch."[136] Burns's methods were, by design, an open secret, and policemen exploited the damnable 12th's reputation to secure confessions.[137] Murder suspect Eli Terrell, for example, told a judge that he confessed "only after he had been tripped to the 12th Precinct police station and threatened with a red hot poker."[138]

During the robbery panic, because most bank bandits were white, cops largely beat, choked, and bludgeoned confessions from white robbery suspects. By the early 1930s, as bank heists became less common and as white New Orleanians conflated predatory crime with race, the third degree, in all its forms, focused on African American suspects.[139] This shift also accelerated the intensity of the abuse, for the line between coercing a confession and punishing an insolent African American suspect was murky. When African Americans maintained their innocence, cops often erupted in rage, both because the suspect foiled their effort to close the case and because an African American defied white authority. Every time Loyd D. T. Washington, a forty-one-year-old African American cook, denied killing a white man in Yazoo City, Mississippi, New Orleans detectives grew angrier and more violent. "You know you killed him, Nigger," the lead interrogator roared as he knocked out five of Washington's teeth and broke one of his ribs before another cop interceded and informed the detective that they had arrested the wrong man.[140] "Negroes are beaten and killed by the police," an African American writer explained in 1933, "because the latter have the authority."[141] All at once, such brutality secured convictions, put "the Negro in his place," and served "as vengeance for the fears and perils the policemen are subjected to while pursuing their duties in the Negro community."[142]

When cops principally brutalized African American New Orleanians, race-specific law enforcement enjoyed greater support among white residents, who had expressed shock that detectives used third-degree methods against white suspects, at least in part because such techniques were also applied to African American suspects.[143] With some notable exceptions, white New Orleanians endorsed the brutal treatment of African American residents.[144] During a court hearing to investigate one incident, a group of white men declared that "it is an outrage to prosecute two white men for beating a 'Nigger.'"[145]

Police brutality served to reinforce the racial hierarchy. Between the 1920s and the 1930s, the number of suspects murdered during interrogations quadrupled, and the proportion of African American victims rose from 50 percent to 75 percent.[146] Moreover, when the third degree became an instrument of racial control, such brutality, like shoot-to-kill policing, emerged as a symbol of law-and-order maintenance and became more widely employed.[147] During the first three months of 1933, even though the city's robbery, robbery-homicide, and homicides rates were plunging, the local Prison Aid League received reports of more than two hundred coerced confessions.[148] Six years later the American Civil Liberties Union surveyed 332 cities on their civil rights protections, particularly in police interrogations. New Orleans was one of three cities, joining Little Rock and Tampa, that received the "worst rating" in the nation, with violations of the "rights of Negroes" particularly noted.[149] "Police brutality, to a certain extent, exists in the majority of police departments," the *Louisiana Weekly* added, "but in this city [it] tops them all."[150] The most violent local cops, such as the Grosch brothers, did not deny their methods, and their actions did not impugn the professionalism of the department. To the contrary, they became celebrated guardians of public safety and of the racial hierarchy sustaining law and order.

Police shootings, police brutality, and the notion that aggressive, predatory, unpredictable African Americans needed to be dominated at any cost fed one another during the 1930s, cementing the process through which cops elided racial control with law enforcement. These elements collided and exploded on March 9, 1932. Late in the morning, Percy Thompson, a twenty-seven-year-old African American laborer, broke into a home on South Claiborne Avenue and stole two men's suits, valued at $60.[151] A neighbor summoned the police, reporting that Thompson had run into a nearby house. Shortly after noon, three policemen arrested Thompson for breaking and entering and petty larceny, and they transported him to the Twelfth Precinct—the damnable 12th.[152]

One of the officers, thirty-eight-year-old Cornelius Ford, along with William King, an African American "trusty," brought the suspect to a second-floor cell and began the interrogation. Thompson admitted to the burglary, explaining that he planned to sell the clothing because "I was out of work and I was hungry."[153] When he refused to confess to a series of recent robberies, Patrolman Ford grew impatient and instructed King to "beat him over the head with a rubber hose."[154] According to Thompson, Ford then drew his pistol and "told me he was going to shoot my brains out." Fearing for his life, the suspect pushed King aside, "grabbed" Ford's gun, and began shooting, killing the patrolman and injuring the "trusty."[155] For the next two hours, two hundred members of the newly militarized police force stormed their own precinct house with sawed-off shotguns, submachine guns, "pump guns," and tear-gas bombs. Shortly before 3:00 p.m., Thompson, who had sustained a superficial bullet wound to the leg in the firefight but had killed three cops, agreed to surrender after the police superintendent promised to provide medical attention for him and guaranteed his safe treatment. In the car ride from Charity Hospital, the suspect, according to Detective Vic Swanson, grabbed "me in the chest with his right hand and [with] the left hand he grabbed my revolver and in the scuffle I managed to get my hand on the trigger of my revolver and fired one shot," killing Thompson.[156] The coroner's report suggested a more complicated picture, as the suspect sustained bullet wounds to the chest and groin.[157]

In a single incident, an African American suspect was arrested for a relatively minor offense, suffered a beating with a rubber hose, was threatened with a gun if he failed to confess to a string of robberies, affirmed police suspicions of the dangers posed by such criminals, killed three cops, and was himself killed after purportedly making a furtive move. Very quickly, however, white New Orleanians produced a sanitized narrative of the "Thompson riot." Two months after the incident, one observer suggested that the "mad negro had run amuck for nothing."[158] Similarly, a 1937 newspaper series on "police heroes" averred that the carnage started because "as [Patrolman] Ford entered the cell, Thompson pounced on him without warning, snatching the policeman's gun from its holster."[159] The Thompson spree reminded white New Orleanians of the 1900 race riot involving Robert Charles, an African American resident who shot more than two dozen white residents, barricaded himself in a house, and died during the police assault on the residence.[160] Just as Charles's "race riot" had, for turn-of-the-century whites, illustrated the threat from African American residents, the Thompson incident reinforced white perceptions of the dangers posed by unpredictable African American New Orleanians. It also confirmed African American residents' fears of cops and precinct-house interrogations. Increasingly, both white policemen and African American suspects anticipated violence from one another, heightening the potential for deadly conflict.[161]

Thompson's fatal shooting of three police officers made cops more jittery and more inclined to brook no resistance or defiance from African American suspects. They felt they needed free rein to protect themselves and to employ deadly force. Thompson's rampage became a cautionary tale for municipal policemen and vindicated cops who killed African American suspects in preemptive self-defense. For their part, African American residents, cognizant of Thompson's fate and familiar with the boasting of William Grosch, Lawrence Terrebonne, and other proudly brutal cops, more often resisted, triggering but also justifying cops' use of deadly force.[162] The incident, in short, cemented white and especially police perceptions of young African American men—and vice versa. Between 1920 and March 8, 1932, six policemen died at the hands of African American suspects. From the Thompson shooting until the end of the 1930s, African American residents killed no cops, whereas law enforcers killed twenty-three African American New Orleanians, including four while in police custody.

The local criminal justice system shifted in comparable ways. Before the crime hysteria of the late 1920s, it was nearly dormant, at least in dealing with felonies. During the early 1920s, New Orleans's homicide rate more than doubled, but the homicide conviction rate was 14 percent, reflecting ineptitude at every level.[163] The police barely investigated cases, prosecutors dropped or eliminated charges in the majority of homicides, and juries eschewed guilty verdicts. Even as violent crime rates skyrocketed, cops, prosecutors, and jurors discharged, exonerated, or acquitted nearly all suspects and defendants.

A confluence of factors produced such endemic inaction. Prosecutors, for example, did not trust judges or jurors and insisted that most New Orleanians preferred informal methods of dispute resolution, rather than intrusive state action. Reluctant to take cases to trial, district attorneys routinely dismissed charges and discharged killers. Furthermore, jurors deferred to custom over law, embraced plastic, expansive notions of self-defense and jury nullification, believed that men ought to be permitted to handle problems themselves, and hence seldom returned guilty verdicts. Assumptions about race reinforced this inattention to violent crime. White New Orleanians, who comprised all cops, judges, prosecutors, and jurors, and almost all voters, maintained that African Americans were volatile but that their violence seldom strayed across racial lines. Therefore, African American crime, while unstoppable, need not concern white residents.

The robbery panic of the late 1920s sparked a jarring shift. Criminal justice observers who had been unconcerned about the anemic conviction rate during the spike in violence demanded that bandits must feel the "iron hand of justice," even as the city's homicide rate plummeted.[164] Between the early 1920s and the early 1930s, the proportion of convicted killers leaped by 56.2 percent, peaking in 1933 at 24.2 percent.[165] At its most vigorous level, fewer than one-quarter of homicide cases ended with a conviction, but this represented a dramatic change. In 1922, for instance, only 9.4 percent of killers had faced punishment of any kind. Capital verdicts followed the same pattern. In 1925, when lethal violence in the city crested, jurors sentenced 0.8 percent of killers to death. Yet in 1930, as homicide plunged but robbery-homicide reached its highest level, jurors returned capital verdicts in 5.9 percent of homicide cases.[166]

Anxiety about banditry and predators significantly affected cops, prosecutors, and judges, leading to higher conviction rates in both robbery-homicide and non-robbery-homicide cases. Just as the banditry hysteria unleashed local cops to shoot to kill (and their victims were not typically robbers), the demand for "justice" extended far beyond protection from highwaymen. From the mid-1920s to the early 1930s, conviction rates for robbery-homicide but also for deadly lovers' quarrels, lethal fights between neighbors, and homicides between acquaintances doubled.

The law-and-order crusade, however, unfolded in race-specific ways. Notwithstanding the panic about white bandit gangs, the white conviction rate remained virtually flat from 1920 until the mid-1930s (see figure 5.3). Dramatic fluctuations in the white robbery rate, in the white robbery-homicide rate, and in public demand for justice barely affected the proportion of white killers sent to prison. During the early 1920s, prosecutors convicted 17.4 percent of white killers. During the early 1930s, the conviction rate sagged to 15.5 percent.[167]

The "iron hand of justice" came down almost exclusively on African American suspects. Despite the modest number of black-on-white robbery-homicides, newspaper editors urged the police and the district attorney to punish African American killers, even those whose violence remained within racial lines. By doing so, the *New Orleans Item* argued, "we will have fewer desperadoes like this roaming the streets and roads to run amuck in any direction, at any provocation or none at all."[168] "More convictions in murder cases among negroes," the newspaper's editor explained, "protects white people from the colored killers."[169]

Some elite African Americans made a comparable argument, reflecting class fissures within their community and a tilt toward pragmatism.[170] The editor of the *Louisiana Weekly*, for example, decried the underpolicing of the African American community and insisted that police indifference toward African American crime encouraged the criminal to target his own community. Concerns about the lax morals of working-class African Americans, however, infused his views as well.[171] Though C. C. Dejoie roundly denounced cops' brutality, he also argued that white officials should improve the policing of the African American community—and convict and execute African American murderers—for the sake of the white community. "If when Negroes kill Negroes, they are not punished," he wrote in 1931, "these same men will carry out their depredations against the white people."[172] Two years later, he predicted that "when criminals are allowed to victimize Negroes, you may put it down as certain, that it will not be long before they will prey upon both white and black without the slightest discrimination."[173] The editor hoped that such an argument would motivate city officials to improve policing within the African American community.

Reflecting these diverse pressures, prosecutors began pursuing cases with African American suspects. Consequently, the proportion of African Americans homicide suspects who were convicted soared, jumping by 112.8 percent from the early 1920s to the early 1930s (see figure 5.3). Nearly all of the increase coincided with the robbery panic. In the years after the Great War, Orleans Parish district attorneys convicted African American killers at lower rates than white killers. In 1921, the white homicide conviction rate was nearly three times the African American rate. Eleven years later, the African American conviction rate was four times higher than the white rate. Prosecutors embraced the view that African American New Orleanians who killed within racial lines ultimately posed a threat across racial lines, for the conviction rate for black-on-black homicide leaped by 132.6 percent, twenty-seven times faster than the figure for white-on-white homicide between the early 1920s and the early 1930s. Even at the peak conviction rate, though, only one African American killer in three was convicted. Nonetheless, the courts, like the police, used the power of the state to fortify the racial order of the city. The number of African American New Orleanians sent to the State Penal Farm at Angola for murder and manslaughter rose at the same time as the number of

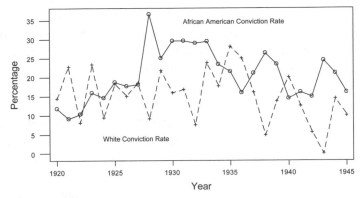

F I G . 5.3. African American and White Conviction Rates, 1920–1945. Source: Police, court, and prison case files.

African American New Orleanians who committed homicide fell. As with police homicide and third-degree interrogations, the prosecutor's office elided race and crime.

Eugene Stanley spearheaded this transformation. The parish district attorney from 1927 until 1935, he reoriented the local criminal justice system, linking crime control to racial control and white supremacy. Stanley helped to convince white New Orleanians that the courts were too lenient toward African American criminals, emboldening predators and thus imperiling respectable society. A self-proclaimed crusader, he focused the racial anxieties of white residents and used them to crystalize Jim Crow prescriptions. Blending racial control and criminal justice reform also proved to be a recipe for electoral success. But Eugene Stanley did not create this elision as much as he exploited the fears of his constituents, who saw race mixing and the defeat of the segregation law, the legal challenges to the racial purity of the electorate and the jury room, and the rampages of Doo-Doom Roberts and Leaval Hubbard as interrelated symptoms of a collapsing racial order.

Like J. Edgar Hoover, Stanley was born in the mid-1890s, hailed from old native stock, worked as a government clerk, attended law school at night, lived with his widowed mother until he was middle-aged, viewed demographic and cultural changes as a threat to social stability, and championed a "relentless war on crime" as a counterbalance to the disorder of the 1920s and 1930s.[174] A lifelong New Orleanian, Stanley attended public schools and began working as a stenographer and secretary in the district attorney's office at the age of nineteen. He studied law at New Orleans's Loyola University at night and passed the bar in 1916. The parish prosecutor, Chandler C. Luzenberg Sr., immediately hired his former clerk as an assistant district attorney. Stanley served in the navy during World War I, after which he returned to his old job.[175] One year later, when a new administration took over local government, Stanley left the prosecutor's office and went into private law practice. In 1925, the Orleans Parish political machine, the Old Regulars, regained power, and Stanley reclaimed his position as an assistant district attorney. Henry Mooney, the parish district attorney, died in 1927, and the machine selected Stanley to succeed him.[176] He ran for election unopposed, capturing 99.8 percent of the vote.[177] Stanley easily won reelection in 1930 and ran unopposed for a third term in 1934.

The thirty-one-year-old district attorney quickly established himself as a law-and-order prosecutor, promising "to see that criminals are punished and that the city is protected from their depredations." His election coincided with the robbery panic and with surging anxieties about the decay of the racial order, and Stanley pledged to use the power of his office to address both issues. He vowed to send "bad criminals" to the penitentiary but also made the defense of white supremacy a core component of his work.[178]

Stanley insisted that he would get tough on criminals and make everyone "feel the demands of the laws of civilized society."[179] He immediately declared his plans "for 'going after' the habitual law violator of New Orleans [and] announced his determination to break up the Saturday pay roll robberies" that besieged the city.[180] Each year the district attorney heralded his office's achievements, proclaiming in 1930, for instance, that his conviction tally "breaks [the] record" and "is believed to be the greatest number of defendants sent to the penitentiary for the crime of robbery."[181] Similarly, Stanley called 1931 "the most successful year in the history of his office" with "the greatest number of convictions with the death penalty in the history of the office."[182] Like many other white New Orleanians, the district attorney held African American residents mainly responsible for crime. In 1927, when the city had the sixth-highest homicide rate in the nation, Stanley maintained that "New Orleans is not crime ridden." "Leaving out of consideration the large negro population," he explained, the "city compared favorably with others."[183]

The district attorney also zealously defended white privilege. When the parish registrar of voters failed to use the "understanding clause" to exclude African American residents, Stanley threatened to indict him for "gross misconduct" and "discrimination against white citizens."[184] Moreover, immediately prior to the 1930 election, the district attorney coauthored a public appeal to white Democrats that he signed "yours in White Supremacy."[185] Five years later, in response to Huey P. Long's promise to help African American

New Orleanians to register to vote, Stanley placed advertisements in leading Louisiana newspapers warning that "at no time in the history of our State has White Supremacy been in greater danger."[186] He pledged "to protect white supremacy in our party at all costs."[187]

Stanley's record as district attorney demonstrated his commitment to white supremacy, his belief that crime was a "negro problem," and his conviction that the vigorous prosecution of African American criminals would restore social order. Unlike his predecessors, Stanley disproportionately prosecuted cases with African American suspects. Although he rarely commented publicly on individual crimes, the district attorney oversaw the handling of more than seven hundred homicide cases and held true to his philosophy about race and crime.

During his first full year as prosecutor, Stanley made racial control the focus of criminal justice in New Orleans. The conviction rate for African American homicide suspects jumped by 102.6 percent, while the rate for white suspects fell by 50.7 percent (see figure 5.3).[188] Between the year before Mooney's death and Stanley's initial full year, the African American homicide conviction rate went from being nearly identical to the white rate to being four times higher. Shifts in crime did not account for this pronounced change. In 1926, African American New Orleanians comprised 64.9 percent of killers and 68.4 percent of those convicted. By contrast, in 1928, they made up 55.4 percent of homicide suspects but 83.3 percent of those convicted.

Over the course of Stanley's tenure as prosecutor, this disparity continued. He produced a 41.6 percent increase in the overall homicide conviction rate, though the rise reflected opposing race-based trends. The white rate dropped by 3.3 percent, while the African American rate surged by 74.2 percent. The conviction rate for African American intraracial homicide jumped by 80.2 percent, and the conviction rate for African American street homicide more than doubled.

He achieved these results largely without relying on judges and juries. Instead, Stanley dropped or eliminated fewer cases with African American suspects but persuaded, cajoled, or pressured more suspects to plead guilty.[189] His efforts worked hand-in-glove with the coerced-interrogation methods of Third Degree Grosch and Buttercup Burns. Armed with signed confessions, Stanley exercised great leverage in negotiations with overwhelmed (and often bloodied) suspects. Although Orleans Parish juries rarely returned capital verdicts, regardless of the race of the defendant, Stanley routinely threatened to seek the death penalty in homicide cases with African American perpetrators, hoping that the suspects would plead guilty to murder with life in prison.

Such a negotiating ploy was of questionable legality; Louisiana law required trials in all murder cases and permitted only juries to "qualify their verdict by adding thereto 'without capital punishment.'"[190] "But the custom," one legal expert noted, "is in the case of negroes to have no trial, but to have them plead guilty without capital punishment and then sentence them to life."[191] With this method, Stanley garnered convictions and avoided the oversight of judges, the unpredictability of juries, and the negative publicity of losing at trial. From 1920 to 1926 (before Stanley's tenure in office) and then from 1928 to 1934 (Stanley's full calendar years as district attorney), the proportion of convicted white killers sentenced to life in prison remained unchanged (at roughly 55 percent), while the proportion of African American inmates with life sentences jumped from 40 percent to 77 percent. Early twentieth-century prosecutors often relied on plea agreements, though, at least for New Orleans, Stanley introduced a stark racial disparity. Prosecutorial discretion and the rule of law worked in the unapologetic service of white supremacy under Eugene Stanley.

In 1935, Stanley lost a power struggle with Huey P. Long and resigned from office.[192] Charles A. Byrne, a Long supporter, replaced him and no longer focused as squarely on using the criminal justice system as a mechanism of racial control. During Byrne's tenure, the white homicide conviction climbed, the African American conviction rate tumbled, and the proportion of African American inmates sentenced to life terms dropped by half. In 1939, the Old Regulars recaptured the district attorney's office, and the racial disparities of the Stanley years quickly returned.

During the interwar period, African American New Orleanians suspects in felonies went from being underpoliced, underprosecuted, and underconvicted to being overpoliced, overprosecuted, and overincarcerated.[193] State-level data echoed these new institutional priorities. During the 1930s, the Louisiana Penal Farm's white inmate population rose by 39 percent, while its African American population increased by 143 percent.[194] Jim Crow criminal justice flowered.

*

During the late 1920s and the early 1930s, crime and punishment moved in opposite directions for African American New Orleanians. While lethal violence dropped, policing became more aggressive, interrogations more coercive, conviction rates soared, and punishment became more draconian. Beginning in the late 1920s, homicide fell sharply, but public and especially predatory violence seemed more terrifying. In particular, Julius Roberts's interracial murders shocked white New Orleanians, contributing to a crime panic and igniting their fears that racial controls were failing and that their African Americans neighbors and acquaintances might, at any moment, "run amuck" and kill them.

A nearly moribund local criminal justice system sprang to life and focused on punishing African American New Orleanians and shoring up the racial order in the process. The peculiar intersection of a small increase in predatory crime, particularly robbery, and widespread white concerns about flagging racial controls led city and especially police officials to link high-profile murders to social disorder. In response, municipal leaders turned to the criminal justice system to supplement and even supplant racial custom. As white residents linked African Americans with predatory violence, they increasingly relied on the police and the courts to maintain public order. Very quickly, cops became crime fighters and were encouraged to catch (and punish) African American criminals at any cost. Shoot-to-kill policing emerged as a badge of professional law enforcement, while unflinching, violent, constitutionally prohibited interrogation methods enjoyed white support, even as they were denounced throughout the nation. White New Orleanians hailed the use of vicious crime-fighting methods to rid the city of African American predators, for such techniques simultaneously protected residents from terrifying killers and reaffirmed the racial hierarchy. Prosecutions changed in parallel ways, focusing on African American suspects and employing methods that were likely unlawful but that appealed to anxious white New Orleanians.

Even as African American homicide plummeted, violent crime became a race issue, and the criminal justice system emerged as a core mechanism to protect white residents by controlling African American residents. Between 1925 and 1932, paradoxically interrelated shifts occurred. The African American homicide rate fell by 58 percent. Yet the African American homicide conviction rate rose by 54.7 percent, the rate of police homicide against African American New Orleanians increased by 160 percent, and the proportion of convicted African American killers sentenced to life terms in prison swelled by 150 percent. Nor did the law-and-order crusade reduce the African American homicide rate, for most killers still avoided conviction. During the crime panic, residents speculated that African American killers, having tasted blood, would kill again and that their violence would eventually target white city dwellers. Or, as one editor explained, "One crime leads to another, much the same way as the taste of human blood makes a 'killer' of a jungle lion."[195] But there were few recidivist killers in interwar New Orleans. In reality, the best known was Detective William Grosch.

Finally, the racialization of criminal justice in New Orleans was self-perpetuating. Far from reducing crime or promoting racial and social stability, the new focus of criminal justice reinforced the perceptions that fueled racial discord in the city. As police brutality became normative, African American suspects increasingly feared William Grosch's one-way ride and Buttercup Burns's red-hot poker. Consequently, they elected to run or resisted the police. Such responses abetted cops' worries about dangerous, violent suspects and reinforced their inclination to see hip-pocket moves and hence to employ deadly force.[196] This cycle triggered Percy Thompson's "race riot," seemingly justifying both police violence and suspect resistance and making the elision of racial control and crime fighting stronger in the minds of white New Orleanians. Ironically, as crime plunged, particularly African American homicide, a new era of state power and criminal justice authority, dedicated to maintaining the racial order, emerged.

CHAPTER 6

"Cheaper than a Dime Sandwich"

Bernice Roy's 1945 murder confirmed white New Orleanians' worst fears of urban life, street violence, and African American residents. A year earlier, the twenty-three-year-old, unmarried white woman had left her Port Arthur, Texas, home, migrated to New Orleans, and secured lodging in a rooming house and work at an Armour meat-packing plant. After her shift on Friday, November 30, Roy ventured to the French Quarter with two friends. At the Hawaiian Club, she met twenty-three-year-old William F. Mears, a staff sergeant at the nearby Gulfport, Mississippi, Army Air Airfield. A native of Anderson, Indiana, Mears had taken a train to New Orleans that day with two army buddies, arriving at 7:20 p.m. Like many other soldiers, they headed directly to the French Quarter and imbibed at five different bars over the next four hours. In the Hawaiian Club, Mears and "Bernie" Roy danced, and then they visited the Cow Shed, another nightspot. Just before midnight, the young woman explained that she "had to be to work at 6:00 in the morning" and hence needed to return to her boardinghouse. The soldier volunteered "to walk part of the way home with her." The couple strolled north on Tulane Avenue but soon noticed two African American men following them.[1]

Roy became anxious and insisted that they cross the street to avoid the strangers, confiding to her escort that "she was afraid of the negroes." Suddenly, the two men caught up with Mears and Roy. The taller, leaner one, eighteen-year-old Wilbert Powell, jabbed a gun in the soldier's back and barked, "If you want to keep living, keep walking." Powell and his roommate, nineteen-year-old Joseph Besser, both day laborers, marched the couple to a vacant lot behind Dalier's Drug Store, where Powell snatched Mears's wallet, wedding ring, and wristwatch, then said with a scowl, "You m——f, if you want to live, stay back against the wall." Standing a few feet in front of them, Besser pushed Roy to the ground, instructed the 95-pound woman to turn over onto her back, but then slugged her in the face. Roy screamed, attracting the attention of an older African American woman in a bright red coat walking a short distance away. The robbers ordered the woman to "keep on moving," but she remained, her eyes fixed on them. Powell panicked and screeched to Besser, "Let's go," and the men fled.[2] When they were approximately thirty feet from the vacant lot, Wilbert Powell wheeled around and fired one shot with a .38 caliber US Army revolver he had stolen a few days earlier.[3] The bullet struck Roy between the eyebrows, piercing her ethmoid bone and penetrating the frontal lobe of her brain.[4] She lost consciousness and at 4:20 p.m. on December 3, 1945, died from her injuries, without regaining consciousness.

Newspaper accounts of the murder included horrifying details, revealing that Besser had attempted to rape Roy before being frightened away by the woman in the red coat.[5] William Mears's initial statement to the police, taken four hours after the crime, described no such attempted "aggravated criminal attack," and the autopsy report failed to confirm this rumor.[6] Nor did the physician who initially treated Roy find any evidence, such as torn clothing, of a sexual assault.[7] Yet every newspaper article on the crime, invoking the unmistakable euphemism of the day, focused on the predator's attempt to commit an "aggravated criminal attack" on Bernice Roy.[8]

News of the African American men's armed robbery of a white soldier and the murder and attempted rape of a young white woman shocked white New Orleanians and shaped both the police investigation of the crime and the trial of the killers, feeding stereotypes of race, violence, and their elision. Led by three of the city's fiercest cops—Detective Louis Martinez, who had been convicted of assaulting and beating a fifteen-year-old African American larceny suspect in 1933, Detective John Grosch, known on the streets as "Third Degree Grosch," and Detective Frank Lannes, who had killed three suspects and had been involved in numerous shootings and beatings of African American suspects—police investigators captured Roy's assailants within three hours.[9] First, they apprehended Powell, who immediately confessed to the robbery and the shooting, identified his accomplice, and disclosed the hiding place in the floor of their room where they had stashed Mears's wedding ring and wristwatch; the robbers had dropped the wallet when they ran. Using information they obtained from Powell, the detectives located and arrested Besser, who had served prison time for robbery.

After a night of playing pool, according to their confessions, Powell and

Besser decided to "rob someone (to make some money)." They wandered the surrounding streets in search of a victim until the two men encountered the soldier and the packing-house worker. Powell and Besser then stalked the young couple.[10] At the trial that followed, prosecutors charged the men with capital murder, arguing that they had committed armed robbery, attempted rape, and murder. In presenting their case to the jury, Assistant District Attorneys George Gulotta and Joseph Monie devoted particular attention to the rape allegation, insuring that the trial commanded white public interest. The prosecutors, pandering to voters on the eve of the district attorney's reelection bid, emphasized their tenacious defense of law and order and their unyielding commitment to the protection of white women.[11]

Gulotta and Monie's case, and especially their supporting evidence, evolved during the seven weeks between the crime and the trial. The police report on the shooting described the murder as a robbery gone bad, in which the two skittish criminals became frightened when the unidentified woman in the red coat refused to be cowed, and Powell fired his revolver in the direction of the victims as he fled. Although the African American suspects had confessed to the robbery of a white soldier and the murder of a white woman, virtually insuring that they would be convicted of a capital crime, Powell and Besser vehemently denied attempting a sexual assault.[12] Yet at trial, the prosecution introduced a signed confession in which Besser also admitted to attempted rape.[13]

Sergeant Mears's account of the crime also shifted between his statement to the police on the night of the attack and his courtroom testimony. Shortly after the shooting, he provided a detailed description of the murder to First Precinct desk sergeant George S. Bengert without any reference to an attempted sexual assault.[14] Moreover, immediately after Powell shot Roy, Mears frantically stopped a streetcar and begged the conductor and passengers for help. His pleas included no mention of an attempted "criminal attack." Rather, he told the passengers on the streetcar, who subsequently made formal statements to the police, that "two negro men had robbed him" and that "a woman was lying in the vacant lot in the rear of the drug store." According to Paul Cucullu, the sixty-year-old white foreman at the Chalmette Laundry Company, Mears insisted that "he did not know the woman and that he was not with the woman and did not know how the woman got hurt," perhaps prevaricating because he was embarrassed for failing to defend Bernice Roy or because he was a married man who had spent the evening drinking and dancing with a single young woman who was engaged to a soldier stationed overseas.[15] Other passengers corroborated this and also told the police that the soldier mainly wept. Thirty-nine-year-old Hilliary J. Rodriguez, who worked at the same laundry as Cucullu, revealed that Mears "kept crying and asking me not to leave him and told me that he did not know what he was going to do."[16] When Mears testified at Powell and Besser's trial, however, his recollections were clear, precise, and perfectly aligned with the prosecution's argument, particularly as he described how Besser "was interrupted in the attempted rape of the deceased by the appearance of an elderly woman."[17]

After deliberating for one hour, the all-white jury returned a guilty verdict. Judge J. Bernard Cocke, a forty-eight-year-old former Orleans Parish district attorney, sentenced Wilbert Powell and Joseph Besser "to die in the electric chair."[18] The convicted men's court-appointed attorneys quickly filed an appeal, charging that a variety of irregularities marred the trial. After a higher court affirmed the verdict, the lawyers petitioned the state pardon board to commute the death sentences to life imprisonment. This effort failed as well.[19]

Immediately after the jury announced its verdict (and four days before voters went to the polls in the Democratic primary election for district attorney), James P. O'Connor, the incumbent district attorney, crowed about the conviction, insisting that without his steady hand and sound judgment "these two vicious killers would have been put back on the street to murder another innocent white woman." Referring to himself in the third person, O'Connor announced on the radio that "the manner in which your district attorney handled the case should be a warning to other would-be criminals."[20] On April 23, 1948, seventy-five people "jammed into the death chamber" at the parish prison and watched the state of Louisiana execute Wilbert Powell and Joseph Besser.[21]

The Roy murder and the trial of Powell and Besser fused powerful social, political, and legal currents in the city, cementing the connection between race and crime in the minds of most white New Orleanians. Both the white newspaper accounts of the case and the arguments of the prosecutors exploited fears that had been festering since the robbery panic of the late 1920s—with stylized images of street crime, interracial violence, and African American predators. The Roy killing also blended the late 1920s hysteria about attacks on innocent white New Orleanians with newer worries about African American violence against soldiers and against white women.[22] Most important, the trial both reflected and reinforced the emerging role of the local criminal justice system as the guardian of social order and white supremacy, a theme bound up with electoral politics in the city—at a time when African Americans comprised one-third of the city's residents but 0.5 percent of its registered voters.[23]

The jarring social, economic, and institutional changes of the 1930s and early 1940s exaggerated trends in crime and punishment—and magnified the disjuncture between them. On the one hand, the Great Depression contributed to the sharp drop in New Orleans homicide and to significant shifts in the character of violence that distorted white perceptions of crime and hence the operation of the local criminal justice system. On the other hand, World War II widened racial disparities in policing and punishment. Criminal justice in New Orleans became yoked to white supremacy, as the social changes triggered by the economic crisis and the war hardened white notions of African American predators preying on white victims and helped to recast the police and the courts as bulwarks against threats to the racial hierarchy. Even as African American homicide rates decreased, white commentators decried the rising threat from African American residents. One journalist, emphasizing African Americans' casual resort to lethal violence, explained that "life is cheap in New Orleans, cheaper than a dime sandwich, a five-cent coin, a second-hand beer glass."[24] Informal mechanisms of racial control, ranging from the direct action of mobs to the subtler influence of racial etiquette, no longer sufficed. During the 1930s and early 1940s, aggressive policemen and zealous district attorneys replaced the inattentive cops and lackadaisical prosecutors of the early 1920s, and racial disparities in law enforcement became, in the minds of most white New Orleanians, integral tools for preserving social order and white supremacy. Jim Crow had come of age.

*

Violent crime plunged during the 1930s, in New Orleans and throughout the nation. Municipal leaders and police officials recognized that the local murder rate had begun falling during the late 1920s and continued to drop through the decade of the Great Depression, for they gathered crime data and submitted the figures to federal authorities.[25] But violence somehow felt more menacing than ever and became a lightning rod in local politics. Police superintendents continued to argue that vicious criminals lurked everywhere and that only the determined efforts of cops preserved law and order. Similarly, candidates for mayor and especially for district attorney routinely emphasized the threat from below and the need for stronger, more aggressive measures to combat predators on the streets of the city and to safeguard white supremacy.[26]

All the while, violent crime plummeted in New Orleans during the 1930s. The robbery rate fell by nearly two-thirds and the homicide rate by one-third.[27] White homicide dropped particularly fast, tumbling by 61.5 percent. African American homicide slumped as well, shrinking by 32.7 percent. The more modest change in African American violence, however, was misleading, since homicide rates for these New Orleanians had begun spiraling downward during the late 1920s (see figure 4.7). Between 1925 and 1940, New Orleans's homicide rate contracted by 58.6 percent (see figure 4.1), with the white level dipping by 56.9 percent and the African American rate by 70.2 percent.[28]

Far from fueling lethal violence, the Great Depression transformed urban society in ways that accelerated the decrease in homicide. The economic crisis sparked a series of interrelated demographic changes that significantly reduced the potential for violent encounters. As the effects of the Wall Street collapse spread across the nation and the local economy faltered, New Orleans no longer attracted large numbers of migrants. The rate of population growth dropped by 57.8 percent. More important, the proportion of residents in their twenties and early thirties fell, as did the percentage of unmarried adults in the city.[29] Depression-era New Orleans had a larger share of middle-aged, married, more settled, and less volatile residents.

The demographic profile of local killers shifted accordingly. While the majority were under thirty during the 1920s, most homicide assailants were over thirty during the 1930s, and the mean age of killers climbed by nearly six years between the late 1920s and the mid-1940s—not because older residents became more pugnacious but because the proportion of younger assailants waned. Similarly, leveling sex ratios gradually reduced the social instability and recreational violence fueled by the shortage of dating and mating partners.[30] Simply put, the economic shockwaves from the Great Depression reduced the pool of city dwellers most likely to engage in violent behavior. Soaring unemployment rates also limited the disposable income that residents could spend on alcohol and at bars, racetracks, gambling halls, and brothels.[31] The blend of relatively fewer young, carousing men and less money to lavish on leisure activities depressed the city's infamous wild night life, resulting in fewer drunken brawls, fewer deadly fights between jealous suitors, and fewer whiskey-inflamed domestic quarrels. The rising cost and falling accessibility of guns dovetailed with these population and economic shifts and made the city less homicidal as well.

In combination, demographic changes and hard times tamed social life in New Orleans during the 1930s—at least by comparison with the Roaring Twenties. But the steep drop in lethal violence was merely one effect of a larger process. Despite soaring levels of poverty, the death rate from all causes dipped by 23.7 percent from 1929 through 1940. Even as the Great Depression made daily life more difficult, New Orleanians led less raucous, more stable, and healthier lifestyles.[32] They died from accidents at lower rates, succumbed from cirrhosis and most other diseases less frequently, and murdered one another less often.[33] Nor were such shifts unique to New Orleans. Nationally, the unemployment rate averaged 16.7 percent during the Great Depression, yet average lifespan surged by four years.[34]

These demographic changes had a cumulative effect on violence, for New Orleans homicide rates rose and fell in consort with overall death rates. Mortality soared during the 1920s, shattering families, fracturing social relations, and reinforcing the hard-living, hard-drinking, and hard-fighting atmosphere of Roaring Twenties New Orleans.[35] Although homicides comprised less than 2 percent of deaths, for the 1920–45 era, both the homicide rate and the overall mortality rate peaked in 1925. During the lean years of the 1930s, by contrast, death rates from accidents, disease, and lethal violence plunged.[36] New Orleans's infant mortality rate dropped by 33.4 percent, the motor vehicle fatality rate by 28.3 percent, and the homicide rate by 32.3 percent.[37]

Reflecting these demographic shifts and buttressing the behavioral changes they produced, family life became more stable for New Orleanians during the Great Depression.[38] Fewer households struggled to deal with the loss of a young child, endured the early death of a parent, lost the primary breadwinner, or confronted the tensions that accompanied remarriage and stepchildren. As the proportion of middle-aged and married city residents rose, domestic life flourished. The birth rate for African American women soared above the white rate, and infant mortality plummeted, across racial lines.[39] The size of African American households increased, and the number of families with lodgers fell.[40] Nuclear family members, therefore, comprised a growing proportion of both African American and white households. The drop in infant deaths and the increasing absence of lodgers reduced some of the tensions that had roiled domestic relations during the 1920s, contributing to a 55.4 percent drop in the home homicide rate. The rate of jealousy-fueled killings and lethal lovers' quarrels erupting in private residences, for example, tumbled by 39.1 percent between the 1920s and the 1930s.

The city's changing social geography reinforced these trends during the 1930s. Although housing construction flagged during the Great Depression, white New Orleanians continued to leave the southern portion of the city and resettle in the newly drained areas to the north, fleeing from African American residents in the process. Back-alley pockets of African American residents expanded into the older downtown housing stock abandoned by white New Orleanians.[41] Tiny, atomized enclaves grew into neighborhoods, facilitating the development of social networks and community institutions. Furthermore, during the 1930s, segregated public housing projects opened on the eastern edge of the city, concentrating the African American population.[42] The maturation of the streetcar system amplified these shifts, which had two effects. First, racial segregation increased.[43] Second, the sorting of people and land not only separated residents by race but also produced more specialized land-use patterns. When New Orleanians, white and African American alike, left the crowded, jumbled, mixed-use real estate on the high ground near the river, private space became more distinct, residential and leisure areas developed, and boardinghouses replaced lodging in private residences for single young New Orleanians. These ecological changes, however, affected white and African American residents in very different ways and contributed to new, race-specific trends in violence during the 1930s.

White homicide, which had reached its high-water mark for the era in 1924, dropped during the late 1920s and continued to fall through the 1930s, despite—or perhaps because of—the effects of the Great Depression (see figure 6.1). Between 1924 and 1930, the white rate dipped by 18.7 percent, and it plunged by nearly two-thirds during the 1930s. New Orleans's white homicide rate decreased by 68.7 percent between 1924 and 1940.

The nature of white lethal violence shifted as much as the rate of homicide, and changes in the character of conflict, reflecting the demographic and ecological transformations of the period, accounted for much of the downward spiral. Domestic life commanded an enhanced role in white New Orleanians' social lives. The proportions of unmarried residents and young adults in the white population contracted, and the share of white households with lodgers dropped from 8.4 percent in 1930 to 3.2 percent a decade later.[44] Compared with the 1920s, white New Orleans had a larger share of residents in their

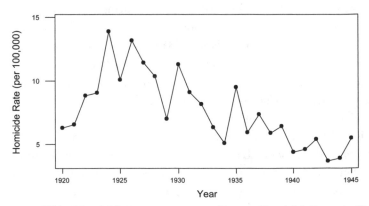

F I G . 6 . 1 . White Homicide Rates, 1920–1945. Source: Homicide Reports, Department of Police, New Orleans.

thirties and forties, residing in family units, and living farther away from the bordellos, barrooms, bustle, and brawls along the river. Domestic life became more private and more cloistered.

In combination, these shifts transformed white violence. With an older population, higher rates of marriage, larger houses, and segregated neighborhoods, white social life—and white violence along with it—increasingly revolved around the home and private space. The rate of lethal violence in white homes dropped modestly between the 1920s and the 1930s, but the proportion of white homicides committed in private residences more than doubled from 1924 to the start of World War II, rising from 18.2 percent to 37.5 percent. By 1945, 42.1 percent of the homicides committed by white New Orleanians occurred in homes. Despite surging fears of street crime, by the late 1930s kitchens and bedrooms in private dwellings became the most violent places in the city for white residents.

Spouses increasingly committed white home homicides. During the early 1920s, deadly fights between domestic partners accounted for one-third of white lethal violence in private residences. By the early 1940s, the figure had ballooned to 52.2 percent. Both the killers and their victims became older over time as well. The etiology of white domestic violence changed markedly, and spousal homicide no longer erupted from the tensions typical of recently married young residents. The proportion of white spousal homicides triggered by drunken fights, for example, fell by 53.2 percent, and the share sparked by jealousy dropped by 18.2 percent. Instead, white spouse killings increasingly occurred after a woman challenged her husband's authority, most often by attempting to dissolve the marriage. Unemployed or underemployed husbands, insecure about their status as breadwinners, became particularly sensitive about their patriarchal authority during the Great Depression.[45] Such triggers were not new but became predominant during the 1930s.

As white home life became more private and family centered, women, at least in violent encounters, became more assertive. Wives committed 32.4 percent of white spousal homicides during the 1920s and 42.5 percent during the 1930s. The aging and settling of the population also allowed informal social networks to expand and provided women with readier access to friends and especially relatives who could shelter them from violent partners.[46] White wives became more willing to leave abusive marriages and less inclined to reconcile. Furious that their wives had defied them, flouted patriarchal authority, usurped control over the future of the unions, and thus humiliated them, many husbands threatened domestic partners who vowed to separate or pursued, stalked, and assaulted their estranged wives. Escaping from toxic marriages, however, often succeeded, and the white wife-killing rate fell by 15.7 percent between the 1920s and the 1930s. But when white husbands murdered their wives, the proportion of such homicides ignited by women rejecting their partners' pleas and demands to "return home" nearly doubled, rising from 33.3 percent during the 1920s to 58.8 percent during the 1930s.

In many ways, John LaHood, a seaman, was a typical 1930s white wife killer. During his marriage to Vera Higginbotham, he "beat his wife unmercifully." After Vera, a telephone operator, refused to endure his abuse any longer and moved in with her sister and her husband, John commanded her to reconcile. To the contrary, she initiated divorce proceedings, and his anger turned into rage.[47] John LaHood followed his estranged wife to a movie house on June 16, 1932, where they scuffled.[48] Vera LaHood struck her husband with her parasol and announced, "I don't want to talk with you at all, talk to my lawyer."[49] Later that evening, Mrs. David Mann heard her brother-in-law's voice in Vera's bedroom. Moments later a gunshot rattled the house, and Mann found her sister unconscious on her bed with a bullet wound to her chest.[50]

White husband killing changed even more sharply during the 1930s. The rate of this violence leaped by 42.1 percent from the 1920s to the 1930s, and the homicides increasingly hinged on men's attempts to assert their patriarchal authority and women's efforts to resist such control. During the 1930s, nearly two-thirds of homicidal wives killed in self-defense, shooting husbands who abused them, attacked them when they attempted to separate, or threatened them when they refused to reconcile. Wife beating likely did not increase between the 1920s and the 1930s as much as women refused to abide such mistreatment and defended themselves, sometimes with lethal force.

Forty-two-year-old Jennie Estrade shot her husband after enduring years of physical abuse. She explained the final explosion of violence to police captain Alfred Malone, noting that Herman Estrade, the forty-two-year-old manager of an ice house, "beat me often." Jennie also revealed that "once he shot me with a rifle. I left him several times, but he would beg me to come back to him, and I always did."[51] Finally, on August 18, 1938, the couple bickered, and Herman locked Jennie out of the house after she threatened to leave him again.[52] She summoned her sister and her husband, who cajoled Herman into allowing him to come in. After that, Herman permitted Jennie to reenter their home.

But that was not the end of the altercation. Herman Estrade fumed to his brother-in-law that "I work all day and when I come home she raises all kind of hell, I'm tired of it."[53] Jennie Estrade insisted that she only wanted to gather her clothes.[54] The seething husband immediately threatened his wife, snarling to her, she said, that "if I didn't get out he'd throw something at me."

When Herman "followed me and kept cursing me," Jennie told police officers shortly afterward, "I then got the gun out of the Vanity drawer and shot him. He then came towards me and I shot him again, he continued coming towards me so I shot him a third time."[55] The first bullet struck Herman in the left forearm, the second hit him squarely in the chest, and the third traveled through his right arm and lodged in his abdomen.[56] When Captain Malone took Estrade's dying declaration and inquired why his wife had shot him, he said it was for "nothing."[57] The Estrade shooting bore the defining characteristics of 1930s white spousal and home homicides, occurring between middle-aged residents, in a bedroom, with a gun, and after years of wife beating. Furthermore, the final, lethal battle exploded after the woman announced her intention to seize control over the union and dissolve it.

With the increasing privatization of social life, white lethal violence moved out of public space. While the white home homicide rate dipped during the 1930s, the rate of white public violence plummeted. From the mid-1920s to the early 1940s, the white street homicide rate dropped by 73.9 percent (see figure 6.2). The proportion of white homicides that erupted on streets slumped as well, from 55.8 percent in 1924 to 28.6 percent in 1940. Even white drunken brawls shifted into homes. During the mid-1920s, 8.3 percent of white lethal drunken brawls exploded in homes and 41.7 percent in the streets of the city, often just outside French Quarter "soft-drink establishments." Two decades later, one-third of white brawl homicides occurred in private residences and one-sixth on the streets.

As white violence migrated from streets and bars into homes, the relationship between assailants and their victims shifted. While white homicide

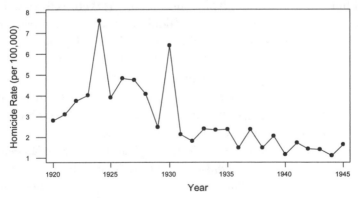

F I G . 6 . 2 . White Street Homicide Rates, 1920–1945. Source: Homicide Reports, Department of Police, New Orleans.

fell overall, the contraction disproportionately occurred in fights between acquaintances and between strangers. Rates of homicide by white acquaintances and strangers dropped by two-thirds. By the mid-1930s, relatively few white homicides occurred in public settings. At the same time, the increasingly aggressive and militarized police committed a rising proportion of public white homicides. During the mid-1920s, New Orleans cops accounted for 26.1 percent of street killings by white residents. Two decades later, law enforcers committed 42.9 percent of such homicides.[58]

Taken together, these shifts redefined white perceptions of crime, race, and violence. White homicide decreased during the 1930s and early 1940s, but white public violence plummeted and increasingly consisted of cops purportedly protecting (white) public safety. In 1930, white residents comprised 51.2 percent of the assailants in street homicides. By 1945, only 13.9 percent of street killers were white—fewer than one in seven in a city whose population was more than two-thirds white. Lethal violence by white New Orleanians did not stop, but it moved indoors and nearly disappeared from public view; for the most visible, high-profile crimes in the city during the 1930s and early 1940s, white killers, other than cops, virtually vanished, and white violence became invisible.[59] The ebbing white homicide conviction rate echoed this shift, as white concerns about white desperadoes evaporated. Between 1935 and 1945, the white homicide conviction rate plunged by 64.4 percent. During the early 1940s, Orleans Parish prosecutors secured convictions in one-tenth of homicide cases with white suspects.

For African American New Orleanians, shifts in violence proved to be both similar and radically different, and these trends unfolded in ways that accelerated the demonization of African American residents and the institutionalization of Jim Crow. The demographic shifts of the 1930s crossed racial lines, as did the accompanying privatization of domestic space. By comparison with the 1920s, the city's African American population during the 1930s had a higher proportion of middle-aged, married, and long-settled residents.[60]

The mix of relatively older, married adults and better-balanced sex ratios encouraged family formation, and the number of young children and the size of families swelled. Falling death rates accelerated the demographic transformation of African American New Orleans from a migrant hub to a more stable community. During the 1930s, African American New Orleanians endured unemployment rates double those of white residents and were four times more likely to live in dwellings in need of major repair.[61] Furthermore, African American New Orleanians continued to face unrelenting discrimination from physicians and hospitals.[62] Yet the African American death rate fell by 35.6 percent, and the African American infant mortality rate dropped by 29.7 percent, nearly mirroring the decrease in the African American homicide rate, which tumbled by one-third during the decade.[63] Not only did families grow, but early death—of both children and adults—disrupted fewer African American households. At the same time, the proportion of families with lodgers dipped from 15.4 percent to 8.4 percent.[64] African American homes became more family centered.

The changing composition of African American domestic space dramatically reduced home violence. Between 1925 and 1940, the rate of homicides occurring in African American homes plunged by 81.5 percent (see figure 6.3). In addition, the proportion of African American homicides occurring in residences contracted from 35.6 percent during the mid-1920s to 20 percent during the early 1940s.[65]

A confluence of factors contributed to the sharp drop. First, when guns became less affordable, fights generated fewer fatalities, and the rising prices of guns, in combination with high poverty rates among African American New Orleanians, particularly reduced the use of firearms and the resulting death toll. During the mid-1920s, killers relied on guns in 68.7 percent of the African American homicides committed in homes. By the late 1930s, the figure dropped to 31.7 percent.[66] The proportion of home homicides committed with knives rose from 20.5 percent to 58.5 percent. More victims, however, survived stab wounds than bullet wounds; even if the number of attempted murders in private dwellings had remained constant, the body count would have dipped.

But the number of violent quarrels in these homes likely fell as the compo-

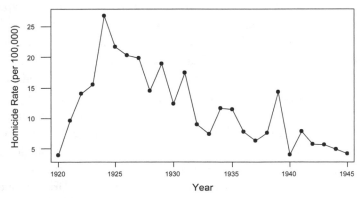

FIG. 6.3. African American Home Homicide Rates, 1920–1945. Source: Homicide Reports, Department of Police, New Orleans.

sition of their homes changed.[67] African American families less often housed unrelated lodgers or unmarried younger brothers and cousins, and crowding reinforced the flow of boarders out of private homes. By the late 1930s, as African American families increased, the size of African American dwelling units decreased, and 63.4 percent had three rooms or fewer, compared with 22 percent of white residential units.[68] The adults remaining in private residents were more often married, relatively older, and parents, all of which tamped down violence. Mature adults were less likely to engage in drunken brawls or to organize home craps games than had the 1920s lodgers.

Dramatic shifts in the morphology of African American home homicide echoed these changing lifestyles and priorities. During the mid-1920s, 62.8 percent of the killers were under thirty years of age. By the late 1930s, 66.7 percent were over thirty. Similarly, the proportion of home homicides involving acquaintances and neighbors dropped by nearly two-thirds. The presence of children in the home discouraged violence as well, and the combination of higher birth rates and lower African American infant mortality rates generated solidarity between parents and pushed raucous activities outside of domestic space.[69] During the mid-1920s, 21.1 percent of African American male-on-male homicides occurred in private dwellings. Two decades later, only 6.3 percent of such lethal violence occurred in homes. Reflecting the same shifts in social life, during the 1920s, one-fifth of African American homicides from drunken brawls occurred in private homes. By the 1930s, the figure had dropped to one-seventh, and it fell to one-thirty-third during the early 1940s.

In short, the African American home homicide rate waned as the proportion of young single men in these dwellings dropped. Instead, the lethal violence in domestic space was increasingly confined to fights between spouses. During the mid-1920s, spousal homicide accounted for 36.4 percent of African American home homicides. By the mid-1940s, the proportion had soared to 68.8 percent. The rate of African American spousal homicide also decreased during this period, reflecting the larger share of middle-aged partners, the higher proportion of parents, and the greater reliance on knives, combining to reduce the number of violent quarrels and the number of fatalities from domestic fights. During the 1930s, half of the drop in the African American home homicide rate came from the dip in the proportion of single men in these households and the other half from a decrease in lethal spousal violence.

Shifts in domestic life transformed the character of African American spousal violence. African American women, even more than white women, assumed increasing control of domestic space and committed a rising share of spousal homicides; in 1925, they committed 52.9 percent of African American partner homicides, and two decades later the proportion rose to 64.3 percent. Similarly, the triggers for such violence changed. During the 1920s, when the African American population was younger, domestic partners typically quarreled over household control, with battles over prosaic matters sparking deadly disputes. A decade later, lethal violence more often erupted after African American wives attempted to dissolve marital unions and their domestic partners challenged the women's exercise of power—similar to the trend in white family violence. The proportion of spouse killers who were separated from their partners climbed by 39.5 percent between the 1920s and the 1930s. The Depression-fueled surge in African American unemployment—and racial disparities in relief support—exacerbated such tensions, challenging men's authority within the household and leading to violent defenses of patriarchy.[70]

In 56.5 percent of 1930s African American wife killings, the deadly fight began when a husband attempted to force his estranged spouse to reconcile, compared with 13.8 percent during the 1920s. Three days after the couple separated, for example, Dave Mays followed Vera Gasper to a neighbor's home, burst into the kitchen, announced, "You will come home forever," and murdered his common-law partner.[71] Similarly, Willie Green attacked and murdered his common-law wife, Dorothy Stewart, one month after she left him and moved in with her brother. Five months pregnant at the time, Stewart, a domestic servant, insisted that she would no longer endure the "cruel beatings." On June 17, 1933, Green, a porter at a local drugstore, confronted Stewart after she left church and "demanded of her to make an immediate promise of reconciliation and come back with him at once." Stewart answered, "No, I am through [with you]. I cannot stand your beatings," whereupon Green drew a paring knife, pounced on his estranged partner, and stabbed her seven times.[72]

African American husband killing changed in comparable ways. Whereas disputes over routine household matters were the leading triggers for such violence during the previous decade, by the 1930s African American wives more often killed after their estranged husbands attempted to compel them to reconcile. Thirty-six-year-old Joseph Landry, a Mississippi-born laborer, attacked his estranged common-law wife two months after she threw him out of her house; he suffered a fatal stab wound in the confrontation that followed. Lucia Porea explained to police investigators that Landry came to her home "and asked me to go back with him to live and I refused him, and he then struck me with his fist in my face." After Porea "pushed him out of the kitchen door," the furious, drunken man returned, "struck me again with his fist, and I then picked up a knife which was lying on a table . . . and I then cut him."[73]

A cluster of overlapping factors accounted for the rising proportion of husbands who died in such encounters. This shift partly reflected the long-standing relative autonomy of African American women. But the decreasing access to firearms also redounded to the advantage of African American women and left an increasing number of abusive husbands on the parish coroner's dissection table. During the mid-1920s, 58.8 percent of African American spouse killers dispatched their partners with guns, while 41.8 percent used knives. Two-thirds of wife killers shot their spouses, compared with 45 percent of husband killers. As the supply of firearms dwindled and the price climbed, fewer African American New Orleanians relied on guns. By the late 1930s, 38.5 percent of African American wife killers and 16.7 percent of husband killers shot their partners; instead, 61.5 percent of wife killers and 72.2 percent of husband killers stabbed their spouses.

When guns disappeared from African American homes, women more often triumphed in violent domestic quarrels. Wives were more skilled with knives than their husbands. African American women had long carried ice picks and paring knives, sometimes for protection and sometimes for practical reasons, such as food preparation.[74] Many abusive husbands quickly discovered that they were attacking women who were armed and well prepared to defend themselves. Thirty-year-old Beatrice Brown, for example, "read[i]ly admitted" fatally stabbing her thirty-seven-year-old common-law husband, Alex Jackson, after he punched her and shoved her against a wall.[75] She told police officers that "Alex said come out bitch I am going to stomp your ass out. He then grabbed ahold of me by my arms and dragged me outside beating me, I then took an ice pick out of my bosom . . . and stabbed at him."[76] Reporting on this homicide and a similar one, the *Louisiana Weekly* wryly observed that those "responsible for the deaths of two men last Sunday in different domestic quarrels were two women, the so-called weaker sex. In both instances the common-law mates of the deceased men proved to be the wielders of a death dealing ice pick and knife."[77] Similarly, when Lucius Coleman began to beat his wife, Louise Coleman "reached for her head where she had a pocket knife hidden in her hair" and "thrust the knife into his chest."[78]

The setting for many violent domestic quarrels also benefited African American wives. Men frequently attacked their partners in kitchens, affording women a wide range of sharp and bladed weapons, such as ice picks, carving knives, butcher knives, and meat cleavers. Alice Carter, for example, explained that "I was stirrin' chicken with a butcher knife, and he [Ulysses

Watson, her thirty-nine-year-old common-law husband] kept botherin' me and I just swung around my hand to shove him off. Well, it was the hand with the butcher knife in it."[79] Likewise, Irma Turner grabbed "off of the kitchen table an old ice pick" and "stabbed him [her common-law husband] once in the chest, once in the abdomen and once on the left arm."[80] Other women were sewing when their partners became abusive and defended themselves with scissors.[81]

Years of carving meat, chopping vegetables, slaughtering chickens, and mending clothes gave African American women a decided advantage in knife fights. After Lillie Johnson rejected Henry Perry's plea to reconcile, informing him that she "did not want to be bothered [with] him," the angry, estranged husband pulled out a knife. "I seen that his knife was open," Johnson revealed to the police. "I then took my pocket knife out of my purse, he then cut at me and I cut him."[82] According to the parish coroner, Johnson stabbed her partner in the neck, severing his jugular vein, and below the right eye.[83] Thirty-six-year-old Gertrude Morris gloated about her "juggin" prowess, boasting to police investigators at the Second Precinct that Wellington Boudray "pulled his knife and I pulled my knife, and I won."[84] Far from guns offsetting men's physical strength and thus being the great equalizer in fights, it was knives that enabled women to repel their attackers—often with deadly results.

But even as women committed the lion's share of spousal homicides, the overall rate of such lethal violence plummeted during the 1930s. Spousal homicide rates plunged by 56.8 percent during the 1930s, and the African American home homicide rate dropped by 67.2 percent. More stabbing victims survived their injuries; more estranged wives found protection in the homes of relatives; older partners engaged in fewer bloody quarrels; the parents of the 1930s were less likely to kill one another than childless couples of the 1920s; and the sharp contraction in the number of single young male lodgers removed a major trigger for domestic conflict.

Some violence, however, was displaced rather than eliminated, as deadly quarrels migrated from domestic space to public settings—moving in the opposite direction of white violence. Between the mid-1920s and the late 1930s, the African American street homicide rate fell by 54.3 percent, but nearly four-fifths of this drop occurred during the late 1920s. The rate changed little during the 1930s. Yet the proportion of African American homicides occurring in streets and bars nearly doubled. Until the early years of the Great Depression, African American residents committed more homicides in private residences than in any other setting. In the mid-1930s, however, the streets became the most homicidal places for African American New Orleanians. During the late

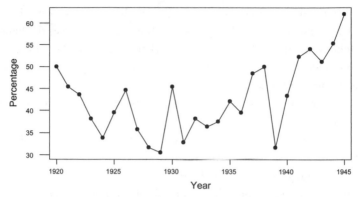

F I G . 6 . 4 . Proportion of African American Homicides Occurring in the Streets, 1920–1945. Source: Homicide Reports, Department of Police, New Orleans.

1920s, less than one-third of African American lethal violence erupted on the streets, but by the mid-1940s, the proportion approached two-thirds (see figure 6.4). In 1945, African American New Orleanians committed homicides in the streets at nearly five times the home homicide rate.[85]

The shifting locus of this violence contributed to changes in the character of African American homicide, which would distort white attitudes toward race and hence the operation of the criminal justice system. When young single men left private residences, African American violence became increasingly bound up with the rhythms of street life; the slice of the population spending time in public settings at night largely determined who would be involved in deadly fights. The proportion of unmarried killers jumped; the percentage of lethal fights between acquaintances and strangers surged; the number of late-night and early-morning homicides ballooned; and the combatants in deadly quarrels became poorer, reflecting the demography of the streets. For example, because social activity on the streets came alive late at night and a rising proportion of African American homicides occurred in public settings, the percentage of after-midnight African American killings doubled between the 1920s and the 1930s. As the social and racial geography of New Orleans changed, violence followed African American young men to late-night street life.

Cross-cutting pressures caused the level of African American street homicides to remain relatively flat after 1930. On the one hand, the cohort of single young men contracted during the 1930s, reducing the pool of aggressive street-corner brawlers. The expansion of African American neighborhoods and the thickening of social and community networks also discouraged raucous, violent behavior.[86] Moreover, the shift from guns to knives lessened the death toll in public violence, as more injured combatants survived their wounds. In 1930, African American killers relied on guns in 60 percent of street homicides and 66.7 percent of saloon homicides. A decade later, they used firearms in 30 percent of street killings and 33.3 percent of lethal bar fights. Knife homicides in 1940 accounted for 61.5 percent of deadly street quarrels and 57.1 percent of saloon deaths. Similarly, nonparticipants, ranging from barkeepers and friends to cops, more often broke up knife battles and fisticuffs in public settings during the 1930s than in fights with guns in private dwellers during the 1920s. Such factors prevented many quarrels from spiraling into homicides.

Countervailing pressures, however, insured that the rate of street violence remained high; during the 1930s, the African American street homicide rate was nearly double the overall white rate and more than five times the white street homicide rate. Public settings late at night produced an alchemy that fueled disputes, as single young, poor African American men struggled to establish status in front of their peers. Reflecting the demographic changes of the period, these New Orleanians were slightly older than their 1920s counterparts. At nearly thirty years old, mostly unmarried, and trapped on the lowest rungs of the occupational ladder during a horrific economic crisis, these men faced uncertain prospects for securing stable work, attracting sexual partners, and establishing families. As a consequence, they found other ways to affirm their status. Minor disputes and trivial disagreements became freighted with symbolic significance and rapidly degenerated into tests of reputation and mettle.[87] An audience of friends and acquaintances heightened the stakes, insuring that the victors in brawls gained respect in the eyes of peers, and the losers sacrificed both their status and their blood.[88]

Again and again, young single African American men on street corners and in alleys traded punches or jugged one another over pennies won and lost in craps games or over trivial affronts.[89] These battles were as much about masculinity as white husbands' violence against their estranged wives. Henry Brown, for example, killed John Tatum in a dispute over $1.50 in chips during a sidewalk card game on November 20, 1939. Brown taunted Tatum, commanding him to "give me my chips when I come back, or your mamma will get a present of a cold box of dead meat," which triggered a deadly fight.[90]

In some homicides, the link between minor disagreements and lethal affirmations of masculine authority was explicit. Sterling Watkins killed Louis Peique in a street-corner dispute over a twenty-cent debt from "Coon Can," a card game. Watkins, who had won the pot, demanded payment, but Peique announced, "No Mother Fucker. I am keeping that because I am Louis Peique the man and you aint getting nothing from me." Watkins told police investigators Peique "then reached in his pocket and started to pull out his knife and I stabbed him in the chest."[91] Gathered together on street corners, late at night, surrounded by peers, poor, single African American men, without families or stable jobs to establish their social standing, performed their status through violent rituals, responding to slights and affronts with bricks and knives.[92] While such public contests had occurred during the 1920s (and before), this violence became the leading form of African American homicide during the 1930s.

In sum, African American violence shifted in two significant ways during this period. First, it decreased sharply. Between 1929 and 1940, the African American homicide rate fell by 58.9 percent. Even though the rate of street violence changed modestly during this period, home violence plunged, spearheading the drop in African American homicide. Second, African American lethal violence became more concentrated in the streets and late at night, making such homicide more public and hence more alarming to white New Orleanians. African American street violence constituted a soaring proportion of a plummeting rate. But its visibility cast a longer shadow than its frequency.[93] In 1930, African American New Orleanians committed 48.8 percent of all street homicides. A decade later, the proportion jumped to 76.5 percent, and by 1945 they committed 86.1 percent of New Orleans street killings (see figure 6.5). On the eve of World War II, the African American street homicide rate was 11.8 times the white one.

At the same time, black-on-white street homicide fell. Such violence was rare, constituting 3.7 percent of all homicides and 6.7 percent of street homicides during the 1930s. Black-on-white crime accounted for 8.2 percent of New Orleans homicides in 1930. A decade later, the figure had tumbled 1.6 percent. Simply put, white residents faced scant risk from African American New Orleanians. Yet the specter of African American predators butchering innocent white New Orleanians became so entrenched in the white imagination that it evolved into a trope during the 1930s.[94] White criminals concocted stories of vicious African American desperadoes to mask their own violent behavior or suspicious activities. Repeatedly, white killers and purported crime victims told police investigators that a "negro bandit," "negro bandit murderer," or "unidentified negroes" had attacked them or robbed and murdered their friends.[95] Further exploiting this stereotype, white holdup men, according to one local journalist, were "known to blacken their faces before committing crimes."[96] Some of these fabricated accounts proved

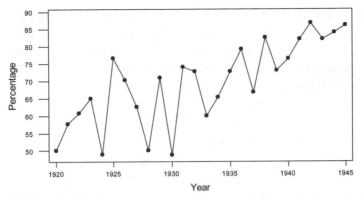

F I G . 6.5. Proportion of Street Homicides with African American Assailants, 1920–1945. Source: Homicide Reports, Department of Police, New Orleans.

to be so formulaic and implausible that detectives, hardly zealous protectors of the civil liberties of African American residents, quickly exposed the ruses.[97] Fifty-six-year-old Alexander Biri, for example, fatally shot a coworker, thirty-one-year-old Anthony Vitrano, in a dispute over money on August 13, 1932. Both men were white. Using his own gun, Biri then shot himself in the leg, summoned the police, and reported that a "negro bandit" had robbed their service station, wounded him, and murdered his colleague. Detectives, however, uncovered glaring "discrepancies"; four months later the killer confessed.[98] The quick resort to blaming the "negro bandit" revealed the depth of white attitudes toward crime and race during the 1930s.

Ghosts of African American mashers shaped policing. During the 1930s, the "dragnet" emerged as cops' default strategy when they suspected that an African American resident had robbed or murdered a white New Orleanian. "Sweeps," or mass arrests, were not new but became racialized. Patrolmen often raided gambling halls, for example, during the 1920s. Later practices, however, lacked the focus of earlier sweeps, which typically targeted specific gaming houses or particular saloons. The new dragnet, an African American newspaper explained, "amounts to arresting practically all the Negroes in New Orleans."[99] Immediately after Edward Melancon's high-profile murder, on March 21, 1932, for example, policemen launched a massive manhunt to apprehend the white grocer's African American killer, arresting more than nine hundred African American residents—or one out of every forty-eight African American men in the city. Patrolmen then transported the suspects to the "school for identification," where police clerks searched, photographed, and fingerprinted the men. This sweep constituted the largest dragnet in the city's history.[100] A year later, Frank Lannes, who later served as one of the lead detectives on the Bernice Roy murder case, orchestrated the arrest of 540 African American men after a series of burglaries of uptown white houses. Four "finger-print experts" spent the next eight hours photographing and fingerprinting the men, only one of whom was held as a suspect.[101]

Dragnets served multiple purposes during the 1930s. While such trawling operations rarely netted the perpetrator of the specific crime that precipitated them, precinct sergeants routinely charged many of the suspects with weapon possession or booked them for vagrancy, loitering, using profane language, or disorderly conduct. In 1943, an African American newspaper editor noted the unabashed racial bias: "Police don't round up and make wholesale arrests of whites when a white man murders another or holds up another."[102] Even when dragnets failed to catch killers, this method of "crime repression" became a tool of racial control, justifying the harassment of young African American men, enjoying support from white residents (and voters), and creating high-visibility spectacles that bolstered the purported link between race and violence.[103] White New Orleanians watched intently as the police paraded African American suspects to precinct houses, a ritual that affirmed the zealous efforts of law enforcers and underscored the race of the suspected predators.

As the connection between street violence and African American men grew stronger, the threshold for police violence against African American residents fell. By the late 1930s, New Orleans cops increasingly shot African American residents suspected of being prowlers or because the young men refused to halt on command. During the early 1940s, more African American suspects were fatally shot for refusing to halt than for any other cause, surpassing the "furtive movement" as a trigger for police killings.[104] Robbery and murder suspects, however, received the roughest treatment from detectives while in police custody, for these were the signature predators of the era. African American "bandits" with criminal records—often dubbed "police characters" or "old offenders"—faced the most brutal and deadly interrogations; detectives were certain that they could be coerced into confessing to myriad violent crimes.

The murder of Aaron Boyd on June 17, 1938, typified these crime-fighting trends. At 9:40 p.m. on June 16, Boyd, a thirty-eight-year-old laborer, boarded a Napoleon Avenue streetcar. Witnesses testified that he immediately flashed a kitchen knife, pressed it against the ribs of the conductor, twenty-four-year-old Joseph Stassi, and demanded his leather money bag. Boyd grabbed the satchel and fled, making off with $2.55—in nickels. Stassi and three white passengers chased the "highway robber" to his home and alerted the police.[105]

Shortly after 10:00 p.m., according to neighbors, Boyd surrendered without incident to six cops.[106] The police report described the arrest as routine and uneventful.[107] The officers then transported Aaron Boyd to the Seventh Precinct station. At 3:00 a.m., police doorman Fred Achor conducted his rounds of the precinct cell block and discovered Boyd's lifeless body.[108] The parish coroner conducted an autopsy and found that Boyd had died from "violence," specifically "hemorrhage and shock following rupture of liver. Bruised area across upper abdomen about 3 inches with ecchymosis of skin and soft structures. Slight swelling over left cheek. Abrasion with discoloration of a small particle of skin of left finger. Brush burn and contusion of left shin." But Dr. C. Grenes Cole ruled the cause of death "undetermined," leading to a formal investigation.[109]

Police Superintendent George Reyer instructed the commander of the Seventh Precinct, Captain Edward Smith, to launch an official inquiry and to report his findings to Detective John "Third Degree" Grosch.[110] Newspapers ran unsubstantiated reports that Boyd had been ferried to a number of precinct houses before landing at the Seventh, suggesting that detectives stashed the suspect "on ice" in order to interrogate him without interference.[111] Other rumors described waves of detectives entering and leaving Boyd's cell in the four hours between his arrival at the station and Achor's discovery of the corpse.[112]

Smith's formal report, however, painted an entirely different picture, one in stark contrast to the arrest report and to the version offered by Boyd's neighbors. According to the official investigation, "nothing improper was done to Boyd." Rather, the "negro bandit suspect" sustained his injuries trying to avoid arrest.[113] Smith's report detailed how Boyd attempted to scale a fence in his yard and make his escape. When he was restrained by patrolmen, Boyd "fell from the fence on two [tree] stumps," presumably rupturing his liver.[114] Such an injury notwithstanding, the suspect then scuffled with policemen while resisting arrest, resulting in the bruises and contusions. But officers Elmo Evans and Peter Ory "used only such force as was necessary to effect his arrest."[115] In their testimony to Smith, the patrolmen invoked the formulaic language for a deranged, violent African American predator, asserting that Boyd "appeared to be out of his mind or under the influence of narcotics."[116] The report also included statements from thirteen policemen, many of whom provided the same word-for-word descriptions of the arrest, transport, and interrogation of the suspect.[117] Furthermore, the investigation underscored that Boyd was an "old offender," arrested twenty-one previous times, though mostly for minor offenses, such as fighting and using profane language.[118] Hence, the formal inquiry simultaneously denied that precinct cops employed excessive force and portrayed Aaron Boyd as the kind of dangerous predator who needed to be apprehended at any cost, thus justifying the use of force that the report maintained never occurred.

Grosch concurred with Captain Smith's report and announced that "no further action would be taken."[119] "The incident is closed," District Attorney Charles A. Byrne ruled.[120] Although newspapers matter-of-factly noted how the initial police report and the civilian witness testimony contradicted Smith's final report, only civil rights groups expressed outrage. The Louisiana League for the Preservation of Constitutional Rights, for example, warned that such "flagrant use of arbitrary and dictatorial methods by the police" ran "closely parallel to the way Fascism first arose both in Italy and Germany."[121]

A series of similar cases, where African American suspects mysteriously died in police custody, followed Boyd's killing and highlighted cops' increasingly aggressive responses to African American street violence, the complicity of parish district attorneys and coroners, and the widespread popular (white) support for such an approach to crime fighting. In 1939, after a white civil rights activist voiced concern about endemic police violence against African American suspects, he received death threats, some invoking the precise methods employed by detectives. "One more crack out of you in regard to all this (nigger) protection, we'll run you out of this city," one letter warned. "We better not hear another word from you, one way or another, in regard to (niggers) or we will take you out for a ride + I'll guarantee you'll never mention (niggers) again."[122] In another such case, three years later, two members of a grand jury complained that "this was case of a policeman shooting a 'nigger,' and that was all right."[123]

World War II exaggerated and politicized these trends, bolstering the purported connection between race and crime as well as forging a link between African American street violence and threats to the war effort. The war buoyed the local economy, and the docks boomed once again. Furthermore, Jackson Barracks, on the eastern edge of the city, became a major staging center for soldiers heading overseas, and the Gulfport Army Airfield sixty-five miles east of New Orleans, funneled wave after wave of visitors, like William Mears, to the area. On weekends, soldiers packed French Quarter bars and the streets surrounding raucous saloons and nightclubs.

The sudden arrival of large numbers of young men, flush with cash, affected violent crime in New Orleans in three overlapping ways. First, it stimulated the local economy. If the economic downturn had dampened drinking, carousing, and brawling, the return to prosperity fueled disorder and violence.[124] The city's homicide rate, which had been tumbling since 1925, rose by 7.8 percent between 1940 and 1945, and the drunken-brawl homicide rate increased by 11.9 percent.

Second, the soldiers not only brought cash to New Orleans; they also arrived with guns. For the first time since the late 1920s, US Army revolvers became plentiful in New Orleans, and pawnshops and hardware stores once again offered cheap firearms, as many drunken servicemen unwittingly left their weapons behind when they staggered back to their bases. A few days before Wilbert Powell shot Bernice Roy, for example, he stole the .38 caliber revolver, stamped "U.S. Army," used in the murder.[125] During the war years, many killers also used secondhand military firearms.[126] New Orleans's gun homicide rate rose by 47.2 percent between 1940 and 1945, after having plunged since the mid-1920s.

Third, the hard-drinking soldiers imbibed, gambled, and quarreled with other young men in public settings late at night, particularly African American New Orleanians, who disproportionately lived and socialized in the older neighborhoods hugging the river and near the French Quarter. As in the early 1920s, where single young men drank and collided, fights abounded. The rate at which strangers killed one another increased sixfold between 1940 and 1945, and the rate of African American stranger homicide rose more than ninefold. Similarly, the African American street homicide rate, which had changed little since the early 1930s, leaped by 122.8 percent during the war years, while the African American gun homicide rate surged by 126.2 percent. White New Orleanians, more often living and socializing farther to the north, had limited contact with the soldiers, and their rates of violence and gun use remained relatively flat.

Many of the deadly fights occurred late at night and crossed racial lines, as white soldiers clashed with African American residents. The proportion of interracial killings, while modest, nearly doubled during the war, rising from 8 percent of homicides in 1940 to 15.7 percent in 1945, when eleven such lethal fights occurred. More important, the share of whites killed by African American assailants quadrupled, from 7.7 percent in 1940 to 30.4 percent five years later. The rate of black-on-white homicide, which had been dropping since 1930, leaped nearly sevenfold between 1940 and 1945 (see figure 6.6). The number of such homicides remained small, but these deadly brawls, which typically erupted in public settings, seemingly provided concrete, flesh-and-blood evidence confirming the racial fears that haunted white New Orleanians. According to white newspapers, African American bandits targeted the soldiers, who often arrived in the city with money in their pockets. "Most of the victims in

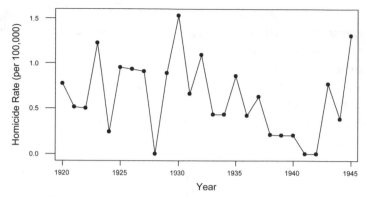

FIG. 6.6. Black-on-White Homicide Rates, 1920–1945. Source: Homicide Reports, Department of Police, New Orleans.

recent holdups have been service men," the *New Orleans Item* reported in the summer of 1943, "and the robbers were Negroes."[127] The *New Orleans Times-Picayune* concurred, writing that "during the last two months a score or more soldiers and sailors have been held up and robbed by Negroes."[128]

The hyperpatriotism of the war years introduced a new, combustible element to this panic. When African American New Orleanians robbed or killed white soldiers, the violence, according to journalists, endangered the war effort, similar to white depictions of the Los Angeles Zoot Suit Riots and the Detroit Race Riot of 1943.[129] In New Orleans, this perspective extended to white victims with any direct link to the war.

Peter Sansone's murder, on August 18, 1943, and particularly reactions to it, fused these exaggerated popular currents and accelerated shifts in the core mission of the local criminal justice system. Just after midnight, Matilda O'Connor, a fifty-three-year-old white nurse at the French Hospital, called the Fourth Precinct station to say that she had peered out a second-floor window in Ward 2C and saw an "unknown man had been shot at Derbigny [Street] near Orleans Street and that he was lying on the sidewalk." O'Connor observed "a man who appeared to be a colored man walking down N. Derbigny Street from Orleans and when he reached the body lying on the sidewalk he stopped when he got in front of the man lying down and then three other unknown men who appeared to be colored then walked up . . . and began searching the man who was lying down." When pressed for additional details, O'Connor cautioned that the street was dark, that she was ninety feet away, that the men who rifled the dead man's pocket "appeared to be colored," but that she could not identify them.[130] This telephone call ignited a panic and unleashed savage criticism of the police.

Police officers rushed to the scene and found the body of Peter Sansone, a fifty-three-old shipyard worker, who had been shot in the chest from close range.[131] Newspapers provided copious coverage of the murder and the police investigation. Although O'Connor stated that she did not see the shooting and that the men who approached the body and searched Sansone's pockets merely "appeared to be colored," crime-beat reporters immediately identified the killers as "four Negro bandits." Captain Edward Theard, the commander of the Fourth Precinct, added that the murderers were likely "members of a gang of Negro bandits who have shot and cut several service men and civilians."[132] Similarly, reporters transformed the victim from a shipyard worker to a "war worker."[133] The police seemed powerless to protect white New Orleanians and war workers.

Editors demanded action, and politicians demanded results. The district attorney threatened "a shakeup of the police department, if it were necessary to control crime here."[134] The police chief responded with an aggressive campaign to catch Sansone's killer, rout African American predators, and safeguard white residents, particularly soldiers and war workers. The day after the murder he "ordered the arrest of all Negroes found prowling around the streets late at night."[135] Detective John Grosch oversaw the initiative, and Detective Frank Lannes directed the "special patrol" rounding up suspects.[136] Within twenty-four hours, Lannes's patrol arrested seventy-four African American men.[137] On the following day, the count jumped to 223, but on the day that the arrest toll surpassed 500, police officials "admitted that they were without a clue which might lead to the solution of the killing."[138] Nonetheless, the mass arrests continued and accelerated. By early September, the dragnet had yielded nearly 1,000 suspects, none of whom had any connection to the murder of Peter Sansone.[139]

The police failed to solve the case but used the sweep to affirm their commitment to the overlapping goals of racial control and crime control, at least in part in order to counter public criticism. Police clerks searched, photographed, and fingerprinted all the men they apprehended. As in earlier dragnets, they charged dozens with weapon possession and vagrancy and held others because they "failed to have in their possession their draft registration cards."[140] Cops filed loitering charges against suspects who did not have "legitimate reasons for being on the streets late at night."[141] The "wholesale arrests" of African American men became both a political salve and a default reaffirmation of the increasingly blurred goals of white supremacy and crime fighting.[142]

Not surprisingly, racial disparities in homicide conviction rates and execution rates widened during the early 1940s. Prosecutors continued to drop and dismiss charges against most homicide suspects, and juries rarely found suspects guilty. Fewer than one killer in seven was convicted during the early 1940s, and the overall conviction rate dropped by 24.9 percent between the 1930s and the early 1940s. The rate for white killers tumbled by 39.4 percent. But the conviction rate in black-on-white homicide cases ballooned by 36.2 percent during the early 1940s, and the rate of execution for African American defendants more than doubled.[143] Perhaps even more significant, a sizable number of African American men ensnared in the sweeps and dragnets following high-profile interracial crimes subsequently spent time in the parish prison on vagrancy or loitering charges. The ripple effects of the reactions to the Sansone murder and similar homicides exaggerated the transformations of both criminal justice and race relations in the city.

At the same time, however, these social, cultural, political, and institutional changes generated an increasingly powerful backlash from African American New Orleanians. During the 1920s, class tensions fragmented the city's African American population. The established Creole elite responded to racial discrimination cautiously. Working within the established power structure, they relied in their personal ties to city officials and rejected aggressive, strident challenges to the racial order. As a consequence, civil rights organizations, particularly the NAACP, remained toothless and lacked support from the larger African American community. When Jim Crow gradually established a binary racial hierarchy in the city, this process undermined the status of the Creole elite and slowly eroded social divisions within African American New Orleans. These changes enabled a younger, more impatient generation to supplant the older African American leadership and to assume prominent roles in civic and civil rights organizations. As a result, the NAACP, for example, grew stronger, more forceful, and gained wider support in the community.[144]

No issue galvanized the African American community more than police violence. Thus, Jim Crow criminal justice, the increasing use of third-degree methods, the rising body count from police violence, and the greater frequency of racial dragnets at least episodically unified African American residents into a political force, contesting the racialized criminal justice of the 1930s and 1940s.[145] The murder of Aaron Boyd and other African American suspects generated even greater unity and more strident responses from civil rights organizations.

National and international events reinforced this development and provided new ways for African American New Orleanians to challenge Jim Crow criminal justice. Rhetorically, civil rights leaders began to compare the local police to Hitler's storm troopers, describing police brutality as the "Nazification of New Orleans."[146] Civil rights organizations also exploited political currents. Again and again, after African American suspects died in police custody, civil rights groups reported the incidents to Justice Department or Interior Department officials, recognizing that these incidents embarrassed New Dealers and jeopardized the flow of federal housing and relief funds from Washington to New Orleans politicians.[147] In 1939, Harold N. Lee, a Tulane University philosophy professor and the president of the Louisiana League for the Preservation of Constitutional Rights, confided that "we are now in a position to make the police in New Orleans more or less acutely uncomfortable on the score of brutality and illegal arrests." Lee added that "we have them [city and police officials] on the run through two channels, the State Attorney's office and the Federal authorities."[148] Lee alerted Justice Department officials to police violence, and at the peak of the dragnets after the Sansone murder, the local NAACP office employed the same strategy.[149] The city's Negro Ministerial Alliance, the Federation of Civic Leagues, and other civil rights groups also flexed their muscles to combat Jim Crow law enforcement.

New Orleans detectives, particularly the Grosch brothers, unwittingly fortified this backlash when they began to use their preferred methods of brutality against white dissidents, especially labor organizers.[150] William Grosch, for example, established his authority by repeatedly taking African American suspects "for a ride" and threatening to kill them—or actually killing them. But many white residents bristled when the detective used this tactic against white members of the Congress of Industrial Organizations or, in 1939, when his brother, John Grosch, publicly and defiantly endorsed the use of overtly illegal third-degree interrogation techniques.[151]

Informal mechanisms for contesting Jim Crow criminal justice grew stronger as well during the 1940s. Just as police violence energized civil rights organizations, this brutality mobilized neighborhood residents. On June 17, 1943, Patrolman John Licali, while investigating a report of a domestic dispute at the home of Felton and Veola Robinson, asserted that the twenty-nine-year-old husband attacked him and made a furtive movement for a weapon. In response, Licali fatally shot Felton Robinson.[152] Shortly after Robinson died, police investigators returned to the scene to search for a gun. African American women from the neighborhood, however, quickly unnerved the law enforcers, pouring into the Robinsons' home and crowding the cops. Rosa Joseph, Felton Robinson's sister-in-law, confronted the policemen, pointedly asking, "Which one of you shot him?" The normally aggressive, brazen officers suddenly became sheepish, remarking that the victim "looked like a nice fellow" and then scurrying out of the home, without finding any weapon.[153] While such demonstrations did not stop police shootings of African Americans residents, these informal efforts represented another way in which residents resisted Jim Crow criminal justice.

Even in the face of such challenges, however, the conflation of race and crime grew stronger. Through the early 1940s, cops continued to brutalize and kill African American New Orleanians, though the most overt cases of police violence became sources of controversy and embarrassment for city officials. Other responses to the purported threat posed by African American residents, such as dragnets, persisted, and racial disparities in convictions, sentencing, and incarceration widened. While Jim Crow criminal justice became self-perpetuating, it also fueled opposition to police tactics and jump-started the development of the local civil rights movement during the middle decades of the twentieth century.[154]

*

The Great Depression transformed crime and punishment in New Orleans in three interconnected ways. First, the economic collapse altered the composition of the city's population and thus both reduced homicide and changed the nature of violence. As unemployment surged, migration to New Orleans ebbed, and family life became more private. These demographic shifts, in combination with changes in the availability of guns, caused homicide rates to plummet. Domestic violence decreased particularly sharply. At the same time, the morphology of intimate homicide changed. During the raucous 1920s, husbands had typically slaughtered their wives. But by the 1930s, women committed a rising proportion of spouse killings. Furthermore, the deadly fights more frequently erupted when men attacked partners fleeing from abusive marriages, and the women defended themselves using lethal force.

Second, the social and economic pressures of the 1930s triggered race-based shifts in the locus of New Orleans violence. White homicide fell and became largely confined to domestic space. But African American violence, which also slumped during the 1930s, became concentrated in public settings, especially in the streets of the city. Such shifts made African American homicide more visible and reshaped white perceptions of social order and race relations.

Third, the Great Depression, in combination with the social changes fueled by World War II, accelerated the growing disjuncture between crime and punishment in New Orleans. Policing and criminal justice became increasingly disconnected from crime. White New Orleanians, for example, largely ignored African American homicide during the early 1920s, when such violence surged. By the late 1920s and 1930s, white residents, and the political and law enforcement officials beholden to them, grew alarmed about African American predators robbing and murdering innocent whites, despite the precipitous drop in African American homicide and the very modest and sinking rate of interracial crime in the city. The concentration of African American homicide in public space and its resulting visibility, rather than its frequency, redefined the policing of race in New Orleans. For African American residents, punishment increased at the same time that crime decreased. During the war years, when African American homicide, especially interracial violence, inched upward, the alarm turned to hysteria, and isolated high-profile crimes, such as the 1945 murder of Bernice Roy, provided a justification for widening racial disparities in policing.

In sum, the cumulative weight of demographic and ecological developments, a robbery panic, changes in the market for guns, shifts in the locus of violent crime, the Great Depression, and World War II transformed the relationship between crime and punishment, the role of the police in local society, and the mission of the criminal justice system in New Orleans. As a result of the collision of these locational, institutional, cultural, and political forces, white criminals became invisible to the police, and white New Orleanians viewed African American violence as a threat to social order and elided race with crime, even as levels of African American homicide plunged. By the dawn of World War II, efforts to preserve the racial hierarchy and measures to fight crime merged. In the process, African American New Orleans went from being underpoliced to being overpoliced, and the city's frenzied response to African American street violence triggered an ominous pivot toward more aggressive law enforcement, mass arrests, and prosecutorial zeal as mechanisms of racial control.

Conclusion

Racial disparities in criminal justice were not fixed in twentieth-century America. To the contrary, they developed and changed over time and in response to social, cultural, legal, and political pressures. In New Orleans, the core elements of such discriminatory practices—the overpolicing of the African American community, race-based patterns of coercive interrogation, police brutality, police homicide, and differential rates of arrest, prosecution, conviction, incarceration, and execution—mushroomed during the interwar period and in counterintuitive reaction to trends in criminal violence. Paradoxically, racial disparities in policing and punishment expanded as rates of African American homicide plunged. White New Orleanians largely ignored African American violent crime when it occurred at high levels and became terrified of such violence just as African American homicide became relatively uncommon. And in response to a threat that was fast disappearing, white residents, led by brutal cops and demagogic politicians, embraced law and order as a tool of racial control and redefined the city's criminal justice system, initiating a transformation that metastasized over the course of the twentieth century.[1]

Homicide exploded in New Orleans during the early 1920s. The surge touched virtually every segment of the population and crossed racial lines, and the city's homicide rate more than doubled between 1920 and 1925. But the spike was particularly pronounced among African American New Orleanians, whose homicide rate leaped by 155.5 percent. White lethal violence rose as well, though by a more modest 60.6 percent. During the first half of the decade, the African American homicide rate ballooned from five to eight times the white rate. By the middle of the decade, African American residents comprised roughly a quarter of the population but almost three-quarters of the city's killers and homicide victims. Especially for African American New Orleanians, blood flowed in the streets.

Yet cops and prosecutors typically ignored violent crime and demonstrated particular indifference toward African American murder. The police conducted halfhearted investigations and gathered little evidence, and the Orleans Parish district attorney dismissed, dropped, and eliminated the lion's share of cases, discharging most suspects before they entered a courtroom. Prosecutors were especially quick to release African American suspects. On the rare occasions when homicide cases proceeded to trial, jurors routinely acquitted the killers. While the murder rate skyrocketed during the early 1920s, making New Orleans one of the most violent cities in the nation, the district attorney secured convictions in only one-seventh of homicides. But the criminal justice system was unusually toothless when the suspected killer was African American. Parish prosecutors charged and convicted a higher proportion of white than African American suspects, and even jurors and judges showed a greater inclination to punish white killers. Juries seldom convicted any defendants, yet white convicted killers were twice as likely as African American defendants to be convicted of murder (rather than manslaughter). Racial discrimination seared daily life in early 1920s New Orleans, though the local criminal justice system demonstrated mainly disinterest when African American residents committed or fell victim to criminal violence.[2]

Instead, policemen, prosecutors, jurors, and judges, all of whom were white, viewed African American violence as unstoppable, insisting that murderous volatility represented an immutable element of African American character. But criminal justice officials also argued that such bloodletting was unimportant, for it nearly always remained safely confined within the African American community. Hence, this violence, no matter its frequency, posed scant threat to white New Orleanians and therefore was ignored. As a result, early 1920s law enforcers and prosecutors made fewer arrests and secured fewer indictments or convictions for African American assailants, and jurors and judges dispensed shorter sentences and returned fewer capital verdicts for African American killers. Not surprisingly, the local criminal justice system evinced even less interest in apprehending, prosecuting, and punishing those who killed African American New Orleanians, convicting these assailants at half the proportion of those who committed homicide against white residents. The killers of African Americans were never executed.

Such indifference toward African American violence had two significant consequences. First, it left these residents unprotected. African American

New Orleanians learned that they could not rely on local cops, prosecutors, jurors, or judges for protection or redress. Crime victims (or potential victims) could either do nothing or seize the initiative and resort to informal methods of conflict resolution, such as aggressive self-help, to mediate disputes, deter attacks, or secure some measure of justice. Self-reliance, however, came at a high cost, for it spurred violent responses to challenges and assaults, contributing to the skyrocketing murder rate among African American New Orleanians during the early 1920s. Second, this soaring level of violence reinforced white stereotypes about emotionally unstable, drug-crazed, knife-wielding, gun-toting African American residents, which, in turn, bolstered notions of white supremacy and buttressed the view that African American homicide was unstoppable and should be overlooked by law enforcers.

But white attitudes toward crime and race shifted abruptly during the late 1920s and early 1930s. White New Orleanians, and the city officials and parish prosecutors they elected, suddenly worried that African American violence would eventually bleed across racial lines and that volatile, savage killers would ultimately prey upon them. This jarring change in white perceptions of African American violence occurred just as African American crime rates slumped. During the late 1920s, the African American homicide rate tumbled by more than half; by 1933, it had dropped by nearly two-thirds. Nor did the rate of black-on-white violence change appreciably.

Three overlapping shifts redefined the relationship between race and criminal justice, transforming race relations and legal institutions in the process. First, a crime panic magnified the anxieties of white New Orleanians, despite the decrease in violence in the city. A slight increase in robbery and robbery-homicide fueled the hysteria and sparked white calls for more aggressive law enforcement. National currents helped to ignite this panic, as chilling press accounts of predatory criminals, such as Edward Hickman in Los Angeles, and celebrity bank robbers, publicized by J. Edgar Hoover, transfixed public attention. Sensational, often salacious reports of vicious desperadoes and thrill killers shaped and exaggerated reactions to local crime. In banner headlines, New Orleans newspapers described the brazen exploits of white bandits and the murderous predations of irrational, savage African American killers. As the panic gripped the city during the late 1920s, for example, New Orleanians learned about Julius "Doo-Doom" Roberts, the African American day laborer who murdered the widowed white shopkeeper Annie Flink and her fourteen-year-old son, Henry, in 1929, fleeing with a handful of loose change. For white New Orleanians, Roberts became the public face of violent crime. Suddenly concerned about their own vulnerability, they demanded police protection.

Second, during the late 1920s and the early 1930s white residents worried that the racial etiquette and behavioral boundaries that had long preserved social order were crumbling. A confluence of factors catalyzed this anxiety. Changes in the social ecology, in combination with the successful legal challenge to the local racial zoning ordinances in 1927, elicited panic about race mixing in New Orleans. At the same time, many white residents believed that African American New Orleanians were becoming bolder and more violent, a development abetted by new forms of transportation. They worried, for instance, about increasingly aggressive, insolent African American drivers flouting racial convention and asserting dominance on the streets. White New Orleanians also grew anxious about African Americans "masquers" attacking white residents during Mardi Gras. Many watched nervously as a younger generation of local civil rights activists attempted to overturn the exclusion of African American New Orleanians from the voter rolls and from juries during the early 1930s, potentially jeopardizing white control over local politics and the courts. White supremacy appeared to be under siege; custom seemed incapable of stemming the assault. Government, and especially the criminal justice system, white residents believed, needed to fill the breach and shore up the fast-decaying racial order.

Third, patterns of violent crime changed dramatically during the late 1920s and the early 1930s, and in ways that reinforced white fears of racial disorder. Both homicide and mortality rates dropped sharply. Death became less omnipresent as the Roaring Twenties gave way to the Great Depression. But lethal violence seemed more shocking and unsettling as murder (and death) became less common. Officials who casually dismissed violent crime as a "Negro problem" during the mid-1920s, when the city was among the national leaders in murder, reacted with alarm during the early 1930s, even though New Orleans's homicide rate had plunged by half and the city no longer ranked in the top thirty in lethal violence.

The changing ecology of murder, in part, produced this response. As the homicide rate plummeted, the spatial context of lethal violence shifted. White homicide dropped but also increasingly occurred in homes, making such violence less visible. Although African American homicide decreased more precipitously, it also moved to other settings, leaving the domestic sphere and more often erupting in public space, particularly on the streets. Between the early 1930s and the mid-1940s, the African American homicide rate fell by half. More important in framing white perceptions of race and violence, the proportion of street homicides committed by African American New Orleanians rose from under half to nearly nine-tenths. Thus, during a period of white panic about racial instability, white violence largely disappeared from public view. By contrast, African American homicide became more visible and more menacing, even as it became less common.

While white fears of faltering racial boundaries and collapsing racial conventions mounted, voters, virtually all of whom were white, looked to the police and demanded that law enforcers become a fighting unit, armed and prepared to meet the African American threat to (white) public safety with force. They pleaded for stronger, more unyielding criminal justice. At a time when white residents comprised 99.1 percent of registered voters in the city, candidates for public office, such as District Attorney Eugene Stanley, exploited such racial anxieties, promising to safeguard white supremacy, and used the crime panic to secure victories at the polls. Law and order became a balm for white anxieties about racial instability.

This alchemy elided African Americans and crime and spearheaded a dramatic shift in law enforcement. Racial control and crime control overlapped, blurred, and blended in the 1930s, redefining policing in the city. Derided as corrupt, feckless political hacks during the early 1920s, cops became racial warriors during the 1930s. Not only did patrolmen more often rely on force, even deadly force, in making arrests, they also increasingly targeted African American assailants. Abetting this transformation, policemen, with the enthusiastic support of jittery white residents, employed greater brutality against African American suspects to buttress the beleaguered racial hierarchy. As the Great Depression eroded the material advantages enjoyed by white New Orleanians, street cops used their authority, their billy clubs, and their service revolvers to defend and to affirm their class and racial supremacy.[3]

During the 1930s, law enforcers also began to employ "dragnets" or "sweeps" in response to high-profile violent crimes with African American assailants and white victims. New Orleans cops had made mass arrests before, but now they employed this tool nearly exclusively against African American suspects. In response to the murder of Peter Sansone in 1943, for instance, police officials ordered the apprehension of "all Negroes found prowling around the streets late at night."[4] Reflecting the vanishing boundary between racial control and crime fighting, patrolmen arrested nearly a thousand African American men, none of whom was connected to the murder, but police clerks charged dozens of them with loitering, vagrancy, suspicious behavior, using profane language, and similar offenses and funneled them to the parish prison.

Police shootings of suspects changed in lockstep, increasing in frequency and more often directed at African American New Orleanians. As white anxieties about racial disorder and criminal violence soared and fused, city officials militarized the police and commanded local cops to "shoot to kill." The threshold for killing a suspect decreased as the pressure to combat African American predators increased. Police use of deadly force was not new but changed during the 1930s. Whereas cops most often killed armed white bandits during the 1920s, by the 1930s, patrolmen increasingly shot unarmed African Americans who appeared disorderly or uncompliant—so-called "bad niggers." The infinitely plastic "hip-pocket move" or "furtive movement" justification persuaded prosecutors and jurors in virtually every such shooting, even when the "advancing suspect" reaching for his gun proved to be unarmed and was shot in the back of the head.

New Orleans detectives emerged as even more zealous defenders of the racial order during the 1930s, and the coerced confession, though denounced nationally, became a symbol of professional policing in the city, as long as the suspect was African American. Municipal and parish officials who publicly rejected the use of third-degree interrogation tactics defended employing such measures against "vicious" African American suspects. When detectives inflicted fatal beatings on African American "police characters," such as Aaron Boyd in 1938, prosecutors and grand jurors exonerated them. District attorneys and juries even overlooked police assassinations of African American suspects, particularly the victims of Detective William Grosch's notorious "one-way rides." Once again, such brutality had occurred earlier in the century but became a tool of racialized crime fighting during the 1930s.

The combination of shifts in the spatial context of violence and surging racial anxieties produced a new law enforcement model in New Orleans. Informal mechanisms of vigilante violence merged with the rule of law, for cops did not eschew violent methods of maintaining "order" so much as they adapted such tactics to fit their expansive new mandate. Beatings, for example, migrated from the streets to interrogation rooms in precinct houses, and New Orleans law enforcers justified and expanded racial violence in the service of preserving social stability. Even as city officials celebrated the crime-fighting success of the police department, old-school cops, who blatantly tortured African American suspects and openly boasted about it, became heroes. With their trademark brutality, the Grosch brothers, for example, rose from supernumerary patrolmen during the 1920s to leading police officials during the 1940s.[5] Parish prosecutor Eugene Stanley exemplified the new politics of race in the criminal justice system and merged a law-and-order agenda with a fierce defense of white supremacy, enjoying great success until a more ruthless demagogue, Huey P. Long, outmaneuvered him.

Stanley's transformation of the criminal justice system, however, endured. The conviction rate for African American killers surged, climbing to double the white level by the late 1930s. In 1943, Orleans Parish prosecutors secured the conviction of 24.4 percent of African American homicide suspects and zero percent of white killers. Sentencing trends followed the same racially disparate trajectory. During the mid-1920s, 91.7 percent of convicted white killers and 50 percent of convicted African American killers received prison terms of ten years or longer. Two decades later, 25 percent of white convicts but 64.3 percent of African American inmates were sentenced to ten years or longer at the State Penal Farm at Angola. The shift in execution rates was even more pronounced. During the early 1920s, jurors returned capital verdicts on white killers twice as often as on African American killers. But by the early 1940s, judges and jurors reserved execution exclusively for African American killers. New Orleans criminal justice, shorn of the rough justice of opening decades of the century, achieved comparably racialized ends with its commitment to the rule of law.

The wider social, economic, and political changes of the 1930s and 1940s fueled and reinforced these shifts. The Great Depression indirectly contributed to the decrease and transformation of lethal violence in the city, shrinking the number of young bachelors in the population, reducing drinking, gambling, and brawling, and pricing firearms beyond the reach of the poorest New Orleanians. Moreover, reactions to the economic crisis of the 1930s promoted state formation. Just as relief agencies matured and expanded their authority, the police and the courts enjoyed robust growth and established more formal and more powerful mechanisms to defend older notions of race and power. World War II cemented these changes. White voters—that is, nearly everyone who cast a ballot in New Orleans—more than ever associated African American men with predatory violence and demanded that their bulked-up law enforcers preserve a racialized definition of social order.

The flowering of Jim Crow criminal justice, however, also generated a backlash that eventually challenged this version of the rule of law. The explicit, bald racial disparities in criminal justice that emerged during the interwar era blunted class divisions in the African American community and thus helped to launch an increasingly powerful civil rights movement. By the late 1940s, the efforts of New Orleans activists began to bear fruit, and city officials consented to appoint African Americans to the municipal police force.[6] Furthermore, the number of African American New Orleanians who were registered to vote skyrocketed, from 609 in 1940 to more than 13,000 in 1948.[7] A long-established, deeply entrenched cop culture resisted these changes, though African American residents contested the institutional world forged by Buttercup Burns, the Grosch brothers, and Eugene Stanley during the 1930s.[8]

In many respects, New Orleans was unique, and the relationship between race and criminal justice in the city unfolded in distinctive ways. From the bayous of Orleans Parish and the raucous bars in the French Quarter to the pitched battles between the Long machine and New Orleans's Old Regulars, local conditions shaped violence, reactions to crime, and the paradoxical institutional responses. A 1940 magazine article captured the city's trademark quirks and oddities, describing New Orleans as "an easy-going, pleasure-loving, colorful, odoriferous, church attending city whose dead are buried aboveground and whose politics is carried on underground."[9]

But, for all of New Orleans's eccentricities, the emergence of racial disparities in criminal justice in the city did not occur in isolation. National currents and wider pressures influenced both patterns of crime and trends in criminal justice. In fundamental ways, the changes that occurred in the city mirrored shifts in crime and punishment across the United States. The demographic transformations of the era, ranging from the waves of migrants who moved to cities during the prosperous 1920s to the sharp drop in mortality during the Great Depression, altered patterns of violence in New Orleans, too. Similarly, J. Edgar Hoover's crusade to establish the authority of the fledgling FBI, which helped to trigger the crime panic of the late 1920s and early 1930s, accelerated changes in public perceptions of violence and in law enforcement prescriptions in every corner of the nation.

Although New Orleans's distinctive conditions dictated the specific fluctuations in criminal violence during this period, local patterns of homicide roughly followed national urban trends. In cities throughout the United States, for example, rates of lethal violence surged during the early 1920s and peaked during the middle years of the decade. Between 1924 and 1926, Boston, Chicago, Philadelphia, Detroit, and other American cities also reached their highest homicide levels for the interwar period. Similarly, New Orleans's sharp drop in lethal violence during the Great Depression mirrored national trends. The homicide rate there plunged by 42.8 percent between 1929 and 1940, compared with dips of 46 percent in Birmingham, 41.8 percent in New

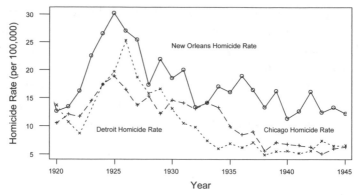

F I G . 7 . 1 . New Orleans, Detroit, and Chicago Homicide Rates, 1920–1945. Source: U.S. Morality Statistics; Uniform Crime Reports.

York City, 44.3 percent in Chicago, and 66.3 percent in Detroit. In short, while local conditions shaped the precise magnitude of peaks and valleys of lethal violence, New Orleans's overall homicide rate trajectory paralleled those of the nation's major urban centers during the 1920–45 period (see figure 7.1).

More fragmentary data suggest that other American cities experienced transformations in policing and criminal justice similar to those in New Orleans. For southern urban centers, such as New Orleans and Memphis, race relations shaped policing, but the shift toward more aggressive law enforcement was not confined to cities in the region. For example, Chicago policemen also employed deadly force more often between the mid-1920s and the early 1930s. A toxic side effect of the crime panic of the era, New Orleans's rate of police homicide spiked by 62.1 percent from 1925 to 1931, while Chicago's rate leaped by 60.3 percent (see figure 7.2).[10] Third-degree interrogations, and the violence that accompanied coercive interrogation techniques, persisted and likely worsened in Chicago and other cities as well, despite the national crusade to eliminate such practices.[11] While the Grosch brothers set the tone for police conduct in New Orleans during the 1930s and early 1940s, every big-city police department no doubt had comparable veteran detectives who played similar roles and trained younger cops.[12]

State and national incarceration data also indicate that New Orleans's practices echoed wider trends in criminal justice. Throughout the United States, violent crime, including homicide and robbery, plunged during the Great Depression, yet rates of incarceration surged. Between 1929 and 1940, the nation's homicide rate dropped by 29.5 percent.[13] The incarceration rate, however, jumped by 32.7 percent. Imprisonment levels were extremely low during the high-crime 1920s and dramatically higher during the low-crime 1930s. Less crime produced more punishment during this era, with incarceration rates rising by 22 percent in Louisiana, 37.8 percent in Illinois, 38 percent in Massachusetts, 23.6 percent in Pennsylvania, and 70.4 percent in New York during the Great Depression (see figure 7.3).[14] Trends in capital punishment shifted in similar ways, reaching their highest level in US history in 1935, as murder rates plummeted. In short, the disjuncture between crime and punishment extended far beyond New Orleans.

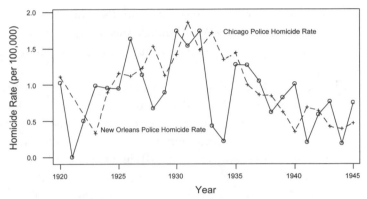

FIG. 7.2. Police-Homicide Rates in New Orleans and Chicago, 1920–1945. Source: Homicide Reports, Department of Police, New Orleans; Thorsten Sellin, *The Death Penalty* (Philadelphia: American Law Institute, 1959), 60.

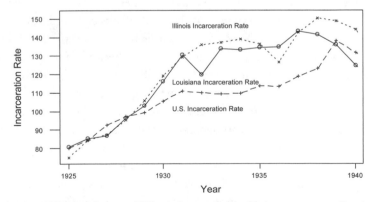

FIG. 7.3. US, Louisiana, and Illinois Incarceration Rates, 1925–1940. Source: Patrick A. Langan, John V. Fundis, Lawrence A. Greenfeld, and Victoria W. Schneider, "Historical Statistics in State and Federal Institutions, Yearend 1925–1986," NCJ-111098, Bureau of Justice Statistics, US Department of Justice, May 1988, pp. 5–7.

Aggregate-level figures hint at emerging racial disparities in policing outside of New Orleans as well. Between 1930 and 1940, for example, the African American inmate population at Louisiana's maximum-security penal farm increased at nearly four times the rate of the white population, even though the African American homicide rate dropped by 29.8 percent.[15] In stark contrast to the 1920s, cops and sheriffs pursued African American suspects during the 1930s. FBI arrest data for the 1933–40 period revealed similar disproportionalities at the national level. The US homicide rate fell by 36.1 percent during this span. The white homicide arrest rate dipped by 8 percent, while the African American homicide arrest rate swelled by 25.4 percent. Comparable shifts occurred in robbery arrest rates, with the white level decreasing by 41.8 percent and the African American rate increasing by 23.4 percent.[16] Across the nation, police departments focused on apprehending African American suspects.

Similarly, the racial disparities in sentencing that developed in New Orleans during the 1930s were also evident at the state and national levels. In Louisiana, African Americans comprised 43.5 percent of the convicts executed during the 1920s, 63.3 percent during the 1930s, and 68.8 percent during the 1940s, shifts entirely unrelated to trends in crime.[17] Furthermore, African Americans made up a soaring proportion of those executed for murder nationally during the 1930s, rising from 38.8 percent at the start of the decade to 58.1 percent in 1940.[18] While distinctive social, political, and legal forces shaped racial disparities in New Orleans, parallel race-based differentials in criminal justice mushroomed from coast to coast during the 1930s.

A tangle of local and national pressures shaped trends in lethal violence, institutional responses to crime, and the politics of race that, in turn, transformed criminal justice in New Orleans during the interwar period. The mismatch between crime and punishment, however, became more pronounced over the course of the twentieth century, locally and nationally. Between 1990 and 2000, the US homicide rate dropped by 41.5 percent, yet the nation's incarceration rate rose by 63.7 percent.[19] Equally telling, the number of executions for murder surged by 270 percent, notwithstanding the sharp decrease in this crime.[20] Racial disparities widened as well. By the early twenty-first century, the United States imprisoned African American residents at a higher rate than South Africa incarcerated black residents at the peak of apartheid.[21] New Orleans's 1930s race-based differentials in convictions, sentencing, and incarceration, therefore, paled by comparison to late twentieth- and early twenty-first-century trends. But the pivot to the modern disjuncture between crime and punishment emerged between World War I and World War II.

Considered one of the most violent departments by the late 1930s, for example, the New Orleans police led the nation in civilian brutality complaints during the 1980s and 1990s.[22] In sum, shifting patterns of homicide, and white reactions to African American violence, triggered dramatic changes in law enforcement in interwar New Orleans, generating racial disparities in policing, prosecutions, and sentencing, and forging the roots of modern mass-arrest and mass-incarceration practices. The forces unleashed between 1920 and 1945 persisted, grew stronger, and shaped the criminal justice system of the early twenty-first century.

ACKNOWLEDGMENTS

For a decade, I accumulated debts relating to this project, and hence I am delighted to thank colleagues and friends and to repay them, in this very modest way, for their professional and personal generosity. I wrote this book in isolation, planted in front of my computer and surrounded only by Charlie and Millie, my faithful-but-demanding dogs. Yet I was never alone as I undertook the research, formulated my ideas, and composed the manuscript. Rather, dedicated archivists, accomplished scholars, and wonderful friends provided support and advice at every turn.

I could not have tackled this topic without the assistance of skilled archivists and librarians. I am particularly grateful to Irene Wainwright. The head archivist of the Louisiana Division/City Archives and Special Collections at the New Orleans Public Library when I began the project, Irene helped me find and secure access to key primary sources, directed me to material with which I was often unfamiliar, patiently answered my questions, and provided all manner of professional support. I have never worked with a more knowledgeable and accommodating archivist. The interlibrary loan staff at the Smathers Library at the University of Florida provided essential support as well. I flooded them with requests for obscure articles and seemingly endless runs of early twentieth-century newspapers, and they were efficient and resourceful.

Four student research assistants also helped me. I am pleased to thank to Jessica Vena, Tamar Ditzian, and Eric Poche for their careful work. Robert Zuchowski, then a graduate student at Loyola University New Orleans, provided stellar research assistance. Smart, creative, and diligent, he was tireless in hunting down material for me.

Over the lifespan of this project, I received generous support from my home institution, the University of Florida. The Department of History, and particularly my department chairs, created an environment that encouraged scholarship. Sean Adams was especially helpful and assisted in myriad ways, including arranging for me to have financial support from the department's Subvention Fund. Brennan Ryan, a former student, provided unexpected and much-appreciated support. The College of Liberal Arts and Sciences made important contributions at two crucial points. I launched this project with research funds from a Waldo W. Neikirk Term Professorship and completed the book during a sabbatical year provided by the college.

It has been an absolute joy to work with the University of Chicago Press. I have always had good experiences with university press editors, but Tim Mennel, an executive editor at the University of Chicago Press, has been the best. He has been extraordinarily accommodating and professional and offered astute comments on the manuscript. Tim Gilfoyle, the series editor for the University of Chicago Press, deserves special thanks. From our first discussion about this project, he has been enthusiastic and intellectually generous. Tim also provided me with an invaluable close reading of the manuscript, drawing from his expertise in the field and his experience as a series editor. His perceptive comments and thoughtful suggestions, always constructive, significantly improved the book both substantively and stylistically. I feel very fortunate to have worked with Tim. The press's anonymous readers offered well-informed, insightful reviews that also strengthened my analysis and sharpened my argument.

Friends could not have been more helpful. They commented on conference papers, drafts of journal articles, and chapters of the book. Moreover, they directed me to sources, shared their research, introduced me to new ideas, and encouraged me to work through my unformed, often half-baked interpretations. Many of these scholars are not historians, and they guided me to methodological and theoretical perspectives from their home disciplines, ranging from psychology and law to sociology and criminology. One of the delights of working in this research area has been discovering a circle of scholars and friends for whom such collegiality is the norm. Even as I peppered them with questions and inundated them with essays and chapters to read, they remained unfailingly generous and constructive. Listing their names is hardly adequate repayment for the intellectual debts I incurred along the way, but nonetheless I am pleased to thank Mark Fondicaro, Leonard Beeghley,

Doug Eckberg, Dee Wood Harper, Sara Bacon, Barry Latzer, Dave Khey, Cynthia Grant Bowman, Elizabeth Dale, Joe Spillane, Tom Gallant, Brandon Jett, Khalil Gibran Muhammad, the late Eric Monkkonen, David Johnson, the late Eric Schneider, Randy Roth, and the late Arnie Hirsch. I am especially indebted to Matt Gallman and Carolyn Conley. They read every word of every conference paper, article, and book chapter, provided trenchant comments, and always did so with good cheer and remarkable speed.

Another group of friends provided less-tangible but also important support, particularly during a recent health crisis. In addition to Matt and Carolyn, Dave Colburn, Nina Caputo, Mitch Hart, Juliana Barr, Luise White, Richard Scher, Aida Hozic, and Mark Hirsch have been extremely generous. My sister and brother-in-law, Nancy and Jim Olsen, have been terrific as well. I am also grateful that they have put up with my research obsessions and allowed me to hijack the conversation at numerous dinner parties and holiday celebrations. Much too frequently, someone made the mistake of asking a benign, polite question about my research, and I proved unable to resist the impulse to prattle on and on about the amygdala and implicit bias, the correlation between mortality rates and economic cycles, or the lethality of gunshot wounds versus stabbing injuries—hardly the stuff of light-hearted, dinner-party banter.

Finally, and most important, I want to thank Barbara Mennel, though I am not sure where to begin. She read every article and chapter and always offered incisive and constructive comments. I also besieged her with the fragments, heaping mountains of tables and graphs in her direction and saddling her with all the inchoate ideas and clumsy sentences that tormented me. But her contributions to this book extended far beyond intellectual help. Barbara's love, companionship, and generosity have sustained me for the past decade.

A dataset including every homicide occurring in New Orleans between 1920 and 1945—a total of 2,118 cases—provided the foundation for my analysis of crime and punishment in this study. To construct this file, I consulted a wide range of sources, used each to add and verify information, and assembled the information, layer by layer and source by source. Police case files formed the core layer.[1] New Orleans policemen responding to reports of lethal violence completed a printed form on every case they investigated. At the top of these "Homicide Reports," the officers recorded basic demographic information, noting the name, address, age, race, and occupation of both the "person killed" and the "accused." In addition, policemen identified the location, time, and weapon used in each homicide, indicated who reported the crime or discovered the corpse and when he or she contacted the local precinct house, and listed witnesses. Each record also included a "Detailed Report," cataloging the crime scene, summarizing witnesses' accounts of the homicide, recounting the events leading up to the violence, and describing the deadly encounter. This narrative typically filled two pages, though some were brief and others extended for many pages. At the conclusion of each case record, the policemen indicated the disposition of the body—in a local hospital or sent directly to the morgue. Many of the reports included updates on the cases, such as the recommendations of the district attorney or the status of ongoing investigations, particularly when the suspects were not immediately apprehended.

For the second layer of information, I consulted coroner's records, examining both the coroner's Record Book Journals, which constituted a kind of intake ledger, and the individual autopsy reports on every corpse in the city between 1920 and 1945.[2] Each entry in the Journal listed the name, address, sex, race, age, marital status, occupation, "time in city," place of birth, and the date and time of death of the decedent. I used such information to corroborate the demographic data contained in the police files and to add demographic information about each victim, such as his or her marital status and place of birth. Every autopsy report featured a detailed explanation of the cause of death, noting the specific nature of the injuries. The reports also identified the location of death and provided still more demographic information, such as the height and weight of the corpse.[3] Once again, I added this information to the dataset and verified the information culled from the police files and the coroner's intake registers.

The coroner's records identified more homicide victims than the police files. But this discrepancy reflected the distinct missions of the police and the coroner. The police reports included cases in which homicide victims were killed in the city and represented the start of a criminal investigation. By contrast, the coroner's files identified those who died in the city and focused on the cause of death. Because New Orleans was the major urban center in a rural region, country sheriffs and relatives often transported badly injured rural dwellers to the city's hospitals for treatment. If they died in New Orleans, typically in Charity Hospital, these victims were autopsied by the parish coroner and listed in his records, even though they had been shot in New Iberia or stabbed in Ponchatoula. Using the information on the location where the injuries were inflicted, I eliminated countryside cases from my dataset, and then the police and coroner's lists of homicide victims became nearly identical, with a difference of only 1 percent, indicating that the police files were virtually complete. Not surprisingly, the tiny number of New Orleans cases included in the coroner's records but missing from the police records often involved police homicides. Detectives who dispensed fatal beatings to suspects sometimes chose to label such deaths "accidental." In these instances, I deferred to the coroner's determination of the cause of death (and to his descriptions of the nature of the injuries) and added the cases to my homicide dataset. When I then compared the total number of homicide cases for each year with other sources—annual tallies from the local health department, federal mortality records, FBI reports (after 1930), Frederick Hoffman's yearly reviews of homicide, and occasional newspaper counts—the figures roughly matched, though Hoffman culled his figures from federal mortality records, and hence both sources, like the coroner's files, included cases where the violence took place in the hinterland but the death occurred in the city. This record-linkage technique, the checking and rechecking protocol, confirmed the comprehensiveness of the police reports and the completeness of my dataset. A 1946 external investigation of the city's police department, which offered a scathing overall assessment of the institution, termed the "local records of homicide" "complete" as well.[4] It would be naïve to conclude that my list of homicides—and therefore my dataset—is, in fact, complete, though, based on comparisons with numerous other sources, it appears to be close to complete. Moreover, with more than two thousand total cases, a few missing homicides would have little effect on the quantitative evidence at the heart of my analysis.

Eight years (1920, 1932–34, 1936–37, 1940, and 1944), however, are missing from the police homicide reports. Drawing from the coroner's records, I identified the homicide cases from these years and added them to the dataset. Hence, I am confident that my data files include nearly every New Orleans homicide between 1920 and 1945.

Beginning with the police and coroner's reports, I then created two files. First, I assembled a file that combined every homicide into a single dataset for quantitative analysis. With 2,118 cases and forty-six different variables for each case, the dataset included demographic information about both the victim and the killer, such as age, race, place of birth, and occupation. Furthermore, I included data about each homicide, noting, for example, the setting where the violence occurred, the time and day of the altercation, the weapon used in the attack, the motive of the killer, and the relationship between the assailant and the victim. In addition, each case included information on the legal disposition of the homicide, indicating whether the killer was tried and convicted, the length of his or her prison sentence, and the number of years served in state penal institutions.

The second file focused on qualitative evidence and particularly drew from the narrative portion of the Homicide Reports. I was especially interested in the triggers for the bloody clashes and the background context that explained why seemingly trivial disputes exploded into vicious murders. Such information, however, tended to be subjective and sometimes contrived as killers attempted to shift blame to their victims, as witnesses offered conflicting or self-serving accounts, and as white cops drew facile and hasty conclusions about the wellsprings of violence in African American homes and neighborhoods.

Next, I traced every killer and every victim into census records.[5] This source provided more demographic data, which corroborated or refined the information drawn from police files and coroner's records. Furthermore, census data placed individuals within households, revealing the presence of lodgers and children in homes and the marital status of killers and victims. Once again, such data enabled me to confirm, revise, or add precision to the background information in my dataset.

I then traced every assailant to correctional institutions. Needless to say, only convicted killers appeared in census enumerations or the convict files of the Louisiana State Penal Farm at Angola.[6] These sources, especially the convict records, yielded new details about convicted killers, including information about their levels of literary, descriptions of their bodies (noting scars and tattoos), the amount of the time the inmates served, and any disciplinary problems that surfaced at the correctional institution. If the coroner's records helped to complete the profiles of the victims, the prison records provided fuller portraits of the killers.

New Orleans newspapers formed the next layer for both my dataset and my qualitative file. I traced every homicide into four local newspapers, the *New Orleans Times-Picayune*, the *New Orleans Item*, the *New Orleans States*, and the city's African American newspaper, the *Louisiana Weekly*, which commenced publication in 1925.[7] I found accounts of 89.2 percent of the homicides in these newspapers. Coverage, however, varied wildly but predictably, depending on the details of the cases and the backgrounds of the killers and victims. Some reports, particularly accounts of African American domestic violence appearing in white dailies, were brief and perfunctory, largely serving as filler on the interior pages of the newspapers. Other homicides commanded careful, comprehensive treatment, and crime-beat reporters tracked and recounted every twist and turn, describing the crimes, the arrests and interrogations of the suspects, the court testimony, and the disposition of the cases as they moved through the criminal justice system. Still other newspaper coverage tended to be almost voyeuristic. Not surprisingly, the *Louisiana Weekly* provided the richest and most judicious reporting on cases involving African American New Orleanians. During this era, crime-beat reporters had nearly unfettered access to homicide suspects and frequently interviewed killers as they sat in police station cells. Journalists even observed detectives' and prosecutors' interrogations of the assailants. Thus, newspapers frequently summarized or even printed full transcripts of interrogations and confessions. Editors also published suicide notes and salacious explanations from friends, relatives, and enemies of both the killers and their victims. Newspapers printed sensational, almost lurid stories of the murders that stirred public anxieties, that offered morality tales, or that exposed the steamy underbelly of life in a city already regarded as scandalous.

Such newspaper accounts, though occasionally filled with rumors and unsupported allegations, provided rich detail, particularly for my qualitative file. Reading every day's editions of these newspapers also provided crucial context, enabling me to understand developments in criminal justice unrelated to specific homicide cases. Reporters tracked changing police strategies, shifts in local political currents that influenced law enforcement and sentencing, and popular reactions to crime and disorder in the city.

I also traced every homicide through a remarkable set of police records containing transcripts of witness testimony.[8] The files include verbatim statements by witnesses to the homicides but also some transcripts of interrogations of suspects and even a few transcripts of interviews with dying homicide victims, typically conducted at local hospitals. These extraordinary records have survived for 1930–33, 1935–38, 1940–42, and 1945. In every way, the witness files are uneven. With no discernable pattern, some case files include numerous witness testimonies, while other homicides do not appear in the records. Moreover, some of the testimony is brief and nonsubstantive, while other transcripts are lengthy, detailed, gossip filled, and immensely revealing about the process through which prosaic disagreements triggered brutal murders. The transcripts seem true to the testimony of the witnesses, for the language is often crude, profane, and filled with the kinds of grammatical mistakes that clerks typically correct. Witnesses always signed the accounts, with an *X* when they were illiterate. These documents provide a unique window into daily life in the roughest neighborhoods of early twentieth-century New Orleans as killers, victims, and witnesses spoke for themselves and provided open-ended, free-form explanations for the homicides. Hence, the statements of witnesses added significantly to the qualitative file, injecting a level of context that is difficult to find, since even trial testimony is typically shaped and guided by attorneys.

Court records constituted the next layer of sources on crime and punishment in the city. Two caches of such records have survived. First, the City Archives holds dozens of manuscript files for the period between 1920 and 1933.[9] As with the witness files, some case records have survived, while others have not. These files often contain a full range of documents, including interview transcripts, court filings and petitions, witness lists, receipts for expenses, such as the cost of transporting suspects or the fees paid to expert witnesses, and even medical records. Other case files hold only the formal document charging the suspect with manslaughter or murder. The information included in these records provided new information for my dataset, particularly about the motive of the killers and his or her background, as well as rich material for my qualitative file, especially when transcripts of interviews and interrogations with suspects survived.

Case files from the Supreme Court of Louisiana constitute the second set of court records.[10] Held at the Earl K. Long Library at the University of New Orleans, the collection includes homicide trials in which defendants appealed verdicts to the state's highest court. Thus, these are formal, printed appellate records. In some cases, appeals hinged on particular testimony, and therefore the relevant excerpts from trial transcripts, many of which are lengthy, are contained in the records. Moreover, every file included sentencing information. As a result, the Supreme Court records provide both additional detail for the dataset and narrative material for the qualitative file.

Finally, I consulted a broad range of other primary sources to understand the social and political context of New Orleans between 1920 and 1945. Institutional records proved to be especially useful. The papers of the New Orleans branch of the National Association for the Advancement of Colored People, for example, provided important perspectives on race relations and civil rights in the city, while the papers of the Louisiana League for the Preservation of Constitutional Rights overflowed with rich material on police brutality.[11] Similarly, two very different investigations of the New Orleans police offered a context for understanding law enforcement in the city and particularly for making sense of police violence.[12] A broad range of guidebooks, travel accounts, and ethnographies, particularly Allison Davis and John Dollard's *Children of Bondage*, provided valuable insights into local conditions as well.[13]

I analyzed the dataset of homicide cases using both descriptive and inferential statistics. To understand the relationships between and among variables, for example, I relied on frequency distributions, two-, three-, four-, and five-way cross-tabulations, and multiple regression analysis. Perhaps as in every large dataset, there was some unevenness. My coding protocol was cautious; wherever possible, I checked each entry against multiple primary sources and relied on common sense to resolve discrepancies. If four sources indicated a killer was between twenty-three and twenty-seven years of age and the fifth source listed him as seventy-five, I assumed that the correct age was roughly twenty-five. But there were judgment calls, particularly in determining motives and relationships between assailants and victims, and the dataset sometimes had missing information, such as the details about killers who were never identified or apprehended. Fortunately, the overwhelming majority of assailants, unapologetic about their actions, remained on the crime scene, and often crowed about their triumphs until patrolmen carted them away.

Calculating conviction rates and charting sentencing patterns proved to be particularly challenging. Here I especially relied on consulting a wide range of sources, since no single one provided information on the legal disposition of cases. Many of the police files included updates that revealed the fate of the killer. Trial records always provided this information, though the lion's share of killers never saw the inside of a courtroom. Newspapers typically covered court proceedings and also published lists of convicts being transported to correctional facilities and lists of those who escaped from the State Penal Farm. Local newspapers printed announcements of prisoners seeking pardons and commutations as well. Executions elicited widespread interests, and New Orleans newspapers always covered hangings and electrocutions. Furthermore, I looked for convicted killers in the records of the institution that would incarcerate them, the State Penal Farm at Angola.

But most cases disappeared from the public record without explanation. Contemporary legal scholars termed this the "mortality rate" for cases, since the records suddenly disappeared and were said to have died.[14] In nearly all such cases, prosecutors "dropped," "dismissed," or "eliminated" the charges without explanation and discharged the suspects. During this era, district attorneys in Louisiana (and in most other states) had "practically unlimited" discretion and could (and did) make charges and cases disappear with the sweep of a pen.[15] Thus, according to early twentieth-century legal experts, the cases that disappeared without a trace were dropped or dismissed through the exercise of prosecutorial discretion. The mortality rate of my homicide cases, fluctuating in the two-thirds range, was consistent with the findings revealed in 1920s "crime surveys."[16] Moreover, my figures roughly matched the rate identified by a 1931 researcher, who had access to court files that have not survived.[17] Furthermore, the proportion of convictions that I calculated was very close to those episodically published in newspapers or announced by district attorneys.[18] The figures, however, never matched perfectly. Newspaper conviction statistics, like the conviction rates trumpeted by local prosecutors, always indicated the number of guilty pleas or verdicts secured in a given year. My dataset was organized by the date of the crime, rather than by the date of the conviction. Hence, when prosecutions extended across calendar years, my figures failed to align precisely with those calculated by journalists and district attorneys. But the numbers remained very close. In short, my calculations of the efficiency of the New Orleans criminal justice system matched the estimates and conclusions of 1920s and 1930s analysts.

Analyzing the evidence in the qualitative file posed different challenges. Some witness testimony, for example, was simply unreliable. Early twentieth-century New Orleanians, needless to say, did not use the phrase "implicit bias," but in an age when overt racism was normative, eyewitness observers were even more likely than modern witnesses to see what they expected and to offer descriptions that neatly conformed to their racial ideologies. Moreover, killers, victims, and witnesses distorted their testimony and even prevaricated for myriad reasons—as is the case in modern police investigations and courtroom testimony.

Furthermore, the volume of source material reflected an endemic mismatch between newspaper coverage and typicality. The most extreme, unusual, strange cases commanded the greatest public interest, while the commonplace forms of lethal violence seemed entirely uninteresting to crime-beat reporters and newspaper readers. Even district attorneys, because they were elected officials and eager to please their constituents, tended to pursue the spectacular cases, those fueled by bizarre circumstances, more often than they prosecuted assailants who committed ordinary, prosaic homicides. African American attacks on white New Orleanians, for example, comprised 3.4 percent of the city's homicides between 1920 and 1945. Yet this tiny cluster of cases dominated newspaper coverage of violent crime. Moreover, policemen vigorously investigated such cases, and the prosecutors who were content to drop charges in two-thirds of homicide cases aggressively tried these killers and secured both convictions and capital verdicts. As a consequence, there was an inverse relationship between the volume of surviving material and the typicality of cases. Newspaper coverage and court records, though immensely revealing about the operation of the criminal justice and the behavior of New Orleanians, conveyed a skewed picture of violent crime in the city, and scholars consulting only these records run the risk of mistaking the "barnacles for the boat."[19] To avoid overlooking the proverbial boat, I relied on quantitative evidence to guide my examination of qualitative evidence and used the confessions, dying declarations, witness statements, courtroom testimony, and the observations of local journalists, judges, and politicians to explain the trends that emerged from the larger quantitative analysis.

In sum, *Murder in New Orleans: The Creation of Jim Crow Policing* employed the methodologies of microhistory. Tapping local records and employing record-linkage and data-analysis techniques, I created 2,118 detailed case files, combined them into a single dataset, gathered qualitative evidence, interwove them, and explored New Orleans homicide in order to examine wider, translocal trends in early twentieth-century crime and punishment. I checked entries in my dataset against multiple sources, and I used descriptive and inferential statistics to identify larger patterns, to guide my interpretations of qualitative sources, and to connect New Orleans currents to broader social and legal changes. These overlapping methodological approaches shaped my analysis of the ways in which patterns of lethal violence, shifts in criminal justice, and trends in race relations collided and influenced one another in New Orleans and in other American cities between 1920 and 1945.

NOTES

INTRODUCTION

1. "Pistol Toters Are Assailed by Dr. Matas," *New Orleans Times-Picayune*, January 27, 1926, p. 3.

2. The statistician Frederick L. Hoffman tracked homicide rates during the early twentieth century, culling data from federal mortality figures. See Hoffman, "The Homicide Record for 1925," *The Spectator* 116 (April 1, 1926): 4, 37–38; Hoffman, "The Homicide Record of 1927," *The Spectator* 120 (March 29, 1928): 8, 40–41; Hoffman, "The Homicide Record for 1929," *The Spectator* 124 (March 20, 1930): 19; Hoffman, "Murder and the Death Penalty," *Current History* 28 (June 1928): 408–10. For a perceptive analysis of Hoffman's controversial views about race and crime, see Khalil Gibran Muhammad, *The Condemnation of Blackness: Race, Crime, and the Making of Urban America* (Cambridge, MA: Harvard University Press, 2010), 35–87.

3. Homicide "rates" consist of the number of homicides in a year per 100,000 residents. The same is true for segments of the population—e.g., the male homicide rate is the annual number of homicides committed by males per 100,000 male residents. Unlike raw numbers, rates can be compared from group to group or place to place, regardless of the specific size of the local population.

4. Because I explore the link between crime and punishment, an eclectic range of theoretical perspectives informs my analysis. Particularly important are Donald Black, "Crime as Social Control," *American Sociological Review* 48 (February 1983): 34–45; Tom R. Tyler, *Why People Obey the Law* (New Haven, CT: Yale University Press, 1990); Robert J. Sampson and Dawn Jeglum Bartusch, "Legal Cynicism and (Subcultural?) Tolerance of Deviance: The Neighborhood Context of Racial Differences," *Law and Society Review* 32 (December 1998): 777–804; Gary LaFree, *Losing Legitimacy: Street Crime and the Decline of Social Institutions in America* (Boulder, CO: Westview, 1998); Elijah Anderson, *Code of the Street: Decency, Violence, and the Moral Life of the Inner City* (New York: Norton, 1999); Roger V. Gould, *Collision of Wills: How Ambiguity about Social Rank Breeds Conflict* (Chicago: University of Chicago Press, 2003); Martin Daly and Margo Wilson, *Homicide* (Hawthorne, NY: Aldine de Gruyter, 1988); Michael P. Johnson, *A Typology of Domestic Violence: Intimate Terrorism, Violent Resistance,*

and Situational Couple Violence (Boston: Northeastern University Press, 2008); Malcolm D. Holmes and Brad W. Smith, *Race and Police Brutality: Roots of an Urban Dilemma* (Albany: State University of New York Press, 2008); Jennifer L. Eberhardt, Phillip Atiba Goff, Valerie J. Purdie, and Paul G. Davies, "Seeing Black: Race, Crime, and Visual Processing," *Journal of Personality and Social Psychology* 87 (December 2004): 876–93.

5. For the emergence of a binary racial framework in interwar New Orleans, see Allison Davis and John Dollard, *Children of Bondage: The Personality Development of Negro Youth in the Urban South* (Washington, DC: American Council of Education, 1940), xxvi, 135; Allison Davis, "How It Feels to be Lower Caste" (typescript), Series V, Subseries 3, Box 32, Folder 14, p. 31, Allison Davis Papers, Special Collections Research Center, University of Chicago, Chicago, IL; *Sunseri v. Cassagne*, 191 La. 209 (1938); Alecia P. Long, *The Great Southern Babylon: Sex, Race, and Respectability in New Orleans, 1865–1920* (Baton Rouge: Louisiana State University Press, 2004), 222–23; Michelle Brattain, "Miscegenation and Competing Definitions of Race in Twentieth-Century Louisiana," *Journal of Southern History* 71 (August 2005): 621–58; Arnold R. Hirsch, "Simply a Matter of Black and White: The Transformation of Race and Politics in Twentieth-Century New Orleans," in *Creole New Orleans: Race and Americanization*, ed. Arnold R. Hirsch and Joseph Logsdon (Baton Rouge: Louisiana State University Press, 1992), 318. The primary sources relating to homicide in early twentieth-century New Orleans, ranging from police files and coroner's inquest reports to trial records, identified killers, victims, and witnesses, without exception, as either "white" or "Negro"/"Colored." White cops, coroners, court reporters, attorneys, census takers, prison officials, and journalists never used categories such as "Creole," "Mulatto," or "Quadroon." Nor did African American New Orleanians employ these terms. Even in sources in which African American residents spoke for themselves, such as in the transcripts of witness testimony, confessions, dying declarations, or articles about violence in the local African American newspaper, they relied on a binary racial framework. I am confident that white police clerks and court reporters did not alter the language of these documents, for witness statements, for example, were often filled with profanities and frequently used the label "Nigger"—but never any of the more fluid racial categories employed so commonly in the city during earlier periods. In part, this might have reflected the class backgrounds of those most often involved in violent episodes. Whereas "Creole" residents dominated the African American socioeconomic and cultural elite in the city, nearly all homicide victims, killers, and witnesses were drawn from the local working class. More important, Jim Crow policies and cultural conventions increasingly squeezed African American residents into a single racial category during this period. A similar process, begun earlier in the century, folded New Orleanians of European extraction into a single racial rubric. At the end of the nineteenth century, many native-born residents viewed Italian immigrants, particularly Sicilian newcomers, as racially distinct. In part because of worsening black-white relations, these immigrants became, in the eyes of old-stock, white New Orleanians, paler or whiter over time. By the 1920s, the hitherto "swarthy," "dark" immigrants became "white" in census records, police files, trial transcripts, and coroner's reports. On these racial transformations, see Louise R. Edwards-Simpson, "Sicilian Immigration to New Orleans, 1870–1910: Ethnicity, Race and Social Position in the New South" (Ph.D. dissertation, University of Minnesota, 1996). Local legal records also employed a binary framework regarding sexual orientation. In only a single homicide between 1920 and 1945 (the fatal stabbing of Willie Jackson on November 27, 1943) did any source allude to a gay killer or victim.

6. In 1920, immigrants comprised at least one-quarter of the residents of most major American cities, including Detroit, Boston, New York City, Chicago, Buffalo, San Francisco, Seattle, Newark, and Cleveland, making New Orleans an outlier. See Niles Carpenter, *Immigrants and Their Children, 1920* (Washington, DC: Government Printing Office, 1927), 24.

7. The one caveat to this statement concerns infanticide. In New Orleans, and elsewhere in the early twentieth-century United States, police officers and prosecutors typically did not include the killing of infants in the criminal offense of "homicide."

8. To confirm this, I compared police records with coroner's reports and found nearly identical "homicide" designations. Thus, local cops and the physicians who conducted autopsies defined homicide the same way.

9. Drew Gilpin Faust termed crime "an inherently political notion," noting that it "exists less in objective reality than in the eye of the beholder." But this cautionary tale applies to non-homicides more than to homicides, for cases of lethal violence, while often dismissed by prosecutors, judges, or jurors as "self-defense" or "justifiable homicide," were, in fact, systematically identified and recorded. Scholars consulting and cross-checking police records, coroner's records, public health records, newspaper tallies, and myriad other sources have confirmed this view. See Faust, "Southern Violence Revisited," *Reviews in American History* 13 (June 1985): 208.

10. For a discussion of this methodological issue by a leading scholar of homicide, see Martin Daly, *Killing the Competition: Economic Inequality and Homicide* (New Brunswick, NJ: Transaction, 2016), 13.

11. For important studies that link rates of American lethal violence to broader social changes, see Roger Lane, *Violent Death in the City: Suicide, Accident, and Murder in Nineteenth-Century Philadelphia* (Cambridge, MA: Harvard University Press, 1979); Roger Lane, *Roots of Violence in Black Philadelphia, 1860–1900* (Cambridge, MA: Harvard University Press, 1986); Roger Lane, *Murder in America: A History* (Columbus: Ohio State University Press, 1997); Eric H. Monkkonen, *Murder in New York City* (Berkeley: University of California Press, 2001); Randolph Roth, *American Homicide* (Cambridge, MA: Harvard University Press, 2009); Barry Latzer, *The Rise and Fall of Violent Crime in America* (New York: Encounter Books, 2016).

12. For important works on Jim Crow that shaped my analysis, see Gunnar Myrdal, *An American Dilemma: The Negro Problem and Modern Democracy*, 2 vols. (1944; rpt. with an introduction by Sissela Bok, New Brunswick, NJ: Transaction, 1962); Stephen A. Berrey, *The Jim Crow Routine: Everyday Performances of Race, Civil Rights, and Segregation in Mississippi* (Chapel Hill: University of North Carolina Press, 2015); Grace Elizabeth Hale, *Making Whiteness: The Culture of Segregation in the South, 1890–1940* (New York: Vintage, 1998); Jennifer Ritterhouse, *Growing Up Jim Crow: How Black and White Children Learned Race* (Chapel Hill: University of North Carolina Press, 2006); Stephanie Cole and Natalie J. Ring, eds., *The Folly of Jim Crow: Rethinking the Segregated South* (Dallas: Texas A&M Press, 2012); Jane Dailey, Glenda Elizabeth Gilmore, and Bryant Simon, eds., *Jumpin' Jim Crow: Southern Politics from Civil War to Civil Rights* (Princeton, NJ: Princeton University Press, 2000). Adam Fairclough termed the period between the late 1930s and the mid-1950s "the first act of a two-act play" about the civil rights movement in Louisiana. See Fairclough, *Race and Democracy: The Civil Rights Struggle in Louisiana, 1915–1972* (Athens: University of Georgia Press, 1995), xii.

13. The appendix provides a detailed description of these sources—and a discussion of how I used them.

14. For late twentieth-century New Orleans, see Leonard N. Moore, *Black Rage in New Orleans: Police Brutality and African American Activism from World War II to Katrina* (Baton Rouge: Louisiana State University Press, 2010). For late twentieth-century developments in criminal justice in the United States, see Michelle Alexander, *The New Jim Crow: Mass Incarceration in the Age of Colorblindness* (New York: New Press, 2010); Jonathan Simon, *Governing through Crime: How the War on Crime Transformed American Democracy and Created a Culture of Fear* (New York: Oxford University Press, 2007); Todd R. Clear and Natasha A. Frost, *The Punishment Imperative: The Rise and Failure of Mass Incarceration in America* (New York: New York University Press, 2014); William J. Stuntz, *The Collapse of American Criminal Justice* (Cambridge, MA: Harvard University Press, 2011); Elizabeth Hinton, *From the War on Poverty to the War on Crime: The Making of Mass Incarceration in America* (Cambridge, MA: Harvard University Press, 2016).

CHAPTER 1

1. "Report of Homicide of Thomas J. Peppitone," January 18, 1923, Homicide Reports, Department of Police, City of New Orleans, City Archives/Louisiana Division, New Orleans Public Library, New Orleans, LA [hereafter "Homicide Reports"]; "Former Member of Terminal Gang Shot and Killed," *New Orleans Times-Picayune*, January 19, 1923, pp. 1, 2. Police records identified the victim as "Peppitone," while newspaper accounts referred to him as "Pepitone."

2. "Former Member of Terminal Gang Shot and Killed," *New Orleans Times-Picayune*, January 19, 1923, pp. 1, 2.

3. "Slayer Silent after Killing of Pepitone," *New Orleans Item*, January 19, 1923, p. 10.

4. "Ray Warns City Thuggery Looms under Behrman," *New Orleans Times-Picayune*, January 26, 1925, p. 28.

5. "Slayer Silent after Killing of Pepitone," *New Orleans Item*, January 19, 1923, p. 10.

6. "Ray Warns City Thuggery Looms under Behrman," *New Orleans Times-Picayune*, January 26, 1925, p. 28.

7. "Murder of Stassi Is Charged to Two," *New Orleans States*, October 15, 1920, p. 1.

8. "Joe Mandot Is in Danger of Having Bond Forfeited," *New Orleans Times-Picayune*, February 19, 1919, p. 8.

9. "Forty-Seven Face Night Recorder; 11 Draw Fines," *New Orleans Times-Picayune*, October 25, 1923, p. 7; "Joe Mandot Puts On His Fighting Face and Brings Man He Bonded into Court," *New Orleans Item*, February 19, 1919, p. 1; "Stassi Suspect on Bond Arrested by Police Sunday," *New Orleans States*, February 21, 1921, p. 8; "Thomas Pepitone Captured in Raid," *New Orleans Times-Picayune*, February 21, 1921, p. 3.

10. "Former Member of Terminal Gang Shot and Killed," *New Orleans Times-Picayune*, January 19, 1923, p. 2; "Gangsters Open War, One Killed in Fight," *New Orleans States*, January 19, 1923, p. 6.

11. "Report of Homicide of Christian Burkhardt," July 17, 1923, Homicide Reports; "Slayer Silent after Killing of Pepitone," *New Orleans Item*, January 19, 1923, p. 10.

12. "Gangsters Open War, One Killed in Fight," *New Orleans States*, January 19, 1923, p. 1.

13. "Former Member of Terminal Gang Shot and Killed," *New Orleans Times-Picayune*, January 19, 1923, p. 2.

14. "Report of Homicide of Thomas J. Peppitone," January 18, 1923, Homicide Reports.

15. "Gangsters Open War, One Killed in Fight," *New Orleans States*, January 19, 1923, pp. 1, 6.

16. "'Not Guilty' Verdict for Kenney in Killing," *New Orleans Item*, January 18, 1923, p. 1.

17. For southern honor, see Bertram Wyatt-Brown, *Southern Honor: Ethics and Behavior in the Old South* (New York: Oxford University Press, 1982). The dramatic shifts in New Orleans homicide between 1920 and 1945 were inconsistent with an "ethic of honor." Rates of violence fluctuated sharply and correlated with situational and structural changes in the city. Scholars embracing the notion of southern honor emphasize long-term continuity, with the social psychologists Richard E. Nisbett and Dov Cohen suggesting that this cultural code was "impervious to change." Thus, the changing levels of New Orleans violence, in combination with the absence of rules and rituals for conflict during this era, suggest that the ethic of honor fails to explain local homicide. See Nisbett and Cohen, *Culture of Honor: The Psychology of Violence in the South* (Boulder, CO: Westview, 1996), 93. Furthermore, as Martin Daly has explained, honor-based culture is not the only explanation for the quick resort to violence, particularly in response to personal insults. See Daly, *Killing the Competition: Economic Inequality and Homicide* (New Brunswick, NJ: Transaction, 2016).

18. "Harris, Accused as Woman Killer, Still at Liberty," *New Orleans Times-Picayune*, May 22, 1923, p. 2.

19. Jeffrey S. Adler, "'Spineless Judges and Shyster Lawyers': Criminal Justice in New Orleans, 1920–1945," *Journal of Social History* 49 (Summer 2016): 904–27.

20. In 1925, African American New Orleanians committed ninety-one homicides.

21. Douglas Eckberg, "Crime, Law Enforcement, and Justice," in *Historical Statistics of the United States*, vol. 5, *Governance and International Relations*, ed. Susan B. Carter, Scott Sigmund Gartner, Michael R. Haines, Alan L. Olmstead, Richard Sutch, and Gavin Wright (New York: Cambridge University Press, 2006), 239; Frederick L. Hoffman, "The Increase in Murder," *Annals of the American Academy of Political and Social Science* 125 (May 1926): 21–22.

22. *Mortality Statistics, 1920, vol. 21* (Washington, DC: Government Printing Office, 1922), 64–65; *Mortality Statistics, 1925, vol. 26* (Washington, DC: Government Printing Office, 1927), 65–85. These figures were based on the number of people who died from homicide in specific cities—rather than the number of people who were killed in the cities. In rural states, victims of violent crime were often sent to urban hospitals. When they died, the deaths were included in the city's homicide figures, blurring the distinction between those who died in the city and those who were killed in the city. While the gap was typically modest, officials in New Orleans and especially in Memphis complained that such data overstated the level of violence in their communities. Frederick L. Hoffman, a statistician for the Prudential Insurance Company, used the mortality data to write newspaper articles and an annual column on homicide for the insurance industry journal, *The Spectator*. Therefore, Hoffman relied on the higher figures, slightly exaggerating violence in many southern cities. For heated discussions of Hoffman's articles, see "The Homicide Record," *New Orleans States*, April 8, 1930, p. 8; Hoffman, "Homicide

Report of Memphis," *The Spectator* 112 (May 15, 1924): 11; J. J. Durrett and W. G. Stromquist, "A Study of Violent Deaths Registered in Atlanta, Birmingham, Memphis and New Orleans for the Years 1921 and 1922" (pamphlet; Memphis: City of Memphis, 1923); Andrew A. Bruce and Thomas S. Fitzgerald, "A Study of Crime in the City of Memphis, Tennessee," *Journal of the American Institute of Criminal Law and Criminology* 19 (August 1928): 3–124; "Misleading Homicide Figures," *Memphis Commercial Appeal*, December 1917, p. 6; "Explains Memphis Homicide Statistics," *The Spectator* 100 (February 21, 1918): 95; "Homicide in Memphis, Tenn.," *The Spectator* 114 (June 4, 1925): 7.

23. *Mortality Statistics, 1920, vol. 21*, 64–65; *Mortality Statistics, 1925, vol. 26*, 65–85, 93–108. For data, see Frederick L. Hoffman, "The Homicide Record for 1925," *The Spectator* 116 (April 1, 1926): 38; Hoffman, *The Homicide Problem* (Newark, NJ: Prudential Press, 1925); H[arrington] C[ooper] Brearley, *Homicide in the United States* (Chapel Hill: University of North Carolina Press, 1932), 209–16.

24. Bruce and Fitzgerald, "A Study of Crime," 23; Hoffman, "The Homicide Record for 1925," 38; "10,000 Murdered in America in 1923," *New York Times*, May 8, 1924, p. 31; "America Leads the World," *New York Times*, August 13, 1924, p. 14.

25. "Lowest Death Rate," *New Orleans Item*, March 18, 1922, p. 6.

26. On the sources that I consulted to assemble this dataset and the methods I employed to analyze the quantitative evidence, see the appendix.

27. These figures are based on the number of homicides per 100,000 residents over the age of fifteen.

28. Prohibition-related violence, including turf battles between criminal enterprises, accounted for 4.3 percent of early 1920s homicides—a total of fourteen killings.

29. For example, see Louis Armstrong, *Satchmo: My Life in New Orleans* (New York: Prentice Hall, 1954), 27; "Crime and Criminals," *New Orleans Item*, April 8, 1922, p. 6; Davis and Dollard, *Children of Bondage*, 49–50, 270. For important approaches to this issue, see Donald Black, "Crime as Social Control," *American Sociological Review* 48 (February 1983): 34–45; Tom R. Tyler, *Why People Obey the Law* (New Haven, CT: Yale University Press, 1990); Gary LaFree, *Losing Legitimacy: Street Crime and the Decline of Social Institutions in America* (Boulder, CO: Westview, 1998); Robert J. Sampson and Dawn Jeglum Bartusch, "Legal Cynicism and (Subcultural?) Tolerance of Deviance: The Neighborhood Context of Racial Differences," *Law and Society Review* 32 (December 1998): 777–804.

30. "Doctor Scores Toting of Guns," *New Orleans States*, January 27, 1926, p. 13.

31. "More Gunshot Wounds Given Treatment at Hospital Here than in Any Other U.S. City," *New Orleans Item*, April 22, 1925, p. 1.

32. Like other southern cities, New Orleans attracted more young women, who found work as domestic servants, than young men, who more often sought factory jobs and migrated to northern industrial centers.

33. Daphne Spain, "Race Relations and Residential Segregation in New Orleans: Two Centuries of Paradox," *Annals of the American Academy of Political and Social Science* 441 (January 1979): 89; H[arlan] W. Gilmore, "The Old New Orleans and the New: A Case for Ecology," *American Sociological Review* 9 (August 1944): 392; Harlan W. Gilmore, Warren Breed, A. L. Johnson, Leonard Reissman, and Cliff W. Wing, *1950 New Orleans Population Handbook* (New

Orleans: Urban Life Research Institute, 1953), 12; Peirce F. Lewis, *New Orleans: The Making of an Urban Landscape*, 2nd ed. (Santa Fe, NM: Center for American Places, 2003), 66.

34. New Orleans Tax Revision Commission, *A Fiscal and Administrative Survey of the City of New Orleans* (New Orleans: Brandao, 1934), 109; Lewis, *New Orleans*, 64.

35. *Fifteenth Census of the United States: 1930, Population, vol. II* (Washington, DC: Government Printing Office, 1933), 19.

36. For the housing shortage, see *Fourteenth Census of the United States Taken in the Year 1920, vol. II, Population* (Washington, DC: Government Printing Office, 1922), 1271.

37. Spain, "Race Relations and Residential Segregation in New Orleans," 90.

38. New Orleanians with mixed racial ancestry, many of them more affluent than the residents employed as servants, less often resided in these "back-yard" pockets, though the racial landscape of the city changed dramatically during this period, and a more binary racial hierarchy emerged by the 1930s. For the "back-yard pattern," see Karl E. Taeuber and Alma F. Taeuber, *Negroes in Cities: Residential Segregation and Neighborhood Change* (Chicago: Aldine, 1965), 190; Lewis, *New Orleans*, 97.

39. T. J. Woofter, *Negro Problems in Cities* (New York: Doubleday, 1928), 70–71.

40. Seeking factory employment and uneasy about competing for work against African American residents, southern and eastern European immigrants typically preferred northern industrial centers. Richard Campanella, "An Ethnic Geography of New Orleans," *Journal of American History* 94 (December 2007): 705–10; Niles Carpenter, *Immigrants and Their Children, 1920* (Washington, DC: Government Printing Office, 1927), 24.

41. Gilmore et al., *1950 New Orleans Population Handbook*, 14; Woofter, *Negro Problems in Cities*, 62.

42. *Mortality Statistics, 1920, vol. 21*, 226–27; *Mortality Statistics, 1925, vol. 26*, 70–71; Charles S. Johnson, *The Negro in American Civilization: A Study of Negro Life and Race Relations in the Light of Social Research* (New York: Henry Holt, 1930), 153.

43. "Report of Homicide of Mrs. Joseph Oppenheimer," June 24, 1924, Homicide Reports.

44. "Report of Homicide of Charles L. Robinson," February 19, 1923, Homicide Reports; "Youth Is Killed While on Porch with Relatives," *New Orleans Times-Picayune*, February 20, 1923, p. 1.

45. "Suit for Divorce Is Filed against Slayer," *New Orleans Times-Picayune*, February 27, 1923, p. 9; "Testimony of Edward E. Woolfero," *State of Louisiana v. Woolfero*, Criminal District Court, Docket #12253, 1923, Section C Case Files, City Archives/Louisiana Division, New Orleans Public Library, New Orleans, LA [hereafter "Criminal District Court Files"].

46. "Special Charge No. 22," "Testimony of Edward E. Woolfero," *State of Louisiana v. Woolfero*, Criminal District Court Files.

47. "First Story of Uptown Murder Is Told," *New Orleans States*, February 20, 1923, p. 1.

48. "Testimony of Thelma Robinson," *State of Louisiana v. Woolfero*, Criminal District Court Files.

49. "Stepfather Slays Youth: Had to Do It, Is Comment of Woolfero," *New Orleans Item*, February 20, 1923, p. 9.

50. "Report of Homicide of Charles L. Robinson," February 19, 1923, Homicide Reports.

51. "Homicide Report of Leta Pichon," February 14, 1922, Homicide Reports; "Lawyers' Tilts Delay Pichon's Slaying Trial," *New Orleans Item*, June 21, 1922, p. 1.

52. "Bad Booze Leads to Wife Murder," *New Orleans States*, February 14, 1922, p. 4; "Woman Stabbed to Death in Row about 25 Cents," *New Orleans Times-Picayune*, February 15, 1922, p. 1.

53. "Pichon Boy Testifies to Save His Father," *New Orleans States*, June 22, 1922, p. 1.

54. "First Story of Murder Told by Two Children," *New Orleans States*, February 15, 1922, p. 4.

55. "Pichon's Son, in Testimony, Helps Father," *New Orleans Item*, June 22, 1922, p. 1.

56. "Jury Gets Pichon Case after Eight Days of Hearing," *New Orleans Times-Picayune*, June 24, 1922, p. 2.

57. "Bad Booze Leads to Wife Murder," *New Orleans States*, February 14, 1922, p. 4.

58. "Pichon Boy Testifies to Save His Father," *New Orleans States*, June 22, 1922, p. 18.

59. "Homicide Report of Leta Pichon," February 14, 1922, Homicide Reports.

60. "Pichon Says Other Man Figured in Case," *New Orleans States*, February 23, 1922, p. 2.

61. "Woman Stabbed to Death in Row about 25 Cents," *New Orleans Times-Picayune*, February 15, 1922, p. 1; "Bad Booze Leads to Wife Murder," *New Orleans States*, February 14, 1922, p. 4.

62. Woofter, *Negro Problems in Cities*, 79; *Fifteenth Census of the United States: 1930, Population, vol. VI*, 67.

63. *Mortality Statistics, 1920, vol. 21*, 226–27; *Mortality Statistics, 1925, vol. 26*, 70–71.

64. Nearly half of white killers and victims held semiskilled jobs.

65. See the appendix for an explanation of my methodology. Data from newspaper reports and a 1931 Tulane University master's thesis indicate that my conviction figures are extremely accurate. For more data on conviction rates, see Adler, "Spineless Judges and Shyster Lawyers," 904–27, and Tennie Erwin Daugette, "Homicide in New Orleans" (M.A. thesis, Tulane University, 1931), 10–13.

66. The "conviction rate" rate is the proportion of homicide cases that ended with a conviction.

67. "'Safe Business' Is Law Breaking, So Records Show," *New Orleans Times-Picayune*, June 19, 1924, p. 6.

68. St. Clair Adams, "Delays Now Strangling Justice in New Orleans' Criminal Courts," *New Orleans Item*, May 8, 1925, p. 12.

69. Louis Vyhnanek, *Unorganized Crime: New Orleans in the 1920s* (Lafayette, LA: Center for Louisiana Studies, 1998), 29–48.

70. "Boy Accuses Robert Cass before Death," *New Orleans Item*, March 27, 1925, p. 2.

71. "Report of Homicide of Eugene Fabre," March 11, 1926, Homicide Reports.

72. "Report of Homicide of Fred North," August 30, 1926, Homicide Reports.

73. For example, see Armstrong, *Satchmo*, 77.

74. "Murder Laid to Cobbler's Slayer," *New Orleans States*, November 17, 1920, p. 2.

75. See Robert H. Marr, *The Criminal Jurisprudence of Louisiana* (New Orleans: Hansell & Bro., 1923), 115–26.

76. "Report of Homicide of Ralph Otillio," August 27, 1922, Homicide Reports.

77. "Four Shots Bring Eight-Year Feud to Tragic Close," *New Orleans Times-Picayune*, August 28, 1922, p. 1.

78. "'I Shot to Save My Life,' Says Slayer, 51," *New Orleans Item*, August 28, 1922, p. 2.

79. "Expect Grand Jury Laundry Report Friday," *New Orleans Item*, September 22, 1922, p. 3.

80. For the unwritten law, see Rupert B. Vance and Waller Wynne Jr., "Folk Rationalizations in the 'Unwritten Law,'" *American Journal of Sociology* 39 (January 1934): 483–92; Brearley, *Homicide in the United States*, 51; Thomas J. Kernan, "The Jurisprudence of Lawlessness," *Loyola Law Journal* 4 (April 1923): 143; Robert M. Ireland, "The Libertine Must Die: Sexual Dishonor and the Unwritten Law in the Nineteenth-Century United States," *Journal of Social History* (Fall 1989): 27–44; Hendrik Hartog, *Man and Wife in America* (Cambridge, MA: Harvard University Press, 2000), 219–37.

81. "Shooting Victim Dies at Hospital," *New Orleans Times-Picayune*, July 24, 1923, p. 5.

82. "Father Tells of Tragedy; Hint Jealousy," *New Orleans Item*, July 16, 1923, p. 1.

83. "Invokes Unwritten Law," *New Orleans Item*, July 16, 1923, p. 1.

84. "Husband Charged with Murdering Friend of Wife," *New Orleans Times-Picayune*, November 23, 1921, p. 1.

85. "Report of Homicide of Sam Lala," November 22, 1921, Homicide Reports.

86. "Unwritten Law Frees Husband," *New Orleans States*, July 28, 1922, p. 4; "Grocer Freed on 'Unwritten Law,'" *New Orleans Times-Picayune*, July 28, 1922, p. 23.

87. Marr, *The Criminal Jurisprudence of Louisiana*, 127–28. For more on this concept, see Richard Maxwell Brown, *No Duty to Retreat: Violence and Values in American History and Society* (New York: Oxford University Press, 1991).

88. Chandler C. Luzenberg, "Motion for a New Trial" and "Request for Special Charge," *State of Louisiana v. Edward E. Woolfero*, Criminal District Court Files.

89. Article XIX, Section 9 of the Louisiana Constitution declared that the jury "shall be judges of the law and of the facts." See *Constitution of the State of Louisiana, Adopted in Convention at the City of Baton Rouge, June 18, 1921* (Baton Rouge: Ramires-Jones, 1921), 119; *Louisiana v. Vinson*, 37 La. Ann. 792 (1885).

90. Richard A. Dowling, "Charge to the Jury," *State of Louisiana v. Edward E. Woolfero*, Criminal District Court Files; Marr, *The Criminal Jurisprudence of Louisiana*, 727–29.

91. *State of Louisiana v. Matt Seminary, alias Joe Nelson*, Docket #28587, April 28, 1927, pp. 2–3, Section E Case Files, Louisiana Supreme Court Case Files, Historical Archives of the Supreme Court of Louisiana, Earl K. Long Library, University of New Orleans, New Orleans, LA [hereafter "Louisiana Supreme Court Case Files"].

92. Daugette, "Homicide in New Orleans," 56.

93. Grand juries "no billed" 22.2 percent of killers, and the police failed to apprehend one-seventh of suspects. Using 1925 data, Daugette found that 71.9 percent of homicides cases with white defendants did not reach trial. My data for 1925 homicides indicate that 75.9 percent of cases did not reach trial. It is not clear how Daugette counted the cases in which killers committed suicide or the cases in which arrests were made later. These methodological issues likely account for the small difference in percentages. See Daugette, "Homicide in New Orleans," 10.

94. Ibid.

95. For example, "Boutwell Freed in Criminal Court on Slaying Writ," *New Orleans Times-Picayune*, November 23, 1928, p. 2.

96. Pamela Tyler, *Silk Stockings and Ballot Boxes: Women and Politics in New Orleans, 1920–1965* (Athens: University of Georgia Press, 1996), 28.

97. This figure is based on 141 cases.

98. Kernan, "The Jurisprudence of Lawlessness," 146–47.

99. "Woman Burglar Killer Wants Her Pistol Back," *New Orleans Times-Picayune*, January 9, 1925, p. 3; "Report of Homicide of Simon Green," January 8, 1925, Homicide Reports.

100. "Report of Homicide of Reginald Harris," March 15, 1922, Homicide Reports.

101. "Kills Neighbor for Thief; No Charges Filed," *New Orleans Item*, March 16, 1922, p. 2.

102. None of the fifteen killers was convicted.

103. The legal scholar Carolyn B. Ramsey also found high conviction rates in uxoricide cases. See Ramsey, "Domestic Violence and State Intervention in the American West and Australia, 1860–1930," *Indiana Law Journal* 86 (Winter 2011): 185–256.

104. See John Dollard, *Caste and Class in a Southern Town* (New York: Doubleday Anchor, 1937); Davis and Dollard, *Children of Bondage*; Allison Davis, Burleigh B. Gardner, and Mary Gardner, *Deep South: A Social Anthropological Study of Caste and Class* (Chicago: University of Chicago Press, 1941); Allison Davis, "Caste, Economy, and Violence," *American Journal of Sociology* 51 (July 1945): 7–15. Also see Gunnar Myrdal, *An American Dilemma: The Negro Problem and Modern Democracy*, 2 vols. (1944; rpt. with an introduction by Sissela Bok, New Brunswick, NJ: Transaction, 1962); Stephen A. Berrey, *The Jim Crow Routine: Everyday Performances of Race, Civil Rights, and Segregation in Mississippi* (Chapel Hill: University of North Carolina Press, 2015).

105. C. J. O'Niell, "Dissenting Opinion," May 23, 1927, pp. 1–3, *State v. Jesse Tolivar*, Section E Case Files, Docket #34080, Criminal District Court Files; Guy B. Johnson, "The Negro and Crime," *Annals of the American Academy of Political and Social Science* 217 (September 1941): 96–97.

106. For an important discussion of this issue, see Khalil Gibran Muhammad, *The Condemnation of Blackness: Race, Crime, and the Making of Urban America* (Cambridge, MA: Harvard University Press, 2010).

107. "Hanging Only Cure for Homicides, Says Molony," *New Orleans Item*, July 6, 1924, p. 1. Also see "Roeling and Healy Join in Plea for Capital Verdicts as 1925 Brings More Deaths of Violence," *New Orleans Times-Picayune*, January 2, 1926, p. 6; "A Study of Violent Deaths," *New Orleans Times-Picayune*, August 8, 1924, p. 8; Brearley, *Homicide in the United States*, 97–116; H[arrington] C[ooper] Brearley, "The Negro and Homicide," *Social Forces* 9 (December 1930): 247–53; Kenneth E. Barnhart, "A Study of Homicide in the United States," *Birmingham-Southern College Bulletin* 25 (May 1932): 7–37; Frederick L. Hoffman, "Murder and the Death Penalty," *Current History* 28 (June 1928): 408–10; Hoffman, "The Increase in Murder," 23–24.

108. For the "murder-town" label, see Bruce and Fitzgerald, "A Study of Crime," 3.

109. "Hanging Only Cure for Homicides, Says Molony," *New Orleans Item*, July 6, 1924, p. 1. Also see Jesse E. Steiner, "Crime and the Foreign Born: New Orleans," *National Commission on Law Observance and Enforcement, No. 10: Crime and the Foreign Born* (Washington, DC: Government Printing Office, 1931), 341. For a defense of Memphis's homicide record, see

Bruce and Fitzgerald, "A Study of Crime," 23. New Orleans and Memphis officials disputed Hoffman's conclusions in part because they felt that he paid inadequate attention to the "negro problem." See Hoffman, "Murder and the Death Penalty," 408. Hoffman's critics also argued that, by relying on mortality statistics, he held Memphis and New Orleans responsible for homicides that occurred in the surrounding regions.

110. "Murder Penalties," *New Orleans Item*, November 16, 1925, p. 10.

111. "More Gunshot Wounds Given Treatment at Hospital Here than in Any Other U.S. City," *New Orleans Item*, April 22, 1925, p. 1.

112. "High Homicide Record Here Due to Large Black Population," *New Orleans Times-Picayune*, September 24, 1924, p. 2.

113. This figure is based on 221 cases.

114. Thirteen cases of black-on-white homicide occurred in the city during the early 1920s. By comparison, there were thirty-three white-on-black homicides, accounting for 8.7 percent of lethal violence during this period.

115. "Hanging Only Cure for Homicides, Says Molony," *New Orleans Item*, July 6, 1924, p. 1.

116. These figures exclude homicides in which the killer committed suicide. Interracial homicides made up 12.7 percent of cases. For white-on-black homicides, the conviction rate was 9.1 percent, and for black-on-white homicides, the rate was 30.8 percent—meaning that even at the higher rate more than two-thirds of killers escaped punishment.

117. New Orleans experienced no lynchings during this period, and, therefore, the lower conviction rate for African American killers was not the product of white residents relying on extralegal forms of "justice." Juries, however, rarely returned capital verdicts during this period. Two of 141 white killers received death sentences, compared with two of 221 African American killers.

118. "Murder Penalties," *New Orleans Item*, November 16, 1925, p. 10.

119. Davis and Dollard, *Children of Bondage*, 6. Also see Allison Davis, "The Socialization of the American Negro Child and Adolescent," *Journal of Negro Education* 8 (July 1939): 272; David L. Cohn, *Where I Was Born and Raised* (Boston: Houghton Mifflin, 1935), 107.

120. "Gun Toting," *Louisiana Weekly*, June 25, 1927, p. 6. For similar, though more subdued, conclusions, see "An Unusual Case," *New Orleans Item*, August 22, 1927, p. 4; "Hanging Only Cure for Homicides, Says Molony," *New Orleans Item*, July 6, 1924, p. 3.

121. "High Homicide Record Here Due to Large Black Population," *New Orleans Times-Picayune*, September 24, 1924, p. 2.

122. "Check the Criminal," *Louisiana Weekly*, April 13, 1929, p. 6. Although African American New Orleanians were hardly eager to work with cops, who were simultaneously brutal and indifferent, surviving evidence challenges police assertions that these residents refused to cooperate in homicide investigations. Brandon Jett found that police and court records overflowed with cases in which African American crime victims and witnesses, for diverse reasons, worked with police investigators. Thus, police explanations for their feeble efforts to clear African American intraracial homicide cases seem self-serving and, at least in part, a convenient justification for indifference. See Jett, "African Americans and the Police in the Jim Crow South, 1900–1945" (Ph.D. dissertation, University of Florida, 2017).

123. "Enforcement Needed," *Louisiana Weekly*, April 14, 1928, p. 6.

124. "Will Justice Be Meted Out," *Louisiana Weekly*, September 3, 1927, p. 6. Also see "The Value of Negro Life," *Louisiana Weekly*, January 29, 1927, p. 6. Elite and middle-class African American residents, though concerned about police brutality, implored city officials to provide greater police protection for their community. See "The Value of Negro Life," *Louisiana Weekly*, January 29, 1927, p. 6; "Enforcement Needed," *Louisiana Weekly*, April 14, 1928, p. 6; "Killings Continue," *Louisiana Weekly*, May 19, 1928, p. 6. For studies that discuss the demands of "respectable" African Americans for improved policing, see Elijah Anderson, *Code of the Street: Decency, Violence, and the Moral Life of the Inner City* (New York: Norton, 1999); Michael Javen Fortner, *Black Silent Majority: The Rockefeller Drug Laws and the Politics of Punishment* (Cambridge, MA: Harvard University Press, 2015).

125. See "Policeman Jailed after Terrorizing Negroes at Wake," *New Orleans Times-Picayune*, December 28, 1930, p. 1; "Big Knives and Pistol Found on Negro Pair by Observing Police Officer," *New Orleans Item*, January 2, 1921, p. 5; Myrdal, *An American Dilemma* 2:542. Early twentieth-century ethnographers noted that many white southerners embraced this binary framework. See Charles S. Johnson, *Patterns of Negro Segregation* (New York: Harper & Brothers, 1943), 299; Davis, Gardner, and Gardner, *Deep South*, 503; Hortense Powdermaker, *After Freedom: A Cultural Study in the Deep South* (New York: Viking, 1939), 40; Johnson, "The Negro and Crime," 97.

126. John C. O'Connor, Augustus G. Williams, and William J. O'Hara, "Appeal from the District Court: Original Brief on Behalf of Defendant and Appellant," *State of Louisiana v. Andrew Wiebelt*, Docket #29325, May 16, 1928, pp. 18–19, Section A Case Files, Louisiana Supreme Court Case Files.

127. Davis, Gardner, and Gardner, *Deep South*, 503.

128. Pierce's upper body was covered with "cut scars"—on his stomach, left shoulder, back, and left cheek. See "Convict Record of Milton Pierce," Louisiana State Penitentiary Records, vol. 32 (1930), p. 676, accessed via Ancestry.com, September 1, 2015.

129. "Report of Homicide of Alice Royal," February 26, 1929, Homicide Reports.

130. "Testimony of [Police] Captain William Bell," *State of Louisiana v. Milton Pierce*, Docket #30045, June 8, 1929, p. 50, Louisiana Supreme Court Case Files. Also see Dollard, *Caste and Class in a Southern Town*, 282–83.

131. Such expressions of prosecutorial discretion reflected district attorneys' indifference, rather than the intervention of influential white patrons. For the latter phenomenon, see Lisa Lindquist Dorr, *White Women, Rape, and the Power of Race in Virginia, 1900–1960* (Chapel Hill: University of North Carolina Press, 2004), 97–111.

132. Daugette, "Homicide in New Orleans," 10. These figures are based on the number of "nolle prossed" cases relatives to the number of homicide cases with suspects in custody. Also see Johnson, "The Negro and Crime," 99.

133. Daugette, "Homicide in New Orleans," 15; "Check the Criminal," *Louisiana Weekly*, April 13, 1929, p. 6.

134. "Hanging Only Cure for Homicides, Says Molony," *New Orleans Item*, July 6, 1924, p. 3.

135. Dollard, *Caste and Class in a Southern Town*, 281; Davis, Gardner, and Gardner, *Deep South*, 520; Bruce and Fitzgerald, "A Study of Crime," 82; Johnson, "The Negro and Crime," 98.

136. See Daugette, "Homicide in New Orleans," 10. According to her data, in 1925, jurors acquitted 38.5 percent of African American defendants whose cases went to trial, compared with 22.2 percent of white defendants.

137. For "emotional restraint," see Davis, Gardner, and Gardner, *Deep South*, 520. For assertions of African Americans' inability to exercise self-control, see Hoffman, "The Increase in Murder," 23; Bruce and Fitzgerald, "A Study of Crime," 23; H[arrington] C[ooper] Brearley, "The Pattern of Violence," in *Culture in the South*, ed., W[illiam] T. Couch (Chapel Hill: University of North Carolina Press, 1935), 690. For a perceptive analysis of the ways in which Hoffman and other social scientists used quantitative data to support such a view, see Muhammad, *The Condemnation of Blackness*, 35-87.

138. Testimony of Dr. C. V. Unsworth, *State of Louisiana v. William Brodes*, Docket #26270, September 14, 1923, pp. 37-38, Section C Case Files, Louisiana Supreme Court Case Files.

139. "Crime and Vice," *New Orleans Item*, July 18, 1922, p. 8; "Crime and Criminals," *New Orleans Item*, April 8, 1922, p. 6.

140. "Crime and Criminals," *New Orleans Item*, April 8, 1922, p. 6. Memphis observers offered the same explanation. See Bruce and Fitzgerald, "A Study of Crime," 20.

141. N. E. Humphrey, "Charge to the Jury," *State of Louisiana v. William Johnson*, Section A Case Files, Docket #35869, pp. 7-8, October 1926, Criminal District Court Files.

142. "Prompt Trials, Death Penalty Urged by Jury," *New Orleans Item*, March 3, 1925, p. 18.

143. "Killings Continue," *Louisiana Weekly*, May 19, 1928, p. 6.

144. Bruce and Fitzgerald, "A Study of Crime," 32.

145. Davis, Gardner, and Gardner, *Deep South*, 520. Also see Hortense Powdermaker, "The Channeling of Negro Aggression by the Cultural Process," *American Journal of Sociology* 48 (May 1943): 753.

146. "Will These Murders Out?" *Louisiana Weekly*, April 18, 1931, p. 6.

147. For related analyses, see Dollard, *Caste and Class in a Southern Town*, 280; Davis, "Caste, Economy, and Violence," 11-12.

148. Davis, "The Socialization of the American Negro Child and Adolescent," 272. For a similar analysis, see Elijah Anderson, "Violence and the Inner-City Street Code," in *Violence and Childhood in the Inner City*, ed. Joan McCord (Cambridge, Eng.: Cambridge University Press, 1997), 1-15.

149. Sampson and Bartusch term this "legal cynicism." See "Legal Cynicism and (Subcultural?) Tolerance of Deviance," 777-804. Some African American residents manipulated local enforcers into assisting them. For a perceptive analysis of this strategy, see Jett, "African Americans and the Police in the Jim Crow South, 1900-1945."

150. "Check the Criminal," *Louisiana Weekly*, April 13, 1929, p. 6; Davis and Dollard, *Children of Bondage*, 270.

151. For police brutality, see K. Stephen Prince, "Remembering Robert Charles: Violence and Memory in Jim Crow New Orleans," *Journal of Southern History* 83 (May 2017): 297-328; William Ivy Hair, *Carnival of Fury: Robert Charles and the New Orleans Race Riot of 1900* (Baton Rouge: Louisiana State University Press, 1976); Leonard B. Moore, *Black Rage in New Orleans: Police Brutality and African American Activism from World War II to Hurricane Katrina* (Baton Rouge: Louisiana State University Press, 2010).

152. Armstrong, *Satchmo*, 78.

153. Ibid., 166–67.

154. Powdermaker, *After Freedom*, 174; Robert Russa Moton, *What the Negro Thinks* (New York: Doubleday, 1929), 41. Also see Anderson, "Violence and the Inner-City Street Code," 15.

155. Dollard, *Caste and Class in a Southern Town*, 271, 281.

156. "'Runs Amuck'—Or Desperation," *Louisiana Weekly*, April 23, 1933, p. 6; Dollard, *Caste and Class in a Southern Town*, 271–72; "Uses Her Wicked Blade on Rival," *Louisiana Weekly*, July 9, 1932, p. 1; Armstrong, *Satchmo*, 164–65; "Statement of Fanny Gaines relative to the fatal cutting of one Sam Hollins," October 4, 1935, Transcripts of Statements of Witnesses to Homicides, New Orleans Police Department, City of New Orleans, City Archives/Louisiana Division, New Orleans Public Library, New Orleans, LA [hereafter "Statements of Witnesses"]. Also see Davis, "The Socialization of the American Negro Child and Adolescent," 272; Leroy G. Schultz, "Why the Negro Carries Weapons," *Journal of Criminal Law, Criminology, and Police Science* 53 (December 1962): 476–83; Cohn, *Where I Was Born and Raised*, 107.

157. Racial disparities in homicide widened dramatically during the early 1920s, but even in 1920 the African American homicide rate was nearly quintuple the white rate. As Louis Armstrong explained, the existing failure of legal institutions already encouraged African American residents to be aggressively self-reliant, helping to account for this gap. The demographic and social changes of the early 1920s, however, heightened the potential for interpersonal violence and thus sharply increased the racial homicide disparity of the era. See Armstrong, *Satchmo*, 78, 166–67.

158. Testimony of Mary Williams, *State of Louisiana v. Milton Pierce*, Docket #30045, June 8, 1929, p. 27, Louisiana Supreme Court Case Files.

159. In short, this was not what the criminologist Marvin E. Wolfgang termed a "subculture of violence," where culture-based codes mandated aggression in particular circumstances. The violence was not grounded in African American cultural traditions. Instead, it was situational, a reaction to institutional failure and increasing social instability. When social conditions changed, as chapter 4 explains, homicide rates abruptly dropped, a shift far too sudden to be the product of "culture." It is implausible that deeply engrained, long-established cultural forces fueled African American violence during the early 1920s but then suddenly weakened sharply in the late 1920s, when homicide rates plunged. For Wolfgang's theory, see Wolfgang, *Patterns in Criminal Homicide* (Philadelphia: University of Pennsylvania Press, 1958); Marvin E. Wolfgang and Franco Ferracuti, *The Subculture of Violence: Toward an Integrated Theory in Criminology* (London: Tavistock, 1967). For a thoughtful, recent adaptation of Wolfgang and Ferracuti's argument, see Barry Latzer, *The Rise and Fall of Violent Crime in America* (New York: Encounter Books, 2016).

160. Davis and Dollard, *Children of Bondage*, 50. Also see Daly, *Killing the Competition*, 130.

161. Davis and Dollard, *Children of Bondage*, 50, 80. Also see Schultz, "Why the Negro Carries Weapons," 479; Jennifer Ritterhouse, *Growing Up Jim Crow: How Black and White Children Learned Race* (Chapel Hill: University of North Carolina Press, 2006), 98.

162. "Signs of the New Negro," *Louisiana Weekly*, August 29, 1931, p. 6; "Statement of Julia Jones relative to murder of Mary Frazier," July 16, 1940, Statements of Witnesses; Schultz, "Why the Negro Carries Weapons," 480.

163. Davis, "The Socialization of the American Negro Child and Adolescent," 272.

164. Armstrong, *Satchmo*, 27. Recent scholarship has established that children exposed to violence are more likely to engage in violent behavior themselves. See Anderson, "Violence and the Inner-City Street Code,"13; Miriam K. Ehrensaft and Patricia Cohen, "Contributions of Family Violence to the Intergenerational Transmission of Externalizing Behavior," *Prevention Science* 13 (August 2012): 370, 383; Miriam K. Ehrensaft, Patricia Cohen, Jocelyn Brown, Elizabeth Smailes, Henian Chen, and Jeffrey G. Johnson, "Intergenerational Transmission of Partner Violence: A 20-Year Prospective Study," *Journal of Consulting and Clinical Psychology* 71 (August 2003): 749.

165. Davis and Dollard, *Children of Bondage*, 25.

166. "Alleged Slayer Free, Witnesses Remain in Prison," *New Orleans Times-Picayune*, July 18, 1924, p. 7.

167. Armstrong, *Satchmo*, 77–78.

168. "Report of Homicide of Benny Williams," July 6, 1924, Homicide Reports.

169. "Alleged Slayer Free, Witnesses Remain in Prison," *New Orleans Times-Picayune*, July 18, 1924, p. 7.

170. "Convict Record of Willie Freeman," Louisiana State Penitentiary Records, vol. 24 (1922–24), p. 104, accessed via Ancestry.com, September 9, 2015.

171. "Report of Homicide of Hilda Mount," September 2, 1928, Homicide Records; "Convict Record of Beatrice Washington," Louisiana State Penitentiary Records, vol. 30 (1928–29), p. 404, accessed via Ancestry.com, September 13, 2015.

172. "Hanging Only Cure for Homicides," *New Orleans Item*, July 6, 1924, p. 3.

173. "A Natural Result," *New Orleans Item*, February 8, 1926, p. 12.

174. Dollard, *Caste and Class in a Southern Town*, 280. For related views, see Davis, Gardner, and Gardner, *Deep South*, 520; Powdermaker, *After Freedom*, 174.

175. For a theoretical perspective on the impact of such forces, see Robert Agnew, *Pressured into Crime: An Overview of General Strain Theory* (Los Angeles: Roxbury Publishing, 2006), 146.

176. For a related analysis of the construction of "race," see Karen E. Fields and Barbara J. Fields, *Racecraft: The Soul of Inequality in American Life* (London: Verso, 2012), 17.

CHAPTER 2

1. "Report of Homicide of Willie Hutton," November 12, 1922, Homicide Reports, Department of Police, City of New Orleans, City Archives/Louisiana Division, New Orleans Public Library, New Orleans, LA [hereafter "Homicide Reports"]; "Pine Kindlings Start Row That Ends in Killing," *New Orleans Times-Picayune*, November 13, 1922, p. 3.

2. African American New Orleanians committed 237 spousal homicides.

3. For the robbery panic, see Claire Bond Potter, *War on Crime: Bandits, G-Men, and the Politic of Mass Culture* (New Brunswick, NJ: Rutgers University Press, 1998).

4. New Orleanians overwhelmingly ignored Prohibition, and local saloons, renamed "soft-drink parlors," remained in operation through the 1920s and early 1930s. See "Drunkenness in New Orleans Has Tripled during 8 Years; 12,788 Arrested Last Year," *New Orleans Item*, May 8, 1925, p. 1; Harry T. Brundidge, "New Orleans Is Called the Wettest Spot of Country;

Other Places Merely Damp," *New Orleans Item*, August 9, 1925, pp. 1, 2; "Orleans Votes 14 to 1 against Prohibition Law," *New Orleans States*, April 4, 1930, p. 4; Joy Jackson, "Prohibition in New Orleans: The Unlikeliest Crusade," *Louisiana History* 19 (Summer 1978): 261–84.

5. Charles E. Hall, *Negroes in the United States, 1920–1932* (Washington, DC: Government Printing Office, 1935), 55.

6. See James R. Grossman, *Land of Hope: Chicago, Black Southerners, and the Great Migration* (Chicago: University of Chicago Press, 1989); Allan H. Spear, *Black Chicago: The Making of a Negro Ghetto, 1890–1920* (Chicago: University of Chicago Press, 1967); William M. Tuttle Jr., *Race Riot: Chicago in the Red Summer of 1919* (New York: Atheneum, 1975).

7. Hall, *Negroes in the United States, 1920 1932*, 85.

8. *Mortality Statistics, 1920, vol. 21* (Washington, DC: Government Printing Office, 1922), 64–65; *Mortality Statistics, 1925, vol. 26, pt. I* (Washington, DC: Government Printing Office, 1927), 282–314. Discrimination in northern cities played a significant role in the increase in violence as well. See Jeffrey S. Adler, *First in Violence, Deepest in Dirt: Homicide in Chicago, 1875–1920* (Cambridge, MA: Harvard University Press, 2006), 120–58; Jeffrey S. Adler, "Murder, North and South: Violence in Early Twentieth-Century Chicago and New Orleans," *Journal of Southern History* 74 (May 2008): 297–324.

9. Demographic changes do not, by themselves, determine homicide rates. Inequality, discrimination, political and cultural pressures, and numerous other factors—as well as the interaction of these forces—play important roles. Nonetheless, across times and space, there is a strong correlation between an excess of young men and high rates of violence. See David Courtwright, *Violent Land: Single Men and Social Disorder from the Frontier to the Inner City* (Cambridge, MA: Harvard University Press, 1996); Eric H. Monkkonen, *Murder in New York City* (Berkeley: University of California Press, 2001), 56–61; Jeffrey S. Adler, "'On the Border of Snakeland': Evolutionary Psychology and Plebeian Violence in Industrial Chicago, 1875–1920," *Journal of Social History* 36 (Spring 2003): 541–60. For an influential interdisciplinary and theoretical perspective on this issue, see Martin Daly and Margo Wilson, *Homicide* (Hawthorne, NY: Aldine de Gruyter, 1988).

10. In New Orleans in 1920, African American women held 95.7 percent of jobs in domestic service. See *Fourteenth Census of the United States Taken in the Year 1920, vol. IV, Occupations* (Washington, DC: Government Printing Office, 1923), 1157; Harlan Gilmore and Logan Wilson, "The Employment of Negro Women as Domestic Servants in New Orleans," *Social Forces* 22 (March 1944): 318–23.

11. Hall, *Negroes in the United States, 1920–1932*, 85.

12. *Fourteenth Census of the United States Taken in the Year 1920, vol. II, Population*, 320; *Fifteenth Census of the United States: 1930, Population, vol. II* (Washington, DC: Government Printing Office, 1933), 764.

13. For a related argument, see Courtwright, *Violent Land*, 52. The biopsychologist Nigel Barber argues that societies with a surplus of women tend to be extremely violent, as men become more impulsive and aggressive in their competition for sexual partners when "marital markets" tilt in their favor. See Barber, "The Sex Ratio and Female Marital Opportunity as Historical Predictors of Violent Crime in England, Scotland, and the United States," *Cross-Cultural Research* 37 (November 2003): 373–92; Barber, "Countries with Fewer Males Have

More Violent Crime: Marriage Markets and Mating Aggression," *Aggressive Behavior* 35 (January/February 2009): 49–56.

14. *Fifteenth Census of the United States: 1930, Occupations by States, vol. IV*, 631.

15. *Fourteenth Census of the United States Taken in the Year 1920, vol. IV, Occupations*, 801; *Fifteenth Census of the United States: 1930, Occupations by States, vol. IV*, 631.

16. Allison Davis and John Dollard, *Children of Bondage: The Personality Development of Negro Youth in the Urban South* (Washington, DC: American Council of Education, 1940), xxiv. Also see Hortense Powdermaker, *After Freedom: A Cultural Study in the Deep South* (New York: Viking, 1939), 146.

17. For related discussions, see Powdermaker, *After Freedom*, 145; Charles S. Johnson, *Shadow of the Plantation* (Chicago: University of Chicago Press, 1934), 48.

18. *Fifteenth Census of the United States: 1930, Population, vol. VI*, 539.

19. Davis and Dollard, *Children of Bondage*, 74. Also see John Dollard, *Caste and Class in a Southern Town* (New York: Doubleday Anchor, 1937), 414.

20. Jeffrey S. Adler, "'I Wouldn't Be No Woman if I Wouldn't Hit Him': Race, Patriarchy, and Spousal Homicide in New Orleans, 1921–1945," *Journal of Women's History* 27 (Autumn 2015): 27; Davis and Dollard, *Children of Bondage*, 74. Men's control over housing, by contrast, represented a "structural constraint," compounding women's difficulties in escaping abusive relationships. See Michael P. Johnson, "Patriarchal Terrorism and Common Couple Violence: Two Forms of Violence against Women," *Journal of Marriage and the Family* 57 (May 1995): 284.

21. For a related argument, see M. P. Baumgartner, "Violent Networks: The Origins and Management of Domestic Conflict," in *Aggression and Violence: Social Interactionist Perspectives*, ed. Richard B. Felson and James Tedeschi (Washington, DC: American Psychological Association, 1993), 209–31.

22. "Charity Hospital Appeal," *New Orleans States*, April 3, 1923, p. 12; "Find Hospitals Lack Finances," *New Orleans Item*, June 5, 1927, p. 5; "Apology Offered," *Louisiana Weekly*, March 13, 1926, p. 1.

23. For the development of the city's African American community, see Donald E. Devore, *Defying Jim Crow: African American Community Development and the Struggle for Racial Equality in New Orleans, 1900–1960* (Baton Rouge: Louisiana State University Press, 2015); Michele Grigsby Coffey, "Providing for Our Communities, Protecting Our Race, Proving Ourselves: African American Activism and Protest in Depression Era New Orleans" (Ph.D. dissertation, University of South Carolina, 2010); Sharlene Sinegal DeCuir, "Attacking Jim Crow: Black Activism in New Orleans" (Ph.D. dissertation, Louisiana State University, 2009).

24. For example, see "Mistreated; Kills Mate," *Louisiana Weekly*, October 14, 1939, p. 2. For a theoretical perspective on such institutional discrimination, see Kimberle Crenshaw, "Mapping the Margins: Intersectionality, Identity Politics, and Violence against Women of Color," *Stanford Law Review* 43 (July 1991): 1241–99.

25. Donald Black, "Crime as Social Control," *American Sociological Review* 48 (February 1983): 41.

26. Dollard, *Caste and Class in a Southern Town*, 414. Also see Johnson, "Patriarchal Terrorism and Common Couple Violence," 284.

27. Adler, "'I Wouldn't Be No Woman if I Wouldn't Hit Him,'" 28.

28. For one example, see "Was Crazed by Jibes and Tales of Other Loves," *New Orleans Item*, November 1, 1927, p. 1.

29. Powdermaker, *After Freedom*, 149; E. Franklin Frazier, *The Negro Family in the United States* (1939; rpt. Notre Dame, IN: University of Notre Dame Press, 2001), 133–34; Johnson, *Shadow of the Plantation*, 40–46.

30. Cynthia Grant Bowman, "A Feminist Proposal to Bring Back Common Law Marriage," *Oregon Law Review* 75 (Fall 1996): 712–13; Nancy Cott, *Public Vows: A History of Marriage and the Nation* (Cambridge, MA: Harvard University Press, 2000), 31; Laura Edwards, "'The Marriage Covenant Is at the Foundation of All Our Rights': The Politics of Slave Marriages in North Carolina after Emancipation," *Law and History Review* 14 (Spring 1996): 108; Göran Lind, *Common Law Marriage: A Legal Institution for Cohabitation* (New York: Oxford University Press, 2008), 261–303.

31. For example, see "Statement of Bessie Walker relative to her cutting Rogers Matthews," January 13, 1938, Transcripts of Statements of Witnesses to Homicides, New Orleans Police Department, City of New Orleans, City Archives/Louisiana Division, New Orleans Public Library, New Orleans, LA [hereafter "Statements of Witnesses"].

32. "Report of Homicide of Charles Phillips," April 1, 1924, Homicide Reports.

33. Edwards, "The Marriage Covenant Is at the Foundation of All Our Rights," 108; Max Rheinstein, "The Law of Divorce and the Problem of Marital Stability," *Vanderbilt Law Review* 9 (June 1956): 644.

34. "Statement of Katherine Boyd in reference to the murder of one, Lawrence Lomax," March 29, 1936, Statements of Witnesses.

35. Edna Dunn, interview data, July 6, 1938, Series V, Subseries 2, Box 31, Folder 10, p. 81, Allison Davis Papers, Special Collections Research Center, University of Chicago, Chicago, IL [hereafter "Davis Papers"].

36. Johnson, *Shadow of the Plantation*, 72.

37. Katherine M. Franke, "Becoming a Citizen: Reconstruction Era Regulation of African American Marriages," *Yale Journal of Law and the Humanities* 11 (Summer 1999): 252; Anthony E. Kaye, *Joining Places: Slave Neighborhoods in the Old South* (Chapel Hill: University of North Carolina Press, 2007), 52–82.

38. Brenda E. Stevenson, *Life in Black and White: Family and Community in the Slave South* (New York: Oxford University Press, 1996), 233.

39. The high filing fee was no accident. By creating such an obstacle, white officials encouraged freedpeople to remain in informal domestic unions. But couples cohabitating not in formal marriages could be arrested and prosecuted for fornication and adultery. Hence, white lawmakers promoted common-law unions among African Americans and then criminalized those living in common-law unions. See Franke, "Becoming a Citizen," 278.

40. Peter W. Bardaglio, *Reconstructing the Household: Families, Sex, and the Law in the Nineteenth-Century South* (Chapel Hill: University of North Carolina Press, 1995), 200; Hendrik Hartog, *Man & Wife in America: A History* (Cambridge, MA: Harvard University Press, 2000), 99; Edwards, "The Marriage Covenant Is at the Foundation of All Our Rights," 85–86, 108; Franke, "Becoming a Citizen," 303–4.

41. Stevenson, *Life in Black and White*, 226–34; Franke, "Becoming a Citizen," 253–57; Edwards, "The Marriage Covenant Is at the Foundation of All Our Rights," 96.

42. For notions of respectability, see Anastasia C. Curwood, *Stormy Weather: Middle-Class African American Marriages between the Two World Wars* (Chapel Hill: University of North Carolina Press, 2010).

43. Frazier, *The Negro Family in the United States*, 133–45; Dollard, *Caste and Class in a Southern Town*, 153; Rheinstein, "The Law of Divorce and the Problem of Marriage Stability," 644; Charles D. Marshall, "The Necessity of Ceremony in a Putative Marriage," *Tulane Law Review* 10 (April 1936): 441; Catherine Augusta Mills, "Implication of the Repeal of Louisiana Civil Code Article 1481," *Louisiana Law Review* 48, no. 5 (1988): 1206.

44. See Davis and Dollard, *Children of Bondage*, 95; Johnson, *Shadow of the Plantation*, 33, 41, 66.

45. Powdermaker, *After Freedom*, 152.

46. May Bamforth Hubert, "The Annulment of Marriage in Louisiana," *Tulane Law Review* 24 (December 1949): 228; Walter O. Weyrauch, "Informal and Formal Marriage—An Appraisal of Trends in Family Organization," *University of Chicago Law Review* 28 (Autumn 1960): 105.

47. For example, see Clarence J. Dowling, "Motion for New Trial," *State of Louisiana v. William Johnson*, Criminal District Court, Section A Case Files, Docket #35869, October 1926, City Archives/Louisiana Division, New Orleans Public Library, New Orleans, LA.

48. "Report of Homicide of Rogers Matthews," January 14, 1938, Homicide Reports; "Statement of Bessie Walker relative to her cutting Rogers Matthews," January 13, 1938, Statements of Witnesses.

49. "Statement of Anna Bates relative to one Bessie Walker cutting which resulted in the death of her Common Law Husband, Rogers Matthews," January 14, 1938, Statements of Witnesses.

50. "Report of Homicide of Rogers Matthews," January 14, 1938, Homicide Reports.

51. "Stabbed by Wife: Husband Is Dead," *New Orleans Times-Picayune*, January 15, 1938, p. 3.

52. Edwards, "The Marriage Covenant Is at the Foundation of All Our Rights," 108; Franke, "Becoming a Citizen," 303.

53. Thus, these husbands were unable to use "economic subordination" to control their wives. See Johnson, "Patriarchal Terrorism and Common Couple Violence," 284.

54. "Kills Cave Man in Brawl," *Louisiana Weekly*, August 20, 1932, p. 1.

55. "Statement of Joe Neason relative to the murder of one Ernestine Caldwell," March 27, 1938, Statements of Witnesses.

56. It is possible that this figure reflected the proportion of African American residents living in common-law marriages. Because census data and other demographic sources blurred the distinction between common-law and state-certified marriages, it is impossible to determine the percentages of marriages in either category. But recent scholarship argues that rates of spousal homicide, particularly against women, are higher in common-law unions. See Douglas A. Brownridge, "Understanding Women's Heightened Risk of Violence in Common-Law Unions: Revisiting the Selection and Relationship Hypothesis," *Violence against Women* 10 (June 2004): 645–47.

57. For an important analysis of the ways in which ambiguous hierarchy generates violence,

see Roger V. Gould, *Collision of Wills: How Ambiguity about Social Rank Breeds Conflict* (Chicago: University of Chicago Press, 2003).

58. Sociologists term such demands for authority a "control tactic." See Johnson, "Patriarchal Terrorism and Common Couple Violence," 291.

59. "Report of Homicide of Oscar Pierce," January 21, 1935, Homicide Reports.

60. "Report of Homicide of Lilly May Tucker," March 12, 1925, Homicide Reports; "Report of Homicide of Viola Lee," August 24, 1928, Homicide Reports.

61. "Report of Homicide of James Taylor," May 14, 1939, Homicide Reports.

62. Social psychologists refer to such coercive acts as "contingent threats." See James T. Tedeschi and Richard B. Felson, *Violence, Aggression, and Coercive Actions* (Washington, DC: American Psychological Association, 1994), 169. Most African American spousal homicides were victim precipitated. See Richard B. Felson and Steven Messner, "Disentangling the Effects of Gender and Intimacy on Victim Precipitation in Homicide," *Criminology* 36 (May 1998): 407.

63. "Report of Homicide of Noah Matthews," January 14, 1923, Homicide Reports.

64. Abstract of Interviews on Edna Dunn, interview by Mrs. Davis, interview transcript, May–November 1938, Series V, Subseries 2, Box 31, Folder 9, p. 1, Davis Papers.

65. Davis and Dollard, *Children of Bondage*, 270.

66. "Statement of Zelia Johnson relative to her Murdering one Johnny McGee," May 17, 1930, Statements of Witnesses.

67. "Wife Says She Killed Ex-Mate: Dead Boy's Mother Says 'Other Man Did It,'" *Louisiana Weekly*, July 15, 1939, p. 2.

68. "Statement of one Leona Walker in reference to her striking her Common-Law husband, [*sic*] Randell Gettridge," January 21, 1935, Statements of Witnesses.

69. "Inquest Report on Wandell Gettredge," January 21, 1935, Coroner's Reports, Coroner's Office, City of New Orleans, Parish of Orleans, State of Louisiana, City Archives/Louisiana Division, New Orleans Public Library, New Orleans, LA [hereafter "Coroner's Reports"].

70. "Mistreated; Kills Mate," *Louisiana Weekly*, October 14, 1939, p. 1.

71. "Report of Homicide of Percy Payton," October 7, 1939, Homicide Reports; "Inquest Report on Percy Peyton [*sic*]," October 7, 1939, Coroner's Reports.

72. "Mistreated; Kills Mate," *Louisiana Weekly*, October 14, 1939, pp. 1, 2.

73. "Statement of Anna Bates relative to one Bessie Walker cutting which resulted in the death of her Common Law Husband, Rogers Matthews," January 14, 1938, Statements of Witnesses.

74. "Homicide Report of Gordon McKay," April 15, 1938, Homicide Reports.

75. "Homicide Report on Edward Francis," June 13, 1931, Homicide Reports.

76. "Statement of Anna Nelson relative to the murder of one Nelson Corner," January 7, 1933, Statements of Witnesses; "Inquest Report on Nelson Corner Jr.," January 3, 1933, Coroner's Reports.

77. "Report of Homicide of Henry Long," March 2, 1924, Homicide Reports; "Inquest Report on Henry Long," March 2, 1924, Coroner's Reports.

78. "Report of Homicide of Louis Bruneau," November 12, 1928, Homicide Reports; "Report of Homicide of Edward Sanders," February 25, 1929, Homicide Reports.

79. "Report on Homicide of Archie McGee," September 8, 1930, Homicide Reports; "Statement of Mary Moses in relation to Sarah Gates stabbing her common law Husband Archie McGee," September 8, 1930, Statements of Witnesses.

80. "Statement of Estelle Brown relative to the murder of Norma Bat," July 28, 1931, Statements of Witnesses; "Kills Cave Man in Brawl," *Louisiana Weekly*, August 20, 1932, p. 1; "Report of Homicide of Willie Bingham," September 13, 1938, Homicide Reports.

81. In wife killings in African American common-law marriages, 53.2 percent of assailants used guns. Nearly two-thirds of killers relied on .38 caliber revolvers, and most of the rest used .32 caliber revolvers.

82. "Kills Wife, Then Wounds Himself," *New Orleans Times-Picayune*, March 6, 1939, p. 11.

83. Dollard, *Caste and Class in a Southern Town*, 270.

84. For more on this form of domestic violence, see Jennifer E. Loveland and Chitra Raghavan, "Coercive Control, Physical Violence, and Masculinity," *Violence and Gender* 14 (March 2017): 5–10.

85. "Man Kills Woman Who Left Him for Husband," *New Orleans Item*, August 24, 1928, p. 2; "Report of Homicide of Viola Lee," August 24, 1928, Homicide Reports.

86. "Common-Law Husbands Squabble," *Louisiana Weekly*, April 2, 1938, p. 1.

87. "Murder Charge Filed against Young Husband," *New Orleans Times-Picayune*, August 13, 1925, p. 5; "Husband Denied Right to Attend Bride's Funeral," *New Orleans Times-Picayune*, August 14, 1925, p. 13; "Homicide Report of Lilly Butler," August 13, 1925, Homicide Reports.

88. "Palmer says, 'I Don't Want to Go to Gallows,'" *Louisiana Weekly*, March 11, 1939, p. 1; "Kills Estranged Wife and Sister, Wounds Himself," *New Orleans Times-Picayune*, March 2, 1939, p. 7; "Inquest Report on Juanita Palmer," March 1, 1939, Coroner's Reports.

89. "Homicide Report of Morise Miles," August 17, 1929, Homicide Reports; "Wife's Defender Slain by Negro," *New Orleans Item*, August 9, 1929, p. 1.

90. The sociologist Donald Black terms abandonment "a marital death penalty." See Black, *Moral Time* (New York: Oxford University Press, 2011), 46. For a different perspective, from evolutionary psychologists, see Daly and Wilson, *Homicide*, 196–202.

91. "Homicide Report of Leonze Mackie," September 11, 1926, Homicide Reports; "Wife Kills Negro, Waits for Police," *New Orleans Times-Picayune*, September 12, 1926, p. 2.

92. Richard Sterner, *The Negro's Share: A Study of Income, Consumption, Housing and Public Assistance* (New York: Harper & Brothers, 1943), 49.

93. T. J. Woofter, *Negro Problems in Cities* (New York: Doubleday, 1928), 86.

94. *Fifteenth Census of the United States: 1930, Population, vol. VI*, 67.

95. Ibid., 59, 537; Sterner, *The Negro's Share*, 55.

96. Sterner, *The Negro's Share*, 54, 55. Also see Charles S. Johnson, *The Negro in American Civilization: A Study of Negro Life and Race Relations in the Light of Social Research* (New York: Henry Holt, 1930), 207.

97. "Homicide Report of Joe Gilbert," November 19, 1922, Homicide Reports; "Beats Companion to Death after Dice Game Fight," *New Orleans Item*, November 20, 1922, p. 3.

98. Spousal conflict was the leading trigger for African American home homicide during the early 1920s, followed by jealousy between rivals and fights over dice or craps games.

99. "Homicide Report of Thomas Smith," November 4, 1924, Homicide Reports.

100. For an analysis that explores the impact of the amount of time spent in particular settings, see Lawrence E. Cohen and Marcus Felson, "Social Change and Crime Rate Trends: A Routine Activity Approach," *American Sociological Review* 44 (August 1979): 588–608.

101. "Common-Law Husbands Squabble," *Louisiana Weekly*, April 2, 1938, p. 4.

CHAPTER 3

1. "Report of Homicides of Leonedie Lee Moity and Theresa Alfano Moity," October 27, 1927, Homicide Reports, Department of Police, City of New Orleans, City Archives/Louisiana Division, New Orleans Public Library, New Orleans, LA [hereafter "Homicide Reports"]; "Find 2 Women Beheaded: Slayer Cuts Off Head, Arms and Legs of Victims," *New Orleans Item*, October 27, 1927, p. 1. The police report identified the neighbor as Nettie Douglas, but newspaper accounts and court records listed her as Nedda Douglas. Similarly, the police report listed Mrs. Joseph Moity as Leonedie, while other documents identified her as Leonide.

2. "Report of Homicides of Leonedie Lee Moity and Theresa Alfano Moity," October 27, 1927, Homicide Reports; "Find 2 Women Beheaded: Slayer Cuts off Head, Arms and Legs of Victims," *New Orleans Item*, October 27, 1927, p. 1.

3. "Moity's Second Confession Read: Try to Prove Insanity in 'Sailor' Yarn," *New Orleans Item*, March 1, 1928, p. 6; "Moity's Story Shaken: Now He's Only 'Pretty Sure' Sailor Slew 2," *New Orleans Item*, October 31, 1927, p. 6.

4. "Report of Homicides of Leonedie Lee Moity and Theresa Alfano Moity," October 27, 1927, Homicide Reports; "Moity's Story," *New Orleans Item*, November 1, 1927, pp. 1, 6; "Henry Moity Bares Story of Life, Love," *New Orleans Item-Tribune*, November 6, 1927, pp. 1, 2, 3; "Moity's Second Confession Read: Try to Prove Insanity in 'Sailor' Yarn," *New Orleans Item*, March 1, 1928, p. 6; "Statement [to the police] of Mrs. Alcee Lecamu relative to the murder of Mrs. Joseph Moity and Mrs. Henry Moity," October 27, 1927, *State of Louisiana v. Henry Moity*, Criminal District Court, Section E Case Files, Docket #40877–78, November 1927, City Archives/Louisiana Division, New Orleans Public Library, New Orleans, LA [hereafter "Criminal District Court Files"]; "Statement of Henry Moity," October 30, 1927, *State of Louisiana v. Henry Moity*, Criminal District Court, Section E Case Files, Docket #40877–78, November 1927, p. 1, Criminal District Court Files; "Examination of Henry Moity," October 30, 1927, *State of Louisiana v. Henry Moity*, Criminal District Court, Section E Case Files, Docket #40877–78, November 1927, p. 5, Criminal District Court Files; "'Dirty Trick,' Henry Played, Says Moity," *New Orleans Item*, October 28, 1927, p. 10. In various documents, Lecamu's first name appears as Alcide, Alice, and Alcee, though she signed her name as Alcee.

5. "Moity's Second Trial Monday," *New Orleans States*, June 17, 1928, p. 4.

6. "Henry Moity Bares Story of Life, Love," *New Orleans Item-Tribune*, November 6, 1927, p. 2.

7. With parental consent, children in Louisiana could legally marry at age twelve. See "Child Marriage," *New Orleans Item*, March 4, 1929, p. 8; "Henry Moity Bares Story of Life, Love," *New Orleans Item-Tribune*, November 6, 1927, p. 3.

8. "Henry Moity Bares Story of Life, Love," *New Orleans Item-Tribune*, November 6, 1927, p. 2; "Sought," *New Orleans Item*, October 28, 1927, p. 1.

9. "Henry Moity Bares Story of Life, Love," *New Orleans Item-Tribune*, November 6, 1927, p. 3.

10. "Coroner Blames Dual Tragedy on City Life: Wives Giddy over Variety He Believes," *New Orleans Item*, October 30, 1927, p. 1; "Judge Charbonnet Willing to Accept Verdict on Sunday," *New Orleans Times-Picayune*, March 4, 1928, p. 4.

11. "Find 2 Women Beheaded: Slayer Cuts Off Head, Arms and Legs of Victims," *New Orleans Item*, October 27, 1927, p. 1. Three weeks before the murders, Joe and Leonie Moity separated and sent their children to live with relatives in New Iberia.

12. "Coroner Blames Duel Tragedy on City Life: Wives Giddy over Variety He Believes," *New Orleans Item*, October 30, 1927, p. 1; "Man Believed Hiding near Crime Scene," *New Orleans Item*, October 28, 1927, p. 10.

13. "Coroner Blames Dual Tragedy on City Life: Wives Giddy over Variety He Believes," *New Orleans Item*, October 30, 1927, p. 1; "Was Crazed by Jibes and Tales of Other Loves," *New Orleans Item*, November 1, 1927, p. 1.

14. "Moity Babies Won't Miss 2 Mothers Now," *New Orleans Item*, October 28, 1927, p. 10; "Moity's Second Confession Read: Try to Prove Insanity in 'Sailor' Yarn," *New Orleans Item*, March 1, 1928, p. 6; "Moity Sanity Is Puzzle, Say Own Alienists," *New Orleans Item*, March 3, 1928, p. 2; "Judge Charbonnet Willing to Accept Verdict on Sunday," *New Orleans Times-Picayune*, March 4, 1928, p. 4.

15. "Was Crazed by Jibes and Tales of Other Loves," *New Orleans Item*, November 1, 1927, p. 1.

16. "Henry Moity Bares Story of Life, Love," *New Orleans Item-Tribune*, November 6, 1927, p. 3; "Statement of Henry Moity," October 30, 1927, *State of Louisiana v. Henry Moity*, Criminal District Court, Section E Case Files, Docket #40877–78, November 1927, p. 1, Criminal District Court Files.

17. "Judge Charbonnet Willing to Accept Verdict on Sunday," *New Orleans Times-Picayune*, March 4, 1928, p. 4; "Henry Moity Bares Story of Life, Love," *New Orleans Item-Tribune*, November 6, 1927, p. 3.

18. "Love Editor Sees Murderer's Children Meet Him in Prison," *New Orleans Item-Tribune*, November 6, 1927, p. 3.

19. "Examination of Henry Moity," November 1, 1927, *State of Louisiana v. Henry Moity*, Criminal District Court, Section E Case Files, Docket #40877–78, November 1927, p. 10, Criminal District Court Files; "Statement of Henry Moity," October 30, 1927, *State of Louisiana v. Henry Moity*, Criminal District Court, Section E Case Files, Docket #40877–78, November 1927, p. 15, Criminal District Court Files; "Moity's Story," *New Orleans Item*, November 1, 1927, p. 6.

20. "Judge Charbonnet Willing to Accept Verdict on Sunday," *New Orleans Times-Picayune*, March 4, 1928, p. 4.

21. "Henry Moity Calm Hearing Sentence," *New Orleans Times-Picayune*, April 10, 1928, p. 9.

22. At other moments, Moity expressed regrets, commenting, "I wish I had not done it. . . . I still hate my wife for the sorrow she brought me. I'm more sorry for the children's sake than hers." See "Was Crazed by Jibes and Tales of Other Loves," *New Orleans Item*, November 1, 1927, p. 1. In still another confession, he showed remorse, stating, "I'm sorry as hell that I killed

her. I still love her." See "Henry Moity Denies He'll Play Insane," *New Orleans Item*, November 2, 1927, p. 8.

23. "Moity Off to Start Life Term," *New Orleans Item*, July 6, 1928, p. 1.

24. "Moity's 'Dad' Collapses: Faints While Visiting Son in Jail Cell," *New Orleans Item*, November 5, 1927, p. 1.

25. "Slayer Loses Calm, 10 Men in Jury Box," *New Orleans Item*, February 28, 1928, p. 1.

26. "Was Crazed by Jibes and Tales of Other Loves," *New Orleans Item*, November 1, 1927, p. 1.

27. "Coroner Blames Dual Tragedy on City Life: Wives Giddy over Variety He Believes," *New Orleans Item*, October 30, 1927, p. 1.

28. "Moity's Second Trial Monday," *New Orleans States*, June 17, 1928, p. 4.

29. "Moity Sentenced for Two Killings, Requests Pardon," *New Orleans Times-Picayune*, June 4, 1935, p. 15.

30. For "diabolical," see "Was Crazed by Jibes and Tales of Other Loves," *New Orleans Item*, November 1, 1927, p. 1. Between 1920 and 1945, white New Orleanians committed eighty-seven spousal homicides.

31. For the 1920–45 period, the African American rate was seven times higher.

32. The mean age for white spouse killers was 38.9, while the mean for African Americans was 31.7.

33. In African American spousal homicides, 45.8 percent of killers used guns.

34. This gap did not merely reflect race-based differences in suicide, for the white suicide rate during this period was less than three times the African American rate.

35. It is impossible to determine the proportion of New Orleanians living in common-law unions, though this marital arrangement enjoyed greater popularity among African American residents.

36. Michael P. Johnson, "Patriarchal Terrorism and Common Couple Violence: Two Forms of Violence Against Women," *Journal of Marriage and the Family* 57 (May 1995): 283–94; Michael P. Johnson, *A Typology of Domestic Violence: Intimate Terrorism, Violent Resistance, and Situational Couple Violence* (Boston: Northeastern University Press, 2008), 5–6. Also see William R. Downs, Barb Rindels, and Christine Atkinson, "Women's Use of Physical and Non-physical Self-Defense Strategies during Incidents of Partner Self-Defense," *Violence against Women* 13 (January 2007): 29.

37. "Report of Homicide of Mrs. Jack White," May 1, 1935, Homicide Reports.

38. "Statement of Mrs. Laurie Larson relative to Jack White killing his wife and committing suicide," May 1, 1935, Transcripts of Statements of Witnesses to Homicides, New Orleans Police Department, City of New Orleans, City Archives/Louisiana Division, New Orleans Public Library, New Orleans, LA [hereafter "Statements of Witnesses"].

39. "Girl Bride Who Kills Husband Is Freed," *New Orleans Item*, December 26, 1922, p. 2.

40. "Man Faces Charge of Manslaughter in Woman's Death," *New Orleans Times-Picayune*, February 26, 1927, p. 15.

41. "Report of Homicide of Mrs. Callie Piper," February 25, 1927, Homicide Reports.

42. "Statement of Mrs. William Welch in relative [sic] to her Husband William A. Welch, being fatally stabbed by his Step Son Joseph Sellen," February 3, 1945, Statements of Witnesses.

43. "Statement of Amelia J. Reike relative to shooting and fatally injuring her husband Franke Reike," May 31, 1937, Statements of Witnesses.

44. For example, see "Kills Her Husband in Defense of Child," *New Orleans Times-Picayune*, March 12, 1922, p. 1. Also see Johnson, *A Typology of Domestic Violence*, 26, 50.

45. "Girl Bride Who Kills Husband Is Freed," *New Orleans Item*, December 26, 1922, p. 2.

46. Eugenie Cressy, "Dying Declaration," April 28, 1924, *State v. Max Cressy*, Section E Case Files, Docket #23782, Criminal District Court Files.

47. "Youth Who Shot Father to Death Freed without Bail on Self-Defense Plea," *New Orleans Times-Picayune*, August 4, 1932, p. 1.

48. "Woman Not Held for Killing Mate," *New Orleans States*, March 13, 1922, p. 4.

49. "Scissors Grinder Admits Killing Wife with Ax," *New Orleans Times-Picayune*, June 23, 1926, p. 1.

50. "Wife Is Slain as She Prays for Her Life," *New Orleans Item*, April 15, 1921, pp. 1, 5.

51. "Statement of Mrs. G. Weiss in relation to Mr. William A. Welch being fatally stabbed by his step son Joseph Sellen," February 3, 1945, Statements of Witnesses.

52. Scholarship on modern domestic violence has found a similar pattern. See Johnson, "Patriarchal Terrorism and Common Couple Violence," 286.

53. Among cohabiting spouse killers, 56.5 percent of men and 80.8 percent of women used guns.

54. The overwhelming majority of abusive marriages did not end with a violent death. Rather, men terrorized their wives for decades.

55. In white spousal homicides involving cohabiting partners, twenty-six of the forty-nine killers were women.

56. Linda Gordon reached the same conclusion. See Gordon, *Heroes of Their Own Lives: The Politics and History of Family Violence* (New York: Penguin, 1988), 274. Also see Downs, Rindels, and Atkinson, "Women's Use of Physical and Nonphysical Self-Defense Strategies during Incidents of Partner Self-Defense," 30.

57. "Mrs. Dietz Is Liberated on Defense Plea," *New Orleans Item*, September 15, 1924, pp. 1, 2; "Mrs. Corso Weeps on Stand: Almost Falls from Chair in Collapse," *New Orleans Item*, November 29, 1927, p. 21.

58. "'I Hope He Dies,' Says Mrs. Nick," *New Orleans Item*, October 23, 1925, p. 1.

59. "Harris Made Will on Death Bed: Was Warned Plans to Wed Meant Death," *New Orleans Item*, March 12, 1928, p. 6.

60. "Husband's Slayer Will Be Allowed to Attend Rites," *New Orleans Times-Picayune*, February 28, 1936, p. 36.

61. "Policeman Shot by Wife Dies of Wounds; Mate to Face Charges of Murder," *New Orleans Times-Picayune*, February 27, 1936, p. 3.

62. Also see Johnson, *A Typology of Domestic Violence*, 35.

63. "Women Asking Protection Are Jailed," *New Orleans Times-Picayune*, November 9, 1922, p. 1.

64. "Woman Faints as Policeman Is Dismissed," *New Orleans Item*, December 1, 1922, p. 1; "Women Asking Protection Are Jailed," *New Orleans Times-Picayune*, November 9, 1922, p. 1.

Also see Elicka S. L. Peterson, "Murder as Self-Help: Women and Intimate Partner Homicide," *Homicide Studies* 3 (February 1999): 33.

65. "Man Believed Hiding near Crime Scene," *New Orleans Item*, October 28, 1927, p. 10; "Examination of Henry Moity," October 30, 1927, *State of Louisiana v. Henry Moity*, Criminal District Court, Section E Case Files, Docket #40877–78, November 1927, p. 5, Criminal District Court Files.

66. "Wife Held for Murder of Mate Slain with Butcher Knife after Day-Long Row," *New Orleans Times-Picayune*, December 7, 1936, p. 6.

67. In this respect, police inaction fueled aggressive self-help across racial lines. For violence and self-help, see Donald Black, "Crime as Social Control," *American Sociological Review* 48 (February 1983): 34–45; Russell P. Dobash, R. Emerson Dobash, Margo Wilson, and Martin Daly, "The Myth of Sexual Symmetry in Marital Violence," *Social Problems* 39 (February 1992): 81.

68. "Wife Who Killed Edgar Bouligny, War Hero, Freed," *New Orleans Times-Picayune*, May 19, 1931, p. 2.

69. "First Wounded American Is Slain in Home," *New Orleans Item*, May 18, 1931, p. 3.

70. "Mrs. Corso Weeps on Stand: Almost Falls From Chair in Collapse," *New Orleans Item*, November 29, 1927, p. 1.

71. "World Smiles on Wife Who Slew Husband," *New Orleans Item*, March 13, 1922, p. 2; "Kills Husband in Defense of Child," *New Orleans Times-Picayune*, March 13, 1922, p. 1.

72. "'I Hope He Dies,' Says Mrs. Nick," *New Orleans Item*, October 23, 1925, p. 1.

73. See Johnson, *A Typology of Domestic Violence*, 10; Downs, Rindels, and Atkinson, "Women's Use of Physical and Nonphysical Self-Defense Strategies during Incidents of Partner Self-Defense," 40.

74. "Wife Released after She Kills Man with Gift," *New Orleans Times-Picayune*, December 27, 1922, p. 4.

75. "Held for Fatal Shooting of Mate," *New Orleans Times-Picayune*, September 22, 1945, p. 5.

76. "'I Hope He Dies,' Says Mrs. Nick," *New Orleans Item*, October 23, 1925, pp. 1, 2.

77. "Report of Homicide of Edgar Bouligny," May 18, 1931, Homicide Reports.

78. "Railroad Shop Foreman Shot Dead by Wife," *New Orleans Times-Picayune*, October 4, 1925, p. 1.

79. "First American Wounded in War Killed by Mate," *Baton Rouge State Times Advocate*, May 18, 1931, p. 4.

80. "Wife Held for Murder of Mate Slain with Butcher Knife after Day-Long Row," *New Orleans Times-Picayune*, December 7, 1936, p. 6.

81. In spousal homicides among white cohabiting couples, 9.1 percent of wife killers held skilled positions, compared with 26.9 percent of husband killers.

82. Because my research focuses exclusively on homicide, it is impossible to determine how frequently separation spared women from spousal violence.

83. Thirty-six such spousal homicides occurred in this period. Social scientists have found the same pattern in modern wife killing. See Holly Johnson and Tina Hotton, "Losing Control: Homicide Risk in Estranged and Intact Intimate Relationships," *Homicide Studies* 7 (February

2003): 59–62, 70; Carolyn Rebecca Block and Antigone Christakos, "Intimate Partner Homicide in Chicago over 29 Years," *Crime and Delinquency* 41 (October 1995): 506; Margo Wilson and Martin Daly, "Spousal Homicide Risk and Estrangement," *Violence and Victims* 8 (Spring 1993): 4.

84. For a similar pattern, see Wilson and Daly, "Spousal Homicide Risk and Estrangement," 6.

85. Among separated white wife killers, 34.6 percent were in their forties, compared with 17.4 percent among cohabiting white wife killers.

86. By comparison, 25 percent of estranged husband killers and 15.4 percent of cohabiting husband killers attempted suicide.

87. "Moity Babies Won't Miss 2 Mothers Now," *New Orleans Item*, October 28, 1927, p. 10; "Judge Charbonnet Willing to Accept Verdict on Sunday," *New Orleans Times-Picayune*, March 4, 1928, p. 4.

88. "Examination of Henry Moity," November 1, 1927, *State of Louisiana v. Henry Moity*, Criminal District Court, Section E Case Files, Docket #40877–78, November 1927, p. 5, Criminal District Court Files.

89. "Slayer Must Face Charge of Murder for Second Killing," *New Orleans Times-Picayune*, March 5, 1928, p. 2.

90. "2nd Victim of Jealous Killer Dies," *New Orleans Item*, September 3, 1928, p. 1.

91. "Third Victim of Love-Maddened Murder-Suicide Dies," *New Orleans Times-Picayune*, September 14, 1928, p. 1.

92. "Report of Homicide of Louise Godwin," February 12, 1922, Homicide Reports.

93. "Husband Kills Estranged Wife as Babe Looks On," *New Orleans Times-Picayune*, June 15, 1926, p. 1.

94. "Homicide Report of Margueret Ferguson," June 14, 1926, Homicide Reports.

95. "Worker Cuts Wife's Throat and Takes Poison after Reconciliation Is Refused," *New Orleans Times-Picayune*, February 12, 1939, p. 1.

96. The men often promised to be better husbands. None invoked religious prohibitions against divorce to support the pleas for reconciliation.

97. "Kills His Wife but Prevented Taking Own Life," *New Orleans Times-Picayune*, October 12, 1924, p. 10; "2nd Victim of Jealous Killer Dies," *New Orleans Item*, September 13, 1928, p. 10; "Man Slays Wife Then Kills Self as Girl Watches," *New Orleans Times-Picayune*, February 13, 1922, p. 2.

98. "Slayer of Wife Mutters in Cell of Saving Neck," *New Orleans Times-Picayune*, September 3, 1926, p. 1; "Husband, Fearing Desertion, Slays Young Wife, Self," *New Orleans Times-Picayune*, September 30, 1928, p. 1.

99. "Girl Cowers as Man Hacks Wife's Throat and Takes Poison," *New Orleans Item*, February 11, 1939, p. 1.

100. "Henry Moity Bares Story of Life, Love," *New Orleans Item-Tribune*, November 6, 1927, p. 3.

101. For a related pattern, see Gordon, *Heroes of Their Own Lives*, 258.

102. Early twentieth-century Chicago women expressed similar sentiments. See Jeffrey S. Adler, *First in Violence, Deepest in Dirt: Homicide in Chicago, 1875–1920* (Cambridge, MA: Harvard University Press, 2006), 64–65. Sociologists and criminologists studying modern

spousal homicide have found that women now typically leave to escape abuse. See Johnson, *A Typology of Domestic Violence*, 53.

103. See "His Conscience Cheers, Tortures Wife-Killer," *New Orleans Item*, February 26, 1931, p. 2; "Report of Homicide of Mrs. William D. Wiggins," November 25, 1923, Homicide Reports.

104. Theresa Moity and Edna Badua, for example, included such taunts.

105. "Husband Kills Estranged Wife as Babe Looks On," *New Orleans Times-Picayune*, June 15, 1926, p. 1.

106. "Baby, 4, Tells How Mother Was Slain," *New Orleans Item*, June 15, 1926, p. 2.

107. "Jury Gets Case of Patrolman in Slaying of Wife," *New Orleans Times-Picayune*, February 26, 1937, p. 1.

108. "Moity's Second Confession Read: Try to Prove Insanity in 'Sailor' Yarn," *New Orleans Item*, March 1, 1928, p. 6.

109. "Statement of Henry Moity," October 30, 1927, *State of Louisiana v. Henry Moity*, Criminal District Court, Section E Case Files, Docket #40877–78, November 1927, p. 15, Criminal District Court Files; "Moity's Story," *New Orleans Item*, November 1, 1927, p. 6.

110. "Husband Gives Up and Confesses He Shot Wife to Death," *New Orleans Times-Picayune*, February 26, 1931, p. 1; "Slayer of Wife Mutters in Cell of Saving Neck," *New Orleans Times-Picayune*, September 3, 1926, p. 1.

111. "Report of Homicide of Louise Godwin," February 12, 1922, Homicide Reports.

112. "Man Slays Wife Then Kills Self as Girl Watches," *New Orleans Times-Picayune*, February 13, 1922, p. 2.

113. "Kills Wife as She Laughs," *New Orleans Item*, October 12, 1924, p. 1.

114. "Cuts Throat of Victim as She Sleeps," *New Orleans Item*, September 2, 1926, pp. 1, 9.

115. "Moity's Story," *New Orleans Item*, November 1, 1927, p. 6.

116. "Report of Homicide of Margueret Ferguson," June 14, 1926, Homicide Reports; "Orleanian Calmly Admits Slaying; Says She Was in the Wrong," *New Orleans Item*, April 22, 1939, p. 2; "Report of Homicide of Camile Pennino," February 27, 1931, Homicide Reports; "Husband Calls Officers after Slaying of Wife," *New Orleans Times-Picayune*, May 16, 1937, p. 1; "Waiter Kills Woman, Badly Wounds Wife," *New Orleans Times-Picayune*, April 1, 1922, p. 2.

117. "Man Cuts Wife's Throat and Own in Death Pact," *New Orleans Times-Picayune*, November 26, 1923, p. 9.

118. "Baby, 4, Tells How Mother was Slain," *New Orleans Item*, June 15, 1926, p. 2; "Kills Wife as She Laughs," *New Orleans Item*, October 12, 1924, p. 1.

119. "Report of Homicide of June Crumpley," April 22, 1939, Homicide Reports.

120. "Estranged Wife Lured from Work, Slain by Husband," *New Orleans Times-Picayune*, September 5, 1925, p. 1.

121. "Waiter Kills Woman, Badly Wounds Wife," *New Orleans Times-Picayune*, April 1, 1922, p. 2.

122. "Fatal Shooting Admitted by Goodwin, Assert Three as State Ends Testimony," *New Orleans Item*, February 25, 1937, p. 2.

123. "Report of Homicide of Edith B. Lane Ney," September 30, 1941, Homicide Reports.

124. Martin Daly and Margot Wilson, *Homicide* (New York: Aldine de Gruyter 1988), 205.

125. "Man Slays Wife Then Kills Self as Girl Watches," *New Orleans Times-Picayune*, February 13, 1922, p. 2.

126. "Shot to Death in Apartment," *Baton Rouge State Times Advocate*, March 9, 1938, p. 13; "Husband Kisses and Slays 40-Year-Old Want-Ad Wife in Vieux Carre Apartment," *New Orleans Times-Picayune*, March 10, 1938, p. 2. His self-inflicted wound was superficial.

127. "Statement of Mrs. Sylvester Lorio relative to Mrs. Oliver Stevens being shot by her estranged husband, Oliver Stevens," December 1, 1945, Statements of Witnesses. The scholarship on such homicide-suicide is replete with cases of men using this specific language. See Wilson and Daly, "Spousal Homicide Risk and Estrangement," 3; Margo Wilson and Martin Daly, "An Evolutionary Psychological Perspective on Male Sexual Proprietariness and Violence against Wives," *Violence and Victims* 8 (Fall 1993): 279.

128. For example, see "Kills Wife as She Laughs," *New Orleans Item*, October 12, 1924, p. 1; "Moity's Second Confession Read: Try to Prove Insanity in 'Sailor' Yarn," *New Orleans Item*, March 1, 1928, p. 6.

129. See M. P. Baumgartner, "Violent Networks: The Origins and Management of Domestic Conflict," in *Aggression and Violence: Social Interactionist Perspectives*, ed. Richard B. Felson and James Tedeschi (Washington, DC: American Psychological Association, 1993), 209–31.

130. Evolutionary psychologists argue that older men seek to control their young partners' reproductive capacity. See Wilson and Daly, "An Evolutionary Psychological Perspective on Male Sexual Proprietariness and Violence against Wives," 283–85.

131. "Kills Wife and Self in Front of Daughter," *New Orleans Item*, February 13, 1922, p. 3.

132. "Kills Bride, Self as Her Love Cools," *New Orleans Item*, September 30, 1928, p. 12.

133. *Fifteenth Census of the United States: 1930, Population, vol. II* (Washington, DC: Government Printing Office, 1933), 76, 764.

134. Ibid., 59. Disparate rates of poverty, malnutrition, infant mortality, and disease contributed as well.

135. See Donald E. Devore, *Defying Jim Crow: African American Community Development and the Struggle for Racial Equality in New Orleans, 1900–1960* (Baton Rouge: Louisiana State University Press, 2015).

136. Baumgartner, "Violent Networks," 213–22.

137. The sociologist Roger V. Gould argues that clear lines of power reduce conflict and that the potential for violence is greatest in social settings where such lines are most ambiguous. See Gould, *Collision of Wills: How Ambiguity about Social Rank Breeds Conflict* (Chicago: University of Chicago Press, 2003).

138. *Fifteenth Census of the United States: 1930, Occupations, by States, vol. IV*, 631; *Fifteenth Census of the United States: 1930, Population, vol. VI*, 539.

139. The psychologist John Archer argues that independent women are more likely to employ violence against their husbands. See Archer, "Cross-Cultural Differences in Physical Aggression between Partners: A Social-Role Analysis," *Personality and Social Psychology Review* 10 (May 2006): 133–53. Also see Catherine P. Cross and Anne Campbell, "Women's Aggression," *Aggression and Violent Behavior* 16 (September–October 2011): 395.

140. "Denies Badua's Plea to Attend Funeral," *New Orleans Times-Picayune*, October 14, 1924, p. 14.

141. "Crazed Brother Killed Women for Infidelity, Joseph Moity Declares," *New Orleans Times-Picayune*, October 28, 1927, p. 12.

142. Prosecutors and judges, coming from the city's upper classes, proved less supportive, viewing wife killers as a dangerous element within white society, a group whose savagery jeopardized elite claims of white supremacy. But criminal courts typically punished violent husbands only after they murdered their wives.

CHAPTER 4

1. "Report of Homicide of Joseph Isom," April 15, 1930, Homicide Reports, Department of Police, City of New Orleans, City Archives/Louisiana Division New Orleans Public Library, New Orleans, LA [hereafter "Homicide Reports"].

2. "Statement of Harry Jones, relative to killing one Joseph Isom," April 16, 1930, Transcripts of Statements of Witnesses to Homicides, New Orleans Police Department, City of New Orleans, City Archives/Louisiana Division, New Orleans Public Library, New Orleans, LA [hereafter "Statements of Witnesses"].

3. "Statement of Joe Glenn relative to the murder of a negro whom he knew as Kuse," April 15, 1930, Statements of Witnesses.

4. "Statement of Harry Jones, relative to killing one Joseph Isom," April 16, 1930, Statements of Witnesses.

5. "Statement of Horace Williams relative to a negro being stabbed to death," April 15, 1930, Statements of Witnesses.

6. "Inquest Report on Joseph Isom," April 15, 1930, Coroner's Reports, Coroner's Office, City of New Orleans, Parish of Orleans, State of Louisiana, City Archives/Louisiana Division, New Orleans Public Library, New Orleans, LA [hereafter "Coroner's Reports"].

7. "Report of Homicide of Joseph Isom," April 15, 1930, Homicide Reports.

8. Richard Sterner, *The Negro's Share: A Study of Income, Consumption, Housing and Public Assistance* (New York: Harper & Brothers, 1943), 362.

9. Frederick L. Hoffman, "The Homicide Record for 1925," *The Spectator* 116 (April 1, 1926): 38.

10. Frederick L. Hoffman, "The Homicide Record of 1934," *The Spectator* 134 (June 20, 1935): 13.

11. For racial etiquette, see Bertram Doyle, *The Etiquette of Race Relations: A Study in Social Control* (Chicago: University of Chicago Press, 1937); Charles S. Johnson, *Patterns of Negro Segregation* (New York: Harper & Brothers, 1943); Grace Elizabeth Hale, *Making Whiteness: The Culture of Segregation in the South, 1890–1940* (New York: Vintage, 1998); Stephen A. Berrey, *The Jim Crow Routine: Everyday Performances of Race, Civil Rights, and Segregation in Mississippi* (Chapel Hill: University of North Carolina Press, 2015); Jennifer Ritterhouse, *Growing Up Jim Crow: How Black and White Southern Children Learned Race* (Chapel Hill: University of North Carolina Press, 2006). For rough justice, see Elizabeth Dale, *Criminal Justice in the United States, 1789–1939* (New York: Cambridge University Press, 2011); Michael J. Pfeifer, *Rough Justice: Lynching and American Society, 1874–1947* (Urbana: University of Illinois Press, 2004).

12. Arnold R. Hirsch, "Simply a Matter of Black and White: The Transformation of Race and Politics in Twentieth-Century New Orleans," in *Creole New Orleans: Race and American-ization*, ed. Arnold R. Hirsch and Joseph Logsdon (Baton Rouge: Louisiana State University Press, 1992), 268.

13. Pamela Tyler, *Silk Stockings & Ballot Boxes: Women & Politics in New Orleans, 1920–1965* (Athens: University of Georgia Press, 1996), 28.

14. Riley E. Baker, "Negro Voter Registration in Louisiana, 1879–1964," *Louisiana Studies* 4 (Winter 1965): 338–39.

15. "97,713 Qualified to Vote in State Election April 17," *New Orleans Times-Picayune*, March 25, 1928, p. 11; Alan Maclachlan, "Up from Paternalism: The New Deal and Race Relations in New Orleans" (Ph.D. dissertation, University of New Orleans, 1998), 20. For the all-white primary, see *Smith v. Allwright*, 321 U.S. 649 (1944).

16. Gunnar Myrdal, *An American Dilemma: The Negro Problem and Modern Democracy*, vol. 1 (New York: Pantheon, 1944), 498.

17. See Donald Black, "Crime as Social Control," *American Sociological Review* 48 (February 1983): 34–45.

18. Newspaper clipping, editorial from the *New Orleans Item*, August 1, 1932, files of the New Orleans branch of the National Association for the Advancement of Colored People in the Papers of the NAACP, Part 12, Reel 14, Series A, ed. John H. Bracey Jr. and August Meier, University Publications (Bethesda, MD, 1991) [hereafter "NAACP Papers"]; Monroe N. Work, ed., *Negro Year Book: An Annual Encyclopedia of the Negro, 1931–32* (Tuskegee, AL: Tuskegee Institute Press, 1931), 47; Johnson, *Patterns of Negro Segregation*, 94.

19. "Bill to Restrict Negro Buildings Is Introduced," *New Orleans Times-Picayune*, September 10, 1924, p. 7; T. J. Woofter, *Negro Problems in Cities* (New York: Doubleday, Doran, 1928), 70; *Harmon v. Tyler*, 273 U.S. 668 (1927); *Harmon v. Tyler* (October 1926), reprinted in *Harmon v. Tyler*, U.S. Supreme Court Transcript of Record with Supporting Pleadings (Farmington Hills, MI: Gale, 2011); Hirsch, "Simply a Matter of Black and White," 268.

20. Joy Jackson, "Prohibition in New Orleans: The Unlikeliest Crusade," *Louisiana History* 19 (Summer 1978): 262.

21. Woofter, *Negro Problems in Cities*, 215.

22. "Charity Hospital Appeal," *New Orleans States*, April 3, 1923, p. 12; "Find Hospitals Lack Finances," *New Orleans Item-Tribune*, June 5, 1927, p. 5.

23. See "Apology Offered," *Louisiana Weekly*, March 13, 1926, p. 1; "Clear Doctor Who Refused to Help Negro," *Louisiana Weekly*, November 23, 1929, p. 1; "Ambulance Attendant Urged Sick Man to Take Car Fare," *Louisiana Weekly*, December 3, 1932, p. 1.

24. "Find Hospitals Lack Finances," *New Orleans Item-Tribune*, June 5, 1927, p. 5.

25. Social scientists have argued that a loss of faith in the legitimacy of political and legal institutions fuels crime. See Tom R. Tyler, *Why People Obey the Law* (New Haven, CT: Yale University Press, 1990); Gary LaFree, *Losing Legitimacy: Street Crime and the Decline of Social Institutions in America* (Boulder, CO: Westview, 1998); Randolph Roth, *American Homicide* (Cambridge, MA: Harvard University Press, 2009).

26. Louis Vyhnanek, *Unorganized Crime: New Orleans in the 1920s* (Lafayette, LA: Center for Louisiana Studies, 1998), 54–55.

27. Harry T. Brundidge, "New Orleans Is Called the Wettest Spot of Country; Other Places Merely Damp," *New Orleans Item*, August 9, 1925, pp. 1, 2.

28. Arthur V. Lashly, "Homicide (in Cook County)," in *The Illinois Crime Survey*, ed. John H. Wigmore (Chicago: Illinois Association for Criminal Justice, 1929), 594, 637; John Landesco, "Organized Crime in Chicago," in Wigmore, *The Illinois Crime Survey*, 923–31; James Boudouris, "A Classification of Homicides," *Criminology* 11 (February 1974): 532.

29. Patricia Sullivan, *Days of Hope: Race and Democracy in the New Deal Era* (Chapel Hill: University of North Carolina Press, 1996), 21.

30. Jackson, "Prohibition in New Orleans," 261, 269.

31. Brundidge, "New Orleans Is Called the Wettest Spot of Country"; Vyhnanek, *Unorganized Crime*, 53.

32. Jackson, "Prohibition in New Orleans," 269.

33. "Orleans Votes 14 to 1 against Prohibition Law," *New Orleans Times-Picayune*, April 4, 1930, p. 4.

34. "Drunkenness in New Orleans Has Tripled during 8 Years; 12,788 Arrested Last Year," *New Orleans Item*, May 8, 1925, p. 1.

35. "Drunks' Drunkest in 1924, Figures Say," *New Orleans Times-Picayune*, May 9, 1925, p. 6.

36. "Drunkenness in New Orleans Has Tripled during 8 Years; 12,788 Arrested Last Year," *New Orleans Item*, May 8, 1925, p. 1.

37. Jackson, "Prohibition in New Orleans," 280.

38. Vyhnanek, *Unorganized Crime*, 51; Jackson, "Prohibition in New Orleans," 267.

39. "Not So Bad," *New Orleans Item*, March 6, 1924, p. 14.

40. Jackson, "Prohibition in New Orleans," 268.

41. "Report of Homicide of August Hasler," March 5, 1928, Homicide Reports.

42. Vyhnanek, *Unorganized Crime*, 68.

43. Ibid., 56, 87–88.

44. Lashly, "Homicide (in Cook County)," 594, 637; Boudouris, "A Classification of Homicides," 532.

45. *Sixteenth Census of the United States: 1940, Population, vol. II* (Washington, DC: Government Printing Office, 1943), 427; *Fourteenth Census of the United States Taken in the Year 1920, vol. II, Population* (Washington, DC: Government Printing Office, 1922), 500; *Fifteenth Census of the United States: 1930, Population, vol. II* (Washington, DC: Government Printing Office, 1933), 764; *Sixteenth Census of the United States: 1940, Population, vol. IV*, 895.

46. *Sixteenth Census of the United States: 1940, Population, vol. II*, 426.

47. *Fifteenth Census of the United States: 1930, Population, vol. VI*, 67; *Sixteenth Census of the United States: 1940, Population, vol. IV*, 900.

48. Charles E. Hall, *Negroes in the United States, 1920–1932* (Washington, DC: Government Printing Office, 1935), 183; *Sixteenth Census of the United States: 1940, Population, vol. IV*, 894–95.

49. *Sixteenth Census of the United States: 1940, Population, Differential Fertility*, 225–26, 233; *Fifteenth Census of the United States: 1930, Population, vol. II*, 59; *Sixteenth Census of the United States: 1940, Population, vol. IV*, 900.

50. *Sixteenth Census of the United States: 1940, Population, vol. II*, 434.

51. This is not to suggest that family life became harmonious. Rather, as Roger V. Gould has argued, symmetry in social relations typically fuels conflict and instability. See Gould, *Collision of Wills: How Ambiguity about Social Rank Breeds Conflict* (Chicago: University of Chicago Press, 2003).

52. For young men and violence, see David T. Courtwright, *Violent Land: Single Men and Social Disorder from the Frontier to the Inner City* (Cambridge, MA: Harvard University Press, 1996); Eric H. Monkkonen, *Murder in New York City* (Berkeley: University of California Press, 2001), 55–104; Rosemary Gartner, "Age and Homicide in Different National Contexts," in *The Crime Conundrum: Essays on Criminal Justice*, ed. Lawrence M. Friedman and George Fisher (Boulder, CO: Westview, 1997), 61–74.

53. Harlan W. Gilmore, Warren Breed, A. L. Johnson, Leonard Reissman, and Cliff W. Wing, *1950 New Orleans Population Handbook* (New Orleans: Urban Life Research Institute, 1953), 12.

54. Michele Grigsby Coffey, "*State v. Guerand*: A Study of Racial Violence, Justice, and Injustice in the Jim Crow South" (M.A. thesis, Baylor University, 2002), 78–79; Karl E. Taeuber and Alma F. Taeuber, *Negroes in Cities: Residential Segregation and Neighborhood Change* (Chicago: Aldine, 1965), 190; Peirce F. Lewis, *New Orleans: The Making of an Urban Landscape*, 2nd ed. (Santa Fe, NM: Center for American Places, 2003), 41.

55. Lewis, *New Orleans*, 68–69; George Campanella, *Geographies of New Orleans: Urban Fabrics before the Storm* (Lafayette, LA: Center for Louisiana Studies, 2006), 18, 60.

56. Daphne Spain, "Race Relations and Residential Segregation in New Orleans: Two Centuries of Paradox," *Annals of the American Academy of Political and Social Science* 441 (January 1979): 90; Gilmore et al., *1950 New Orleans Handbook*, 13.

57. Lewis, *New Orleans*, 97.

58. Allison Davis and John Dollard, *Children of Bondage: The Personality Development of Negro Youth in the Urban South* (Washington, DC: American Council of Education, 1940), xxvi, 135. Also see Allison Davis, "How It Feels to Be Lower Caste" (typescript), Series V, Subseries 3, Box 32, Folder 14, p. 31, Allison Davis Papers, Special Collections Research Center, University of Chicago, Chicago, IL; Alecia P. Long, *The Great Southern Babylon: Sex, Race, and Respectability in New Orleans, 1865–1920* (Baton Rouge: Louisiana State University Press, 2004), 222.

59. Davis and Dollard, *Children of Bondage*, xxvi.

60. These sources no longer used terms such as "Creole," "Mulatto," or "Quadroon." By the late 1930s, white officials had codified this binary racial hierarchy, as Louisiana adopted a "one-drop" definition of race. See *Sunseri v. Cassagne*, 191 La. 209 (1938).

61. Sharlene Sinegal DeCuir, "Attacking Jim Crow: Black Activism in New Orleans" (Ph.D. dissertation, Louisiana State University, 2009), 3–5, 88, 145–47, 153, 173; Maclachlan, "Up from Paternalism," 34; Brandon T. Jett, "African Americans and the Police in the Jim Crow South, 1900–1945" (Ph.D. dissertation, University of Florida, 2017), 99–120; Rachel L. Emanuel and Alexander P. Tureaud Jr., *A More Noble Cause: A. P. Tureaud and the Struggle for Civil Rights in Louisiana* (Baton Rouge: Louisiana State University Press, 2011), 61–65, 86–91; Adam Fairclough, *Race and Democracy: The Civil Rights Struggle in Louisiana, 1915–1972* (Athens: University of Georgia Press, 1995), 49.

62. Newspaper clipping, editorial from the *New Orleans Item*, August 1, 1932, files of the New Orleans branch of the National Association for the Advancement of Colored People in the Papers of the NAACP, Part 12, Reel 14, NAACP Papers.

63. Fairclough, *Race and Democracy*, 66; Emanuel and Tureaud, *A More Noble Cause*, 44–65; DeCuir, "Attacking Jim Crow," 174; Maclachlan, "Up from Paternalism," 44.

64. See Michele Grigsby Coffey, "Providing for Our Communities, Protecting Our Race, Proving Ourselves: African American Activism and Protest in Depression Era New Orleans" (Ph.D. dissertation, University of South Carolina, 2010).

65. Ibid., 161–207; Michele Grigsby Coffey, "*The State of Louisiana v. Charles Guerand*: Interracial Sexual Mores, Rape Rhetoric, and Respectability in 1930s New Orleans," *Louisiana History* 54 (Winter 2013): 53–72.

66. Harold N. Lee to Mr. Musgrove, September 24, 1939, Papers of the Louisiana League for the Preservation of Constitutional Rights, Harold Newton Lee Papers, Manuscripts Collection 245, Louisiana Research Collection, Howard-Tilton Memorial Library, Tulane University, New Orleans, LA; "League Demands Action to Assure Rights of Public," *New Orleans Times-Picayune*, August 2, 1939, p. 3; Jett, "African Americans and the Police in the Jim Crow South, 1900–1945," 153–59.

67. For the early development of the local civil rights movement, see Fairclough, *Race and Democracy*.

68. The sociologist Robert J. Sampson argues that such "collective efficacy" generates social cohesion and reduces crime and disorder. See Sampson, *Great American City: Chicago and the Enduring Neighborhood Effect* (Chicago: University of Chicago Press, 2012), 152–78.

69. For examinations of this process, see Donald E. Devore, *Defying Jim Crow: African American Community Development and the Struggle for Racial Equality in New Orleans, 1900–1960* (Baton Rouge: Louisiana State University Press, 2015); Coffey, "Providing for Our Communities, Protecting Our Race, Proving Ourselves"; DeCuir, "Attacking Jim Crow"; Maclachlan, "Up from Paternalism."

70. "Report of Homicide of Henry Sambrone," November 12, 1931, Homicide Reports; "Inquest Report on Henry Sam Baronne [*sic*]," November 12, 1931, Coroner's Reports.

71. "Report of Homicide of Joseph Gomez," October 10, 1929, Homicide Reports.

72. M. P. Baumgartner, "Violent Networks: The Origins and Management of Domestic Conflict," in *Aggression and Violence: Social Interactionist Perspectives*, ed. Richard B. Felson and James Tedeschi (Washington, DC: American Psychological Association, 1993), 209–31.

73. "Report of Homicide of Cecil McNair," August 26, 1931, Homicide Reports.

74. Testimony of Dimitry Saik, *State of Louisiana v. Fred Kelly*, Docket #30352, November 12, 1929, p. 12, Section C Case Files, Louisiana Supreme Court Case Files, Historical Archives of the Supreme Court of Louisiana, Earl K. Long Library, University of New Orleans, New Orleans, LA [hereafter "Louisiana Supreme Court Case Files"].

75. William J. O'Hara, "Motion for New Trial," *State of Louisiana v. Fred Kelly*, Docket #30352, November 12, 1929, p. 22, Section C Case Files, Louisiana Supreme Court Case Files; "Convict Record of Fred Kelly," Louisiana State Penitentiary Records, vol. 31 (1929–30), p. 73, accessed via Ancestry.com, September 2, 2015.

76. "Report of Homicide of Jules Saik," August 15, 1929, Homicide Reports.

77. During the 1920s, when disputes more often unfolded in homes, the guns kept on mantels or stashed in closets had been more readily accessible during quarrels.

78. For bullet injuries, see "More Gunshot Wounds Given Treatment at Hospital Here than in Any Other U.S. City," *New Orleans Item*, April 22, 1925, p. 1. Even with modern trauma care, the mortality rate for gunshot wounds is quadruple the rate for stab wounds. See Roger Band, Rama A. Salhi, Daniel N. Holena, Elizabeth Powell, Charles C. Branas, and Brendan G. Carr, "Severity-Adjusted Mortality in Trauma Patients Transported by Police," *Annals of Emergency Medicine* 63 (May 2014): 611.

79. "Murder Charged Filed in Death," *New Orleans Item*, March 17, 1935, p. 11.

80. For "cutting scrapes," see "An Unusual Case," *New Orleans Item*, August 22, 1927, p. 4.

81. H[arrington] C[ooper] Brearley, *Homicide in the United States* (Chapel Hill: University of North Carolina Press, 1932), 71.

82. Frederick L. Hoffman, "Letter to the Editor," *New York Times*, October 19, 1930, p. 52.

83. Robert J. Spitzer, *Guns across America: Reconciling Gun Rules and Rights* (New York: Oxford University Press, 2015), 186–89.

84. "Gun Toting," *New Orleans States*, March 22, 1930, p. 4.

85. Robert H. Marr, *The Criminal Jurisprudence of Louisiana* (New Orleans: Hansell & Bro., 1923), 350–51.

86. "Big Knives and Pistol Found on Negro Pair by Observing Police Officer," *New Orleans Item*, January 2, 1921, p. 5; "20 'Pistol-Toters' Must Face Court," *New Orleans Times-Picayune*, January 5, 1926, p. 7; "Loses Life over Ten Cent Bet," *Louisiana Weekly*, October 2, 1937, p. 2; "City-Wide Negro Roundup Follows in Wake of Murder," *New Orleans Item*, August 19, 1943, p. 1. For a related analysis, see Khalil Gibran Muhammad, *The Condemnation of Blackness: Race, Crime, and the Making of Urban America* (Cambridge, MA: Harvard University Press, 2010), 240–68.

87. Such use of the criminal law is consistent with Emile Durkheim's theory of deviance. See Durkheim, *The Division of Labor in Society* (1933; rpt. New York: Free Press, 1984), 58–61.

88. "Molony Scores 'Gun-Toting' Evil in Underworld," *New Orleans Times-Picayune*, May 25, 1923, p. 3.

89. "Prompt Trials, Death Penalty Urged by Jury," *New Orleans Item*, March 3, 1925, p. 18.

90. "Pistol Toters Are Assailed by Dr. Matas," *New Orleans Times-Picayune*, January 27, 1926, p. 3.

91. "Hanging Only Cure for Homicides, Says Molony," *New Orleans Item*, July 6, 1924, p. 1.

92. Brearley, *Homicide in the United States*, 74.

93. Frederick L. Hoffman, *The Homicide Problem* (Newark, NJ: Prudential Press, 1925), 4; William McAdoo, "Crime and Punishment: Causes and Mechanisms of Prevalent Crimes," *Scientific Monthly* 24 (May 1927): 418.

94. Julius Rosenwald, 1930, quoted in Brearley, *Homicide in the United States*, 74.

95. "Hanging Only Cure for Homicides, Says Molony," *New Orleans Item*, July 6, 1924, p. 1.

96. McAdoo, "Crime and Punishment," 418.

97. For example, see "Classified Ads," *New Orleans States*, May 25, 1924, p. 12.

98. "Gun-Toting," *New Orleans States*, March 22, 1930, p. 4; "Persuaded to Take Blame, He Testifies," *New Orleans Item*, June 24, 1920, p. 6. For "'Saturday night' weapons," see "Prowler

Surprised by Woman Escaper After Chase by 100 Orleanians," *New Orleans Item*, September 23, 1920, p. 20.

99. "Examination of Henry Moity," October 30, 1927, *State of Louisiana v. Henry Moity*, Criminal District Court, Section E Case Files, Docket #40877–78, November 1927, p. 86, Louisiana Supreme Court Case Files.

100. "Report of Homicide of Joseph Harris," July 27, 1921, Homicide Reports.

101. "Report of Homicide of Hugh Macelus," September 29, 1921, Homicide Reports; "Report of Homicide of Sam Lala," November 22, 1921, Homicide Reports.

102. "Classified Ads," *New Orleans Item*, August 27, 1922, p. 12.

103. Lee Kennett and James La Verne Anderson, *The Gun in America: The Origins of a National Dilemma* (Westport, CT: Greenwood Press, 1975), 194.

104. "Classified Ads," *New Orleans Item*, July 22, 1934, p. 21; "Classified Ads," *New Orleans Times-Picayune*, December 4, 1934, p. 34.

105. For example, see "Robbery Report of Carrol Dulberger," February 14, 1925, p. 505, Robbery Reports, Offense Reports, New Orleans Police Department, City of New Orleans, City Archives/Louisiana Division, New Orleans Public Library, New Orleans, LA [hereafter "Offense Reports"]; "Robbery Report of Allan R. Mayo," January 5, 1935, Residence Robbery Reports, Offense Reports.

106. "Report of Homicide of George Bensfield," August 15, 1938, Homicide Reports; "Statement of Louis Sapp relative to the murder of one Harold Bourg," November 28, 1935, Statements of Witnesses.

107. Dollard and Davis, *Children of Bondage*, 80; John Dollard, *Caste and Class in a Southern Town* (New York: Doubleday Anchor, 1937), 271–72.

108. Sterner, *The Negro's Share*, 362; Sullivan, *Days of Hope*, 21; Coffey, "Providing for Our Communities, Protecting Our Race, Proving Ourselves," 23–25.

109. Figure 4.4 does not disaggregate by occupational group.

110. Garen J. Wintemute, "Firearms as a Cause of Death in the United States, 1920–1982," *Journal of Trauma* 27 (May 1987): 533; Douglas Eckberg, "Crime, Law Enforcement, and Justice," in *Historical Statistics of the United States*, vol. 5, *Governance and International Relations*, ed. Susan B. Carter, Scott Sigmund Gartner, Michael R. Haines, Alan L. Olmstead, Richard Sutch, and Gavin Wright (New York: Cambridge University Press, 2006), 239.

111. "Statement of Anselmo Garcia relative to the murder of George Bensfield," August 15, 1938, Statements of Witnesses.

112. "Report of Homicide of George Bensfield," August 15, 1938, Homicide Reports.

113. "Report of Homicide of Mabel Slack," December 7, 1935, Homicide Reports.

114. "Statement of Cleo Wiley relative to being charged with the murder of Mabel Slack," December 7, 1935, Statements of Witnesses; "Inquest Report on Mabel Slack," December 7, 1935, Coroner's Reports.

115. "Statement of Ethel Daniels relative to the fatal cutting of Sam Hollins," October 4, 1935, Statements of Witnesses; "Report of Homicide of Sam Hollins," October 4, 1935, Homicide Reports; "Inquest Report on Samuel Holland" [*sic*], October 4, 1935, Coroner's Reports.

116. Dean Gordon B. Hancock, "Between the Lines," *Louisiana Weekly*, June 26, 1943, p. 10.

CHAPTER 5

1. "Report of Homicides of Mrs. Anna Flink and Henry Sylvester Flink," April 13, 1929, Homicide Reports, Department of Police, City of New Orleans, City Archives/Louisiana Division, New Orleans Public Library, New Orleans, LA [hereafter "Homicide Reports"]. Police records identified Mrs. Flink as "Anna," though other sources listed her as "Annie."

2. "Testimony of Anna Van Val," *State of Louisiana v. Julius Roberts*, Docket #30539, February 27, 1929, p. 90, Section D Case Files, Louisiana Supreme Court Case Files, Historical Archives of the Supreme Court of Louisiana, Earl K. Long Library, University of New Orleans, New Orleans, LA [hereafter "Louisiana Supreme Court Case Files"]; "Two Held in Ax Murders after Quiz," *New Orleans Item*, April 14, 1929, p. 3.

3. For the panic and celebrity bandits, see Claire Bond Potter, *War on Crime: Bandits, G-Men, and the Politics of Mass Culture* (New Brunswick, NJ: Rutgers University Press, 1998).

4. "Homicide Reports of Mrs. Anna Flink and Henry Sylvester Flink," April 13, 1929, Homicide Reports.

5. "Statement of Julius Roberts," *State of Louisiana v. Julius Roberts*, Criminal District Court, Docket #48235, April 15, 1929, Section C Case Files, City Archives/Louisiana Division, New Orleans Public Library, New Orleans, LA [hereafter "Criminal District Court Files"].

6. "Testimony of Anna Van Val," *State of Louisiana v. Julius Roberts*, February 27, 1929, p. 91, Louisiana Supreme Court Case Files.

7. "Statement of Julius Roberts," *State of Louisiana v. Julius Roberts*, April 15, 1929, Criminal District Court Files; "Testimony of Charles Flink," *State of Louisiana v. Julius Roberts*, Docket #30559, February 27, 1930, pp. 113–14, Louisiana Supreme Court Case Files.

8. "Statement of Julius Roberts," *State of Louisiana v. Julius Roberts*, April 15, 1929, Criminal District Court Files.

9. Ibid.

10. "Inquest Reports on Annie Flink and Henry Sylvester Flink," April 13, 1929, Coroner's Reports, Coroner's Office, City of New Orleans, Parish of Orleans, State of Louisiana, City Archives/Louisiana Division, New Orleans Public Library, New Orleans, LA [hereafter "Coroner's Reports"]. For the death of Henry Flink Sr., see "Deaths," *New Orleans States*, April 1, 1928, p. 2.

11. "Saved by Technicality," *New Orleans States*, May 7, 1929, p. 6; "Particeps Criminis," *New Orleans Times-Picayune*, April 17, 1929, p. 10.

12. For important discussions of this topic, see Bertram Doyle, *The Etiquette of Race Relations: A Study of Social Control* (Chicago: University of Chicago Press, 1937); John Dollard, *Caste and Class in a Southern Town* (New York: Doubleday Anchor, 1937); Stephen A. Berrey, *The Jim Crow Routine: Everyday Performances of Race, Civil Rights, and Segregation in Mississippi* (Chapel Hill: University of North Carolina Press, 2015); Jennifer Ritterhouse, *Growing Up Jim Crow: How Black and White Children Learned Race* (Chapel Hill: University of North Carolina Press, 2006).

13. "Statement of Julius Roberts," *State of Louisiana v. Julius Roberts*, April 15, 1929, Criminal District Court Files.

14. "Action Needed," *New Orleans Item*, October 7, 1929, p. 10; "Driver of Bandit Car Is Given Life Term in New Orleans," *Baton Rouge Times Advocate*, January 28, 1932, p. 15.

15. "Hanging Only Cure for Homicides, Says Molony," *New Orleans Item*, July 6, 1924, p. 1; "Action Needed," *New Orleans Item*, October 7, 1929, p. 10.

16. Data on robberies are difficult to gather, for robberies often went unreported. The police maintained reports of robberies, though burglaries comprised the majority of the cases. See "Robbery Reports," Offense Reports, New Orleans Police Department, City of New Orleans, City Archives/Louisiana Division, New Orleans Public Library, New Orleans, LA [hereafter "Offense Reports"]. FBI data, gathered in the *Uniform Crime Reports*, calculated reported robberies, beginning in 1931. The comparative figures came from 1931 data. See "Total Offenses Reported for 1931," *Uniform Crime Reports* 2 (December 1931): 16–17; "Felonious Homicide and Robbery, 1930–31, 58 Cities over 100,000 Population," *Uniform Crime Reports* 3 (July 1932): 8.

17. See Potter, *War on Crime*; Elliott J. Gorn, *Dillinger's Wild Ride: The Year That Made America's Public Enemy Number One* (New York: Oxford University Press, 2009).

18. "Report of Homicide of Frank Pipitone," March 15, 1930, Homicide Reports.

19. "Arrest Suspect after Bandit Kills Man," *New Orleans States*, March 16, 1930, p. 10.

20. "Inquest Report on Frank Pipitone," March 15, 1930, Coroner's Reports.

21. "Statement of Captain Charles Volz to a [*sic*] unknown white man throwing a [*sic*] automatic pistol out of a Blue green automobile," March 15, 1930, Transcripts of Statements of Witnesses to Homicides, New Orleans Police Department, City of New Orleans, City Archives/Louisiana Division, New Orleans Public Library, New Orleans, LA [hereafter "Statements of Witnesses"].

22. "Capture 3rd Suspect in Killing of Policeman," *New Orleans States*, December 25, 1930, p. 2.

23. "Report of Homicide of Ernest A. Grillott," December 24, 1930, Homicide Reports; "Inquest Report on Ernest Adrian Grillot," December 24, 1930, Coroner's Reports.

24. "Infuriated Throng Threatens Lynching," *New Orleans Times-Picayune*, December 25, 1930, p. 3.

25. "Ito Jacques Sentenced to Hang in June," *Louisiana Weekly*, April 23, 1932, p. 1.

26. "Policeman Shot by Negro Bandit Dying of Wounds," *New Orleans Times-Picayune*, November 24, 1930, p. 3; "Four Bandits Convicted of Rizzo Murder," *New Orleans Times-Picayune*, February 28, 1931, p. 1.

27. "Policeman Shot by Negro Bandit Dying of Wounds," *New Orleans Times-Picayune*, November 24, 1930, p. 3.

28. "War on Bandits Drives Them to N. O., Says Saint," *New Orleans Item*, November 24, 1930, p. 1.

29. "Bandit-Murderers," *New Orleans Times-Picayune*, January 1, 1931, p. 10.

30. "Four Bandits Convicted of Rizzo Murder," *New Orleans Times-Picayune*, February 28, 1931, p. 4.

31. Emanuel H. Lavine, *The Third Degree: A Detailed and Appalling Exposé of Police Brutality* (Garden City, NY: Garden City Publishing, 1930), 227.

32. "Crazed Orleans Negro Killed by Officer's Shot," *Baton Rouge State Times Advocate*, April 7, 1930, p. 3.

33. The robbery figures were culled from late 1920s police department Offense Reports. I

examined every report and separated robberies from burglaries and larcenies. Because many New Orleanians likely failed to report robberies, this figure is suggestive rather than definitive. The race of the robbers roughly mirrored the composition of the population. Robbery-homicide figures, drawn from the Homicide Reports, were more precise.

34. "Statement of Sanders Watkins," April 26, 1932, Statements of Witnesses.

35. "Statement of Leaval Hubbard," April 26, 1932, Statements of Witnesses.

36. "Statement of Sanders Watkins," April 26, 1932, Statements of Witnesses; "Killer at Victim's Funeral," *New Orleans Item*, April 26, 1932, p. 4.

37. "Three Boys Held for Killing Tamale Vendor," *New Orleans Times-Picayune*, August 17, 1940, p. 13; "Statement of Jacob Vildhinsen relative to having been shot by an unknown negro," July 8, 1940, Statements of Witnesses.

38. "Crime and Vice," *New Orleans Item*, July 18, 1922, p. 8; Allison Davis, Burleigh B. Gardner, and Mary Gardner, *Deep South: A Social Anthropological Study of Caste and Class* (Chicago: University of Chicago Press, 1941), 520; "Behind the High Rate of Homicide," *Louisiana Weekly*, December 12, 1942, p. 10; Thorsten Sellin, "The Negro and the Problem of Law Observance and Administration in the Light of Social Research," in *The Negro in American Civilization: A Study of Negro Life and Race Relations in the Light of Social Research*, ed. Charles S. Johnson (New York: Henry Holt, 1930), 443–44.

39. For a sociological analysis of this phenomenon, see Joel Best, *Random Violence: How We Talk about New Crimes and New Victims* (Berkeley: University of California Press, 1999), 93–118.

40. "Son of Murdered Man Pleading for Work," *New Orleans States*, April 26, 1932, p. 1; "Killer at Victim's Funeral," *New Orleans Item*, April 26, 1932, p. 4.

41. Robert M. Fogelson, *Big-City Police* (Cambridge, MA: Harvard University Press, 1977), 117–92.

42. Louis Vyhnanek, *Unorganized Crime: New Orleans in the 1920s* (Lafayette, LA: Center for Louisiana Studies, 1998), 32; Bruce Smith, *The New Orleans Police Survey* (New Orleans: Bureau of Governmental Research, 1946), 1–3, 34, 26.

43. "Hanging Only Cure for Homicides, Says Molony," *New Orleans Item*, July 6, 1924, p. 1.

44. "Ray Warns City Thuggery Looms under Behrman," *New Orleans Times-Picayune*, January 26, 1925, p. 25.

45. "Police Budget to Drop 143 Men from Ranks in '23," *New Orleans Times-Picayune*, December 28, 1922, p. 1.

46. For the "discovery" of social problems, see Stephen J. Pfohl, "The 'Discovery' of Child Abuse," *Social Problems* 24 (February 1977): 310–23.

47. "Vows Policy of Action as Police Chief," *New Orleans Item*, May 13, 1925, p. 1.

48. "Ray Threatens Drastic Action to Stop Hold-Ups," *New Orleans Times-Picayune*, October 7, 1929, p. 1.

49. See Best, *Random Violence*, 142–61.

50. "Pay Roll Hold-Ups Stir Ray to War on Bandit Gangs," *New Orleans Times-Picayune*, July 21, 1929, p. 1.

51. "Ray Shifts 50 Officers in War on Holdups," *New Orleans States*, March 20, 1930, p. 1; "Myers, Reyer Plan New War on Bandits," *New Orleans States*, May 6, 1930, p. 1.

52. "Police to Get Machine Guns to Fight Bandits," *New Orleans Item*, March 31, 1926, p. 1.

53. "Orleans Police to Get Machine Gun to Curb Bandits," *New Orleans Times-Picayune*, July 11, 1929, p. 17; "Police to Use Machine Guns to Battle Bandits in Future: 'Shoot to Kill,' Is Order Issued by Superintendent Ray," *New Orleans Item*, July 10, 1929, p. 1.

54. "Bandits Beware," *New Orleans Item*, July 10, 1929, p. 1; "Orleans Police to Get Machine Gun to Curb Bandits," *New Orleans Times-Picayune*, July 11, 1929, p. 17.

55. "Police Squads Proficient with Guns," *New Orleans States*, April 7, 1930, p. 1.

56. "Orleans Police to Get Machine Gun to Curb Bandits," *New Orleans Times-Picayune*, July 11, 1929, p. 17.

57. "Ray to Revive Target Practice So Police Won't Miss Bandits," *New Orleans Item*, June 16, 1929, p. 10.

58. "Orleans Police to Get Machine Gun to Curb Bandits," *New Orleans Times-Picayune*, July 11, 1929, p. 17.

59. For example, "Patrolman Is Cited for Killing Bandits," *New Orleans Times-Picayune*, March 18, 1931, p. 3. Between 1920 and 1945, twenty-three holdup men were killed during robberies, eight of them between 1930 and 1933. Bandits killed seventy-six of their victims.

60. "Police Killings," *New Orleans Item*, August 4, 1927, p. 12.

61. These figures were culled from volumes 2–16 of the FBI's *Uniform Crime Reports*.

62. "15 Die, 12 Wounded in Orleans Hold-Up Cases during Last Year," *New Orleans Times-Picayune*, January 1, 1931, p. 1. The newspaper's tally included robbers who were killed.

63. "Better Policing," *Louisiana Weekly*, December 21, 1929, p. 6.

64. *New Orleans Morning Tribune*, 1929, quoted in "Better Policing," *Louisiana Weekly*, December 21, 1929, p. 6.

65. "Driver of Bandit Car Is Given Life Term in New Orleans," *Baton Rouge Times Advocate*, January 28, 1932, p. 15.

66. "Stanley Invites Allen to Start Suit for Ouster," *New Orleans Times-Picayune*, July 25, 1934, p. 9.

67. J. B. Priestley, "New Orleans: A First Impression," *Harper's Magazine* 176 (May 1938): 595.

68. "Annual Trends, Offenses Known to the Police, 1931–1939," *Uniform Crime Reports* 10 (January 1940): 171.

69. "Police to Use Machine Guns to Battle Bandits in Future: 'Shoot to Kill,' Is Order Issued by Superintendent Ray," *New Orleans Item*, July 10, 1929, p. 1.

70. "Healy Will Set Deadline Limits against Bandits," *New Orleans Times-Picayune*, August 4, 1928, p. 1.

71. *Harmon v. Tyler*, 273 U.S. 668 (1927).

72. *Trudeau v. Barnes*, 65 F.2d 563 (1933); "A Registration Challenge," *Louisiana Weekly*, April 11, 1931, p. 6; Donald E. Devore, *Defying Jim Crow: African American Community Development and the Struggle for Racial Equality in New Orleans, 1900–1960* (Baton Rouge: Louisiana State University Press, 2015), 186–90; Sharlene Sinegal DeCuir, "Attacking Jim Crow: Black Activism in New Orleans" (Ph.D. dissertation, Louisiana State University, 2009), 137–42.

73. "65,000 Negroes Sign Poll Books, Asserts Stanley," *New Orleans Times-Picayune*, May 31, 1935, p. 3.

74. "Called for Jury Service," *Louisiana Weekly*, August 3, 1935, p. 8; "Negroes Qualified for Jury Duty Here," *Louisiana Weekly*, November 5, 1935, p. 7.

75. Charles S. Johnson, *Patterns of Negro Segregation* (New York: Harper & Brothers, 1943), 127.

76. Dollard, *Class and Caste in a Southern Town*, 213; Robert Russa Moton, *What the Negro Thinks* (New York: Doubleday, 1929), 213; Berrey, *The Jim Crow Routine*, 33.

77. Johnson, *Patterns of Negro Segregation*, 125.

78. "Statement of Albert Johnson," *State of Louisiana v. Andrew Wiebelt*, Docket #29325, May 16, 1928, pp. 58, 67, Louisiana Supreme Court Case Files.

79. "Report of Homicide of Lily Johnson," August 23, 1927, Homicide Reports.

80. For example, see "Street Car Segregation," *Louisiana Weekly*, November 6, 1926, p. 6; "Report of Homicide of Joseph Baptiste," November 23, 1924, Homicide Reports.

81. Social psychologists have charted the ways in which implicit bias shapes responses to ambiguous interactions. See H. Andrew Sagar and Janet Ward Schofield, "Racial and Behavioral Cues in Black and White Children's Perceptions of Ambiguously Aggressive Acts," *Journal of Personality and Social Psychology* 39 (October 1980): 590–98.

82. "Student's Slayer Hunted," *New Orleans Item*, March 5, 1930, p. 3; "Killing Mars Mardi Gras," *Louisiana Weekly*, March 8, 1930, p. 1.

83. "Transcript of 'Radio Speech' by Maurice B. Galtan," Station WBW, August 9, 1935, files of the New Orleans branch of the National Association for the Advancement of Colored People in the Papers of the NAACP, Part 12, Reel 15, Series A, ed. John H. Bracey Jr. and August Meier, University Publications (Bethesda, MD, 1991).

84. For the fear of white mobs, see the city attorney's brief in the segregation case. Bertrand I. Cahn, "*Amicus Curiae* Brief," *Harmon v. Tyler* (October 1926), reprinted in *Harmon v. Tyler*, US Supreme Court Transcript of Record with Supporting Pleadings (Farmington Hills, MI: Gale, 2011), 51–53.

85. Except for two outlying years in robbery homicide (1926 and 1931), the trends moved together.

86. Between 1920 and 1945, white robbers murdered twenty-five victims, and New Orleans police officers killed thirty-six white suspects. Although the two trend lines generally moved together, they deviated in 1926 and 1931. During these years, an echo effect from the robbery-homicides committed in the previous years buoyed the police homicide rate. Put differently, the panic from earlier surges in robbery-homicide persisted, leading to more aggressive and more deadly policing.

87. "Report of Homicide of Vernon Floyd," April 27, 1930, Homicide Reports; "Deaths," *New Orleans Item*, April 28, 1930, p. 2; "Inquest Report on Vernon Floyd," April 27, 1930, Coroner's Reports; "Two Bandits Shot Down Fleeing Holdup Scene," *New Orleans Item*, April 27, 1930, p. 1.

88. "Credo Is Promoted for Killing Bandit," *New Orleans Times-Picayune*, May 2, 1930, p. 2.

89. African American robbers murdered thirty-nine victims between 1920 and 1945, while policemen killed seventy African American New Orleanians. Local law enforcers killed sixteen African American suspects between 1930 and 1932 and eleven between 1935 and 1937.

90. Of the thirty-six white victims of police homicide, seventeen were suspected of rob-

bery or burglary. Twenty-three of seventy African American victims were robbery or burglary suspects.

91. "Report of Homicide of Milton Battise," June 29, 1930, Homicide Reports; "Negro Fleeing Arrest Killed by Road Police," *New Orleans Times-Picayune*, June 30, 1930, p. 1. Karl and Mamola belonged to the State Highway Motorcycle Police.

92. "Highway Police Held for Killing Negro Who Fled," *New Orleans Times-Picayune*, July 1, 1930, p. 6.

93. "Report of Homicide of Milton Battise," June 29, 1930, Homicide Reports. The district attorney ruled the shooting justifiable.

94. "Police Kill Man Who Threatens, Resists Arrest," *New Orleans Times-Picayune*, July 28, 1938, p. 8; "Report of Homicide of Paul Henry," August 1, 1927, Homicide Reports; "Statement of Patrolman Joseph P. Tansey, relative to him killing one Dave Hughes," April 6, 1930, Statements of Witnesses; "Hip-Pocket Move Brings Death to Attack Suspect," *New Orleans Times-Picayune*, June 18, 1939, p. 12.

95. "Hip-Pocket Move Brings Death to Attack Suspect," *New Orleans Times-Picayune*, June 18, 1939, p. 12.

96. Frederick L. Hoffman, "The Increase in Murder," *Annals of the American Academy of Political and Social Science* 125 (May 1926): 23; H[arrington] C[ooper] Brearley, "The Pattern of Violence," in *Culture in the South*, ed. W. T. Couch (Chapel Hill: University of North Carolina Press, 1935), 690.

97. "Negro Halted by Bullet after Breaking Away," *New Orleans Times-Picayune*, April 30, 1924, p. 1.

98. Smith, *The New Orleans Police Survey*, 8–9.

99. Jeffrey S. Adler, "'The Killer behind the Badge': Race and Police Homicide in New Orleans, 1925–1945," *Law and History Review* 30 (May 2012): 501–3. See the important scholarship on implicit bias and weapon (mis)identification, such as Jerry Kang, "Trojan Horses of Race," *Harvard Law Review* 118 (March 2005): 1503–19; Jennifer L. Eberhardt, "Imaging Race," *American Psychologist* (February–March 2005): 181–90.

100. "The Average Policeman," *Louisiana Weekly*, October 1, 1927, p. 6. Also see Jonathan Rubinstein, *City Police* (New York: Farrar, Straus & Giroux, 1973), 330; Malcolm D. Holmes and Brad W. Smith, *Race and Police Brutality: Roots of an Urban Dilemma* (Albany, NY: SUNY Press, 2008), 92.

101. Smith, *The New Orleans Police Survey*, 37; Vyhnanek, *Unorganized Crime*, 32.

102. Gunner Myrdal, *An American Dilemma: The Negro Problem and Modern Democracy*, vol. 2 (1944; rpt. with an introduction by Sissela Bok, New Brunswick, NJ: Transaction, 1962), 540.

103. "'The Killer behind the Badge,'" *Louisiana Weekly*, October 3, 1942, p. 10.

104. For a related discussion, see Hannah Arendt, *On Violence* (New York: Harcourt, 1969), 77.

105. Joseph H. Fichter, with the collaboration of Brian Jordan, "Police Handlings of Arrestees: A Research Study of Police Arrests in New Orleans" (unpublished report, Department of Sociology, Loyola University of the South, 1964), 50. Also see Myrdal, *An American Dilemma* 2:535, 2:540.

106. White residents comprised ten of the twenty victims.

107. Between 1931 and 1934, twelve of the eighteen victims were African American, and during the late 1930s, ten of thirteen were African American residents.

108. "Second Man Shot at Gentilly," *Louisiana Weekly*, August 12, 1933, p. 4; "Threat to Shoot Met with Bullet," *New Orleans Times-Picayune*, August 6, 1933, p. 26.

109. Adler, "'The Killer behind the Badge,'" 499–500. Of the 106 police homicides between 1920 and 1945, one policeman was convicted.

110. "The 'Hot Tamale' Decision," *Louisiana Weekly*, November 8, 1941 p. 10; "On Trial; Lads' Bodies Show Cuts, Bruises; Await Verdict," *Louisiana Weekly*, July 31, 1937, p. 4.

111. See Jeffrey S. Adler, "'The Greatest Thrill I Get Is When I Hear a Criminal Say, Yes, I Did It': Race and the Third Degree in New Orleans, 1920–1945," *Law and History Review* 34 (February 2016): 1–44.

112. Zechariah Chafee Jr., Walter H. Pollak, and Carl S. Stern, "The Third Degree," in *National Commission on Law Observance and Enforcement, No. 11: Report on Lawlessness in Law Enforcement* (Washington, DC: United States Government Printing Office, 1931), 52–83; Richard A. Leo, *Police Interrogation and American Justice* (Cambridge, MA: Harvard University Press, 2008), 69; Marilynn S. Johnson, *Street Justice: A History of Police Violence in New York City* (Boston: Beacon Press, 2003), 122–42.

113. Article I, Section 11, *Constitution of the State of Louisiana, Adopted in Convention at the City of Baton Rouge, June 18, 1921* (Baton Rouge: Ramires-Jones, 1921), 3.

114. *Report on Lawlessness in Law Enforcement.*

115. See "Third Degree Has Defenders as Well as Vigorous Critics," *New York Times*, July 24, 1932, XX3.

116. "Molony and Marr Drop 'Third Degree' Battle," *New Orleans Item*, April 22, 1921, p. 12.

117. "Detectives Face Assault Charge in Court Today," *New Orleans Times-Picayune*, January 31, 1923, p. 9; "Head Crushed by Robber, Aged Victim Dies," *New Orleans Item*, July 18, 1923, p. 1.

118. "Crime Board Asks Constitutional Ban on Third Degree," *New Orleans Times-Picayune*, August 11, 1931, p. 15.

119. "Against Third Degree," *New Orleans States*, June 3, 1933, p. 4.

120. "Third Degree Case," *New Orleans States*, May 13, 1932, p. 6.

121. "Grosch Target of Mrs. Purvis Defense Fire," *New Orleans States*, December 16, 1933, p. 2; "Labor Meeting in C.I.O. Row Is Continued," *Baton Rouge State Times Advocate*, July 1, 1938, p. 6; "Bandit in Bank Raid Denies Third Degree Used on Confession," *New Orleans Item*, July 10, 1936, p. 21.

122. "Crime Is Curbed by 'Third Degree,' Asserts Grosch," *New Orleans Times-Picayune*, June 1, 1939, p. 1.

123. "A Fair Hearing," *New Orleans States*, January 12, 1938, p. 6.

124. "Testimony of Edward J. Smith," *State of Louisiana v. James Scarbrough*, Docket #029362, June 2, 1928, Section A Case Files, Louisiana Supreme Court Case Files; "Suspect in Hacking Case Is Denied Writ; One Victim Is Dying," *New Orleans States*, July 20, 1937, p. 21; B. Ogden Chisolm and Hastings H. Hart, "Methods of Obtaining Confessions and Informa-

tion from Persons Accused of Crime," paper presented at the Fifty-First Congress of the American Prison Association, Jacksonville, FL, 1921 (New York: Russell Sage Foundation, 1922), 17.

125. "Testimony of James Scarbrough," *State of Louisiana v. James Scarbrough*, Docket # 029362, June 1928, Section A Case Files, Louisiana Supreme Court Case Files; "On Trial, Lads' Bodies Show Cuts, Bruises; Await Verdict," *Louisiana Weekly*, July 31, 1937, p. 1.

126. "Last Pleas Made to Save Slayers From Scaffold," *New Orleans Times-Picayune*, April 29, 1933, p. 2.

127. James B. LaFourche, "11-Year-Old Witness Tells Court Cops Beat Him and Promised Bicycle for Lie," *Louisiana Weekly*, May 15, 1937, p. 1.

128. "Johnson Saved, but Gets Life Imprisonment," *Louisiana Weekly*, August 30, 1930, p. 1.

129. "Alleged 'Third Degree' Methods Inquiry Will Be Resumed Today," *New Orleans Times-Picayune*, February 25, 1932, p. 1; "Police Methods Come under Fire in Investigation," *New Orleans Times-Picayune*, February 12, 1932, p. 3; "Two Held Guilty in Holdup Death, Face Life Terms," *New Orleans Times-Picayune*, November 19, 1941, p. 5.

130. "Murder Suspect Tells How Detectives Attempted to Make Him Confess," *Louisiana Weekly*, January 13, 1934, p. 4.

131. "Killing by Detective Put under New Probe," *New Orleans Times-Picayune*, March 5, 1941, p. 5.

132. "Prisoner Pleads Not to Be Beaten," *Louisiana Weekly*, April 8, 1933, p. 1; "Jury Probes Police Case," *New Orleans Item*, March 12, 1941, p. 2.

133. "Board Hears Pleas of 3 Doomed," *Louisiana Weekly*, May 6, 1933, pp. 1, 7.

134. "Healy Promotes 16 on Force, Adds 113 Regular Jobs," *New Orleans Times-Picayune*, September 29, 1928, p. 3.

135. "Capt. James A. 'Buttercup' Burns Dies," *New Orleans States*, May 3, 1933, p. 1.

136. "Court Dismisses Torture Charge against Police," *New Orleans Times-Picayune*, December 7, 1929, p. 2.

137. "Accuse Police Captain of Brutality; to Be Tried," *Louisiana Weekly*, December 7, 1929, p. 1; "Police Disclaim Use of Force to Get Confession," *New Orleans Times-Picayune*, September 24, 1931, p. 6.

138. "Police Disclaim Use of Force to Get Confession," *New Orleans Times-Picayune*, September 24, 1931, p. 6.

139. "Torture Laid to Policemen," *New Orleans Item*, December 1, 1929, p. 4; "A Closed Incident," *Louisiana Weekly*, May 20, 1933, p. 8; "What's behind the Rising Tide of Police Brutality," *Louisiana Weekly*, June 6, 1942, p. 10; "No Excuse for Police Brutality," *Louisiana Weekly*, February 11, 1939, p. 8; Harold N. Lee to John Rouseau, November 1, 1944, Papers of the Louisiana League for the Preservation of Constitutional Rights, Harold Newton Lee Papers, Manuscripts Collection 245, Louisiana Research Collection, Howard-Tilton Memorial Library, Tulane University, New Orleans, LA [hereafter "Louisiana League Papers"].

140. "Statement of Floyd [*sic*] D. T. Washington," September 14, 1939, Louisiana League Papers.

141. "A Closed Incident," *Louisiana Weekly*, May 20, 1933, p. 8.

142. Myrdal, *An American Dilemma* 2:541.

143. "Detectives Suspended; Prisoner's Death Laid to Brutal Flogging," *Louisiana Weekly*, May 14, 1932, p. 1.

144. "21st Amendment Study by Special Session Is Urged," *New Orleans Times-Picayune*, May 27, 1933, p. 2.

145. "2 Detectives Are Found Guilty," *Louisiana Weekly*, June 3, 1933, p. 7.

146. The numbers were modest: two cases in the 1920s and eight in the 1930s. The shift, however, matched trends in police homicide.

147. Some white residents protested police tactics. See the Louisiana League Papers.

148. "Physical Examinations Urged for 'Confessors,'" *New Orleans States*, April 22, 1933, p. 3.

149. "Survey Finds Americans Enjoy but Half of Guaranteed Rights," *Washington Post*, March 6, 1939, p. 24.

150. "Police Brutality," *Louisiana Weekly*, February 3, 1940, p. 8.

151. "Prisoner Fights 200 City Policemen; 3 Are Slain and He Too, Fatally Shot," *Louisiana Weekly*, March 12, 1932, p. 1; "Prisoner Kills Three Police; Is Slain by Detective," *New Orleans Times-Picayune*, March 10, 1932, p. 1.

152. "Statement of Patrolman James Burns," March 9, 1932, Statements of Witnesses,

153. "Statement of Percy Thompson," March 9, 1932, Statements of Witnesses.

154. "Prisoner Fights 200 City Policemen; 3 Are Slain and He Too, Fatally Shot," *Louisiana Weekly*, March 12, 1932, p. 1.

155. "Statement of Percy Thompson," March 9, 1932, Statements of Witnesses.

156. "Statement of Detective Vic Swanson in relation to one Percy Thompson who was shot by Detective Vic Swanson while being in transit from the Charity Hospital to the First Precinct Station," March 10, 1932, Statements of Witnesses.

157. "Inquest Report on Percy Thompson," March 9, 1932, Coroner's Reports.

158. "Letters from the People," *New Orleans Item*, May 26, 1932, p. 12.

159. "Negro Captured and Slain after Dealing Death to Police in 12th Precinct Battle," *New Orleans Item*, June 30, 1937, p. 4.

160. William Ivy Hair, *Carnival of Fury: Robert Charles and the New Orleans Race Riot of 1900* (Baton Rouge: Louisiana State University Press, 1976).

161. Guy B. Johnson, "The Negro and Crime," *Annals of the American Academy of Political and Social Science* 217 (September 1941): 97.

162. "Jury Probes Police Case," *New Orleans Item*, March 12, 1941, p. 2; "'Runs Amuck'—Or Desperation?" *Louisiana Weekly*, April 23, 1933, p. 6.

163. The conviction rate is the proportion of all homicide cases that ended with a conviction. To calculate this rate, I traced every homicide through police and court files, local newspapers, census data on parish and state penal institutions, and convict files from the Louisiana State Penal Farm at Angola. This record-linkage technique yielded figures comparable to the statistics unearthed by the legal reformers of the era. For a fuller discussion, see Jeffrey S. Adler, "'Spineless Judges and Shyster Lawyers': Criminal Justice in New Orleans, 1920–1945," *Journal of Social History* 49 (Summer 2016): 904–27.

164. "Try Alleged Bandits as Killers," *New Orleans States*, March 18, 1930, p. 1.

165. In 1933, the district attorney convicted sixteen of sixty-six killers.

166. Orleans Parish juries returned twenty-nine capital verdicts between 1920 and 1945.

167. Prosecutors convicted 17 of 98 white killers during the early 1920s and 18 of 116 during the early 1930s.

168. "A Natural Result," *New Orleans Item*, February 8, 1926, p. 12.

169. "An Unusual Case," *New Orleans Item*, August 22, 1927, p. 4.

170. For related arguments, see Brandon T. Jett, "African Americans and the Police in the Jim Crow South, 1900–1945" (Ph.D. dissertation, University of Florida, 2017); Elijah Anderson, *Code of the Street: Decency, Violence, and the Moral Life of the Inner City* (New York: Norton, 1999); Michael Javen Fortner, "The 'Silent Majority' in Black and White: Invisibility and Imprecision in the Historiography of Mass Incarceration," *Journal of Urban History* 40 (March 2014): 273–77.

171. "The Value of Negro Life," *Louisiana Weekly*, January 29, 1927, p. 6; "Killings Continue," *Louisiana Weekly*, May 19, 1928, p. 6; "Check the Criminal," *Louisiana Weekly*, April 13, 1929, p. 6.

172. "Will These Murders Out?" *Louisiana Weekly*, April 18, 1931, p. 6. Also see "The Crime Wave," *Louisiana Weekly*, January 14, 1933, p. 8; "Gun Toting," *Louisiana Weekly*, June 25, 1927, p. 6.

173. "The Crime Wave," *Louisiana Weekly*, January 14, 1933, p. 8.

174. "Stanley Is Pledged to a Relentless War on Crime," *New Orleans Item*, May 4, 1930, p. 18. For Hoover, see Richard Gid Powers, *Secrecy and Power: The Life of J. Edgar Hoover* (New York: Free Press, 1987), 1–20.

175. "Stanley Rites Are Conducted," *New Orleans Times-Picayune*, November 13, 1962, pp. 1, 17; "Resignation of Stanley Given Allen," *Baton Rouge Advocate*, July 12, 1935, p. 8; "Made Assistant Attorney," *New Orleans Times-Picayune*, June 15, 1916, p. 5; "Attorney Back from War," *New Orleans Item*, May 3, 1919, p. 8.

176. "Stanley Rites Are Conducted," *New Orleans Times-Picayune*, November 13, 1962, p. 17; "Stanley Looms as Likely Choice of Old Regulars," *New Orleans Times-Picayune*, April 7, 1927, p. 1.

177. "Election Proclamation," *Baton Rouge State Times Advocate*, May 28, 1927, p. 5.

178. "Stanley Is Pledged to a Relentless War on Crime," *New Orleans Item*, May 4, 1930, p. 18.

179. "Eugene Stanley, District Attorney" [political advertisement], *New Orleans Item*, May 6, 1934, p. 27.

180. "Stanley Defends Record of Crime in New Orleans," *New Orleans Times-Picayune*, April 21, 1927, p. 6.

181. "Stanley Breaks Record of Court," *New Orleans States*, February 2, 1930, p. 10.

182. "1101 Convictions Obtained in 1931, Stanley Reports," *New Orleans Times-Picayune*, May 6, 1932, p. 3. Three years later, he repeated this claim. See "Stanley Invites Allen to Start Suit for Ouster," *New Orleans Times-Picayune*, July 25, 1934, p. 9.

183. Frederick L. Hoffman, "The Homicide Record of 1927," *The Spectator* 120 (March 29, 1928): 40–41; "Stanley Defends Record of Crime in New Orleans," *New Orleans Times-Picayune*, April 21, 1927, p. 6.

184. "Favoritism Charged to Barnes by Saint in Ouster Petition," *New Orleans Times-Picayune*, August 15, 1931, p. 1.

185. "Democrats Work for Big Vote Tuesday," *New Orleans States*, April 6, 1930, p. 4.

186. "Warning" [advertisement], *New Orleans States*, May 16, 1935, p. 7. This advertisement

also appeared in the *New Orleans Item*, the *New Orleans Times-Picayune*, the *Baton Rouge Advocate*, and the *Baton Rouge State Times Advocate*.

187. "Lays Negro Vote Activity to Long," *New Orleans States*, May 31, 1935, p. 3.

188. These figures compare 1926 homicide cases with 1928 cases. When the crime occurred late in the year, the legal outcome was often determined in the next calendar year.

189. Tennie Erwin Daugette, "Homicide in New Orleans" (M.A. thesis, Tulane University, 1931), 10. For plea bargaining, see George Fisher, *Plea Bargaining's Triumph: A History of Plea Bargaining in America* (Stanford, CA: Stanford University Press, 2003); William J. Stuntz, *The Collapse of Criminal Justice* (Cambridge, MA: Harvard University Press, 2011), 264.

190. Robert H. Marr, *An Annotated Revision of the Statutes of Louisiana through the Session of 1915* (New Orleans: Hansel & Bro., 1915), 1:531.

191. Harold N. Lee to Bernard D. Mintz, March 7, 1940, Louisiana League Papers.

192. "At Long's dictation," the state legislature stripped Stanley of his authority to appoint his own assistant district attorneys and clerical staff. Instead, the attorney general gained this power, shifting control of the prosecutor's office into the hands of state officials. "Resignation of Stanley Given Allen," *Baton Rouge Advocate*, July 12, 1935, pp. 1, 8; "We Salute Eugene Stanley," *New Orleans Times-Picayune*, July 13, 1935, p. 6.

193. Underpolicing hardly stopped local cops from harassing African Americans.

194. For Angola data, see the manuscript schedules of the Fifteenth and Sixteenth Censuses.

195. "Gun Toting," *Louisiana Weekly*, June 25, 1927, p. 6.

196. "There Is No Excuse," *Louisiana Weekly*, May 20, 1939, p. 8. For a related analysis, see Davis, Gardner, and Gardner, *Deep South*, 503.

CHAPTER 6

1. "Statement of William F. Mears, relative to being a victim of armed robbery by two unknown negroes and assault and shooting of unknown white woman by the two negroes," December 1, 1945, Transcripts of Statements of Witnesses to Homicides, New Orleans Police Department, City of New Orleans, City Archives/Louisiana Division, New Orleans Public Library, New Orleans, LA [hereafter "Statements of Witnesses"].

2. Ibid. "Besser" also appeared as "Bessar" in sources.

3. "Report of Homicide of Bernice Roy," December 1, 1945, Homicide Reports, Department of Police, City of New Orleans, Louisiana City Archives/Division, New Orleans Public Library, New Orleans, LA [hereafter "Homicide Reports"]; "Holdup Shooting Suspects Seized," *New Orleans Times-Picayune*, December 2, 1945, p. 4.

4. Ibid.; "Inquest Report on Bernice Mary Roy," December 3, 1945, Coroner's Reports, Coroner's Office, City of New Orleans, Parish of Orleans, State of Louisiana, City Archives/Louisiana Division, New Orleans Public Library, New Orleans, LA [hereafter "Coroner's Reports"].

5. "Holdup Shooting Suspects Seized," *New Orleans Times-Picayune*, December 2, 1945, p. 4; "Holdup Bullet Fatal to Woman," *New Orleans Times-Picayune*, December 4, 1945, p. 1.

6. "Statement of William F. Mears, relative to being a victim of armed robbery by two unknown negroes and assault and shooting of unknown white woman by the two negroes,"

December 1, 1945, Statements of Witnesses; "Inquest Report on Bernice Mary Roy," December 3, 1945, Coroner's Reports.

7. "Statement of Externe Jack H. Phillips, relative to unknown white woman found lying in vacant lot in rear of Dalier's Drug Store," December 1, 1945, Statements of Witnesses.

8. For example, see "Holdup Bullet Fatal to Woman," *New Orleans Times-Picayune*, December 4, 1945, p. 1.

9. Ibid.; "Indict Two Men in Girl Slaying," *New Orleans Times-Picayune*, December 7, 1945, p. 16; "Report of Homicide of Bernice Roy," December 1, 1945, Homicide Reports. For Martinez, see "Two Detectives Found Guilty of Beating Boy, 15," *New Orleans Times-Picayune*, May 27, 1933, p. 1. For Grosch, see "Labor Hearing in C.I.O. Row Is Continued," *Baton Rouge State Times Advocate*, July 1, 1938, p. 6. For Lannes, see "Workers Alliance Attempt to Stop Funeral Futile," *Louisiana Weekly*, December 4, 1937, p. 1; "Two Confessions Given Death Jury: One Later Denied," *New Orleans Times-Picayune*, July 29, 1937, p. 2.

10. *State of Louisiana v. Bessar et al.*, 213 La. 299 (1948), 302.

11. "O'Connor Proud of Record, Cites Convictions," *New Orleans Times-Picayune*, January 19, 1946, p. 1.

12. "Report of Homicide of Bernice Roy," December 1, 1945, Homicide Reports; "Hold-Up Shooting Suspects Seized," *New Orleans Times-Picayune*, December 2, 1945, p. 4.

13. *State of Louisiana v. Bessar et al.*, 213 La. 299 (1948), 312. The combination of the records of the lead detectives for coercing confessions and confessions that conflicted with the defendants' public statements suggests the possibility that Powell and Besser signed the confessions under duress, though the defense attorneys, one of whom was a seasoned lawyer and former prosecutor, did not make such as allegation, even in their appeal of the verdict. Chandler C. Luzenberg Jr. and Bentley G. Byrnes complained of irregularities in the trial, particularly the judge's unwillingness to let them offer an insanity plea.

14. "Statement of William F. Mears, relative to being a victim of armed robbery by two unknown negroes and assault and shooting of unknown white woman by the two negroes," December 1, 1945, Statements of Witnesses.

15. "Statement of Paul Cucullu, relative to unknown white woman found lying in vacant lot in rear of Dalier's Drug Store, 2000 Tulane Ave., bleeding about face and forehead," December 1, 1945, Statements of Witnesses.

16. "Statement of Mrs. Hilliary J. Rodriguez, relative to unknown white woman found lying in vacant lot in rear of Dalier's Drug Store, 2000 Tulane Ave., bleeding about face and forehead," December 1, 1945, Statements of Witnesses.

17. *State of Louisiana v. Bessar et al.*, 213 La. 299 (1948), 312.

18. "Two Negroes to Die for Slaying of Woman," *Baton Rouge Morning Advocate*, February 12, 1946, p. 11.

19. *State of Louisiana v. Bessar et al.*, 213 La. 299 (1948); "Two Killers Die in Electric Chair," *New Orleans Times-Picayune*, April 24, 1948, p. 5.

20. "O'Connor Proud of Record, Cites Convictions," *New Orleans Times-Picayune*, January 19, 1946, p. 1.

21. "Two Killers Die in Electric Chair," *New Orleans Times-Picayune*, April 24, 1948, p. 5.

22. Very few homicide cases included allegations of attempted rape.

23. Pamela Tyler, *Silk Stockings and Ballot Boxes: Women and Politics in New Orleans, 1920–1965* (Athens: University of Georgia Press, 1996), 28. For the influence of local politics on criminal justice in late twentieth-century America, see William J. Stuntz, *The Collapse of American Criminal Justice* (Cambridge, MA: Harvard University Press, 2011).

24. W. D. Hays Jr., "Human Life Is Cheap in City; 8-Month Record Reveals Nickel, Dime Killings Here," *New Orleans Times-Picayune*, September 20, 1936, p. 27.

25. For the national pattern, see A. Joan Klebba, "Homicide Trends in the United States, 1900–74," *Public Health Reports* 90 (May–June 1975): 196; Barry Latzer, *The Rise and Fall of Violent Crime in America* (New York: Encounter Books, 2016), 44; Roger Lane, *Murder in America* (Columbus: Ohio State University Press, 1997), 248. For the *Uniform Crime Reports*, beginning in 1930, the FBI relied on data supplied by local law enforcers, and New Orleans officials diligently submitted crime figures.

26. For example, see "Eugene Stanley, District Attorney" [political advertisement], *New Orleans Item*, May 6, 1934, p. 27.

27. The robbery figures come from FBI data and cover the period from 1931 to 1940. See "Total Offenses Reported for 1931," *Uniform Crime Reports* 2 (December 1931): 17; "Number of Offenses Known to the Police," *Uniform Crime Reports* 11 (January 1941): 183.

28. The race-specific figures presented here focus on the killers. In 6 percent of homicides, however, neither the police nor witnesses identified the race of the assailant, and thus the race-based sums of local homicides do not precisely equal the total number of homicides.

29. *Fourteenth Census of the United States Taken in the Year 1920, vol. II, Population* (Washington, DC: Government Printing Office, 1922), 320–21; *Sixteenth Census of the United States: 1940, Population, vol. II* (Washington, DC: Government Printing Office, 1943), 426, 894.

30. *Sixteenth Census of the United States: 1940, Population, vol. II*, 427. For detailed analyses of this issue, see David Courtwright, *Violent Land: Single Men and Social Disorder from the Frontier to the Inner City* (Cambridge, MA: Harvard University Press, 1996), 9–25; Eric H. Monkkonen, *Murder in New York City* (Berkeley: University of California Press, 2001), 56–61.

31. Glen H. Elder Jr., *Children of the Depression: Social Change in Life Experience* (Chicago: University of Chicago Press, 1974), 26; Christopher J. Ruhm and William E. Black, "Does Drinking Really Decrease in Bad Times," *Journal of Health Economics* 21 (July 2002): 659–78; Christopher J. Ruhm, "Healthy Living in Hard Times," *Journal of Health Economics* 24 (March 2005): 341–63.

32. Elder, *Children of the Depression*, 284.

33. *Mortality Statistics for 1929, vol. 30* (Washington, DC: Government Printing Office, 1932), 148–49; *Vital Statistics of the United States: 1940, pt. II*, 262–63; Michael R. Haines, "Vital Statistics," in *Historical Statistics of the United States*, vol. 1, *Population*, ed. Susan B. Carter, Scott Sigmund Gartner, Michael R. Haines, Alan L. Olmstead, Richard Sutch, and Gavin Wright (New York: Cambridge University Press, 2006), 458–61, 469–82. For a related, provocative perspective, see Raymond Pearl, *The Rate of Living: Being an Account of Some Experimental Studies on the Biology of Life Duration* (New York: Alfred A. Knopf, 1928), 151. In this study of fruit flies, Pearl, a biologist, concluded that "the length of life depends inversely on the rate of living." Such an interpretation is intriguingly consistent with recent scholarship by public health economists and demographers exploring the relationship between eco-

nomic cycles and mortality rates. See Ruhm, "Healthy Living in Hard Times," 341–63; Ulf-G. Gerdtham and Christopher J. Ruhm, "Deaths Rise in Good Economic Times: Evidence from the OECD," *Economics and Human Biology* 4 (December 2006): 298–316; David Stuckler, Christopher Meissner, Price Fishback, Sanjay Basu, and Martin McKee, "Banking Crises and Mortality during the Great Depression: Evidence from US Urban Populations, 1929–1937," *Journal of Epidemiology and Community Health* 66 (May 2012): 410–19; José A. Tapia Granados, "Increasing Mortality during the Expansions of the US Economy, 1900–1996," *International Journal of Epidemiology* 34 (December 2005): 1194–1202; José A. Tapia Granados and Ana V. Diez Roux, "Life and Death during the Great Depression," *Proceedings of the National Academy of Sciences* 106 (October 13, 2009): 17290–95.

34. Frederick E. Hosen, *The Great Depression and the New Deal: Legislative Acts in Their Entirely (1932–1933) and Statistical Economic Data (1926–46)* (Jefferson, NC: McFarland, 1992), 252, 257; Robert William Fogel, *The Escape from Hunger and Premature Death, 1700–2100: Europe, America, and the Third World* (Cambridge, Eng.: Cambridge University Press, 2004), 37.

35. Many studies argue that exposure to violence contributes to subsequent violent behavior. See Miriam K. Ehrensaft and Patricia Cohen, "Contributions of Family Violence to the Intergenerational Transmission of Externalizing Behavior," *Prevention Science* 13 (August 2012): 370, 383; Miriam K. Ehrensaft, Patricia Cohen, Jocelyn Brown, Elizabeth Smailes, Henian Chen, and Jeffrey G. Johnson, "Intergenerational Transmission of Partner Violence: A 20-Year Prospective Study," *Journal of Consulting and Clinical Psychology* 71 (August 2003): 749.

36. Shifts in infant mortality rates especially tend to mirror changes in homicide. See Martin Daly, *Killing the Competition: Economic Inequality and Homicide* (New Brunswick, NJ: Transaction, 2016), 71.

37. Forrest E. Linder and Robert D. Grove, *Vital Statistics Rates in the United States, 1900–1940* (Washington, DC: Government Printing Office, 1943), 587. Because automobile fatality data for 1930 were unavailable, the motor vehicle rate figures compare 1929 with 1940. See *Mortality Statistics for 1929, vol. 30*, 51; *Vital Statistics of the United States: 1940, pt. II*, 223.

38. For a related perspective, see Robert S. Lynd and Helen Morrell Lynd, *Middletown in Transition: A Study in Cultural Conflicts* (New York: Harcourt, Brace, 1937), 146, 202.

39. *Sixteenth Census of the United States: 1940, Population, Differential Fertility*, 225–26; Linder and Grove, *Vital Statistics Rates in the United States, 1900–1940*, 587.

40. *Fifteenth Census of the United States, 1930, Population, vol. VI* (Washington, DC: Government Printing Office, 1933), 538; *Sixteenth Census of the United States: 1940, Population, vol. IV*, 903.

41. Peirce F. Lewis, *New Orleans: The Making of an Urban Landscape*, 2nd ed. (Santa Fe, NM: Center for American Places, 2003), 67.

42. Lewis, *New Orleans*, 97, 132.

43. Daphne Spain, "Race Relations and Residential Segregation in New Orleans: Two Centuries of Paradox," *Annals of the American Academy of Political and Social Science* 441 (January 1979): 89–90; Karl E. Taeuber and Alma F. Taeuber, *Negroes in Cities: Residential Segregation and Neighborhood Change* (Chicago: Aldine, 1965), 41; Harlan W. Gilmore, Warren Breed, A. L. Johnson, Leonard Reissman, and Cliff W. Wing, *1950 New Orleans Population Handbook*

(New Orleans: Urban Life Research Institute, 1953), 13; H[arlan] W. Gilmore, "The Old New Orleans and the New: A Case for Ecology," *American Sociological Review* 9 (August 1944): 393; Allison Davis and John Dollard, *Children of Bondage: The Personality Development of Negro Youth in the Urban South* (Washington, DC: American Council of Education, 1940), xxvi, 135.

44. *Sixteenth Census of the United States: 1940, Population, vol. IV*, 894; *Sixteenth Census of the United States: 1940, Population, vol. II*, 426; *Fifteenth Census of the United States: 1930, Population, vol. VI*, 538; *Sixteenth Census of the United States: 1940, Population, vol. IV*, 903.

45. For marital authority, see Elder, *Children of the Great Depression*, 30.

46. M. P. Baumgartner, "Violent Networks: The Origins and Management of Domestic Conflict," in *Aggression and Violence: Social Interactionist Perspectives*, ed. Richard B. Felson and James Tedeschi (Washington, DC: American Psychological Association, 1993), 209–31.

47. "Husband Arrested in Fatal Shooting of Estranged Wife," *New Orleans Times-Picayune*, June 20, 1932, p. 1.

48. "Statement of one John LaHood, relative to finding Mrs. John LaHood being found lying across the bed in the second room down stairs at 1431 Polmnyia Street, dead with a gunshot wound in her chest," June 19, 1932, Statements of Witnesses.

49. "Husband Arrested in Fatal Shooting of Estranged Wife," *New Orleans Times-Picayune*, June 20, 1932, p. 1.

50. "Statement of Mrs. David Mann, relative to the finding of Mrs. John LaHood lying across the bed in the second room dead with a gunshot wound in the chest," June 19, 1932, Statements of Witnesses.

51. "Husband Near Death, Asks Police to Release His Wife in Shooting," *New Orleans Item*, August 19, 1938, p. 3.

52. "Report of Homicide of Herman Estrade," August 18, 1938, Homicide Reports; "Husband Near Death, Asks Police to Release His Wife in Shooting," *New Orleans Item*, August 19, 1938, p. 3.

53. "Statement of Peter Milano, relative to |the| shooting of one Mr. Herman Estrade," August 18, 1938, Statements of Witnesses.

54. "Statement of Mrs. Herman Estrade, relative to the shooting of one Herman Estrade," August 18, 1938, Statements of Witnesses.

55. Ibid.

56. "Inquest Report on Herman Joseph Estrade," August 20, 1938, Coroner's Reports.

57. "Statement of Herman Estrade, relative to his being shot by his wife," August 18, 1938, Statements of Witnesses.

58. One of the 106 cops who killed civilians was convicted.

59. For violence and public perceptions, see Joel Best, *Random Violence: How We Talk about New Crimes and New Victims* (Berkeley: University of California Press, 1999).

60. *Sixteenth Census of the United States: 1940, Population: vol. II*, 426, 427, 894–95; *Sixteenth Census of the United States: 1940, Population, Differential Fertility*, 226, 233.

61. Richard Sterner, *The Negro's Share: A Study of Income, Consumption, Housing and Public Assistance* (New York: Harper & Brothers, 1943), 362, 190–91.

62. For example, see "A Fatal Blunder," *Louisiana Weekly*, December 3, 1932, p. 8.

63. *Mortality Statistics for 1929, vol. 30*, 7, 148–49; *Vital Statistics of the United States: 1940,*

pt. II (Washington, DC: Government Printing Office, 1943), 9, 31; Linder and Grove, *Vital Statistics Rates in the United States, 1900–1940*, 587.

64. *Sixteenth Census of the United States: 1940, Population*, vol. *IV*, 903; *Fifteenth Census of the United States: 1930, Population*, vol. *VI*, 538.

65. The rate fell faster than the proportion because overall African American homicide dipped. Nearly all forms of African American homicide dropped, but none more sharply than home violence. As a result, the overall "pie" decreased in size, causing the "proportional" change, which is relative to the whole, to contract more sharply than the "rate."

66. Wealthier than African American residents, white New Orleanians continued to purchase firearms. As a consequence, white gun use fell modestly.

67. Police, public health, and coroners' records document cases of lethal violence. It is impossible, however, to quantify cases in which victims survived assaults. Thus, I am assuming that trends in lethal violence provide hints about nonlethal violence. Such an assumption is a standard practice among scholars of violence.

68. *Fifteenth Census of the United States, 1930, Population*, vol. *VI*, 59; *Sixteenth Census of the United States: 1940: Housing*, vol. *II*, 345; Sterner, *The Negro's Share*, 405.

69. For the effect of children on domestic violence, see Margo I. Wilson and Martin Daly, "Who Kills Whom in Spouse Killings? On the Exceptional Sex Ratio of Spousal Homicides in the United States," *Criminology* 30 (May 1992): 198.

70. For racial disparities in poor relief, see Michele Grigsby Coffey, "Providing for Our Communities, Protecting Our Race, Proving Ourselves: African American Activism and Protest in Depression Era New Orleans" (Ph.D. dissertation, University of South Carolina, 2010), 23–25.

71. "Report of Homicide of Vera Gasper," January 10, 1930, Homicide Reports.

72. "Expectant Mother Is Slain," *Louisiana Weekly*, July 1, 1933, p. 1; "Statement of Harry Moore, relative to the murder of one Dorothy Stewart," June 17, 1933, Statements of Witnesses; "Report of Homicide of Dorothy Stewart," June 18, 1933, Homicide Reports; "Inquest Report on Dorothy Stewart," June 18, 1933, Coroner's Reports.

73. "Statement of Lucia Porea, relative to murder of one Joseph Landry," January 27, 1936, Statements of Witnesses.

74. See John Dollard, *Caste and Class in a Southern Town* (New York: Doubleday Anchor, 1937), 271–72.

75. "Report of Homicide of Alex Johnson," July 2, 1945, Homicide Reports.

76. "Statement of Beatrice Brown, relative to the murder of Alex Jackson," July 1, 1945, Statements of Witnesses.

77. "1 Nabbed on Scene; Other Makes Escape," *Louisiana Weekly*, July 7, 1945, p. 1.

78. "Slays Mate in Domestic Fight," *Louisiana Weekly*, July 15, 1944, p. 6.

79. "Bothers Her; She Cuts Him Short," *New Orleans Item*, March 9, 1943, p. 5.

80. "Report of Homicide of Edmond Dolliole," May 13, 1939, Homicide Reports.

81. See "Report of Homicide of Archie McGee," September 8, 1930, Homicide Reports.

82. "Statement of Lillie Johnson, relative to death [of] one, Henry Perry, her Common-law husband," March 21, 1937, Statements of Witnesses.

83. "Inquest Report on Henry Perry," March 21, 1937, Coroner's Reports.

84. "Both Pull Knives; She Wins; Jailed," *New Orleans Times-Picayune*, February 10, 1937, p. 9; "Statement of Gertrude Morris, relative to cutting Wellington Boudray," February 9, 1937, Statements of Witnesses.

85. Between 1920 and 1945, African American New Orleanians committed 540 homicides on the streets of the city, whereas white residents committed 240 such homicides. In 1945, African Americans committed 31, compared with 5 by whites.

86. Robert J. Sampson terms this "collective efficacy" and argues that it correlates with lower levels of violent and deviant behavior. See Sampson, *Great American City: Chicago and the Enduring Neighborhood Effect* (Chicago: University of Chicago Press, 2012), 149–78.

87. As the social psychologist Martin Daly has noted, such violence does not necessarily point to an ethic of honor or a subculture of violence. He argues that economic inequality offers a more compelling explanation for such behavior. See Daly, *Killing the Competition*; Elijah Anderson, *Code of the Street: Decency, Violence, and the Moral Life of the Inner City* (New York: Norton, 1999).

88. Davis and Dollard, *Children of* Bondage, 271–72.

89. In his study of homicide in midcentury Philadelphia, Marvin E. Wolfgang noted the frequency of such "trivial" triggers. See Wolfgang, *Patterns in Criminal Homicide* (New York: John Wiley & Sons, 1958), 185–99.

90. "Report of Homicide of John Tatum," December 4, 1939, Homicide Reports.

91. "Statement of Sterling Watkins, relative to one Louise Gabile being stabbed," December 27, 1942, Statements of Witnesses; "Report of Homicide of Louis Gabile," December 27, 1942, Homicide Reports. Peique's announcement of his name notwithstanding, police files recorded the victim as "Louis Gabile."

92. This violence does not fit the definition of a "subculture of violence," for it was situational. During the 1920s, such street-corner skirmishes were uncommon. With the demographic, ecological, and economic shifts of the 1930s, however, public, performative violence flared.

93. For a related analysis, see Robert Agnew, *Pressured into Crime: An Overview of General Strain Theory* (Los Angeles: Roxbury Publishing, 2006), 162.

94. For an important, related perspective, see Donald Black and M. P. Baumgartner, "On Self-Help in Modern Society," *Dialectical Anthropology* 12 (March 1987): 33.

95. "Note by Vitrano Supports Theory Officers Declare," *New Orleans Times-Picayune*, August 16, 1936, p. 16; "Murder Charge Holds Biri in Cell," *New Orleans Item*, August 14, 1936, p. 1; "Report of Homicide of Frank Grisaffi," January 9, 1939, Homicide Reports.

96. "Indiscriminate Arrests," *Louisiana Weekly*, August 28, 1943, p. 10.

97. For example, see "The White Man's Burden," *Louisiana Weekly*, May 20, 1933, p. 8; "Story of Being Bound and Gagged Hoax, Youth Confesses to Police," *New Orleans Times-Picayune*, May 12, 1933, p. 6; "Oil Station Manager Is Held by Police in Attendant's Death," *New Orleans Times-Picayune*, August 14, 1936, p. 1.

98. "Police Charge Biri with Murder, Block Effort to Free Him," *New Orleans States*, August 14, 1914, p. 2; "Biri Pleads Guilty in Oil Station Slaying," *New Orleans States*, December 9, 1936, p. 1.

99. "Juvenile Delinquency," *Louisiana Weekly*, September 4, 1943, p. 10.

100. "Bringing Things to Light," *Louisiana Weekly*, April 1, 1932, p. 6; John Bowers, "540 Persons Arrested in Raid: 17-Yr.-Old Boy Caught Later; Confesses to Crime," *Louisiana Weekly*, September 30, 1933, p. 1.

101. John Bowers, "540 Persons Arrested in Raid: 17-Yr.-Old Boy Caught Later; Confesses to Crime," *Louisiana Weekly*, September 30, 1933, p. 1.

102. "Indiscriminate Arrests," *Louisiana Weekly*, August 28, 1943, p. 10.

103. Thorsten Sellin, "The Negro and the Problem of Law Observance and Administration in the Light of Social Research," in *The Negro in American Civilization: A Study of Negro Life and Race Relations in the Light of Social Research*, ed. Charles S. Johnson (New York: Henry Holt, 1930), 447–48. Such police tactics also undermined the legitimacy of local law enforcers. See Robert J. Sampson and Dawn Jeglum Bartusch, "Legal Cynicism and (Subcultural?) Tolerance of Deviance: The Neighborhood Context of Racial Differences," *Law and Society Review* 32 (December 1998): 777–804.

104. In nearly one-third of early 1940s police homicides, cops shot suspects who refused to halt on command.

105. Meigs O. Frost, "Streetcar Bandit Found Dead in Cell at Seventh Precinct," *New Orleans States*, June 17, 1938, p. 3; "Await Cell Death Report," *New Orleans Item*, June 20, 1938, p. 2.

106. "Uncover New Evidence in Aaron Boyd's Death," *Louisiana Weekly*, July 2, 1938, p. 2.

107. Meigs O. Frost, "7th Precinct Commander to Conduct Inquiry," *New Orleans States*, June 18, 1938, p. 2.

108. Meigs O. Frost, "Streetcar Bandit Found Dead in Cell at Seventh Precinct," *New Orleans States*, June 17, 1938, pp. 1, 3.

109. "Inquest Report on Aaron Boyd," June 17, 1938, Coroner's Reports.

110. Meigs O. Frost, "7th Precinct Commander to Conduct Inquiry," *New Orleans States*, June 18, 1938, pp. 1, 2.

111. "Found Lifeless in Jail, Aaron Boyd's Brutal Slaying Is Being Investigated," Associated Negro Press Release, June 30, 1938, typescript, in Papers of the Louisiana League for the Preservation of Constitutional Rights, Harold Newton Lee Papers, Manuscripts Collection 245, Louisiana Research Collection, Howard-Tilton Memorial Library, Tulane University, New Orleans, LA [hereafter "Louisiana League Papers"].

112. "Cell Death Report Due Next Week," *New Orleans Item*, June 18, 1938, p. 1.

113. "Grosch Will Get Report of Smith on Death Probe," *New Orleans Times-Picayune*, June 19, 1938, p. 3; "Clears Police of Blame in Cell Death," *New Orleans States*, June 20, 1938, p. 4.

114. John W. Dickens, "Action in Cell Death Case Asked," letter to the editor, *New Orleans Times-Picayune*, June 24, 1938, p. 10.

115. "Clears Police of Blame in Cell Death," *New Orleans States*, June 20, 1938, pp. 1, 4.

116. "Police End Inquiry in Cell Death," *New Orleans Item*, June 21, 1938, p. 2.

117. "Found Lifeless in Jail, Aaron Boyd's Brutal Slaying Is Being Investigated," Associated Negro Press Release, June 30, 1938, Louisiana League Papers.

118. "Death of Negro in New Orleans Jail Is Mystery," *Baton Rouge Advocate*, June 18, 1938, p. 8; "Reyer Orders Probe of Cell Death," *New Orleans States*, June 18, 1938, p. 2.

119. John W. Dickens, "Action in Cell Death Case Asked," letter to the editor, *New Orleans Times-Picayune*, June 24, 1938, p. 10.

120. "State Attorney Accepts Report in Boyd's Death," *New Orleans Times-Picayune*, June 22, 1938, p. 15.

121. "Police End Inquiry in Cell Death," *New Orleans Item*, June 21, 1938, p. 2; "Important Bulletin," June 30, 1938, Louisiana League Papers.

122. "Anonymous [Letter] to (Nigger Loving) Harold Lee," February 1939, Louisiana League Papers.

123. Harold N. Lee to Henry A. Scheinhaut, Civil Liberties Section, Department of Justice, October 22, 1942, Louisiana League Papers.

124. "Up to the Police," *New Orleans Times-Picayune*, August 20, 1943, p. 10.

125. "Report of Homicide of Bernice Roy," December 1, 1945, Homicide Reports.

126. For example, see "Statement of Saverio Romano, relative to his having shot and killed one, Ernest Rivers," August 23, 1942, Statements of Witnesses; "Report of Homicide of Fannie Lee McDaniels," January 3, 1944, Homicide Reports.

127. "Slain across from Hospital," *New Orleans Item*, August 18, 1943, p. 2.

128. "Gang Is Hunted in Slaying Here," *New Orleans Times-Picayune*, August 19, 1943, p. 1.

129. Edward J. Escobar, *Race, Police, and the Making of a Political Identity: Mexican Americans and the Los Angeles Police Department, 1900–1945* (Berkeley: University of California Press, 1999); Dominic J. Capeci Jr. and Martha Wilkerson, *Layered Violence: The Detroit Rioters of 1943* (Jackson: University of Mississippi Press, 1999).

130. "Report of Homicide of Peter Sansone," August 18, 1943, Homicide Reports.

131. Ibid.; "Inquest Report on Peter Sansone," August 18, 1943, Coroner's Reports.

132. "Gang Is Hunted in Slaying Here," *New Orleans Times-Picayune*, August 19, 1943, p. 1.

133. "Police Jail 223 Negroes as Suspects in Robbery," *New Orleans Item*, August 20, 1943, p. 5.

134. "91 Negroes Jailed in Orleans Drive Against Crime Wave," *Baton Rouge Advocate*, August 30, 1943, p. 12.

135. "Gang Is Hunted in Slaying Here," *New Orleans Times-Picayune*, August 19, 1943, p. 1.

136. "Sansone Murder 'Near Solution,'" *New Orleans Times-Picayune*, August 24, 1943, p. 1; "Police Jail 223 Negroes as Suspects in Robbery," *New Orleans Item*, August 20, 1943, p. 5.

137. "City-Wide Negro Roundup Follows in Wake of Murder," *New Orleans Item*, August 19, 1943, p. 1.

138. "Police Jail 223 Negroes as Suspects in Robbery," *New Orleans Item*, August 20, 1943, p. 5; "Work or Jail Order Faced by Loiterers," *New Orleans Times-Picayune*, August 26, 1943, p. 1.

139. "Police Continue Arrest of Negroes," *Louisiana Weekly*, September 4, 1943, p. 1.

140. "Gang Is Hunted in Slaying Here," *New Orleans Times-Picayune*, August 19, 1943, p. 1; "City-Wide Negro Roundup Follows in Wake of Murder," *New Orleans Item*, August 19, 1943, pp. 1, 2; "Sansone Murder 'Near Solution,'" *New Orleans Times-Picayune*, August 24, 1943, p. 1; "Hunt for Killers Yields Weapons," *New Orleans Times-Picayune*, August 20, 1943, p. 5.

141. "Negro Bandits Rob Gas Man," *New Orleans Item*, August 23, 1943, p. 12.

142. "Work or Jail Order Faced by Loiterers," *New Orleans Times-Picayune*, August 26, 1943, p. 1.

143. During the early 1940s, the conviction rate for black-on-white homicide reached 50 percent, and the execution rate rose to 21.4 percent—triple the 1920s figure.

144. Alan Maclachlan, "Up from Paternalism: The New Deal and Race Relations in New Orleans" (Ph.D. dissertation, University of New Orleans, 1998), 27–28, 32–34, 44, 170–71; Adam Fairclough, *Race and Democracy: The Civil Rights Struggle in Louisiana* (Athens: University of Georgia Press, 1995), 56; Sharlene Sinegal DeCuir, "Attacking Jim Crow: Black Activism in New Orleans, 1925–1941" (Ph.D. dissertation, Louisiana State University, 2009), 45, 88, 174, 186.

145. Leonard N. Moore, *Black Rage in New Orleans: Police Brutality and African American Activism from World War II to Hurricane Katrina* (Baton Rouge: Louisiana State University Press, 2010), 1–5, 21.

146. Telegram from Harold N. Lee to William Green, American Federation of Labor, June 28, 1938, Louisiana League Papers; Henry W. Hermes, "Ice Cream and Cake," letter to the editor, *New Orleans States*, June 9, 1939, p. 6.

147. Harold N. Lee to Henry A. Scheinhaut, Civil Liberties Section, Department of Justice, October 22, 1942, Louisiana League Papers; "Police Continue Arrest of Negroes," *Louisiana Weekly*, September 4, 1943, p. 1; Maclachlan, "Up from Paternalism," 171.

148. Harold N. Lee to Mr. Musgrove, September 24, 1939, Louisiana League Papers.

149. Harold N. Lee to Henry A. Scheinhaut, Civil Liberties Section, Department of Justice, October 22, 1942, Louisiana League Papers; "Police Continue Arrests of Negroes," *Louisiana Weekly*, September 4, 1943, p. 1.

150. The Grosch brothers especially believed that white support for rough justice in the name of maintaining law and order gave them a mandate to use nearly any method for controlling or eliminating threats. See, for example, "Notorized Statement of Bernard D. Mintz," August 1, 1938, Louisiana League Papers; "Notorized Statement of Lee Rattner," July 5, 1938, Louisiana League Papers.

151. "Notorized Statement of Lee Rattner," July 5, 1938, Louisiana League Papers; "Crime Is Curbed by 'Third Degree,' Asserts Grosch," *New Orleans Times-Picayune*, June 1, 1939, p. 1; "Byrne 'Amazed' by Quoted Views on Third Degree," *New Orleans Times-Picayune*, June 3, 1939, p. 3.

152. "Report of Homicide of Felton Robinson," June 17, 1943, Homicide Reports.

153. "Notes from interviews of witnesses of the shooting of Felton Robinson," September 10, 1943, Louisiana League Papers.

154. Fairclough, *Race and Democracy*, xii.

CONCLUSION

1. For the second half of the century, see Leonard N. Moore, *Black Rage in New Orleans: Police Brutality and African American Activism from World War II to Hurricane Katrina* (Baton Rouge: Louisiana State University Press, 2010).

2. This attitude extended to black-on-white homicide during the early 1920s. Prosecutors convicted only one-third of killers in such cases.

3. Joseph H. Fichter, with the collaboration of Brian Jordan, "Police Handlings of Arrest-

ees: A Research Study of Police Arrests in New Orleans" (unpublished report, Department of Sociology, Loyola University of the South, 1964), 32; Gunnar Myrdal, *An American Dilemma: The Negro Problem and Modern Democracy*, vol. 2 (1944; rpt. with an introduction by Sissela Bok, New Brunswick, NJ: Transaction, 1962), 541.

4. "Gang Is Hunted in Slaying Here," *New Orleans Times-Picayune*, August 19, 1943, p. 1.

5. John Grosch retired from the department as the chief of detectives and William Grosch as a lieutenant.

6. Moore, *Black Rage in New Orleans*, 18–42.

7. Pamela Tyler, *Silk Stockings and Ballot Boxes: Women and Politics in New Orleans, 1920–1965* (Athens: University of Georgia Press, 1996), 28; Moore, *Black Rage in New Orleans*, 19.

8. See Moore, *Black Rage in New Orleans*; Adam Fairclough, *Race and Democracy: The Civil Rights Struggle in Louisiana, 1915–1972* (Athens: University of Georgia Press, 1995).

9. David L. Cohn, "New Orleans: The City That Care Forgot," *Atlantic Monthly* 165 (April 1940): 484.

10. For the Chicago figures, see Thorsten Sellin, *The Death Penalty* (Philadelphia: American Law Institute, 1959), 60. These rates, and the slopes charted in figure 7.2, are not disaggregated by race. At least for New Orleans, the sharp drop after the early 1930s mainly reflected the plunge in police homicides with white victims.

11. Elizabeth Dale, *Robert Nixon and Police Torture in Chicago, 1871–1971* (DeKalb: Northern Illinois University Press, 2016).

12. For the role of older cops in establishing departmental norms, see Aaron M. Kohn, "Report of the Special Citizens Investigating Committee of the Commission Council of New Orleans," vol. 1, New Orleans Police Department, April 1954, Louisiana Research Collection, Tulane University Library, New Orleans, LA (typescript), p. 113.

13. Douglas Eckberg, "Crime, Law Enforcement, and Justice," in *Historical Statistics of the United States*, vol. 5, *Governance and International Relations*, ed. Susan B. Carter, Scott Sigmund Gartner, Michael R. Haines, Alan L. Olmstead, Richard Sutch, and Gavin Wright (New York: Cambridge University Press, 2006), 239.

14. Patrick A. Langan, John V. Fundis, Lawrence A. Greenfeld, and Victoria W. Schneider, "Historical Statistics in State and Federal Institutions, Yearend 1925–1986," NCJ-111098, Bureau of Justice Statistics, US Department of Justice, May 1988, pp. 5–7.

15. The incarceration figures were calculated from the manuscript schedules of the 1930 and 1940 federal censuses for the Louisiana State Penal Farm at Angola. For the homicide figures, see *Mortality Statistics, 1931, vol. 32* (Washington, DC: Government Printing Office, 1935), 46; *Vital Statistics of the United States: 1940, pt. II* (Washington, DC: Government Printing Office, 1943), 223.

16. *Uniform Crime Reports* 4 (1933): 21; *Uniform Crime Reports* 4 (1940): 225.

17. These figures were culled from the ESPY data files, accessed at www.deathpenaltyinfo.org/documents/ESPYstate.pdf.

18. Eckberg, "Crime, Law Enforcement, and Justice," 262.

19. Nor is there empirical evidence that rising incarceration rates produced falling rates of violent crime. See Jeremy Travis, Bruce Western, and Steve Redburn, eds., *The Growth*

of Incarceration in the United States: Exploring Causes and Consequences (Washington, DC: National Academies Press, 2014), 130–56.

20. For incarceration and execution data, see "Sourcebook of Criminal Justice Statistics Online," www.albany.edu/sourcebook/pdf/t62/pdf and www.albany.edu/sourcebook/pdf/t686 2010.pdf.

21. Michelle Alexander, *The New Jim Crow: Mass Incarceration in the Age of Colorblindness* (New York: New Press, 2010), 6.

22. "Survey Finds Americans Enjoy but Half of Guaranteed Rights," *Washington Post*, March 6, 1939, p. 24; "The 'Hot Tamale' Decision," *Louisiana Weekly*, November 8, 1941 p. 10; Moore, *Black Rage in New Orleans*, 5.

APPENDIX

1. Homicide Reports, Department of Police, City of New Orleans, City Archives/Louisiana Division, New Orleans Public Library, New Orleans, LA.

2. Record Book Journals, Coroner's Office, City of New Orleans, Parish of Orleans, City Archives/Louisiana Division, New Orleans Public Library, New Orleans, LA.

3. Coroner's Reports, Coroner's Office, City of New Orleans, Parish of Orleans, State of Louisiana, City Archives/Louisiana Division, New Orleans Public Library, New Orleans, LA.

4. Bruce Smith, *The New Orleans Police Survey* (New Orleans: Bureau of Governmental Research, 1946), 18.

5. I traced every killer and victim into the handwritten manuscript schedules of the federal census immediately preceding the date of the homicide—the 1920 census, the 1930 census, or the 1940 census. Thus, for example, I searched the 1930 census for the entries of the individual households of those involved in a 1931 homicide.

6. Convict Records, Louisiana State Penitentiary Records, vols. 24–42 (1920–36), Louisiana State Archives, accessed through Ancestry.com.

7. Rather than relying on keyword searches of digitized newspapers, I pored over every page of every newspaper, spending huge blocks of time yoked to a microfilm reader. Given spelling errors and the quirks of search engines, I found the keyword approach efficient but inadequate. Though less systematically, I also scanned newspapers from Baton Rouge, the state capital, such as the *Baton Rouge Times Advocate*.

8. Transcripts of Statements of Witnesses to Homicides, New Orleans Police Department, City of New Orleans, City Archives/Louisiana Division, New Orleans Public Library, New Orleans, LA.

9. Criminal District Court Case Files, Parish of Orleans, City Archives/Louisiana Division, New Orleans Public Library, New Orleans, LA (1920–33).

10. Louisiana Supreme Court Case Files, Historical Archives of the Supreme Court of Louisiana, Earl K. Long Library, University of New Orleans, New Orleans, LA.

11. Papers of the New Orleans branch of the National Association for the Advancement of Colored People, in the Papers of the NAACP, Part 12, Reels 14–15, Series A, ed. John H. Bracey Jr. and August Meier, University Publications (Bethesda, MD, 1991), microfilm; Papers of the Louisiana League for the Preservation of Constitutional Rights, Harold Newton Lee

Papers, Manuscripts Collection 245, Louisiana Research Collection, Howard-Tilton Memorial Library, Tulane University, New Orleans, LA.

12. Smith, *The New Orleans Police Survey*; Aaron M. Kohn, "Report of the Special Citizens Investigating Committee of the Commission Council of New Orleans," New Orleans Police Department, vols. 1–5, April 1954, Louisiana Research Collection, Tulane University Library, New Orleans, LA (typescript).

13. Federal Writers Project of the Works Progress Administration for the City of New Orleans, *New Orleans City Guide 1938* (Boston: Houghton Mifflin, 1938); David L. Cohn, "New Orleans: The City That Care Forgot," *Atlantic Monthly* 165 (April 1940): 484–91; Allison Davis and John Dollard, *Children of Bondage: The Personality Development of Negro Youth in the Urban South* (Washington, DC: American Council of Education, 1940). Also see the Allison Davis Papers, Special Collections Research Center, University of Chicago, Chicago, IL.

14. C. E. Gehlke, "A Statistical Interpretation of the Criminal Process," in *The Missouri Crime Survey* (New York: Macmillan, 1926), 272. For a fuller discussion of this issue, see Jeffrey S. Adler, "'Spineless Judges and Shyster Lawyers': Criminal Justice in New Orleans, 1920–1945," *Journal of Social History* 49 (Summer 2016): 906–8.

15. Arthur V. Lashly, "Preparation and Presentation of the State's Case," in *The Missouri Crime Survey*, 118; Robert H. Marr, *The Criminal Jurisprudence of Louisiana*, 2nd ed., vol. 1 (New Orleans: Hansell & Bro., 1923), 606–7, 755.

16. Arthur V. Lashly, "Homicide (in Cook County)," in *The Illinois Crime Survey*, ed. John H. Wigmore (Chicago: Illinois Association for Criminal Justice, 1929), 629; Louis N. Robinson, "The Relation of the Police and the Courts to the Crime Problem," in *A Report Submitted to the National Crime Commission* (New York: National Crime Commission, 1928), 8; H[arrington] C[ooper] Brearley, *Homicide in the United States* (Chapel Hill: University of North Carolina Press, 1932), 132.

17. Tennie Erwin Daugette, "Homicide in New Orleans" (M.A. thesis, Tulane University, 1931), 10–13.

18. For example, "'Safe Business' Is Law Breaking, So Record Shows," *New Orleans Times-Picayune*, June 19, 1924, pp. 1, 6.

19. John H. Langbein, "Albion's Fatal Flaws," *Past and Present* 98 (February 1983): 120.